Robert Tomes, Benjamin G Smith

The Great Civil War

A History of the Late Rebellion

Robert Tomes, Benjamin G Smith

The Great Civil War
A History of the Late Rebellion

ISBN/EAN: 9783337401627

Printed in Europe, USA, Canada, Australia, Japan

Cover: Foto ©ninafisch / pixelio.de

More available books at **www.hansebooks.com**

THE

GREAT CIVIL WAR

A HISTORY OF

THE LATE REBELLION

BEING A COMPLETE

NARRATIVE OF THE ORIGIN AND PROGRESS OF THE WAR

WITH

BIOGRAPHICAL SKETCHES OF LEADING STATESMEN

AND

DISTINGUISHED NAVAL AND MILITARY COMMANDERS, ETC.

BY ROBERT TOMES, M.D.

CONTINUED FROM THE BEGINNING OF THE YEAR 1864 TO THE END OF THE WAR

BY BENJAMIN G. SMITH, Esq.

ILLUSTRATED BY HIGHLY FINISHED PORTRAITS, BATTLE SCENES, VIEWS OF FORTS AND BATTLE-FIELDS, COLORED MAPS, PLANS Etc., ALL ENGRAVED ON STEEL, FROM DRAWINGS MADE EXPRESSLY FOR THIS WORK, BY F. O. C. DARLEY, AND OTHER EMINENT AMERICAN ARTISTS.

VIRTUE AND YORSTON
12 DEY STREET, AND 544 BROADWAY, NEW YORK.

Entered, according to Act of Congress, in the year One Thousand Eight Hundred and Sixty-five,

BY VIRTUE & YORSTON,

In the Clerk's Office of the District Court of the United States for the Southern District of New York.

TO

Lieut.-General Winfield Scott,

U. S. A.,

THIS WORK

IS RESPECTFULLY DEDICATED

BY HIS OBEDIENT SERVANTS,

THE PUBLISHERS.

THE GREAT CIVIL WAR:

A HISTORY OF

THE LATE REBELLION.

CHAPTER I.

State Sovereignty; its Honest and Dishonest Advocates.—Northern Conciliation.—Southern Domination.—Northern Independence.—Increased Power of the North.—Alarm at the Encroachments of the South.—The Kansas Struggle.—Organization of the Republican Party.—Nomination of John C. Fremont for President.—His Opinions on Slavery.—An exciting Political Contest.—Election of Buchanan.—Audacious Expressions of Opinion.—Uneasiness of Southern Partisans.—Causes of their Anxiety.—An early Secession Speech of Jefferson Davis.—The Appeals of the Southern Press.—Perversion of the Principles of the Republican Party.—Delusions of Commerce.—Re-establishment of the Slave Trade.—Alliances with the "Cotton Kingdom."—Conspirators in high places.—Illegal use of Public Moneys.—Ill uses of Munitions of War, Navy, etc.—Increased Strength of the Republican Party.—South Carolina first to move toward Disunion.—A Secession Resolution.—A Secession Commissioner.—An emphatic Speech from Brooks, of South Carolina.—Political Conventions.—Division of the Democrats.—Nominations for the Presidency.—Chicago Convention.—Lincoln nominated for President.—Motives of the South in the division of the Democratic Party.—A Secession Message from the Governor of South Carolina.—Suggestions of Treason from a Virginian Governor.—Election of Lincoln as President.

MANY of the political leaders of the extreme Southern States of the American Union had long since boldly asserted that each individual State possessed a sovereignty paramount to that of the united commonwealth of the Republic of the United States of America. Some of these men, deluded by the artful sophistries of the subtle Calhoun, the apostle of the doctrine of "State Rights," in avowing their political heresy, gave expression, it is believed, to an honest conviction. Others, however, influenced by personal interests, sought only to gratify their ambition or to soothe their disappointment by creating a faction from which they hoped to obtain favors they had failed in extorting from the country. In the mean time the people of the Southern States, with the exception perhaps of those of South Carolina, who had been misled by the persuasive plausibilities of their favorite Calhoun, continued to cherish a patriotic sentiment of attachment to the Union.

While the partisan leaders of the South were enabled, through the conciliatory concessions of Northern politicians, to wield the political power of the country to their own purposes of personal and sectional advantage, they shrewdly disguised their selfish designs beneath a mask of traditional regard for the Constitution of the United States. When, however, the North began to grow restless under its subservience to Southern domination, and to manifest a desire for emancipation, the partisan leaders of the South became anxious lest they should lose the political mastery by which they had so long governed a nation in the interests of a faction. Alarmed by these evidences of Northern independence, the Southern leaders asserted their theory of State sovereignty with increased audacity, and threatened to evoke its exercise to the destruction of the Union. They thus hoped to frighten the Northern people, who were known to be fondly devoted to the united country, into renewed submission to Southern control.

The North had, in the mean time, been rapidly gaining in power through the natural increase of population and an immense European immigration. The South had striven to balance this growing ascendancy by an increase of slave States. By artful party combinations, and skillful management of Northern politicians, the partisan leaders of the South for awhile succeeded in their purpose. Texas was annexed at the expense of a war with Mexico, and established a slave State; an intrigue, though it proved abortive, was set on foot to force Spain into the sale of servile Cuba; and finally the Missouri Compromise act was abrogated, for the purpose of admitting the Territories of Nebraska and Kansas as slaveholding States. The Northern people became alarmed at these continued encroachments of the South, and resolutely prepared to check them. In spite of the virtual abrogation of the Missouri Compromise act, by which the new Territory was thrown open to slavery, Kansas, through the efforts of the advocates of free soil, was filled with Northern settlers, and became by the votes of its inhabitants a free State. This, however, was not effected without a struggle. The neighboring slave States had sent in armed bands to resist the Northern immigration, and a bloody strife ensued, which greatly stirred the antagonistic interests and sentiments of the Northern and Southern States.

It was in the course of this bitter contention that the Republican party was formed, to resist the further extension of slavery. It soon gathered to its standard such a force as to threaten a successful opposition to the oldest and most powerful political combinations.

Fully organized, the Republican party met in convention at Philadelphia on the 17th of June, and 1856. nominated John C. Fremont, the eminent explorer, for President. Though a native of South Carolina, he was known to be strongly opposed to the extension of slavery, and in favor of free labor. He, however, objected to any interference with the rights of the Southern States secured to them by the Constitution of the United States, as he thus declared in a letter addressed to some leading members of the Republican party: "I heartily concur," he wrote, "in all movements which have for their object to repair the mischiefs arising from the violation of good faith in the repeal of the Missouri Compromise. I am opposed to slavery in the abstract and upon principle, sustained and made habitual by long-settled convictions. While I feel inflexible in the belief that it ought not to be interfered with where it exists under the shield of State sovereignty, I am as inflexibly opposed to its extension on this continent beyond its present limits." This was probably not only a fair exposition of his individual opinion, on the exciting question of slavery, but of that of the great mass of the Republican party.

The political contest for the Presidency which ensued upon the nomination of Fremont was one of the most stirring of our periodical excitements. The result was the triumph of the candidate of the Democratic party, James Buchanan, for whom the whole South, with the exception of Maryland, whose choice was for Fillmore, had cast its vote. Fremont, however, had received the large suffrage of one hundred and fourteen out of the whole electoral vote of three hundred and six. New York, Ohio, Michigan, Iowa, Wisconsin, and the six New England States were arrayed in favor of the Republican candidate. By the election of their favorite, Mr. Buchanan, the Southern leaders were apparently soothed, and they settled into a temporary political contentment. In the course of the electoral contest, some had audaciously declared that in case of the election of the Republican candidate, the slave States would exercise their self-asserted sovereignty, and secede from the Union. This threat, however, deemed but the angry effusion of political contention, or a mere electioneering *ruse*, was little heeded.

Though exulting in the triumph of the election of their favorite, Buchanan, of whose sympathy with their political views they did not seem to doubt, and by whose elevation to power they had apparently established the security of their own, the political leaders of the South soon began to show evident symptoms of restless discontent. The already acquired and growing strength of the Republican party darkened their prospect of continued domination; the issue of the Kansas struggle had resulted in the defeat of their hope of securing another slave State; freer expositions* of the evils of their cherished institution, and the insurrectionary attempt at Harper's Ferry, aroused their fears; and the audacious prophecies of Republican leaders, who foretold an "irrepressible conflict," threatened them with a resolute opposition. They now began to be hopeless of future triumphs, and prepared, some by open appeals to sectional prejudice, and others by secret means, to dissolve the Union. It was during the year 1858 that Jefferson Davis, United States senator, since President of the self-styled Confederate States, boldly avowed, in a speech at Jackson, Mississippi, these insurrection-

1858.

---

* For example, the publication of Helper's "Impending Crisis."

ary sentiments, which prove that the late rebellion, of which he was the master spirit, had been with him for a long time a "foregone conclusion:" "If an abolitionist," he said, "be chosen President of the United States, you will have presented to you the question of whether you will permit the Government to pass into the hands of your avowed and implacable enemies? Without pausing for an answer, I will state my own belief to be that such a result would be a species of revolution by which the purposes of the Government would be destroyed and the observance of its mere forms entitled to no respect. In that event, in such a manner as should be most expedient, I should deem it your duty to provide for your safety outside of the Union, with those who have already shown the will, and would have acquired the power, to deprive you of your birthright, and to reduce you to worse than the colonial dependence of your fathers."

The Southern press, too, began to urge emphatically the right of secession, and the advantage to the States of the South of separation from the Union. To gain the sympathy of the people, who had yet a traditional reverence for the Government founded by Washington and the patriots of the Revolution, incessant appeals were made alternately to their fears, their passions, and their cupidity. The principles of the Republican party and its leaders were studiously misstated. Their objects were declared to be the abolition of slavery, which they were determined to accomplish, at any hazard to the lives and property of the Southern people. The inhabitants of the sea-ports were deluded with the magnificent prospects of a direct trade with Europe, by which the dwindling cities of the South would be swollen into the importance of Tyre and Carthage, and enriched with the wealth of the whole commercial world. The cupidity, too, and pride of the poorer population, the "mean whites," the Pariahs of the South, who, without property and without enterprise to acquire it, had nothing to fear from the abolition of slavery, or to hope from the promotion of commerce, were aroused by the promise of the re-establishment of the slave-trade, by which the Lazarus of the pine barren would be enabled to count his negroes with the Dives of the rice jungle. The hazards, moreover, of casting off the protection of the powerful Government of the United States and incurring the interposition of its contemned authority were conjured away by the confident assurances that Great Britain and France would eagerly embrace the cause and seek the alliance of the "Cotton kingdom," to which European trade would be forced to do homage.

The people of the South were thus artfully being seduced from their allegiance to the Union while their leaders were conspiring to destroy it. The President, Buchanan, bound in close ties of political sympathy with the prominent partisans of the Southern States, had selected from among them the chief members of his cabinet, to whose guidance he yielded his feeble will, which they seemed to bend unresistingly to their own purposes. The treasury, the army, the navy, and the state, either under the control of Southern conspirators directly, or indirectly through the perhaps unconscious connivance of Northern political allies, were administered to the advantage of a rebellion which had been long contemplated. The public moneys were illegally appropriated for Southern purposes, the ships of war were dispatched to remote parts of the world, munitions of war were profusely distributed among the States of the South, and the offices of the Government both at home and abroad were filled by confederates of the conspirators of the slave States.

In the mean time, the Republican party, with increased strength, was preparing to join in the struggle for political ascendancy with renewed hope. Its undoubted power became so manifest, that the more impatient of the Southern leaders lost all hope of successful opposition within the Union, and began to prepare for open resistance.

South Carolina, with her loyalty to the Union long since weakened by false theories and seditious practices, was the first to move toward secession. On the 30th of November a resolution was offered in the House of Representatives of South Carolina, that "South Carolina is ready to enter, together with other slaveholding States, or such as desire prompt action, into the formation of a Southern confederacy;" and the governor was requested to forward the resolution to the various Southern States. To this succeeded other action toward the same object.

1859.

In the following January, Mr. Memminger, a prominent politician of the State, presented himself at Richmond, as the commissioner of South Carolina to Virginia, and delivered a long speech, in the course of which he argued that the guarantees of the Constitution of the United States were powerless to protect the South, and that it must demand new guarantees if the Union was to be preserved.

1860.

Some of the more impatient of the politicians of South Carolina had anticipated by many years in their rhetorical effusions, this grave action of their State. In 1856, Preston Brooks, a member of the United States Congress from South Carolina, whose emphasis of action was made manifest by his murderous attack upon Senator Sumner, of Massachusetts, delivered these characteristic words to some of his fellow-citizens who were honoring him with a public banquet:

"I tell you, fellow-citizens, from the bottom of my heart, that the only mode which I can think of for meeting the issue is just to tear the Constitution of the United States, trample it under foot, and form a Southern confederacy, every State of which shall be a slaveholding State. I believe it as I stand in the face of my Maker—I believe it on my responsibility to you, as your honored representative, that the only hope of the South is in the South, and that the only available means of making that hope effective is to cut asunder the bonds that tie us together, and take our separate position in the family of nations." These sentiments found a ready echo among the seditiously disposed people of South Carolina.

The period for the electoral struggle for the Presidency was approaching. The conventions for the nomination of candidates had met. The Democratic National Convention assembled on the 25th of April, at Charleston, in South Carolina. Caleb Cushing, of Massachusetts, was elected president, and a platform was adopted. This, however, did not concede to the South all it claimed as "necessary guarantees for the preservation of the Union," and the Southern delegates withdrawing, organized a Southern convention, which met on the 3d of May, but after many ineffectual attempts, failing to agree upon a candidate for the Presidency, adjourned to meet at Richmond. The Democratic National Convention had also adjourned to meet at Baltimore, on the 13th of June. On reassembling, a large number of delegates again withdrew. Those remaining nominated Stephen A. Douglas, of Illinois, for President, and Benjamin Fitzpatrick, of Alabama, for Vice-President. The seceders met and nominated John C. Breckinridge, of Kentucky, then Vice-President of the United States, for President, and for Vice-President, Joseph Lane, of Oregon. These nominations were afterward confirmed by the convention at Richmond. In the mean time a convention, styling itself the "Constitu-

1860.

tional Union," met at Baltimore on the 9th of May, and nominated John Bell, of Tennessee, for President, and Edward Everett, of Massachusetts, for Vice-President.

Again, at Chicago, on the 16th of May, the delegates of that now imposing party, the National Republican, met in convention and nominated Abraham Lincoln, of Illinois, for President, and Hannibal Hamlin, of Maine, for Vice-President.

The leaders of the South had evidently determined to forego the advantage of their usual political combinations with their fellow-partisans of the North, by whose aid they could alone hope to secure their prescriptive importance in the Union. They were willing thus to weaken by division those who were still inclined to succor them in an unavoidable struggle with a party whose power if established they professed to consider fatal to their rights. It would seem that disunion with them was a predetermined act, and that they wished the success of the National Republicans, whom they persisted in denouncing as abolitionists, to justify their contemplated Southern rebellion to the people of the South, whose sensitive anxieties for the security of their slave interests might be readily excited to an angry resistance to the constitutional authorities of the United States. The division of the Democratic party, from which certainly the Southern leaders could have no fears of an invasion of their constitutional rights, threw the election into the power of the Republicans, whom they professed to dread as the avowed enemies of the institutions of the South. The result, easily foreseen, soon occurred. As it became evident that Lincoln would be elected, the conspirators of the South, some of whom were in the highest places of the States and of the Union, began, through message, speech, and the press, to denounce the Republican candidate as an abolitionist, whose purpose, at the head of a powerful party, was to interfere with Southern slavery, and by incendiary appeals to excite the people to resistance. In South Carolina, the conspirators, confident of the sympathy of the misguided people, did not hesitate to declare their rebellious purposes. On the day before the Presidential election, the governor of South Carolina delivered a message to the Legislature, in which he boldly avowed the principles of secession, and recommended the appointment of delegates to a convention to be assembled for the purpose of dissolving all connection with the United States.

Even in Virginia, Governor Letcher, at that early date, did not fear to suggest treason, and declared in his message to the Legislature : " It is useless to attempt to conceal the fact, that in the present temper of the Southern people, it [alluding to the probable election of Lincoln] can not and will not be submitted to. * * * The idea of permitting such a man to have the control and direction of the army and navy of the United States, and the appointment of high judicial and executive officers, postmasters included, can not be entertained by the South for a moment." On November the 6th the election took place, and Abraham Lincoln, as was foreseen, was elected President of the United States. His principles and character will be best illustrated by a cursory history of his life and political career.

CHAPTER II.

Birth of Lincoln.—His Ancestry.—Humble Parentage.—Early Education.—Small Accomplishments extensively Utilized.—Handling of the Axe.—Death of his Mother.—Study of the Bible.—Second Marriage of his Father.—Young Lincoln's earliest Literary Acquirements.—Later pursuits of Learning.—Bodily Development and Accomplishments.—First Trip on a Flat Boat.—A Migration to Illinois.—A feat of "Splitting Rails."—A Hand on a Flat Boat.—Reward of Industry and Integrity.—General Manager of a Shop and Mill.—A Volunteer in the Black Hawk War.—A sudden and unexpected Promotion.—Return to Civil Life.—A Candidate for the Legislature.—A Partnership in a Shop.—Failure.—An extemporaneous Surveyor.—Elected Member of the Legislature.—Good opinion of his Constituents.—Reading Law.—Admission to the Bar.—Professional Success.—Prominent among the Politicians.—A Canvass of the State.—Elected Whig Member of Congress.—His Votes and Opinions on the Slave Question.—Return to practice as a Lawyer.—Member of Whig National Convention.—A Champion of the Republican Party.—Nominated a United States Senator.—Canvass of the State.—Contest with Douglas.—A Victory and a Defeat.—His candid Answers to Questions on Slavery.—Nominated for the Presidency.—Enthusiasm of his Party.—An exciting Canvass.—Elected President.—Sudden Elevation.—" Honest Abe."—Character and Manner.

ABRAHAM LINCOLN was born in Hardin County, Kentucky, on the 12th of February, 1809. From the dark and confused traditions of an humble ancestry, a mole-eyed investigator has traced back the lineage of our President to some forefathers who emigrated from England to America, and settled in Berks County, Pennsylvania, where they were engaged in the tranquil pursuit of farming, and known as peaceful members of the "Society of Friends." One of them, however, the great-grandfather of Abraham Lincoln, removed to Virginia, where his grandson, Thomas Lincoln, the father of the President, was born. The family soon migrated to Kentucky. Here Thomas, Abraham's father, being left poor and uneducated, led the life of an itinerant laborer, ready to put his shoulder to any work that promised a fair day's wages. He, however, on marrying Nancy Hanks, in 1806, gave up his migratory habits, and located himself in Hardin County, where our President was born. Without property and without education, Thomas Lincoln found himself in the unenviable position of one of those "poor whites" who in a society based on slavery are contemned alike by the negro and his master. He therefore determined to emigrate to a free State, where personal labor was deemed no humiliation and honest poverty no disgrace. He accordingly moved, in the autumn of 1816, to Spencer County, Indiana, when his son Abraham had reached the age of eight years. The youth had already, while in Kentucky, picked up some stray scraps of learning, and could not only read and cipher, but write. This rare accomplishment of the juvenile scholar proved invaluable to the Lincoln family and the illiterate neighbors of their forest home in Indiana. They had left relatives and friends in Kentucky, and were naturally desirous of keeping up a correspondence with them. Young Abraham Lincoln's services were accordingly put into requisition as the secretary, not only of his father, who could barely sign his name, and of his mother, who, "though a ready reader, had not been taught the accomplishment of writing," but of many of the other rude settlers of the wilderness. He thus early acquired a facility of expression which proved of good service to him in after years, and aided his future advancement in life.

This, however, was only the occupation of his rare intervals of leisure. He more frequently handled the axe than the pen. A log-house was to be built, and his father's land to be cleared of its forest growth of oaks and hickories. Abraham was young, but well-grown, and wondrously strong for his age, and took to the rude labor with instinctive readiness. "An axe was at once placed in his hands, and from that time until he attained his twenty-third year, when not employed in labor on the farm, he was almost constantly wielding that most useful instrument."*

In 1818, young Lincoln lost his mother, a pious woman of the Baptist persuasion, who had taken care that no Sunday should pass without having a chapter of the Bible read either by herself or one of her children. Her son is said thus to have acquired a familiarity with the words and principles of the Scriptures, which made an abiding impression upon his memory and conduct. His father, however, soon provided himself with another wife, by marrying a Mrs. Sally Johnston, of Kentucky, who proved a worthy substitute to her not-able predecessor. Schooling was too dear, and the necessity of hard work too pressing, to allow of much devotion to study, and Abraham was left chiefly to his own unaided exertions for his education. With barely a year's instruction in all, he succeeded, by diligently reading the few books that fell in his way, in developing his naturally vigorous understanding, and preparing himself for the success which has marked his life. His earliest literary acquisitions, after his spelling-book and the Bible, were a stray copy of Esop's Fables, which he conned until he learned it by heart; the Pilgrim's Progress, Franklin's Autobiography, Weems' picturesque Life of Washington, and Riley's wondrous narrative of travel. At the age of fifteen he earned, by three days work, in reaping a distant neighbor's corn, Ramsay's History of the Revolution, and soon after crowned his arduous pursuit of literature with the acquisition of a copy of Plutarch's Lives. "He studied English grammar after he was twenty-three years of age; at twenty-five he mastered enough of geometry, trigonometry, and mensuration to enable him to take the field as a surveyor; and he studied the six books of Euclid after he had served a term in Congress, and when he was forty years of age, amid the pressure of an extensive legal practice, and of frequent demands upon his time by the public."*

In the mean time, while young Lincoln was striving against every disad-

---

* "Life of Abraham Lincoln." New York, 1860.   * "Life of Abraham Lincoln." New York, 1860.

vantage for mental progress, he was advancing rapidly in physical stature and robustness. His rough backwoods life was hardening his muscle and knitting his stalwart frame, so that he soon became not only foremost in felling a tree or "splitting a rail," but the most noted among his comrades in feats of wrestling, leaping, and throwing the bar. His spirit of independence and adventure was displayed in a trip on a flat-boat to New Orleans, which he made at the age of nineteen, as one of the hands.

The fame of the broad prairies of Illinois, with their seductive promise of cheap lands and natural richness of soil, had reached the Lincoln family, and tempted them to seek its "fresh fields and pastures new." Accordingly, in the spring of 1830, Thomas Lincoln, with his wife and children, abandoned his home in Indiana and journeyed to the new land of promise. Ox-carts loaded with the women folk, the household goods, the farming utensils, and provision of corn and bacon for the journey, and driven by the patriarch and his son, our future President, carried all the hopes and fortunes of the Lincolns to their new home. After a slow and long journey through an unfrequented country, picturesque to the eye with its diversified scenery, but trying to the endurance of the traveler with its mountain acclivities, its deep watercourses, and perplexing forests, they finally arrived in Illinois. Here the Lincolns settled in Macon County, where the strong arm and skilled labor of Abraham, now one-and-twenty years of age, were at once put to service. The summer was mostly spent in building the log-house, as a protection against the storms and frosts of the approaching autumn and winter. The next step was to prepare the bit of prairie which had fallen to the lot of the Lincolns, for a crop of Indian corn. It was now that Abraham accomplished that memorable feat of "splitting the rails" for the ten-acre field, which has subsequently been cultivated to such advantage by the fertilizing rhetoric of political orators.

The winter compelling an intermission of labor on the farm, and the severity of the season restricting the means of livelihood at home, young Lincoln was induced to accept the offer of a neighbor and assist in taking a flat-boat from Beardstown, on the Illinois River, to New Orleans. Having performed this service greatly to the satisfaction of his employer, he was rewarded by him with the appointment of general manager of his shop and mill in New Salem. He had been thus occupied for several months, when, on the breaking out of the Black Hawk war in 1832, he joined a company of volunteers. Lincoln was at once chosen the captain, an unexpected elevation, which he declared gave him more pleasure than any subsequent honor which has fallen to his lot. The war being soon brought to a close, Lincoln returned to civil life, after the brief military career of three months.

On reaching New Salem, he was induced to offer himself as a "Whig" candidate for the Legislature, but was defeated by his Democratic opponent. He now formed a partnership, and buying a stock of goods on credit, opened a country store. He was also appointed postmaster at New Salem. The business, however, not proving successful, nor the office remunerative, he was soon in such pecuniary straits as to be forced to close his doors. His next effort for a livelihood was as an extemporaneous assistant surveyor, for which he readily prepared himself by obtaining a field compass, a chain, and a treatise on surveying.

In 1834, Lincoln was elected a member of the Legislature of Illinois. Although reticent of speech, he by the faithful discharge of his duties, and his personal and political rectitude of conduct, won so much of the good opinion of his constituents that they re-elected him for three successive terms.

Even while practicing as a surveyor, Lincoln had been in the habit of reading books on law. After entering the Legislature, he began to study them with increased attention, and in 1836 had made such progress that he was admitted to the bar. In April of the following year he became a partner of a Mr. John F. Stuart, and removed to Springfield, where he began the practice of his profession. His success as a lawyer was immediate, and he soon attained to such eminence, that he ranked among the chief legal practitioners of the neighborhood. His forte was in the management of jury cases. Though laboriously occupied with his profession, Lincoln took a prominent lead in politics. His sympathies were with the Whigs, and having been chosen a candidate for Presidential elector in 1844, he canvassed the whole State of Illinois and a portion of Indiana in favor of Henry Clay. In 1846 he was elected by the Whigs a member of Congress, and in December, 1847, took his seat in the House of Representatives. Though opposed to the annexation of Texas and the war with Mexico, which had been then brought to a triumphant close by the conquest of the Mexican capital, Lincoln never failed to recognize the good service of our soldiers, and to join in all the congressional votes of acknowledgment and reward.

At an early period Lincoln had manifested those opinions on slavery which secured for him the nomination of the Republican party, and elevated him to his future high position. In a protest which is recorded upon the journal of the Illinois Legislature on the 3d of March, 1837, he united with a fellow-member in saying that: "They believe that the institution of slavery is founded on both injustice and bad policy; but that the promulgation of abolition doctrines tends rather to increase than abate its evils.

"They believe that the Congress of the United States has no power, under the Constitution, to interfere with the institution of slavery in the different States.

"They believe that the Congress of the United States has the power under the Constitution to abolish slavery in the District of Columbia; but that the power ought not to be exercised unless at the request of the people of said District."

His action while in Congress, as after his election to the Presidency, was ever in strict accordance with the scrupulous regard thus early expressed for all constitutional obligations in respect to Southern slavery, but he surely never failed to do his utmost to restrict within its legal bounds an institution which he did not favor. He showed his resolute opposition to its extension by voting, while in Congress, no less than forty-two times for the Wilmot proviso. His action on other questions was in harmony with his professed Whig principles, and a protective tariff, river and harbor improvements, and the sale of the public lands at a low valuation, received his support and vote.

Lincoln, having served in Congress but a single term, returned to the practice of his profession in Springfield. In 1848, however, he was a member of the Whig National Convention, and warmly concurred in the nomination of General Zachary Taylor for the Presidency. In 1849 he was the Whig candidate for the United States Senate, but as the majority of the Legislature of Illinois was Democratic, was beaten by his competitor, General Shields.

The repeal of the Missouri Compromise aroused Lincoln once more to active political effort, and he came forward as a champion of the new Republican party organized to resist the extension of slavery. In the canvass for the choice of a senator in the place of General Shields, he sustained Judge Trumbull, and to his spirited efforts was attributed the triumph of that Republican candidate. So prominent had he now become as a leader of the new party, that in the Republican National Convention of 1856, which nominated John C. Fremont for President, Lincoln was pressed by the delegates from the State of Illinois as a nominee for the Vice-Presidency.

Being nominated on the 2d of June, 1858, by the Republican party of his State, candidate for the United States Senate, in opposition to Douglas, Lincoln canvassed Illinois together with his eminent competitor. Having already, in the struggle between Trumbull and Shields, tested his powers with the "Little Giant," as the partisans of Douglas fondly termed him, in allusion to his combined loftiness of intellect and smallness of stature, Lincoln did not hesitate to challenge his doughty antagonist to another encounter. The political contest which ensued became memorable, and Lincoln exhibited, as a free-soil combatant, such pluck and bottom that he was hailed by the Republicans of Illinois as their favorite champion. They claimed that he had victoriously sustained their principles against the stoutest leader of their antagonists. He, however, with all his vigor of fight, did not succeed in his immediate purpose of gaining the prize of the senatorship. The popular vote, it is true, proclaimed him victor, but his competitor, Douglas, received the suffrage of the State Senate in consequence of the unequal apportionment law of Illinois, which gave the Democrats an undue share of its members. Lincoln, however, had secured for himself, among the expanding Republican party, an importance which obtained for him the nomination for the Presidency, and finally his elevation to that high office.

How far his political views upon the question of slavery did really justify a defiance of the authority of his government, as pretended by those seeking pretexts for rebellion, his own words will prove. In the course of his political contest for the senatorship, Douglas proposed certain questions to him, which are here given, with Lincoln's answers, which present a candid exposition of his opinions.

"*Question* 1. I desire to know whether Lincoln to-day stands pledged, as he did in 1854, in favor of the unconditional repeal of the Fugitive Slave law?

Answer. I do not now, nor ever did, stand pledged in favor of the unconditional repeal of the Fugitive Slave law.

Q. 2. I desire him to answer whether he stands pledged to-day, as he did in 1854, against the admission of any more slave States into the Union, even if the people want them?

A. I do not now, nor ever did, stand pledged against the admission of any more slave States into the Union.

Q. 3. I want to know whether he stands pledged against the admission of a new State into the Union, with such a constitution as the people of that State may see fit to make?

A. I do not stand pledged against the admission of a new State into the Union, with such a constitution as the people of that State may see fit to make.

Q. 4. I want to know whether he stands to-day pledged to the abolition of slavery in the District of Columbia?

A. I do not stand to-day pledged to the abolition of slavery in the District of Columbia.

Q. 5. I desire him to answer whether he stands pledged to the prohibition of the slave-trade between the different States?

A. I do not stand pledged to the prohibition of the slave-trade between the different States.

Q. 6. I desire to know whether he stands pledged to prohibit slavery in all the Territories of the United States, north as well as south of the Missouri Compromise line?

A. I am impliedly, if not expressly, pledged to a belief in the *right* and *duty* of Congress to prohibit slavery in all the United States' Territories.

Q. 7. I desire him to answer whether he is opposed to the acquisition of any new territory, unless slavery is first prohibited therein?

A. I am not generally opposed to honest acquisition of territory; and, in any given case, I would or would not oppose such acquisition, according as I might think such acquisition would or would not aggravate the slavery question among ourselves.

Now, my friends, it will be perceived, upon an examination of these questions and answers, that so far I have only answered that I was not *pledged* to this, that, or the other. The Judge has not framed his interrogatories to ask me anything more than this, and I have answered in strict accordance with the interrogatories, and have answered truly that I am not *pledged* at all upon any of the points to which I have answered. But I am not disposed to hang upon the exact form of his interrogatory. I am rather disposed to take up at least some of these questions, and state what I really think upon them.

As to the first one, in regard to the Fugitive Slave law, I have never hesitated to say, and I do not now hesitate to say, that I think, under the Constitution of the United States, the people of the Southern States are entitled to a Congressional Fugitive Slave law. Having said that, I have had nothing to say in regard to the existing Fugitive Slave law, further than that I think it should have been framed so as to be free from some of the objections that pertain to it, without lessening its efficiency. And inasmuch as we are not now in an agitation in regard to an alteration or modification of that law, I would not be the man to introduce it as a new subject of agitation upon the general question of slavery.

In regard to the other question, of whether I am pledged to the admission of any more slave States into the Union, I state to you very frankly, that I would be exceedingly sorry ever to be put in a position of having to pass upon that question. I should be exceedingly glad to know that there would never be another slave State admitted into the Union; but I must add that, if slavery shall be kept out of the Territories during the territorial existence of any one given Territory, and then the people shall, having a fair chance and a clear field, when they come to adopt the Constitution, do such an extraordinary thing as to adopt a slave constitution, uninfluenced by the actual presence of the institution among them, I see no alternative, if we own the country, but to admit them into the Union.

The third interrogatory is answered by the answer to the second, it being, as I conceive, the same as the second.

The fourth one is in regard to the abolition of slavery in the District of Columbia. In relation to that, I have my mind very distinctly made up. I should be exceedingly glad to see slavery abolished in the District of Columbia. I believe that Congress possesses the constitutional power to abolish it. Yet, as a member of Congress, I should not, with my present views, be in favor of *endeavoring* to abolish slavery in the District of Columbia, unless it would be upon these conditions : *First*, that the abolition should be gradual. *Second*, that it should be on a vote of the majority of qualified voters in the District ; and *third*, that compensation should be made to unwilling owners. With these three conditions, I confess I would be exceedingly glad to see Congress abolish slavery in the District of Columbia, and, in the language of Henry Clay, 'sweep from our capital that foul blot upon our nation.'

In regard to the fifth interrogatory, I must say here, that as to the question of the abolition of the slave-trade between the different States, I can truly answer, as I have, that I am *pledged* to nothing about it. It is a subject to which I have not given that mature consideration that would make me feel authorized to state a position so as to hold myself entirely bound by it. In other words, that question has never been prominently enough before me to induce me to investigate whether we really have the constitutional power to do it. I could investigate it if I had sufficient time to bring myself to a conclusion upon that subject; but I have not done so, and I say so frankly to you here, and to Judge Douglas. I must say, however, that if I should be of opinion that Congress does possess the constitutional power to abolish the slave-trade among the different States, I should still not be in favor of the exercise of that power unless upon some conservative principle, as I conceive it, akin to what I have said in relation to the abolition of slavery in the District of Columbia.

My answer as to whether I desire that slavery should be prohibited in all the Territories of the United States, is full and explicit within itself, and can not be made clearer by any comments of mine. So I suppose in regard to the question whether I am opposed to the acquisition of any more territory unless slavery is first prohibited therein, my answer is such that I could add nothing by way of illustration, or making myself better understood, than the answer which I have placed in writing.

1860. On the 16th of May, the Republican National Convention met at Chicago. After two ballots, which resulted in no choice, Lincoln was chosen on the third, receiving three hundred and fifty-four of the whole four hundred and sixty-five votes.* The election was then made unanimous. The party responded enthusiastically to the choice, and began at once to stir the country with an exciting canvass. The "Wide Awakes," unarmed but uniformed armies of voters, mustered and led by bands of music, were paraded through the streets in marching order by day, and in torchlight processions at night. Illuminated banners, gigantic flags, and posters made the names of Lincoln and Hamlin familiar to every eye and ear. Republican orators, of whom Seward, himself the leading competitor with Lincoln for the nomination of President, was the chief, posted from State to State, city to city, and throughout the rural districts, gathering great crowds and arousing them by their fervid rhetoric to resist the encroachments of slavery, and rally to the standard of the party organized to oppose it.

The divided Democrats and the so-called Unionists were not less demonstrative and industrious in making appeals by means of party emblems, processions, "monster" meetings, and political speeches. The country was never so agitated and party spirit so envenomed. Mutterings, in the mean time,

---

* The whole number of votes was 465, of which 273 were necessary to a choice. On the first ballot, Seward received 173½, Lincoln 102, Cameron 50½, and Bates 48; the rest were scattered. On the second ballot, Seward received 184½, and Lincoln 181; on the third, Lincoln had 354, Seward 102½, Dayton 1, and McLean ½ a vote.

of disaffection came from the South anticipating defeat, but were either not listened to, or scouted as the grumbling of impotent discontent. The clamor of party drowned all but its own voice.

In consequence of the dissensions and divisions of the Democratic party, the Republicans succeeded in electing their candidate. Abraham Lincoln was elected President of the United States, 1860, having received the electoral vote of seventeen States—California, Connecticut, Illinois, Indiana, Iowa, Maine, Massachusetts, Michigan, Minnesota, New Hampshire, New York, Ohio, Oregon, Pennsylvania, Rhode Island, Vermont, and Wisconsin—while the electoral vote of eleven States was given to Breckinridge, of three to Bell, and of two to Douglas. The whole popular vote, however, was only 1,857,610 for the Republican candidate, while that for the other three combined amounted to 2,804,560.

Lincoln, by his election, became at once, from a comparatively obscure person, whose name before his nomination was hardly known beyond the limits of the State of Illinois, the most prominent man in the country. Though acknowledged in his own State as an acute lawyer and skillful politician, he had never been recognized by the country at large as a leading statesman. He had, however, acquired in Illinois such a repute for political and personal integrity, that the people of the North, of all parties, disgusted with the corruption in high places, readily accepted him as a chief magistrate, upon whom they might rely for a strict adherence to his constitutional obligations. The "honest Abe" of his partisans would prove, it was believed, the worthy President of the great Republic.

Personally, Lincoln, who in character and manner had the unreserved and popular characteristics of the Western man, had no pretensions to the stately dignity we are apt to associate with the office of President. Retaining the informal habits of his early life, he was easily accessible, yielding without reserve his ready social sympathy to the first comer. A tall, gaunt man, with bending shoulders like an overweighted Atlas, nearly six feet and a half in height, and of great physical vigor, developed by the rude labor of his earlier, and strengthened by the simple habits of his later years, he was the representative of the sturdy democracy of the country. With none of the pretentious refinements of a fastidious culture, he yet had a naturally vigorous understanding, carefully improved by legal and political study. A certain logical acumen appeared characteristic of his mind, and tracing with untiring pertinacity the windings of an argument, he succeeded in distinguishing the plausible from the true. His mental like his moral character had generally a natural bias for truth, and the nation, in those days of political crime, confidently trusted in his honesty.

CHAPTER III.

The Election of Lincoln a signal and pretext of Insurrection.—The news hailed with joy in South Carolina.—Secession Meetings.—Sympathy of Slave States.—Offer of Aid from Virginia.—Secession Movement in New Orleans.—A Call for an Army in South Carolina.—Resignation of the United States Senators from South Carolina.—Tendency to Rebellion in the other Slave States.—Action of the Legislature of Georgia.—Florida hails the "Gallant Palmetto Flag."—The Governor of Alabama advises to prepare for Secession.—Conventions ordered.—Increase of the Secession Mania in South Carolina.—Flying of the Palmetto Flag, and excited enthusiasm of the People.—An infectious example.—Arming of Georgia.—Commissioners from Mississippi.—Mutual Counsel and Advice.—Arming of the Southern People.—Purchases of Arms from the North.—Increased Barbarity at the South.—Feeling at the North.—Trust in the sentiment of Union.—Hope from Congress and the President.—Disappointment.—President Buchanan's Message.

1860. The election of Lincoln was made the signal in the South, as it was the pretext, for the open defiance of the authority of the Federal Government. The intelligence of the fact was received at Charleston, S. C., with undisguised joy, and the citizens gave vent to their enthusiasm in "long-continued cheering for a Southern confederacy." Meetings were held, where local orators delivered stirring speeches, in which they declared that Southern independence could only be secured by the secession of South Carolina, and were rapturously applauded. The conspirators of the different Southern States interchanged expressions of sympathy and offers of mutual service. From Virginia, even at that early period, came a proffer to South Carolina of a volunteer corps to aid her in her projected rebellion. In New Orleans, placards were posted on the walls of the city inviting the citizens to military organization, and soon "minute men" were mustered in every cotton State.

On the 10th of November a bill was introduced in the Legislature of South Carolina for calling out and equipping an army of ten thousand volunteers, and on the same day was ordered an election for delegates to a convention to take action on the question of secession. This was followed by the resignation by the South Carolina senators of their seats in the Senate of the United States, which was accepted with enthusiasm. Finally, on November 13th, the Legislature adjourned *sine die*, when its preparatory acts of secession were honored by a torch-light procession in the capital of the State.

The other cotton States, though less precipitate than South Carolina in legislative action, gave early indications of their tendency to insurrection. The Legislature of Georgia refused to order the election of a senator to fill a vacancy in the United States Senate. The Governor of Florida sent a telegraphic greeting to the Governor of South Carolina, declaring that "Florida is with the gallant Palmetto flag." The Governor of Alabama advised his fellow-citizens to prepare for secession, and gave notice of his intention to order an election of delegates to a State convention. An extra session of the Legislature of Virginia was called to "take into consideration the condition of public affairs." At the same time great meetings were held at New Orleans, Augusta, Montgomery, Vicksburg, and other Southern cities, in favor of disunion. Each day brought with it a fresh development of the secession mania. The citizens of Charleston gathered in crowds to "inaugurate the revolution." The palmetto flag, the symbol of the State, was hoisted upon tall poles of pine erected for the purpose, and flung out from every public building, hotel, and private residence. Men, women, and children flaunted secession badges, and yielded unresistingly to the common madness.

In the meanwhile the example of South Carolina was infecting her neighbors. The Legislature of Georgia voted Nov. 18. an appropriation of a million of dollars "to arm and equip the State," and ordered an election of delegates to a convention. The Legislature Nov. 30. of North Carolina refused to elect a United States Senator. The Legislature of Mississippi authorized the Nov. 29. governor to appoint commissioners to visit the slaveholding States, to devise means in co-operation for "their common defense and safety." The Legislature Dec. 1. of Florida unanimously passed the bill calling for a convention. The Legislature of Georgia again, unable to check its impatience, Dec. 3. made a further advance toward rebellion by considering a resolution to invite a conference of the Southern States, for mutual counsel in regard to the best means of resistance to the North.

The people of the slave States were daily arming themselves for an anticipated encounter with the Federal authorities they were provoking. Immense purchases of arms and ammunition were made at New York, Boston, and Hartford. The rage against the unsympathetic citizens of the North, who by an unhappy fate chanced to be exposed to their insults and violence, was manifested with increased barbarity.

The loyal citizens of the country, though alarmed by these rebellious indications of the slave States, yet trusted to the sentiment of union to check, and the power as well as the disposition of the Federal Government to repress them. Some looked to Congress, now in Dec. 3. session, for a ready compliance with measures of conciliation and compromise, by which Southern discontent might be soothed by Northern concession. Others trusting in the power of Government, hoped that the chief magistrate, now that his weak will and vacillating purposes could be steadied and directed by congressional resolution, would bind with the fetters of authority the rebellion before it should be aroused in its might.

The message of Buchanan, however, soon dissipated these hopes. Instead of a dignified vindication of authority, Dec. 4. it was an ill-concealed attempt at justification of its contemners, and an open declaration of their impunity. This remarkable document will be always considered a not inefficient promoter of rebellion, and is now recorded as an important fact in its history.

PRESIDENT BUCHANAN'S MESSAGE.

"FELLOW-CITIZENS OF THE SENATE
AND HOUSE OF REPRESENTATIVES:

"Throughout the year since our last meeting, the country has been eminently prosperous in all its material interests. The general health has been excellent, our harvests have been abundant, and plenty smiles throughout the land. Our commerce and manufactures have been prosecuted with energy and industry, and have yielded fair and ample returns. In short, no nation in the tide of time has ever presented a spectacle of greater material prosperity than we have done until within a very recent period.

"Why is it, then, that discontent now so extensively prevails, and the Union of the States, which is the source of all these blessings, is threatened with destruction? The long-continued and intemperate interference of the Northern people with the question of slavery in the Southern States has at length produced its natural effects. The different sections of the Union are now arrayed against each other, and the time has arrived, so much dreaded by the Father of his Country, when hostile geographical parties have been formed. I have long foreseen and often forewarned my countrymen of the now impending danger. This does not proceed solely from the claims on the part of Congress or the Territorial Legislature to exclude slavery from the Territories, nor from the efforts of different States to defeat the execution of the Fugitive Slave law.

"All or any of these evils might have been endured by the South without danger to the Union (as others have been), in the hope that time and reflection might apply the remedy. The immediate peril arises not so much from these causes, as from the fact that the incessant and violent agitation of the slavery question throughout the North for the last quarter of a century, has at length produced its malign influence on the slaves, and inspired them with vague notions of freedom. Hence a sense of security no longer exists around the family altar. This feeling of peace at home has given place to apprehensions of servile insurrection. Many a matron throughout the South retires at night in dread of what may befall herself and her children before the morning. Should this apprehension of domestic danger, whether real or imaginary, extend and intensify itself until it shall pervade the masses of the Southern people, then disunion will become inevitable. Self-preservation is the first law of nature, and has been implanted in the heart of man by his Creator for the wisest purpose; and no political union, however fraught with blessings and benefits in all other respects, can long continue, if the necessary consequence be to render the homes and the firesides of nearly half the parties to it habitually and hopelessly insecure. Sooner or later the bonds of such a union must be severed. It is my conviction that this fatal period has not yet arrived; and my prayer to God is, that he would preserve the Constitution and the Union throughout all generations.

"But let us take warning in time, and remove the cause of danger. It can not be denied that for five-and-twenty years the agitation at the North against slavery in the South has been incessant. In 1835, pictorial handbills and inflammatory appeals were circulated extensively throughout the South, of a character to excite the passions of the slaves; and, in the language of Gen. Jackson, 'to stimulate them to insurrection, and produce all the horrors of a servile war.' This agitation has ever since been continued by the public press, by the proceedings of State and county conventions, and by abolition sermons and lectures. The time of Congress has been occupied in violent speeches on this never-ending subject, and appeals in pamphlet and other forms, indorsed by distinguished names, have been sent forth from this central point, and spread broadcast over the Union.

"How easy would it be for the American people to settle the slavery question forever, and to restore peace and harmony to this distracted country!

"They, and they alone, can do it. All that is necessary to accomplish the object, and all for which the slave States have ever contended, is to be let alone and permitted to manage their domestic institutions in their own way. As sovereign States, they, and they alone, are responsible before God and the world for the slavery existing among them. For this, the people of the North are not more responsible, and have no more right to interfere, than with similar institutions in Russia or in Brazil. Upon their good sense and patriotic forbearance I confess I still greatly rely. Without their aid, it is beyond the power of any President, no matter what may be his own political proclivities, to restore peace and harmony among the States. Wisely limited and restrained as is his power, under our Constitution and laws, he alone can accomplish but little, for good or for evil, on such a momentous question.

"And this brings me to observe that the election of any one of our fellow-citizens to the office of President does not of itself afford just cause for dissolving the Union. This is more especially true if his election has been effected by a mere plurality, and not a majority, of the people, and has resulted from transient and temporary causes, which may probably never again occur. In order to justify a resort to revolutionary resistance, the Federal Government must be guilty of 'a deliberate, palpable, and dangerous exercise' of powers not granted by the Constitution. The late Presidential election, however, has been held in strict conformity with its express provisions How, then, can the result justify a revolution to destroy this very Constitution? Reason, justice, a regard for the Constitution, all require that we shall wait for some overt and dangerous act on the part of the President-elect before resorting to such a remedy.

"It is said, however, that the antecedents of the President-elect have been sufficient to justify the fears of the South that he will attempt to invade their constitutional rights. But are such apprehensions of contingent danger in the future sufficient to justify the immediate destruction of the noblest system of government ever devised by mortals? From the very nature of his office, and its high responsibilities, he must necessarily be conservative. The stern duty of administering the vast and complicated concerns of this Government affords in itself a guarantee that he will not attempt any violation of a clear constitutional right. After all, he is no more than the chief executive officer of the Government. His province is not to make, but to execute, the laws; and it is a remarkable fact in our history, that, notwithstanding the repeated efforts of the Anti-Slavery party, no single act has ever passed Congress, unless we may possibly except the Missouri Compromise, impairing in the slightest degree the rights of the South to their property in slaves. And it may also be observed, judging from the present indications, that no probability exists of the passage of such an act, by a majority of both Houses, either in the present or the next Congress. Surely, under these circumstances, we ought to be restrained from present action by the precept of Him who spake as never man spoke, that 'sufficient unto the day is the evil thereof.' The day of evil may never come, unless we shall rashly bring it upon ourselves.

"It is alleged as one cause for immediate secession, that the Southern States are denied equal rights with the other States in the common Territories. But by what authority are these denied? Not by Congress, which has never passed, and I believe never will pass, any act to exclude slavery from these Territories; and certainly not by the Supreme Court, which has solemnly decided that slaves are property, and, like all other property, their owners have a right to take them into the common Territories, and hold them there under the protection of the Constitution.

"So far, then, as Congress is concerned, the objection is not to anything they have already done, but to what they may do hereafter. It will surely be admitted that this apprehension of future danger is no good reason for an immediate dissolution of the Union. It is true that the Territorial Legislature of Kansas, on the 23d of February, 1860, passed in great haste an act, over the veto of the governor, declaring that slavery 'is, and shall be, forever prohibited in this Territory.' Such an act, however, plainly violating the rights of property secured by the Constitution, will surely be declared void by the judiciary whenever it shall be presented in a legal form.

"Only three days after my inauguration, the Supreme Court of the United States solemnly adjudged that the power did not exist in a Territorial Legislature. Yet such has been the factious temper of the times, that the correctness of this decision has been extensively impugned before the people, and the question has given rise to angry political conflicts throughout the country. Those who have appealed from this judgment of our highest constitutional tribunal to popular assemblies would, if they could, invest a Territorial Legislature with power to annul the sacred rights of property. This power Congress is expressly forbidden, by the Federal Constitution, to exercise. Every State Legislature in the Union is forbidden, by its own Constitution, to exercise it. It can not be exercised in any State except by the people, in their highest sovereign capacity, when framing or amending their State Constitution.

"In like manner it can only be exercised by the people of a Territory represented in a convention of delegates, for the purpose of framing a constitution, preparatory to admission as a State into the Union. Then, and not until then, are they invested with power to decide the question, whether slavery shall or shall not exist within their limits. This is an act of sovereign authority, and not of subordinate territorial legislation. Were it otherwise, then indeed would the equality of the States in the Territories be destroyed, and the right of property in slaves would depend, not upon the guarantees of the Constitution, but upon the shifting majorities of an irresponsible Territorial Legislature. Such a doctrine, from its intrinsic unsoundness, can not long influence any considerable portion of our people, much less can it afford a good reason for a dissolution of the Union.

"The most palpable violations of constitutional duty which have yet been committed, consist in the acts of different State legislatures to defeat the execution of the Fugitive Slave law. It ought to be remembered, however, that for these acts neither Congress nor any President can justly be held responsible. Having been passed in violation of the Federal Constitution, they are, therefore, null and void. All the courts, both State and national, before whom the question has arisen, have from the beginning declared the Fugitive Slave law to be constitutional. The single exception is that of a State court in Wisconsin; and this has not only been reversed by the proper appellate tribunal, but has met with such universal reprobation that there can be no danger from it as a precedent. The validity of this law has been established over and over again by the Supreme Court of the United States with perfect unanimity. It is founded upon an express provision of the Constitution, requiring that fugitive slaves who escape from service in one State to another shall be 'delivered up' to their masters. Without this provision, it is a well-known historical fact that the Constitution itself could never have been adopted by the Convention.

"In one form or other, under the acts of 1793 and 1850, both being substantially the same, the Fugitive Slave law has been the law of the land from the days of Washington until the present moment. Here, then, a clear case is presented, in which it will be the duty of the next President, as it has been my own, to act with vigor in executing this supreme law against the conflicting enactments of State legislatures. Should he fail in the performance of this high duty, he will then have manifested a disregard of the Constitution and laws, to the great injury of the people of nearly one half of the States of the Union. But are we to presume in advance that he will thus violate his duty? This would be at war with every principle of justice and of Christian charity. Let us wait for the overt act. The Fugitive Slave law has been carried into execution in every contested case since the commencement of the present administration; though often, it is to be regretted, with great loss and inconvenience to the master, and with considerable expense to the Government. Let us trust that the State legislatures will repeal their unconstitutional and obnoxious enactments. Unless this shall be done without any necessary delay, it is impossible for any human power to save the Union.

"The Southern States, standing on the basis of the Constitution, have a right to demand this act of justice from the States of the North. Should it be refused, then the Constitution, to which all the States are parties, will have been willfully violated by one portion of them in a provision essential to the domestic security and happiness of the remainder. In that event, the injured States, after having first used all peaceful and constitutional means to obtain redress, would be justified in revolutionary resistance to the Government of the Union.

"I have purposely confined my remarks to revolutionary resistance, because it has been claimed within the last few years that any State, whenever this shall be its sovereign will and pleasure, may secede from the Union, in accordance with the Constitution, and without any violation of the constitutional rights of the other members of the confederacy. That, as each became parties to the Union by a vote of its own people assembled in convention, so any one of them may retire from the Union in a similar manner by the vote of such a convention.

"In order to justify secession as a constitutional remedy, it must be on the principle that the Federal Government is a mere voluntary association of States, to be dissolved at pleasure by any one of the contracting parties. If this be so, the confederacy is a rope of sand, to be penetrated and dissolved by the first adverse wave of public opinion in any of the States. In this manner our thirty-three States may resolve themselves into as many petty, jarring, and hostile republics, each one retiring from the Union, without responsibility, whenever any sudden excitement might impel them to such a course. By this process a union might be entirely broken into fragments in a few weeks, which cost our forefathers many years of toil, privation, and blood to establish.

"Such a principle is wholly inconsistent with the history as well as the character of the Federal Constitution. After it was framed, with the greatest deliberation and care, it was submitted to conventions of the people of the several States for ratification. Its provisions were discussed at length in these bodies, composed of the first men of the country. Its opponents contended that it conferred powers upon the Federal Government dangerous to the rights of the States, while its advocates maintained that under a fair construction of the instrument there was no foundation for such apprehensions. In that mighty struggle between the first intellects of this or any other country, it never occurred to any individual, either among its opponents or advocates, to assert, or even to intimate, that their efforts were all vain labor, because the moment any State felt herself aggrieved she might secede from the Union. What a crushing argument would this have proved against those who dreaded that the rights of the States would be endangered by the Constitution! The truth is, that it was not until many years after the origin of the Federal Government that such a proposition was first advanced.

"It was then met and refuted by the conclusive arguments of General Jackson, who, in his message of 16th January, 1833, transmitted the nullifying ordinance of South Carolina to Congress, employs the following language: 'The right of the people of a single State to absolve themselves at will, and without the consent of the other States, from their most solemn obligations, and hazard the liberty and happiness of the millions composing this Union, can not be acknowledged. Such authority is believed to be utterly repugnant both to the principles upon which the General Government is constituted, and to the objects which it was expressly formed to attain.'

"It is not pretended that any clause in the Constitution gives countenance to such a theory. It is altogether founded upon inference, not from any language contained in the instrument itself, but from the sovereign character of the several States by which it was ratified. But is it beyond the power of a State, like an individual, to yield a portion of its sovereign rights to secure the remainder? In the language of Mr. Madison, who has been called the Father of the Constitution: 'It was formed by the States—that is, by the people in each of the States, acting in their highest sovereign capacity; and formed consequently by the same authority which formed the State constitutions.'

"Nor is the Government of the United States, created by the Constitution, less a government in the strict sense of the term, within the sphere of its powers, than the governments created by the constitutions of the States are, within their several spheres. It is, like them, organized into legislative, executive, and judiciary departments. It operates, like them, directly on persons and things; and, like them, it has at command a physical force for executing the powers committed to it.

"It was intended to be perpetual, and not be annulled at the pleasure of any one of the contracting parties. The old articles of confederation were entitled 'Articles of Confederation and Perpetual Union between the States;' and by the 13th article it is expressly declared that 'the articles of this Confederation shall be inviolably observed by every State, and the Union shall be perpetual.' The preamble to the Constitution of the United States, having express reference to the articles of Confederation, recites that it was established 'in order to form a more perfect union.' And yet it is contended that this 'more perfect union' does not include the essential attribute of perpetuity.

"But that the Union was designed to be perpetual, appears conclusively from the nature and extent of the powers conferred by the Constitution on the Federal Government. These powers embrace the very highest attributes of national sovereignty. They place both the sword and the purse under its control. Congress has power to make war, and to make peace; to raise and support armies and navies, and to conclude treaties with foreign governments. It is invested with the power to coin money, and to regulate the value thereof, and to regulate commerce with foreign nations, and among the several States. It is not necessary to enumerate the other high powers which have been conferred upon the Federal Government. In order to carry the enumerated powers into effect, Congress possesses the exclusive right to lay and collect duties on imports, and in common with the States to lay and collect all other taxes.

"But the Constitution has not only conferred these high powers upon Congress, but it has adopted effectual means to restrain the States from interfering with their exercise. For that purpose it has, in strong prohibitory language, expressly declared that 'no State shall enter into any treaty, alliance, or confederation; grant letters of marque and reprisal; coin money; emit bills of credit; make anything but gold and silver coin a tender in payment of debts; pass any bill of attainder, *ex post facto* law, or law impairing the obligation of contracts.' Moreover, 'without the consent of Congress, no State shall lay any imposts or duties on any imports or exports, except what may be absolutely necessary for executing its inspection laws;' and if they exceed this amount, the excess shall belong to the United States.

"And 'no State shall, without the consent of Congress, lay any duty of tonnage; keep troops, or ships of war, in time of peace; enter into any agreement or compact with another State, or with a foreign power; or engage in war, unless actually invaded, or in such imminent danger as will not admit of delay.'

"In order still further to secure the uninterrupted exercise of these high powers against State interposition, it is provided 'that this Constitution, and the laws of the United States which shall be made in pursuance thereof, and all treaties made, or which shall be made, under the authority of the United States, shall be the supreme law of the land; and the judges in every State shall be bound thereby, anything in the Constitution or laws of any State to the contrary notwithstanding.'

"The solemn sanction of religion has been superadded to the obligations of official duty, and all Senators and Representatives of the United States, all members of State Legislature, and all executive and judicial officers, 'both of the United States and of the several States, shall be bound by oath or affirmation to support this Constitution.'

"In order to carry into effect these powers, the Constitution has established a perfect government in all its forms, legislative, executive, and judicial; and this Government, to the extent of its powers, acts directly upon the individual citizen of every State, and executes its own decrees by the agency of its own officers. In this respect it differs entirely from the Government under the old confederation, which was confined to making requisitions on the States in their sovereign character. This left it in the discretion of each whether to obey or to refuse, and they often declined to comply with such requisition. It thus became necessary, for the purpose of removing this barrier, and, 'in order to form a more perfect union,' to establish a government which could act directly upon the people, and execute its own laws without the intermediate agency of the States. This has been accomplished by the Constitution of the United States.

"In short, the Government created by the Constitution, and deriving its authority from the sovereign people of each of the several States, has precisely the same right to exercise its power over the people of all these States, in the enumerated cases, that each one of them possesses over subjects not delegated to the United States, but 'reserved to the States respectively, or to the people.'

"To the extent of the delegated powers, the Constitution of the United States is as much a part of the Constitution of each State, and is as binding upon its people, as though it had been textually inserted therein.

"This Government, therefore, is a great and powerful government, invested with all the attributes of sovereignty over the special subjects to which its authority extends. Its framers never intended to implant in its bosom the seeds of its own destruction, nor were they, at its creation, guilty of the absurdity of providing for its own dissolution. It was not intended by its framers to be the baseless fabric of a vision which, at the touch of the enchanter, would vanish into thin air, but a substantial and mighty fabric, capable of resisting the slow decay of time, and of defying the storms of ages. Indeed, well may the jealous patriots of that day have indulged fears that a government of such high powers might violate the reserved rights of the States, and wisely did they adopt the rule of a strict construction of these powers to prevent the danger! But they did not fear, nor had they any reason to imagine, that the Constitution would ever be so interpreted as to enable any State, by her own act, and without the consent of her sister States, to discharge her people from all or any of their Federal obligations.

"It may be asked, then, are the people of the States without redress against the tyranny and oppression of the Federal Government? By no means. The right of resistance on the part of the governed against the oppression of their governments can not be denied. It exists independently of all constitutions, and has been exercised at all periods of the world's history. Under it old governments have been destroyed, and new ones have taken their place. It is embodied in strong and express language in our own Declaration of Independence. But the distinction must ever be observed, that this is revolution against an established government, and not a voluntary secession from it by virtue of an inherent constitutional right. In short, let us look the danger fairly in the face: secession is neither more nor less than revolution. It may or it may not be a justifiable revolution, but still it is revolution.

"What, in the mean time, is the responsibility and true position of the Executive? He is bound by solemn oath before God and the country 'to take care that the laws be faithfully executed,' and from this obligation he can not be absolved by any human power. But what if the performance of this duty, in whole or in part, has been rendered impracticable by events over which he could have exercised no control? Such, at the present moment, is the case throughout the State of South Carolina, so far as the laws of the United States to secure the administration of justice by means of the Federal judiciary are concerned. All the Federal officers within its limits, through whose agency alone these laws can be carried into execution, have already resigned. We no longer have a district judge, a district attorney, or a marshal, in South Carolina. In fact, the whole machinery of the Federal Government necessary for the distribution of remedial justice among the people has been demolished, and it would be difficult, if not impossible, to replace it.

"The only acts of Congress on the statute-book, bearing upon this subject, are those of the 28th February, 1795, and 3d March, 1807. These authorize the President, after he shall have ascertained that the marshal, with his *posse comitatus*, is unable to execute civil or criminal process in any particular case, to call forth the militia and employ the army and navy to aid him in performing this service, having first by proclamation commanded the insurgents to disperse and retire peaceably to their respective abodes within a limited time.' This duty can not by possibility be performed in a State where no judicial authority exists to issue process, and where there is no marshal to execute it, and where, even if there were such an officer, the entire population would constitute one solid combination to resist him.

"The bare enumeration of these provisions proves how inadequate they are without further legislation to overcome a united opposition in a single State, not to speak of other States who may place themselves in a similar attitude. Congress alone has power to decide whether the present laws can or can not be amended so as to carry out more effectually the objects of the Constitution.

"The same insuperable obstacles do not lie in the way of executing the laws for the collection of the customs. The revenue still continues to be collected, as heretofore, at the custom-house in Charleston; and should the collector unfortunately resign, a successor may be appointed to perform this duty.

"Then in regard to the property of the United States in South Carolina. This has been purchased for a fair equivalent, 'by the consent of the Legislature of the State,' 'for the erection of forts, magazines, arsenals,' etc., and over these the authority 'to exercise exclusive legislation' has been expressly granted by the Constitution to Congress. It is not believed that any attempt will be made to expel the United States from this property by force; but if in this I should prove to be mistaken, the officer in command of the forts has received orders to act strictly on the defensive. In such a contingency the responsibility for consequences would rightfully rest upon the heads of the assailants.

"Apart from the execution of the laws, so far as this may be practicable, the Executive has no authority to decide what shall be the relations between the Federal Government and South Carolina. He has been invested with no such discretion. He possesses no power to change the relations heretofore existing between them, much less to acknowledge the independence of that State. This would be to invest a mere executive officer with the power of recognizing the dissolution of the confederacy among our thirty-three sovereign States. It bears no resemblance to the recognition of a foreign *de facto* government, involving no such responsibility. Any attempt to do this would, on his part, be a naked act of usurpation. It is, therefore, my duty to submit to Congress the whole question in all its bearings. The course of events is so rapidly hastening forward, that the emergency may soon arise, when you may be called upon to decide the momentous question whether you possess the power, by force of arms, to compel a State to remain in the Union. I should feel myself recreant to my duty were I not to express an opinion on this important subject.

"The question fairly stated is: Has the Constitution delegated to Congress the power to coerce a State into submission which is attempting to withdraw, or has actually withdrawn, from the confederacy? If answered in the affirmative, it must be on the principle that the power has been conferred upon Congress to declare and to make war against a State. After much serious reflection, I have arrived at the conclusion that no such power has been delegated to Congress, or to any other department of the Federal Government. It is manifest, upon an inspection of the Constitution, that this is not among the specific and enumerated powers granted to Congress; and it is equally apparent that its exercise is not 'necessary and proper for carrying into execution' any one of these powers. So far from this power having been delegated to Congress, it was expressly refused by the Convention which framed the Constitution.

"It appears from the proceedings of that body, that on the 31st May, 1787, the clause '*authorizing an exertion of the force of the whole against a delinquent State,*' came up for consideration. Mr. Madison opposed it in a brief but powerful speech, from which I shall extract but a single sentence. He observed: 'The use of force against a State would look more like a declaration of war than an infliction of punishment, and would probably be considered by the party attacked as a dissolution of all previous compacts by which it might be bound.' Upon his motion, the clause was unanimously postponed, and was never, I believe, again presented. Soon afterward, on the 8th June, 1787, when incidentally adverting to the subject, he said: 'Any government for the United States, formed on the supposed practicability of using force against the unconstitutional proceedings of the States, would prove as visionary and fallacious as the Government of Congress,' evidently meaning the then existing Congress of the old confederation.

"Without descending to particulars, it may be safely asserted that the power to make war against a State is at variance with the whole spirit and intent of the Constitution. Suppose such a war should result in the conquest of a State, how are we to govern it afterward? Shall we hold it as a province, and govern it by despotic power? In the nature of things we could not, by physical force, control the will of the people, and compel them to elect Senators and Representatives to Congress, and to perform all the other duties depending upon their own volition, and required from the free citizens of a free State, as a constituent member of the confederacy.

"But if we possessed this power, would it be wise to exercise it under existing circumstances? The object would doubtless be to preserve the Union. War would not only present the most effectual means of destroying it, but would banish all hope of its peaceable reconstruction. Besides, in the fraternal conflict, a vast amount of blood and treasure would be expended, rendering future reconciliation between the States impossible. In the mean time, who can foretell what would be the sufferings and privations of the people during its existence?

"The fact is, that our Union rests upon public opinion, and can never be cemented by the blood of its citizens shed in civil war. If it can not live in the affections of the people, it must one day perish. Congress possess many means of preserving it by conciliation; but the sword was not placed in their hand to preserve it by force.

"But may I be permitted solemnly to invoke my countrymen to pause and deliberate, before they determine to destroy this, the grandest temple which has ever been dedicated to human freedom since the world began? It has been consecrated by the blood of our fathers, by the glories of the past, and by the hopes of the future. The Union has already made us the most prosperous and, ere long, will, if preserved, render us the most powerful nation on the face of the earth. In every foreign region of the globe the title of American citizen is held in the highest respect, and when pronounced in a foreign land it causes the hearts of our countrymen to swell with honest pride. Surely when we reach the brink of the yawning abyss, we shall recoil with horror from the last fatal plunge. By such a dread catastrophe the hopes of the friends of freedom throughout the world would be destroyed, and a long night of leaden despotism would enshroud the nations. Our example for more than eighty years would not only be lost, but it would be quoted as a conclusive proof that man is unfit for self-government.

"It is not every wrong—nay, not every grievous wrong—which can justify a resort to such a fearful alternative. This ought to be the last desperate remedy of a despairing people, after every other constitutional means of conciliation had been exhausted. We should reflect that under this free Government there is an incessant ebb and flow in public opinion. The slavery question, like everything human, will have its day. I firmly believe that it has already reached and passed its culminating point. But if, in the midst of the existing excitement, the Union shall perish, the evil may then become irreparable. Congress can contribute much to avert it by proposing and recommending to the Legislatures of the several States the remedy for existing evils, which the Constitution has itself provided for its own preservation. This has been tried at different critical periods of our history, and always with eminent success. It is to be found in the 5th article providing for its own amendment. Under this article, amendments have been proposed by two thirds of both Houses of Congress, and have been 'ratified by the Legislatures of three fourths of the several States,' and have consequently become parts of the Constitution. To this process the country is indebted for the clause prohibiting Congress from passing any law respecting an establishment of religion, or abridging the freedom of speech, or of the press, or of the right of petition. To this we are also indebted for the bill of Rights, which secures the people against any abuse of power by the Federal Government. Such were the apprehensions justly entertained by the friends of State Rights at that period as to have rendered it extremely doubtful whether the Constitution could have long survived without these amendments.

"Again: the Constitution was amended by the same process after the election of President Jefferson by the House of Representatives, in February, 1803. This amendment was rendered necessary to prevent a recurrence of the dangers which had seriously threatened the existence of the Government during the pendency of that election. The article for its own amendment was intended to secure the amicable adjustment of conflicting constitutional questions like the present which might arise between the governments of the States and that of the United States. This appears from cotemporaneous history. In this connection, I shall merely call attention to a few sentences in Mr. Madison's justly celebrated report in 1799 to the Legislature of Virginia. In this he ably and conclusively defended the resolutions of the preceding Legislature against the strictures of several other State Legislatures. These were mainly founded upon the protest of the Virginia Legislature against the 'Alien and Sedition Acts,' as 'palpable and alarming infractions of the Constitution.' In pointing out the peaceful and constitutional remedies—and he referred to none other—to which the States were authorized to resort on such occasions, he concludes by saying, 'that the Legislatures of the States might have made a direct representation to Congress with a view to obtain a rescinding of the two offensive acts, or they might have represented to their respective senators in Congress their wish that two thirds thereof would propose an explanatory amendment to the Constitution; or two thirds of themselves, if such had been their option, might, by an application to Congress, have obtained a convention for the same object.'

"This is the very course which I earnestly recommend in order to obtain an 'explanatory amendment' of the Constitution on the subject of slavery. This might originate with Congress or the State Legislatures, as may be deemed most advisable to attain the object.

"The explanatory amendment might be confined to the final settlement of the true construction of the Constitution on three special points:

"1. An express recognition of the right of property in slaves in the States where it now exists or may hereafter exist.

"2. The duty of protecting this right in all the common Territories throughout their territorial existence, and until they shall be admitted as States into the Union, with or without slavery, as their constitutions may prescribe.

"3. A like recognition of the right of the master to have his slave, who has escaped from one State to another, restored and 'delivered up' to him, and of the validity of the Fugitive Slave law enacted for this purpose, together with a declaration that all State laws impairing or defeating this right are violations of the Constitution, and are consequently null and void.

"It may be objected that this construction of the Constitution has already been settled by the Supreme Court of the United States, and what more ought to be required? The answer is, that a very large proportion of the people of the United States still contest the correctness of this decision, and never will cease from agitation and admit its binding force until clearly established by the people of the several States in their sovereign character. Such an explanatory amendment would, it is believed, forever terminate the existing dissensions and restore peace and harmony among the States.

"It ought not to be doubted that such an appeal to the arbitrament established by the Constitution itself would be received with favor by all the States of the confederacy. In any event it ought to be tried in a spirit of conciliation before any of these States shall separate themselves from the Union.

"When I entered upon the duties of the Presidential office, the aspect neither of our foreign nor domestic affairs was at all satisfactory. We were involved in dangerous complications with several nations, and two of our Territories were in a state of revolution against the Government. A restoration of the African slave-trade had numerous and powerful advocates. Unlawful military expeditions were countenanced by many of our citizens, and were suffered, in defiance of the efforts of the Government, to escape from our shores, for the purpose of making war upon the unoffending people of neighboring republics with whom we were at peace. In addition to these and other difficulties, we experienced a revulsion in monetary affairs, soon after my advent to power, of unexampled severity and of ruinous consequences to all the great interests of the country. When we take a retrospect of what was then our condition, and contrast this with its material prosperity at the time of the late Presidential election, we have abundant reason to return our grateful thanks to that merciful Providence which has never forsaken us as a nation in all our past trials."

CHAPTER IV.

Meeting of Congress.—Little Hope.—Determination of the Disunionists.—Refusal to Vote—Reasons.—Opposed to Compromise.—Bold Assertions of Southern Senators.—A Programme of Rebellion.—A Menace of Rebellion.—An Appeal for Union.—Caucuses and Conferences.—Failure.—Increased Violence and Hostility.—Bewilderment of the Moderates.—President Buchanan's indisposition to exercise Authority.—His Message an Encouragement to Rebellion. —General Scott's Advice.—Advice not Taken.—Dissension in the Cabinet.—Resignation of Cass.—Continued but ineffectual attempts of Congress.—Firmness of the Republicans.—Speech of Wade.—Resolutions of Crittenden.— The state of Feeling in the Country.—Depression of Trade and Commerce.—Bankruptcy.—Suspension of Specie Payment.—Emptiness of the National Treasury.—Resignation of Cobb.—Appointment of Dix.—A continued belief in the Cessation of Troubles.—Speech of Seward.

1860. Dec. 3 From the very first day of the meeting of Congress it became evident that the distracted country had little to hope from its action. All the members from South Carolina, and most of those from Florida, Alabama, Georgia, and Mississippi, who still retained their seats in the national legislature with a formal affectation of allegiance to the Union, showed at once their obstinate determination to dissolve it. They refused to vote on the resolution, "that so much of the President's message as relates to the present perilous condition of the country be referred to a special committee of one from each State," audaciously declaring, as a reason for their recreancy, that the States to which they owed allegiance had, in their "sovereign" capacity, ordered conventions to consider their relations with the Federal Union, and that they looked to them for an authoritative decision of the question. Some even proclaimed that they were now, and had ever been, opposed to all compromises. The introduction of a resolution expressing fidelity to the Union, and pledging the House to maintain it, was fiercely opposed by the disaffected Southern members, and every indication was given of a predetermined hostility to all efforts at conciliation. Such were the sentiments and action, not only of the Southern members of the less restrained House of Representatives, but of the more composed Senate. Even a senator from North Carolina, a State which was believed to be loyal to the Union, did not hesitate to propose a division of the public property between the North and South, while the senators of Mississippi, Georgia, and Texas declared any attempt on the part of the Federal authorities to resist the progress of insurrection would be opposed by force. The senator* from Georgia, after a bold avowal of the projected rebellion, published by anticipation its programme, and flaunted it in the face of the Senate with the declaration, that "before the 4th of March—before your President is inaugurated—there will be five States, if not eight, that will be out of the Union, and will have formed a constitution for a frame of government." He declared that the South wanted no concessions, and would receive none. "You can not," he added, "stop this revolution. It is not the liberty laws, but the mob law, which the South fears. They do not dread these overt acts, for, without the power of the Federal Government, by force, under the Republican rule, their institution would not last ten years, and they know it. They intend to go out of this Union. Before the 4th of March five States will have declared their independence, and I am satisfied that three other States will follow as soon as the action of the people can be had. Arkansas will call her convention, and Louisiana will follow. And though there is a clog in the way in the lone star of Texas, in the person of the governor, who will not consent to call the Legislature, yet the public sentiment is so strong, that even her governor may be over-ridden; and if he will not yield to that public sentiment, some Texan Brutus may arise to rid his country of this old, hoary-headed traitor. There has been a good deal of vaporing and threatening, but they came from the last men who would carry out their threats. Men talk about their eighteen millions, but we hear a few days afterward of these same men being switched in the face, and they tremble like a sheep-stealing dog. There will be no war. The North, governed by such far-seeing statesmen as the senator from New York, will see the futility of

---
* Mr. Iverson.

this. In less than twelve months a Southern confederacy will be formed, and it will be the most successful government on earth. The Southern States, thus banded together, will be able to resist any force in the world. We do not expect war, but we will be prepared for it, and we are not a feeble race of Mexicans either."

This menace of rebellion was received with a cautious but defiant silence on the part of most of the Republicans, and timid expressions from the moderate men of all parties of a hope of still allaying the fierce temper of the South by the persuasives of conciliation and compromise. Crittenden, of Kentucky, the Nestor of the Senate, appealed to the sentiment of Union by an eloquent exposition of its blessings, and the dangers to the country of its dissolution. "This Union was established," he said, "by great sacrifices, and it is worthy of great sacrifices and great concessions for its maintenance. I trust that there is no senator but who is willing to yield and conciliate, and to compromise, in order to preserve the Union to the nation and to the country. I look with dismay, and something like despair, to the condition of this country when the Union is stricken down and we shall be turned loose to speculate on the foundations of a new government. I look at it with fear and trembling, which predispose me to the most solemn consideration that I am capable of feeling, and to search out, if possible, some means for the reconciliation of the different sections and members of this Union, to see if we can not again restore that harmony and fraternity that belong to the Union which has given us so much blessing and prosperity."

The Senate and House, with brief intervals of adjournment, during which vain attempts were made by caucuses and conferences to appease contention, continued their fruitless deliberations. The representatives of the extreme Southern States became daily more inveterate in their expressions of hostility to the Federal Government, and more outspoken in their expressions of disloyalty. The more moderate men of the South and those of the North seemed bewildered and powerless to counsel or to act.

President Buchanan, surrounded by men whose ill-concealed treason was soon to display itself in open rebellion, showed no disposition to exercise his power in protecting the authority of the Federal Government already boldly defied. His message, manipulated to their purpose by the hands of traitors, had, while it argued against the right of secession, put in a plea for its extenuation on the score of provocation from the North, and by confessing the impotency of the Federal authority to enforce obedience, encouraged the disaffected to rebel, with assurances of impunity. His conduct was in conformity with the assertion in his message, that coercion was unconstitutional, and he studiously withheld every indication of a manifestation of the exercise of executive authority to check the intent or to repress the overt act of rebellion.

ADVICE OF GENERAL SCOTT.

The commander-in-chief, Lieutenant-General Scott, had already at an early period urged upon the President the necessity of prompt measures to thwart the action of threatened secession. "From a knowledge of our Southern population," he wrote in a letter to Mr. Buchanan, "it is my solemn conviction that there is some danger of an early act of rashness preliminary to secession, viz., the seizure of some or all of the following forts: Forts Jackson and St. Philip, in the Mississippi, below New Orleans, both without garrisons; Fort Morgan, below Mobile, without a garrison; forts Pickens and McRae, Pensacola harbor, with an insufficient garrison for one; Fort Pulaski, below Savannah, without a garrison; forts Moultrie and Sumter, Charleston harbor, the former with an insufficient garrison, and the latter without any; and Fort Monroe, Hampton Roads, without a sufficient garrison. In my opinion all these works should be immediately so garrisoned, as to make any attempt to take any one of them by surprise or *coup de main* ridiculous.

"With the army faithful to its allegiance, and the navy probably equally so, and with a Federal Executive for the next twelve months of firmness and moderation, which the country has a right to expect—*moderation* being an element of power not less than *firmness*—there is good reason to hope that the danger of secession may be made to pass away without one conflict of arms, one execution, or one arrest for treason."

This timely advice of the veteran Scott, always vigilant to preserve the Union, was unheeded by the President, whose feeble will was guided by those who were seeking to destroy it. His traitorous associates in the Government threatened to resign, in case he complied with the suggestions of Scott, and extorted from him the pledge not to reinforce the forts. While thus promoting their traitorous purposes with the sanction and under the protection of the Federal Executive, these plotters of rebellion clung to the Government, whose authority they were daily weakening while they were strengthening their own power of ill.

There had been, however, already some dissension in the cabinet in regard to the subject of reinforcing the Southern forts; and when the expediency of sending an additional force to Major Anderson, in command of a feeble garrison at Fort Moultrie, in Charleston harbor, became manifest, two Northern members, Cass and Toucey, earnestly pleaded for it. They were, however, overborne, and the President, hampered by his pledges and controlled by his Southern advisers, sent not a single soldier to sustain the insulted and threatened authority of the Government. Cass, with patriotic indignation at this remissness of duty, resigned his seat in the cabinet.

While the President was thus yielding, unresistingly, to the promoters of rebellion, Congress was continuing its futile attempts to check it by resolutions. The debates, however, became only more angry and the discord more

Oct. 29, 1860.

Dec. 14.

obvious. The secessionists increased in violence and audacity, and the extreme Republicans, provoked to more obstinate resistance, renewed their declarations of opposing all compromises. Wade, the Republican senator for Ohio, said, in a forcible speech:

"We beat you on the plainest and most palpable issue ever presented to the American people, and one which every man understood; and now, when we come to the capital, we tell you that our candidates must and shall be inaugurated—must and shall administer this government precisely as the Constitution prescribes. It would not only be humiliating, but highly dishonorable to us, if we listened to any compromise by which we should lay aside the honest verdict of the people. When it comes to that, you have no government, but anarchy intervenes, and civil war may follow, and all the evils that human imagination can raise may be consequent upon such a course as that. The American people would lose the sheet-anchor of Liberty whenever it is denied on this floor that a majority fairly given shall rule. I know not what others may do, but I tell you, that with that verdict of the people in my pocket, and standing on the platform on which these candidates were elected, I would suffer anything before I would compromise in any way. I deem it no case where we have a right to extend courtesy or generosity. The absolute right, the most sacred that a free people can bestow upon any man, is their verdict that gives him a full title to the office he holds. If we can not stand there we can not stand anywhere, and, my friends, any other verdict would be as fatal to you as to us."

The moderate men of both the North and the South with an amiable persistency still persevered in their endeavors to preserve the national peace by plans of conciliation and compromise. These, however, met with little encouragement from the embittered partisans of extreme opinions, and the hope of "saving the Union" by mutual concessions daily diminished. The resolutions of Mr. Crittenden, of Kentucky, seemed from the high character of the veteran statesman who offered them, to make the greatest impression upon public opinion. These proposed to renew the Missouri Compromise line—prohibiting slavery in the Territory north of 36 deg. 30 min., and protecting it south of that latitude; to admit new States with or without slavery, as their constitutions shall provide; to prohibit the abolition of slavery by Congress in the States; to prohibit its abolition in the District of Columbia so long as it exists either in Virginia or Maryland; to permit the transportation of slaves in any of the States by land or water; to provide for the payment of fugitive slaves, when rescued; to repeal one obnoxious feature of the Fugitive Slave law—the inequality of the fee to the commissioner; to ask the repeal of all the Personal Liberty bills in the Northern States, and effectually to execute the laws for the suppression of the African slave-trade. These were to be submitted to the people as amendments to the Constitution, and to be changed at no subsequent time.

While treason was being uttered in Congress, plotted in the cabinet, and encouraged to overt act in the slave States, unchecked by the national authority, which seemed indisposed, if not incapable of vindicating its supremacy, there was a general feeling of discouragement throughout the country. This was increased by the universal depression in trade and commerce. The great business of the Northern commercial and manufacturing cities with the South had been almost entirely arrested. The Southern merchants made no new, and failed to pay for their old, purchases. The payment of the great debt of three hundred millions of dollars due to the North suddenly stopped, and fears were already entertained that it would never be resumed. The Southern banks having suspended the payment of specie, had so depreciated the value of their currency, that exchange upon the North rose to such a height as almost to preclude remittances from the South whenever there were still found those disposed to make them. Northern merchants, thus suddenly deprived of their Southern resources, were forced into bankruptcy. The banks necessarily sympathized with the ruin of their customers, and although those of New York and Boston were enabled, through the abundance of their resources, to sustain their credit and even to increase their loans, the banks of Philadelphia, Baltimore, Washington, and Richmond suspended specie payment.

To add to this financial embarrassment, the national treasury was threatened with bankruptcy. So little faith had the country in the government as controlled by the Southern advisers of the President, that the secretary of the treasury, Howell Cobb, of Georgia, could only obtain a loan at a discount of 25 per cent. of the usual market rates in periods of national prosperity. Cobb was so perplexed by the financial embarrassments of his department, that, under the pretence of a difference of political views with the President, he resigned, and betook himself to the more congenial work of disturbing the loyalty of his native State. His successor, John A. Dix, of New York, a Northern man, was enabled, however, through the confidence inspired by his integrity and patriotism, to restore the public credit and again fill the treasury.

With all these causes, however, tending to depress the public feeling, there was still a strong belief among Northern people, that the civil troubles would, although none pretended to know how, be soon settled. This seemed to be based upon the supposed attachment to the Union among the people even in South Carolina. How far this belief in the loyalty of the Southern slave States prevailed is well illustrated by a speech of Seward, then senator, now secretary of state. He thus jauntily descanted on the grave subject of Southern disaffection:

"Now, gentleman, my belief about all this is, that whether it is Massachusetts or South Carolina, or whether **Dec. 22.**

it is New York or Florida, it would turn out the same way in each case. There is no such thing in the book, no such thing in reason, no such thing in philosophy, and no such thing in nature, as any State existing on the continent of North America outside of the United States of America. I do not believe a word of it; and I do not believe it for a good many reasons. Some I have already hinted at; and one is, because I do not see any good reason given for it. The best reason I see given for it is, that the people of some of the Southern States hate us of the free States very badly, and they say that we hate them, and that all love is lost between us. Well, I do not believe a word of that. On the other hand, I do know for myself and for you, that, bating some little differences of opinion about advantages, and about prescription, and about office, and about freedom, and about slavery, and all those which are family difficulties, for which we do not take any outsiders in any part of the world into our councils on either side, there is not a state on the earth, outside of the American Union, which I like half so well as I do the State of South Carolina—[cheers]—neither England, nor Ireland, nor Scotland, nor France, nor Turkey; although from Turkey they sent me Arab horses, and from South Carolina they send me nothing but curses. Still, I like South Carolina better than I like any of them; and I have the presumption and vanity to believe that if there were nobody to overhear the State of South Carolina when she is talking, she would confess that she liked us tolerably well. I am very sure that if anybody were to make a descent on New York to-morrow—whether Louis Napoleon, or the Prince of Wales, or his mother [laughter], or the Emperor of Russia, or the Emperor of Austria, all the hills of South Carolina would pour forth their population for the rescue of New York. [Cries of 'Good,' and applause.] God knows how this may be. I do not pretend to know, I only conjecture. But this I do know, that if any of those powers were to make a descent on South Carolina, I know who would go to her rescue. [A voice—'We'd all go.'] We would all go—everybody. ['That's so,' and great applause.] Therefore they do not humbug me with their secession, and I do not think they will humbug you; and I do not believe that, if they do not humbug you and me, they will much longer succeed in humbugging themselves. [Laughter.] Now, fellow-citizens, this is the ultimate result of all this business. These States are always to be together—always shall. Talk of striking down a star from that constellation—it is a thing which can not be done. [Applause.] I do not see any less stars to-day than I did a week ago, and I expect to see more all the while. [Laughter.] The question then is, what in these times—when people are laboring under the delusion that they are going out of the Union and going to set up for themselves—ought we to do in order to hold them in? I do not know any better rule than the rule which every good father of a family observes. It is this. If a man wishes not to keep his family together, it is the easiest thing in the world to place them apart. He will do so at once if he only gets discontented with his son, quarrels with him, complains of him, torments him, threatens him, coerces him. This is the way to get rid of the family, and to get them all out of doors. On the other hand, if you wish to keep them, you have got only one way to do it. That is, be patient, kind, paternal, forbearing, and wait until they come to reflect for themselves. The South is to us what the wife is to her husband. I do not know any man in the world who can not get rid of his wife if he tries. * * * I do not know a man on earth who—even though his wife was as troublesome as the wife of Socrates—cannot keep his wife if he wants to do so ; all that he needs is, to keep his own virtue and his own temper. [Applause.] Now, in all this business I propose that we shall keep our own virtue, which, in politics, is loyalty, and our own temper, which, in politics, consists in remembering that men may differ, that brethren may differ. If we keep entirely cool, and entirely calm, and entirely kind, a debate will ensue which will be kindly in itself, and it will prove very soon either that we are wrong—and we shall concede to our offended brethren—or else that we are right, and they will acquiesce and come back into fraternal relations with us. I do not wish to anticipate any question. We have a great many statesmen who demand at once to know what the North proposes to do —what the Government proposes to do —whether we propose to coerce our Southern brethren back into their allegiance. They ask us, as of course they may rightly ask, what will be the value of fraternity which is compelled? All I have to say on that subject is, that so long ago as the time of Sir Thomas More, he discovered, and set down the discovery in his writings, that there were a great many schoolmasters, and that while there were a very few who knew how to instruct children, there were a great many who knew how to whip them. [Laughter.] I propose to have no question on that subject, but to hear complaints, to redress them if they ought to be redressed, and if we have the power to redress them ; and I expect them to be withdrawn if they are unreasonable, because I know that the necessities which made this Union exist, for these States, are stronger to-day than they were when the Union was made, and that those necessities are enduring, while the passions of men are short-lived and ephemeral. I believe that secession was stronger on the night of the 6th of November last, when a President and Vice-President who were unacceptable to the slave States were elected, than it is now. That is now some fifty days since, and I believe that every day's sun which set since that time, has set on mollified passions and prejudices, and that if you will only give it time, sixty days' more suns will give you a much brighter and more cheerful atmosphere." [Loud and long continued applause.]

CHAPTER V.

The Inaction of Government.—The Bewilderment of the North.—Movement of the South.—Precipitancy of South Carolina.—Election of Convention of South Carolina.—Impatience of Action.—Anticipatory Programme.—Governor Gist's last Message.—Action of other Slave States.—Alabama Declaration of Causes.—Immediate Secession views of the Governor of Florida.—Immediate Secession views of the Governor of Georgia.—Vigilance Committees. —Arming and Equipping.—Conventions called.—Meeting of South Carolina Convention.—Adjournment to Charleston.—Ordinance of Secession.—Manifestation of Popular Feeling in the South.—Audacity of Southern Members of Congress.—Proceedings of South Carolina Convention.—Proclamation of the Act of Secession of South Carolina.— Declaration of Causes.—Withdrawal from Congress of the Members of South Carolina.—Apparent attempts made to check the precipitate action of South Carolina.—Motives of such attempts.—Opposition to Disunion from Maryland. —Union Sentiments in Virginia.—Loyalty of Eastern and Western Virginia contrasted.—Proposed Conferences.— Disposition of Tennessee.—Firm stand for the Union of Johnson and Etheredge.—Letter of Bell, of Tennessee.— Feeling in Kentucky.—Governor Magoffin's Propositions.—Manful resistance of Governor Houston, of Texas.— Silence of Arkansas.—Irresolution of Georgia.—Union eloquence of Alexander H. Stephens.—Feeling in Alabama. —Mississippi.—Louisiana.—How the Propositions of the other Slave States were received by South Carolina.—South Carolina's Assurances.—Force of Example.—Anticipated Effect.—Ordinance of Concurrence.

1860.

WHILE the President, meekly submissive to the influence of his traitorous advisers, was confessing and manifesting impotency; while the national councils, alternately frightened by the defiance of audacious rebels and provoked by their threats, were now striving to soothe them by plans of conciliation and compromise, and again contending with them in angry discussion; while the people of the North, bewildered by the inaction of the Federal authority, the perplexing deliberations of Congress, and the frivolous conjectures of their leaders, seemed doubtful whether to hope or to fear, and willing to yield their destiny to the uncertainties of chance, the South was moving with unhesitating strides toward rebellion.

South Carolina, with characteristic precipitancy, established her claim to precedence in secession. The delegates to the convention called by the act of the Legislature were elected on the 5th of December, to meet on the 17th. The leaders of South Carolina, however, as if impatient of all deliberation, did not await its action. They summoned the people in masses throughout the State, and distinctly announced the programme of rebellion. At a large meeting in Charleston, Mr. Memminger, an able lawyer of that city, and a prominent politician, declared even before the election of the delegates that the convention, within three days of its assembling, would declare South Carolina out of the Union; that a commissioner would be sent to the capital of the United States to treat in regard to the forts and other Federal property, which would be formally demanded, and if not given up, that the armed men of South Carolina would take them. Presuming upon the easy temper of Buchanan, or the corrupt connivance of his traitorous advisers, he did not hesitate

Nov. 30.

to declare that he had no fear of the interference of the President, while he complacently dwelt upon the powerlessness of his successor, who would be too much embarrassed by the difficulty of organizing his government and obtaining the sanction of Congress, to apply coercion to South Carolina, until she had been joined by the other cotton States, when, thus strengthened, she would be able to resist it.

The governor* of the State, in his last message, urged the prospective convention to immediate action.

Dec. 7.

"The delay," he said, "of the convention for a single week to pass the ordinance of secession, will have a blighting and chilling influence upon the action of the other Southern States. The opponents of the movement everywhere will be encouraged to make another effort to rally their now disorganized and scattered forces to defeat our action and stay our onward march. Fabius conquered by delay, and there are those of his school, though with a more unworthy purpose, who, shrinking from open and manly attack, use this veil to hide their deformity, and from a masked battery to discharge their missiles. But I trust they will strike the armor of truth and fall harmless at our feet, and that by the 28th of December no flag but the Palmetto will float over any part of South Carolina."

Great encouragement had already come from the leaders of the other cotton States, who hoped, by the hasty action of South Carolina, to precipitate their fellow-citizens into a separation from that Union for which there might be still a traditional reverence. At an early meeting at Mobile the secession leaders of Alabama had issued a declaration of causes for separation which they emphatically urged. After a long and bitter exposition of the wrongs they had suffered from the North, they declared:

Nov. 13.

"The time has come for us 'to put our house in order,' and, if need be, to stand by our arms.

"We will not give the enemy time to collect his strength and wield the powers of government against us, by waiting for any further 'overt act.' Therefore, be it

"*Resolved*, 1. That the election of Abraham Lincoln to the Presidency upon the principles avowed by the Black Republican party is, in our opinion, a virtual overthrow of the Constitution and of the equal right of the States.

"2. That the idea of submission by the South to the rule of such a man and such a party should be repudiated from one end of her borders to the other.

"3. That in the language of the Constitution of Alabama, under which she was admitted into the Union, 'All political power is inherent in the people, and all free governments are founded on their authority, and intended for their benefit; and, therefore, they have at all times an inalienable and indefeasible right to alter, reform, or abolish their form of government in such manner as they may think expedient.'

"4. That, in the present state of things, it is the deliberate opinion of

* Gist.

this meeting, assembled without distinction of parties, that the State of Alabama should withdraw from the Federal Union without any further delay than may be necessary to obtain in the speediest manner a consultation with other slaveholding States, in the hope of securing their co-operation in a movement which we deem essential to our safety."

It is true that in this document a consultation with other slaveholding States was recommended, with the hope of securing their co-operation, but at the same time it advised immediate action. A meeting was held in Louisiana, at which a similar declaration was suggested.

The Governor of Florida invoked the Nov. Legislature to immediate secession. 26. "For myself," he said, "in full view of the responsibility of my position, I most decidedly declare that, in my opinion, the only hope the Southern States have for domestic peace or safety, or for future respectability and prosperity, is dependent on their action now ; and that the proper action is, secession from our faithless, perjured confederates." Governor Brown, too, of Georgia—a State thought to be extremely reluctant to dissolve its connection with the Union— Dec. had written a letter in favor of early 9. secession. Mississippi had sent commissioners to all the slaveholding States to confer with them on the means "for their common defence and safety." Vigilance committees had been formed in the cotton States, money appropriated for equipping and arming, and conventions called, whose purpose was unequivocally the severance of their connection with the Federal Union.

The Convention of South Carolina assembled on the day appointed, but in consequence of the prevalence of Dec. an epidemic of small-pox at the 17. capital, adjourned from Columbia to Charleston, where, by a unanimous vote on the 20th of December, this, the first formal act of secession, was passed :

"AN ORDINANCE TO DISSOLVE THE UNION BETWEEN THE STATE OF SOUTH CAROLINA AND OTHER STATES UNITED WITH HER UNDER THE COMPACT ENTITLED THE CONSTITUTION OF THE UNITED STATES OF AMERICA:

" We, the people of the State of South Carolina, in convention assembled, do declare and ordain, and it is hereby declared and ordained, that the ordinance adopted by us in convention, on the 23d day of May, in the year of our Lord 1788, whereby the Constitution of the United States of America was ratified, and also all acts and parts of acts of the General Assembly of this State ratifying the amendments of the said Constitution, are hereby repealed, and that the Union now subsisting between South Carolina and other States under the name of the United States of America is hereby dissolved."

That in Charleston and throughout South Carolina the passage of this ordinance should be received with a manifestation of popular joy was expected, that in Mobile, and New Orleans, Memphis, Macon, Norfolk, and even in Baltimore, it should be welcomed by the firing of guns, the cheers of the people, military parades, the singing of the Marseillaise, the decorating of busts of Calhoun with secession cockades, the raising of the Palmetto flag, the burning of bonfires, and the illuminating of the streets, was, if a discouraging, not a surprising, exhibition on the part of an excited and deluded people ; that, however, a member of the Federal Congress, in the very capital of the Union, should venture to applaud this attempt to dissolve it by declaring that " one of the sovereign States of this confederacy has, by the *glorious* act of her people, withdrawn, in vindication of her rights, from the Union,"* and that some of his fellows should clap their hands in sympathetic response, was an audacity of treason as astounding as it was unexampled.

The Convention of South Carolina proceeded rapidly in its work of dissolution. Commissioners were appointed to proceed to Washington, and to treat for a peaceful settlement of the relations between the United States and the "sovereign" State of South Carolina, and negotiate for the transfer of forts and other public property.

Dec. 21.

The newly elected governor, Pickens, proclaimed to the world, in accordance with the act of secession, that "South Carolina is, and has a right to be, a separate, sovereign, free, and independent State, and, as such, has a right to levy war, conclude peace, negotiate treaties, leagues, or covenants, and to do all acts whatever that rightfully appertain to a free and independent State."

Dec. 22.

Dec. 21.

* Mr. Garnet, member of Congress for Virginia.

This was followed by the—

" DECLARATION OF CAUSES WHICH INDUCED THE SECESSION OF SOUTH CAROLINA.

"The people of the State of South Carolina, in convention assembled, on the 2d day of April, A.D. 1852, declared that the frequent violations of the Constitution of the United States by the Federal Government, and its encroachments upon the reserved rights of the States, fully justified this State in their withdrawal from the Federal Union ; but in deference to the opinions and wishes of the other slaveholding States, she forbore at that time to exercise this right. Since that time these encroachments have continued to increase, and further forbearance ceases to be a virtue.

" And now the State of South Carolina having resumed her separate and equal place among nations, deems it due to herself, to the remaining United States of America, and to the nations of the world, that she should declare the immediate causes which have led to this act.

" In the year 1765, that portion of the British empire embracing Great Britain undertook to make laws for the government of that portion composed of the thirteen American Colonies. A struggle for the right of self-government ensued, which resulted, on the 4th of July, 1776, in a declaration, by the Colonies, ' that they are, and of right ought to be, FREE AND INDEPENDENT STATES ; and that, as free and independent states, they have full power to levy war, conclude peace, contract alliances, establish commerce, and to do all other acts and things which independent states may of right do.'

"They further solemnly declared that whenever any 'form of government becomes destructive of the ends for which it was established, it is the right of the people to alter or abolish it, and to institute a new government.' Deeming the Government of Great Britain to have become destructive of these ends, they declare that the Colonies 'are absolved from all allegiance to the British Crown, and that all political connection between them and the state of Great Britain is, and ought to be, totally dissolved.'

"In pursuance of this Declaration of Independence, each of the thirteen States proceeded to exercise its separate sovereignty; adopted for itself a constitution, and appointed officers for the administration of government in all its departments—legislative, executive, and judicial. For purposes of defence they united their arms and their counsels; and in 1778 they entered into a league known as the Articles of Confederation, whereby they agreed to intrust the administration of their external relations to a common agent, known as the Congress of the United States, expressly declaring, in the first article, 'that each State retains its sovereignty, freedom, and independence, and every power, jurisdiction, and right which is not, by this confederation, expressly delegated to the United States in Congress assembled.'

"Under this confederation the war of the Revolution was carried on; and on the 3d of September, 1783, the contest ended, and a definite treaty was signed by Great Britain, in which she acknowledged the independence of the Colonies in the following terms:

"'ARTICLE 1. His Britannic Majesty acknowledges the said United States, viz.: New Hampshire, Massachusetts Bay, Rhode Island and Providence Plantations, Connecticut, New York, New Jersey, Pennsylvania, Delaware, Maryland, Virginia, North Carolina, South Carolina, and Georgia, to be FREE, SOVEREIGN, AND INDEPENDENT STATES; that he treats with them as such; and, for himself, his heirs, and successors, relinquishes all claims to the government, property, and territorial rights of the same and every part thereof.'

"Thus were established the two great principles asserted by the Colonies, namely, the right of a state to govern itself; and the right of a people to abolish a government when it becomes destructive of the ends for which it was instituted. And concurrent with the establishment of these principles was the fact, that each Colony became, and was recognized by the mother country, AS A FREE, SOVEREIGN, AND INDEPENDENT STATE.

"In 1787, deputies were appointed by the States to revise the articles of confederation; and on 17th September, 1787, these deputies recommended, for the adoption of the States, the articles of union known as the Constitution of the United States.

"The parties to whom this constitution was submitted were the several sovereign States; they were to agree or

NEW NATIONAL WORK ON THE LATE REBELLION.

Now Publishing in Parts at 50 cents, and Divisions at $1.

THE GREAT CIVIL WAR:

A HISTORY OF

THE LATE REBELLION;

Being a complete Narrative of the Events connected with the Origin, **Progress**, and Conclusion of the War, with **Biographical Sketches of Leading** Statesmen and Distinguished Military and Naval Commanders, etc., etc.

By ROBERT TOMES, M.D.

Continued from the beginning of the year 1864 to the end of the War,

By BENJ. G. SMITH, Esq.

Illustrated by numerous highly finished Steel Engravings, Colored Maps, Plans, etc., from Drawings by F. O. C. **Darley** and other eminent Artists.

THE four years' war, now happily ended—so remarkable for its sudden outbreak, its unexpected duration, and its entire termination—not only absorbed universal attention at home, but had, during its continuance, a paramount interest for the nations of Europe, and was the subject of constant comment and prophecy on the part of both the friends and enemies of national self-government. It not only displayed the astonishing resources of the country, and exhibited, even while the struggle continued, in the vast armies raised and the persistent spirit of the people, a capacity for war that entitles the United States to the first rank among military nations, but also demonstrated the enduring character of the government and institutions, which have proved themselves able to withstand even the fearful shocks of a gigantic civil war.

A history of this great war will be a necessity to every loyal American. To be without a knowledge of the causes and events of the great struggle for the preservation of the Union would be as inexcusable as to be ignorant of the events which led to its formation.

The present work will be a complete history of the war and of its immediate causes, from the election of Mr. Lincoln and the commencement of actual hostilities by the attack on Fort Sumter, to the evacuation of Richmond and the surrender of the armies of Lee, Johnston, and Kirby Smith. It will contain detailed accounts of the great battles, sieges, marches, and naval operations, a record of political events, remarks on foreign relations, statistical facts with regard to the resources of both the Northern and Southern States, descriptions of fortresses and battle-fields, and a large number of biographical sketches of distinguished commanders and statesmen, to which will be appended a copious and elaborate Index.

Not the least attractive feature of the work will be the large number of beautiful and costly steel engravings, comprising portraits of statesmen and military and naval commanders, Northern and Southern, who have become famous in the course of the war.

Among the illustrations are also splendid bird's-eye views of Fortress Monroe and vicinity, Charleston, Richmond, and New Orleans; representations of battle-scenes, views of forts and battle-fields, sea views, and a number of carefully prepared colored maps and plans, highly useful in making clear the movements and positions of armies.

CONDITIONS OF PUBLICATION.

The work will be printed in a clear, bold type, on superfine, calendered paper, and issued in Parts at Fifty Cents, and Divisions at $1 each.

The illustrations will comprise fifty-four portraits and thirty-six battle-scenes, plans, maps, bird's-eye views, etc.

A Part will be published every two weeks and a Division every month until completed, the whole not to exceed forty-five Parts, at Fifty Cents each.

No subscriber's name received for less than the whole work; and each Part or Division will be payable on delivery, the carrier not being allowed to give credit or receive payment in advance.

VIRTUE & YORSTON, 12 DEY STREET, & 544 BROADWAY, NEW YORK.

And Sold by their Agents in all the Principal Cities of the United States and Canadas.

disagree, and when nine of them agreed, the compact was to take effect among those concurring; and the General Government, as the common agent, was then to be invested with their authority.

"If only nine of the thirteen States had concurred, the other four would have remained as they then were—separate sovereign states, independent of any of the provisions of the Constitution. In fact, two of the States did not accede to the Constitution until long after it had gone into operation among the other eleven; and during that interval, they each exercised the functions of an independent nation.

"By this constitution, certain duties were imposed upon the several States, and the exercise of certain of their powers was restrained, which necessarily impelled their continued existence as sovereign states. But, to remove all doubt, an amendment was added, which declared that the powers not delegated to the United States by the Constitution, nor prohibited by it to the States, are reserved to the States respectively, or to the people. On the 23d May, 1788, South Carolina, by a convention of her people, passed an ordinance assenting to this Constitution, and afterwards altered her own Constitution to conform herself to the obligations she had undertaken.

"Thus was established, by compact between the States, a government with defined objects and powers, limited to the express words of the grant. This limitation left the whole remaining mass of power subject to the clause reserving it to the States or the people, and rendered unnecessary any specification of reserved rights. We hold that the Government thus established is subject to the two great principles asserted in the Declaration of Independence; and we hold further, that the mode of its formation subjects it to a third fundamental principle, namely, the law of compact. We maintain that in every compact between two or more parties, the obligation is mutual; that the failure of one of the contracting parties to perform a material part of the agreement entirely releases the obligation of the other; and that where no arbiter is provided, each party is remitted to his own judgment to determine the fact of failure, with all its consequences.

"In the present case, that fact is established with certainty. We assert that fourteen of the States have deliberately refused for years past to fulfil their constitutional obligations, and we refer to their own statutes for proof.

"The Constitution of the United States, in its fourth article, provides as follows:

"'No person held to service or labor in one State under the laws thereof, escaping into another, shall, in consequence of any law or regulation therein, be discharged from such service or labor, but shall be delivered up, on claim of the party to whom such service or labor may be due.'

"This stipulation was so material to the compact, that without it that compact would not have been made. The greater number of the contracting parties held slaves, and they had previously evinced their estimate of the value of such a stipulation by making it a condition in the ordinance for the government of the territory ceded by Virginia, which obligations and the laws of the General Government, have ceased to effect the objects of the Constitution. The States of Maine, New Hampshire, Vermont, Massachusetts, Connecticut, Rhode Island, New York, Pennsylvania, Illinois, Indiana, Michigan, Wisconsin, and Iowa have enacted laws which either nullify the acts of Congress, or render useless any attempt to execute them. In many of these States the fugitive is discharged from the service of labor claimed, and in none of them has the State Government complied with the stipulation made in the Constitution. The State of New Jersey, at an early day, passed a law in conformity with her constitutional obligation; but the current of anti-slavery feeling has led her more recently to enact laws which render inoperative the remedies provided by her own laws and by the laws of Congress. In the State of New York, even, the right of transit for a slave has been denied by her tribunals; and the States of Ohio and Iowa have refused to surrender to justice fugitives charged with murder, and with inciting servile insurrection in the State of Virginia. Thus the constitutional compact has been deliberately broken and disregarded by the non-slaveholding States; and the consequence follows, that South Carolina is released from her obligation.

"The ends for which this Constitution was framed are declared by itself to be 'to form a more perfect union, to establish justice, insure domestic tranquility, provide for common defence, promote the general welfare, and secure the blessings of liberty to ourselves and our posterity.'

"These ends it endeavored to accomplish by a federal government, in which each State was recognized as an equal, and had separate control over its own institutions. The right of property in slaves was recognized by giving to free persons distinct political rights; by giving them the right to represent, and burdening them with direct taxes for, three-fifths of their slaves; by authorizing the importation of slaves for twenty years; and by stipulating for the rendition of fugitives from labor.

"We affirm that these ends for which this Government was instituted have been defeated, and the Government itself has been destructive of them by the action of the non-slaveholding States. Those States have assumed the right of deciding upon the propriety of our domestic institutions; and have denied the rights of property established in fifteen of the States and recognized by the Constitution; they have denounced as sinful the institution of slavery; they have permitted the open establishment among them of societies, whose avowed object is to disturb the peace of and eloin the property of the citizens of other States. They have encouraged and assisted thousands of our slaves to leave their homes; and those who remain have been incited by emissaries, books, and pictures to servile insurrection.

"For twenty-five years this agitation has been steadily increasing, until it has now secured to its aid the power of the common government. Observing the forms of the Constitution, a sectional party has found within that article establishing the Executive department, the means of subverting the Constitution itself. A geographical line has been drawn across the Union, and all the States north of that line have united in the election of a man to the high office of President of the United States whose opinions and purposes are hostile to slavery. He is to be intrusted with the administration of the common government, because he has declared that that 'government can not endure permanently half slave, half free,' and that the public mind must rest in the belief that slavery is in the course of ultimate extinction.

"This sectional combination for the subversion of the Constitution has been aided, in some of the States, by elevating to citizenship persons who, by the supreme law of the land, are incapable of becoming citizens; and their votes have been used to inaugurate a new policy hostile to the South, and destructive of its peace and safety.

"On the 4th of March next this party will take possession of the Government. It has announced that the South shall be excluded from the common territory, that the judicial tribunal shall be made sectional, and that a war must be waged against slavery until it shall cease throughout the United States.

"The guarantees of the Constitution will then no longer exist; the equal rights of the States will be lost. The slaveholding States will no longer have the power of self-government or self-protection, and the Federal Government will have become their enemy.

"Sectional interest and animosity will deepen the irritation, and all hope of remedy is rendered vain by the fact that the public opinion at the North has invested a great political error with the sanctions of a more erroneous religious belief.

"We, therefore, the people of South Carolina, by our delegates in convention assembled, appealing to the Supreme Judge of the world for the rectitude of our intentions, have solemnly declared that the Union heretofore existing between this State and the other States of North America is dissolved, and that the State of South Carolina has resumed her position among the nations of the world as a separate and independent state, with full power to levy war, conclude peace, contract alliances, establish commerce, and to do all other acts and things which independent states may of right do."

The South Carolina members, at the same time that their State declared its independence, formally withdrew from Congress with a studious expression in their letter to the Speaker of the House of Representatives of a desire to do so with a feeling of "mutual regard and respect for each other, and the hope that in our future relations we may better enjoy that peace and harmony essential to the happiness of a free and enlightened people."

Apparent attempts had been made by some of the political leaders of the South to arrest this precipitate action of South Carolina. Some of these were undoubtedly prompted by a sincere attachment to the Union and a desire to preserve it. Some only affected the sentiment of patriotism, while others, equally resolved upon secession with the men of South Carolina, were desirous of a concert of action, in order to secure strength of effort and certainty of effect by combination. The Governor of Maryland, though beset by a strong secession sentiment in his State, resolutely opposed any indication of opposition to the legitimate authority of the Federal Government. In answer to a memorial of some of the more influential inhabitants of Maryland, urging him to convene the Legislature, he declared:

Nov. 27.
"Identified as I am by birth and every other tie with the South, a slaveholder, and feeling as warmly for my native State as any man can do, I am yet compelled by my sense of fair dealing, and my respect for the Constitution of our country, to declare that I see nothing in the bare election of Mr. Lincoln which would justify the South in taking any steps tending toward a separation of these States. Mr. Lincoln being elected, I am willing to await further results. If he will administer the government in a proper and patriotic manner, we are all bound to submit to his administration, much as we may have opposed his election."

Dec. 6.
At a later period, at a Democratic convention held in the city of Baltimore, the following resolution was passed:

"*Resolved*, That we deplore the action taken by our sister State of South Carolina, and earnestly protest against an ordinance of secession on her part as being unconstitutional, disorganizing, and precipitate, and unfriendly, if not arrogant, toward the counsels and situations of the other slaveholding States; and we believe that such act of secession will weaken and must divide their ultimate position; and while we declare for co-operation, we will firmly resist being dragged into secession. Maryland will not stand as a sentinel at the bidding of South Carolina, and we remind her, by the memories of the Revolution, that such purpose can not be justified; and, in conclusion, in a fraternal spirit, we entreat South Carolina to suspend all farther action until such measures of peaceful adjustment have first been tried and have failed."

Virginia, though many of her leaders, deeply infected with the heresies of Calhoun, were known to regard secession from the United States as an act if not immediately desirable, at any rate legal and justifiable, seemed to stand firm for the Union. Her political writers, in an emphatic protest against the assumed right of South Carolina to individual action, thus rebuked her presumption:

"Throwing aside the question of constitutional right to secede at all, there is something due to comity, to neighborhood associations, to propriety. No man has a 'right,' by setting fire to his own house, to endanger the house of his neighbor. Virginia, in this Union, or out of it as a sovereign, and as potential as South Carolina, has her own interests to look after, her own rights to be secured, her own feelings to be respected—and she will demand this from South Carolina just as much as she would from any other State in the present United States. It would seem as if in the course now pursued, fearing the conservative action of Virginia, and not desiring, in truth, 'a united South,' certain cotton States were for going off by themselves, for the mere sake of 'forming a cotton confederacy,' totally irrespective of other Southern States which do not recognize cotton as their king, and totally regardless of any interests or any views but their own. It used to be a 'united South!' It was formerly disunion and secession for aggression by the General Government. It is now a disunited South—secession on account of the untoward result of a Presidential election! This is not the way to uphold the rights of the States and the rights of the South. It is weakening our own position, and destroying our own strength."

The Virginian leaders, even the most headstrong advocates of States' Rights, seemed desirous of making an effort to hold fast by the Union. At a political banquet in Richmond, "The Union," "Virginia in the Union," and other patriotic toasts, were drunk and responded to with enthusiasm. While there might be doubt of the continued loyalty of Eastern, there was no question of the persistency of that of Western, Virginia, whose proximity to the free States of Illinois and Ohio, and identity of origin, habits, and interests, made them as one people. The loyalty of the East was conditional upon such concessions to the slave power as the most sanguine believers in compromise could hardly anticipate. The loyalty of the West, comparatively free of the entanglement of slave interests, was sincere and unconstrained.

Virginia strove to check the precipitancy of South Carolina by appointing a commissioner to urge an arrest of proceedings until there might be a conference among the slave States.

Tennessee, though her governor was suspected even at that early period of a strong sympathy, if not active concurrence, with the leaders of the rebellion, was apparently indisposed to secession. Her United States senator, and formerly governor, Andrew Johnson, and Emerson Etheredge, a member of the House of Representatives, were among the first to deny emphatically the assumed right of secession, and to call it treason. They both in their respective spheres were the firm assertors of the Federal authority and the resolute opponents of its enemies. Johnson, in the Senate of the United States, while even Northern men were doubting the right of the Government to suppress a rebellion against its authority, thus emphatically argued not only for its existence, but for its exercise:

Dec. 19.

"Have we not the power to enforce the laws in the State of South Carolina, as well as in the State of Vermont or

Dec. 5.

any other State? And notwithstanding they may resolve and declare themselves absolved from all allegiance to this Union, yet it does not save them from the compact. If South Carolina drives out the Federal courts from the State, then the Federal Government has a right to re-establish the courts. If she excludes the mails, the Federal Government has a right and the authority to carry the mails. If she resists the collection of revenue in the port of Charleston, or any other ports, then the Government has a right to enter and enforce the law. If she undertakes to take possession of the property of the Government, the Government has a right to take all means to retain that property. And if they make any effort to dispossess the Government, or to resist the execution of the judicial system, then South Carolina puts herself in the wrong, and it is the duty of the Government to see the judiciary faithfully executed. In 1805, South Carolina made a deed of cession of the land on which these forts stand—a full cession—with certain conditions. The Government complied with the conditions, and has had possession of these forts till this day. And now has South Carolina any right to attempt to drive the Government from that property? If she secedes, and makes any attempt of this kind, does she not come within the meaning of the Constitution, where it speaks of levying war? And in levying war, she does what the Constitution declares to be treason. We may as well talk of things as they are, for if anything can be treason, within the scope of the Constitution, is not levying war upon the Government, treason? Is not attempting to take the property of the Government and expel the Government soldiers therefrom, treason? Is not attempting to resist the collection of the revenue, attempting to exclude the mails, and driving the Federal court from her borders, treason? What is it? I ask, in the name of the Constitution, what is it? It is treason, and nothing but treason."

With a sympathy among many of the political leaders of Tennessee with secession, and an undisguised effort to promote it, there yet seemed to exist among the people throughout the State, but especially in the eastern districts, a firm attachment to the Union. A secession meeting at Memphis was disturbed Nov. by manifestations of opposition on 30. the part of a large gathering of unionists. The Honorable John Bell, of Nashville, who had been a candidate for the Presidency, in a letter in answer to an invitation to an assemblage of secessionists, declared that he was for the Union, that he did not think that the election of Lincoln was a just cause for its dissolution, and that the South, equally with the North, was responsible for the angry sectionalism of feeling which prevailed.

In Kentucky the Union sentiment appeared at this time to be predominant. There was, however, great uneasiness of feeling and a disposition on the part of many of the political leaders of the State to act concurrently with the cotton States, or to demand excessive concessions from the North as the condition of loyalty. Governor Magoffin seemed by this circular sent to the governors of the various slave States, to have made a sincere effort toward conciliation.

"COMMONWEALTH OF KENTUCKY, EXECUTIVE DEPARTMENT, FRANKFORT, *Dec. 9, 1860.*

"Entertaining the opinion that some movement should be instituted at the earliest possible moment to arrest the progress of events which seem to be rapidly hurrying the Government of the Union to dismemberment, as an initiatory step I have, with great diffidence, concluded to submit to the governors of the slave States a series of propositions, and to ask their counsel and co-operation in bringing about a settlement upon them as a basis. Should the propositions be approved, they can be submitted to the assembling legislatures and conventions of the slave States, and a convention of all of said States, or of those only approving, be called to pass upon them, and ask a general convention of all the States of the Union that may be disposed to meet us on this basis for a full conference. The present good to be accomplished would be to arrest the secession movement until the question as to whether the Union can be preserved upon fair and honorable terms can be fully tested. If there be a basis for the adjustment of our difficulties within the Union, nothing should be left undone in order to its development. To this end, it seems to me there should be a conference of the States in some form, and it appears to me the form above suggested would be most effective. I, therefore, as the governor of a State having as deep a stake in the perpetuity of the Union, and at the same time as much solicitude for the maintenance of the institution of slavery as any other, would respectfully beg leave to submit for your consideration the following outline of propositions:

"*First.* Repeal, by an amendment of the Constitution of the United States, all laws in the free States in any degree nullifying or obstructing the execution of the Fugitive Slave law.

"*Second.* Amendments to said law to enforce its thorough execution in all the free States, providing compensation to the owner of the slave from the State which fails to deliver him up under the requirements of the law, or throws obstructions in the way of his recovery.

"*Third.* The passage of a law by Congress compelling the governors of free States to return fugitives from justice, indicted by a grand jury in another State for stealing or enticing away a slave.

"*Fourth.* To amend the Constitution so as to divide all the Territories belonging to the United States, or hereafter to be acquired, between the free and the slave States, say upon the line of the 37th degree of north latitude—all north of that line to come into the Union with requisite population as free States, and all south of the same to come in as slave States.

"*Fifth.* To amend the Constitution so as to guarantee forever to all the States the free navigation of the Mississippi River.

"*Sixth.* To alter the Constitution so

as to give the South the power, say in the United States Senate, to protect itself from unconstitutional and oppressive legislation upon the subject of slavery.

"Respectfully,
"Your obedient servant,
"B. MAGOFFIN."

Governor Houston, of Texas, manfully resisted the progress of the secessionists of that State by refusing to convene the Legislature, and strove to check the precipitancy of South Carolina by recommending a conference of the slave States. The governor of Arkansas uttered no expression of opinion in this crisis, but it was hoped that his silence was an indication that the people were loyal to the Union.

Georgia was evidently still irresolute. Alexander H. Stephens, one of her leading men, afterward Vice-President of the Southern Confederacy, spoke eloquently in behalf of the Union, and the Legislature urged the other slave States, in a circular addressed to them, not to act separately and precipitately.

Dec. 15.

Even in Alabama, at a meeting held in Baldwin County, a unanimous resolution was passed against secession; in Mississippi a large gathering of citizens in Vicksburg expressed the belief by a resolution that there were "yet remedies within the Union;" in Louisiana a leading journal declared that there was a "disposition to move with deliberation and to try all remedies, until means of security and equality in the Union are exhausted, before the State considers the United

Nov. 24.
Nov. 29.
Dec. 15.

States as a foreign government and its citizens as aliens."

South Carolina had, however, treated with contempt this lingering loyalty, and gave no heed to the suggestions of the other slave States. The convention refused to listen to the commissioners of Kentucky and Virginia, and even laid upon the table the proposition of the Legislature of Georgia without reading it. South Carolina was doubtless strengthened in resolution by secret alliances and pledges of conformity on the part of the political leaders in the other slave States, and could estimate at its just value a public affectation of loyalty to the Union by men who had conspired to destroy it. In South Carolina itself the people had been long prepared for secession, and required no persuasions or threats to effect what they impatiently desired. In the other "cotton" States, however, partly from an attachment to the Union and partly from a reluctance to assume the responsibility of dissolving it, there was a hesitating disaffection which could only be quickened to rebellion by the force of example. South Carolina, though professing her willingness and boasting her ability to stand alone, did not doubt that her lead would be soon followed by her sister States.

Confident in this belief, a committee of the convention at Charleston introduced the following ordinance, in which the concurrence in secession of the slaveholding States and their organization into a separate government, were already assumed by anticipation:

Dec. 25.

"*First.* That the conventions of the seceding slaveholding States of the United States unite with South Carolina, and hold a convention at Montgomery, Ala., for the purpose of forming a Southern confederacy.

"*Second.* That the said seceding States appoint, by their respective conventions or legislatures, as many delegates as they have representatives in the present Congress of the United States, to the said convention to be held at Montgomery, and that on the adoption of the constitution of the Southern confederacy, the vote shall be by States.

"*Third.* That whenever the terms of the constitution shall be agreed upon by the said convention, the same shall be submitted at as early a day as practicable to the convention and legislature of each State respectively, so as to enable them to ratify or reject the said constitution.

"*Fourth.* That in the opinion of South Carolina, the Constitution of the United States will form a suitable basis for the confederacy of the Southern States withdrawing.

"*Fifth.* That the South Carolina convention appoint by ballot eight delegates to represent South Carolina in the convention for the formation of a Southern confederacy.

"*Lastly.* That one commissioner in each State be elected to call the attention of the people to this ordinance."

CHAPTER VI

Energetic Action of the Convention at Charleston.—Proclamation for Fasting and Prayer by the President of the United States.—Compromise Committees: their ineffectiveness.—The Senator of Georgia's opinion of them.—Despair of the Senator from Kentucky.—Feeling at the North.—Activity of South Carolina.—Resolution of Inquiry passed by the Charleston Convention in regard to the Federal Forts.—Intense interest of the Charleston people.—Description of the Forts.—Anxiety of Major Anderson.—Hopelessness of the Defence of Fort Moultrie.—A Call of Duty.—A Resolution taken.—Preparations to abandon Fort Moultrie.—Ruse.—Expedition at Night.—In possession of Fort Sumter.—Excitement in Charleston.—The abandoned Federal Forts taken possession of by the South Carolinians.—The condition of Fort Moultrie described.—Seizure of Public Property.—Indignation against Major Anderson.—Anderson assumes the Responsibility.—Energetic Preparations at Charleston for War.—Sympathy from the Gulf States.—Feeling at the North.—The great Robbery of the Indian Trust Fund.—The supposed Criminals.—The order for the removal of Arms from Pittsburg.—Excitement of the Citizens.—Relief in a Mass Meeting.—Fears at the North. The deed of Anderson hailed with enthusiasm.—Newspaper Rhetoric.—The effect at Washington.—Resignation of Floyd.—A strange Correspondence.—Departure of the South Carolina Commissioners from Washington, and Correspondence.

WHILE the convention at Charleston was energetically pursuing its course of independent government, the President at Washington did nothing but bewail the misfortunes of the country in a proclamation of a day to be set apart for humiliation, fasting, and prayer, and Congress continued its futile attempts at compromise. The committees of "Thirty-three" and "Thirteen," appointed to consider and report on the crisis of the country, met, adjourned, and met again

1860.

without any result but the increased conviction that conciliation was impracticable. That there were some sincere efforts made by the moderate men of the South, with the desire of appeasing disunion, may be believed, but that the representatives of the extreme opinions of the cotton States had, if the wish for, not the least expectation of, their success, may be inferred from this telegram dispatched to his constituents by the United States senator from Georgia:

Dec. 23.

"I came here to secure your constitutional rights, and to demonstrate to you that you can get no guarantee for those rights from your Northern confederates.

"The whole subject was referred to a committee of thirteen in the Senate. I was appointed on the committee, and accepted the trust. I submitted propositions which, so far from receiving a decided support from a single member of the Republican party of the committee, were all treated with derision or contempt. A vote was then taken in the committee on amendments to the Constitution, proposed by Hon. J. J. Crittenden, and each and all of them were voted against, unanimously, by the Black Republican members of the committee.

"In addition to these facts, a majority of the Black Republican members of the committee declared distinctly that they had no guarantees to offer, which was silently acquiesced in by the other members.

"The Black Republican members of this committee are representative men of the party and section, and, to the extent of my information, truly represent them.

"The Committee of Thirty-Three on Friday adjourned for a week, without coming to any vote, after solemnly pledging themselves to vote on all the propositions then before them that day. It is controlled by the Black Republicans, your enemies, who only seek to amuse you with delusive hope until your election, that you may defeat the friends of secession.

"If you are deceived by them, it shall not be my fault. I have put the test fairly and frankly. It is decisive against you now. I tell you, upon the faith of a true man, that all further looking to the North for security for your constitutional rights in the Union ought to be instantly abandoned.

"It is fraught with nothing but ruin to yourselves and to your posterity. Secession, by the 4th day of March next, should be thundered from the ballot-box by the unanimous voice of Georgia on the 2d day of January next. Such a voice will be your best guarantee for liberty, tranquility, and glory.

"R. TOOMBS."

The venerable Crittenden, of Kentucky, whose fidelity to the Union was beyond peradventure, even despaired, and seeing no prospect in congressional action of an accommodation, exclaimed, that it was the darkest day of his life—that he was overwhelmed with solicitude for the country, and that nothing but the affection of the people for the Union could restore peace. In the mean while, the people of the North remained in a state between fear and hope. The timid gave expression to their alarms in "union meetings," and petitions counselling concession; while the hopeful deluded themselves with the supposed strength of the loyal men in the South. A few contemplated the possibility of war, but most fondly believed that the country would be spared its horrors.

South Carolina, however, though secured for the present by the pledges of President Buchanan and the corrupt connivance of his cabinet, was yet distrustful of the future, and began to prepare for its possible dangers. A resolution was offered in the convention at Charleston that the governor be requested to communicate in secret session any information he might possess in regard to the condition of forts Moultrie and Sumter, and Castle Pinckney, the number of guns in each, the number of workmen and kind of labor employed, the number of soldiers in each, and what additions, if any, had been made since the 20th of December; also, whether any assurance had been given that the forts would not be reinforced, and if so, to what extent; also, what police or other regulations had been made, if any, in reference to the defences of the harbor of Charleston, the coast, and the State.

Dec. 26.

At the same time the condition of these forts and their capability of defence became a subject of intense interest to the people of South Carolina, who were evidently determined upon possessing themselves of them. A minute survey of the works was made and published, in which the efforts in progress to improve their strength were studiously detailed and exaggerated, with the view of exciting the impatient ardor of the South Carolinians to wrest them from the Federal Government.

This account, as it conveys a tolerably accurate idea of the forts in the harbor of Charleston, is here given as published in the Charleston *Mercury*:

"Fort Moultrie is an inclosed water battery, having a front on the south, or water side, of about 300 feet, and a depth of about 240 feet. It is built with salient and re-entering angles on all sides, and is admirably adapted for defence, either from the attack of a storming party or by regular approaches.

"The outer and inner walls are of brick, capped with stone, and filled in with earth, making a solid wall 15 or 16 feet in thickness. The work now in progress consists in cleaning the sand from the walls of the fort; ditching it around the entire circumference, and erecting a glacis; closing up the postern gates in the east and west walls, and, instead, cutting sally-ports which lead into strong outworks on the southeast and southwest angles, in which twelve-pounder howitzer guns will be placed, enabling the garrison to sweep the ditch on three sides with grape and canister. The northwest angle of the fort has also been strengthened by a bastionette to sustain the weight of a heavy gun which will command the main street of the island. The main entrance has also been better secured, and a trap-door, two feet square, cut in the door for ingress and egress. At this time, the height of the wall from the bottom of the ditch to the top of the parapet is 20 feet. The ditch is from 12 to 15 feet wide at the base, and 15 feet deep. The nature of the soil would not seem to admit of this depth being increased, quicksand having been reached in many places. The work on the south side is nearly finished. The counterscarp is substantially built with plank, and spread with turf. The glacis is also finished. It is composed of sand, and covered with layers of loam and turf, all of which are kept firmly in place by the addition of sections of plank nailed to uprights sunk in the sand, and crossing each other at right angles, making squares of 10 feet each. The purpose of the glacis, which is an inclined plane, is to expose an attacking party to the fire of the guns, which are so placed as to sweep it from the crest of the counterscarp to the edge of the beach. On the north side all the wooden gun-cases have been placed close together on the ramparts, apparently for the purpose of securing it against an escalade, but possibly as a screen for a battery of heavy guns. A good many men are engaged in clearing the ramparts of turf and earth, for the purpose of putting down a very ugly-looking arrangement, which consists of strips of planks four inches wide, one and a half inches thick, and six or eight feet long, sharpened at the point, and nailed down so as to project about three feet horizontally from the top of the walls.

"A noticeable fact in the bastionettes, to which we have above alluded, is the haste in which one of them has been built. The one completed is formed of solid masonry. In constructing the other, however, a framework of plank has been substituted. Against the inside of this wooden outwork loose bricks have been placed. Both bastionettes are armed with a small carronade, and a howitzer pointed laterally so as to command the whole intervening moat by a cross-fire.

"In the hurried execution of these extensive improvements, a large force—about 170 men—are constantly engaged. Additions are daily made to this number, and the work of putting the post in the best possible condition for defence is carried on with almost incredible vigor.

"A few days ago, Colonel Gardiner, who for years had held the commandant's position, and whose courtesy and bearing had won the friendship of all who knew him, was relieved in the command by Major Robert Anderson, of Kentucky. Major Anderson received his first commission as brevet second lieutenant second artillery, July 1st, 1825, was acting inspector-general in the Black Hawk war, and received the rank of brevet captain, August, 1838, for his successful conduct in the Florida war. On September 8th, 1847, he was made brevet-major for his gallant and meritorious conduct in the battle of Molino del Rey.

"The other officers are: Captain Abner Doubleday, Captain T. Seymour, Lieutenant T. Talbot, Lieutenant J. C.

Davis, Lieutenant N. J. Hall—all of the first regiment artillery.

"Captain J. G. Foster and Lieutenant G. W. Snyder, of the engineer corps.

"Assistant Surgeon S. W. Crawford, of the medical staff.

"The force under these gentlemen consists of two companies of artillery. The companies, however, are not full, the two comprising, as we are informed, only about seventy men, including the band. A short time ago two additional companies were expected, but they have not come; and it is now positively stated that there will be, for the present at least, no reinforcement of the garrison.

"While the working-men are doing wonders on the outside, the soldiers within are by no means idle. Field-pieces have been placed in position upon the green within the fort, and none of the expedients of military engineering have been neglected to make the position as strong as possible. It is said that the greatest vigilance is observed in every regulation at this time, and that the guns are regularly shotted every night. It is very certain that ingress is no longer an easy matter for an outsider, and the visitor who hopes to get in must make up his mind to approach with all the caution, ceremony, and circumlocution with which the allies are advancing upon the capital of the Celestial Empire.

"Fort Sumter, the largest of our fortresses, is a work of solid masonry, octagonal in form, pierced on the north, east, and west sides with a double row of port-holes for the heaviest guns, and on the south or land side, in addition to openings for guns, loop-holes for musketry; stands in the middle of the harbor, on the edge of the ship channel, and is said to be bomb-proof. It is at present without any regular garrison. There is a large force of workmen—some one hundred and fifty in all—busily employed in mounting the guns and otherwise putting this great strategic point in order. The armament of Fort Sumter consists of 140 guns, many of them being the formidable ten-inch 'columbiads,' which throw either shot or shell, and which have a fearful range. Only a few of these are yet in position, and the work of mounting pieces of this calibre in the casemates is necessarily a slow one. There is also a large amount of artillery stores, consisting of about 40,000 pounds of powder, and a proportionate quantity of shot and shell. The workmen engaged here sleep in the fort every night, owing to the want of any regular communication with the city. The wharf or landing is on the south side, and is of course exposed to a cross fire from all the openings on that side.

"The fortress most closely commanding the city and its roadstead is Castle Pinckney, which is located on the southern extremity of a narrow slip of marsh land, which extends in a northerly direction to Hog Island Channel. To the harbor side the so-called castle presents a circular front. It has never been considered of much consequence as a fortress, although its proximity to the city would give it importance, if properly armed and garrisoned. From hasty observation, we find that there are about fifteen guns mounted on the parapet; the majority of them are eighteen and twenty-four pounders. Some 'columbiads' are, however, within the walls. There are also supplies of powder, shot, and shell. At present there is no garrison at the post; the only residents are one or two watchmen, who have charge of the harbor light. Some thirty or forty day laborers are employed repairing the cisterns, and putting the place generally in order."

Major Anderson, the Federal officer in command, informed of the action of the convention in regard to the forts, witnessing the public excitement in Charleston, conscious of the intense desire of the people of South Carolina to possess them, and believing that they would not long hesitate to make the attempt, became solicitous about their safety. He had no hope of being able to defend Fort Moultrie, whose feeble and unprotected walls he held with a meagre garrison of only sixty effective men. He despaired of any aid from the Federal Government, for he had been told by the secretary of war, Floyd, how, with a natural regard for the safety of his fellow-conspirators, he had "carefully abstained from increasing the force at this point, or taking any measures which might add to the present excited state of the public mind, or which would throw any doubt on the confidence he feels that South Carolina will not attempt by violence to obtain possession of the public works, or interfere with their occupancy."*

It was not, therefore, surprising that Anderson should write thus despairingly:

"When I inform you that my garrison consists of only sixty effective **Dec.** men, and that we are in a very **24.** indifferent work, the walls of which are only about fourteen feet high, and that we have, within one hundred and sixty yards of our walls, sand-hills which command our work, and which afford admirable sites for batteries and the finest covers for sharp-shooters, and that besides this there are numerous houses, some of them within pistol-shot, you will at once see that, if attacked in force, headed by any one but a simpleton, there is scarce a possibility of our being able to hold out long enough to enable our friends to come to our succor.

"Trusting that God will not desert us in our hour of trial, I am sincerely yours.

"ROBERT ANDERSON,
"Major 1st Artillery, etc."

Anderson, however, was not the man to yield to despair while the call of duty invoked to effort. He accordingly determined, that if Fort Moultrie could not be defended, he would place his meagre garrison in Fort Sumter, which could. His preparations were made with a prudent secrecy. In order to deceive the inhabitants of Sullivan Island, upon which the fort is situated, it was studiously reported among them, that in consequence of the probability

* Verbal Instructions to Major Anderson, Dec. 11, 1860.

OCCUPATION OF FORT SUMTER.

of an attack by the people of Charleston, the wives and children of the garrison were about to be removed to a safer place. Under the cover of this pretext, three schooners were hired, brought up to the wharf, and loaded with what was supposed by the people of the island merely ordinary baggage. These vessels, however, contained not only the women and children, but provisions, munitions of war, and the personal effects of the officers and soldiers. Thus laden, the three schooners put off, and sailed, not to Fort Johnson, on James Island, as had been carefully reported, and for which they apparently steered, but to Fort Sumter, where, after a circuitous course, they finally arrived in the evening and discharged their important burthens. Anderson waited for the darkness of the night before embarking his men. At half-past nine o'clock, row-boats having been got ready, the whole force, with the exception of Captain Foster and eight men, left to dismantle and spike the guns and burn their carriages, pushed off. Before daylight next morning Major Anderson was in full possession of Fort Sumter, with his little garrison. The smoke from Fort Moultrie, still rising at early dawn, was the first to arouse the attention of the people of Charleston. They gathered in excited crowds upon the wharfs and the battery, and anxiously sought the cause. Great alarm spread throughout the town, and the troops were called to arms. Various were the conjectures: some thought that a fresh United States force

Dec. 26.

had arrived; some supposed that Anderson had evacuated the harbor altogether, after having destroyed the fort; but none seemed to suspect his masterly movement. All doubt, however, was soon removed by the arrival in the city of some of the inhabitants of Sullivan's Island.

When the fact became known, the excitement increased. The convention met immediately, and issued orders for the occupation of the deserted Fort Moultrie and the other defences of the harbor by the State troops. The Federal arsenal at Charleston, which had been so generously supplied by the treasonable forecast of the secretary of war, yielded up its stores of arms and ammunition to the eager asserters of "State sovereignty." Colonel Pettigrew, in obedience to the command of the convention, took possession, with two hundred men, of Castle Pinckney, which was found without a man to defend it, but with its entrances barricaded, its guns spiked, its ammunition gone, and its flagstaff prostrate. Lieutenant-Colonel De Saussure, also with two hundred men, proceeded to take possession of the abandoned Fort Moultrie. As he approached, Captain Foster and his eight soldiers, who had been left to destroy the guns and keep nominal possession, pushed off in a row-boat for Fort Sumter.

As soon as the South Carolinians got possession, they commenced to repair the damage effected by Anderson, and to add to the former efficiency and strength of the fort. The condition in which it was found after its abandon-

Dec. 27. ment by the Federal force, is thus minutely described by a writer in the Charleston *Courier:*

"On the way across the harbor, the hoisting of the American flag from the staff of Fort Sumter, at precisely twelve o'clock, gave certain indication that the stronghold was occupied by the troops of the United States. On a nearer approach the fortress was discovered to be occupied, the guns appeared to be mounted, and sentinels were discovered on duty, and the place to give every sign of occupancy and military discipline. The grim fortress frowned defiance on every side; the busy notes of preparation resounded through its unforbidding recesses, and everything seemed to indicate the utmost alacrity in the work on hand.

"Turning toward Fort Moultrie, a dense cloud of smoke was seen to pour from the end facing the sea. The flag-staff was down, and the whole place had an air of desolation and abandonment quite the reverse of its busy look one week ago, when scores of laborers were engaged in adding to its strength all the works skill and experience could suggest.

"In the immediate vicinity of the rear or landside entrance, however, greater activity was noticeable. At the time of our visit, a large force of hands had been summoned to deliver up their implements for transportation to Fort Sumter. Around on every side were the evidences of labor in the fortification of the work. In many places a portion of the defences were strength- ened by every appliance that art could suggest or ingenuity devise; while in others, the uncompleted works gave evidences of the utmost confusion. On all hands the process of removing goods, furniture, and munitions was yet going on. The heavy guns upon the ramparts of the fort were thrown down from their carriages and spiked. Every ounce of powder and every cartridge had been removed from the magazines, and, in fact, everything like small-arms, clothing, provisions, accoutrements, and other munitions of war had been removed off and deposited; nothing but heavy balls and useless cannon remained.

"The entire place was, to all appearances, littered up with the odds, ends, and fragments of war's desolation. Confusion could not have been more complete had the late occupants retired in the face of a besieging foe. Fragments of gun-carriages, etc., broken to pieces, bestrewed the ramparts. Sand-bags and barrels filled with earth crowned the walls, and were firmly imbedded in their bomb-proof surface as an additional safeguard; and notwithstanding the heterogeneous scattering of materials and implements, the walls of the fort evinced a vague degree of energy in preparing for an attack. A ditch some fifteen feet wide and about the same in depth surrounds the entire wall on three sides. On the south side, or front, a glacis has been commenced and prosecuted nearly to completion, with a rampart of sand-bags, barrels, etc.

"On one side of the fort a palisade of palmetto logs is extended around the ramparts as a complete defence against an escalading party. New embrasures have been cut in the walls so as to command the faces of the bastion and ditch. These new defences are all incomplete, and are evidence of the haste with which they were erected. Considering the inferior force, in point of numbers, under his command, Major Anderson had paid particular attention to strengthening only a small part of the fort.

"A greater portion of the labor expended was spent upon the citadel, or centre of the west point of the position. This he had caused to be strengthened in every way; loop-holes were cut, and everything was so arranged that in case a well-concerted attack was made, he would have retired from the outer bastions to the citadel, and afterward blow up the other portions of the fort. For this purpose mines had already been sprung, and trains had been laid ready for the application of the match. The barrack-rooms and every other part of the fort that was indefensible would have gone at a touch.

"On the ramparts of the fort fronting Fort Sumter were nine eight-inch columbiads, mounted on wooden carriages. As soon as the evacuation of the fort was complete, the carriages of these guns were fired, and at the time of visiting the fort yesterday, were nearly consumed, and the guns thereby dismounted. These guns, as well as those constituting the entire armament of the fortress, were spiked before it was abandoned. This is the only damage done the fortification, further than cutting down the flagstaff, and the breaking up of ammunition-wagons to form ramparts on the walls of the fort."

The seizure of the Federal forts was followed by that of the arsenal, the custom-house, and the post-office, upon each of which was raised the Palmetto flag. The South Carolinians were pleased to consider the simple movement of a Federal officer from one Federal fort to another an act of war. "Major Robert Anderson, United States army," wrote a journalist,[*] "has achieved the unenviable distinction of opening civil war between American citizens by an act of gross breach of faith. He has, under counsels of a panic, deserted his post at Fort Moultrie, and under false pretexts has transferred his garrison and military stores and supplies to Fort Sumter."

Another writer[†] declared: "It is due to South Carolina and to good faith that the act of this officer (Major Anderson) should be repudiated by the Government, and that the troops be removed forthwith from Fort Sumter."

The governor of South Carolina demanded of Anderson by what authority he had acted, and what was the object of his movement. Anderson replied, that it was merely a military measure for the purpose only of defence, which he had executed on his own responsibility.

The convention, however, of South Carolina made the act of Anderson the pretext for the most energetic preparations for war. Assuming the whole conduct of government, it organized a mil-

[*] *Courier.*   [†] *Mercury.*

itary force and a complete system of coast defence. The buoys from the channels were removed, the lights in the light-houses extinguished, fortifications built, an army was enlisted, and a most formidable show of defiance to the Federal authorities exhibited everywhere throughout the State. Most of the officers of the United States army and navy who were natives of South Carolina had, on the announcement of its act of secession, resigned from the Federal service and offered their allegiance to the seceded State. South Carolina was thus at once provided with officers capable of organizing its military force and directing the works necessary for its defence.

Throughout the cotton States the movement of Major Anderson was considered an aggressive act, and they showed their disposition to make common cause with South Carolina by liberal offerings of aid. Georgia, Alabama, and even North Carolina, tendered the services of troops.

At the North, public attention had been diverted for a time from South Carolina by exciting events occurring nearer home, which, however, from their supposed relation to the Southern movement, served to increase the general inquietude, and prepare the public for further developments of treason. **Dec. 25.** A great defalcation had been discovered in the Indian trust fund, by which the Government had been defrauded of eight hundred and thirty thousand dollars. Thompson, the secretary of the interior, who had been absent from his Federal post, striving as a secession commissioner from Mississippi to stir up the people of North Carolina to rebellion, was summoned to Washington. His disbursing clerk was absent, and the key of the safe missing. The former was discovered, but the latter was lost. The safe was broken open; no property, however, was found. It was difficult to trace the degree of criminality which belonged to those to whom the trust had been confided. The superiors asserted their innocence, and to the inferior was imputed the crime; but public opinion did not hesitate to charge the secretary of war, Floyd, and the secretary of the interior, Thompson, as accomplices in the fraud, which had been committed, if not for personal advantage, at any rate for the advancement of Southern interests.

Another event, no less exciting, occurred at the same moment. An order had been received from Washington at Pittsburg to send immediately from the Alleghany arsenal there 78 large cannon to Fort Newport, near Galveston, and 48 to Ship Island, near Biloxi, off the coast of Mississippi. **Dec. 25.**

As the government of Buchanan was still guided by those whose fidelity to the Union was suspected, the purpose of this order was naturally supposed to further Southern secession. This aroused the indignation of the citizens of Pittsburg, who expressed a determination not to allow the arms to leave the arsenal. Finally, the excitement of Pittsburg found relief in a "mass meeting," at which resolutions were adopted "declaring loyalty to the Union, and ability to defend themselves against all enemies of the Union; deprecating any interference with the shipment of arms under government orders, however inopportune or impolitic the order might appear; deploring the existing state of things in connection with the administration of important departments of the public service so as to have shaken confidence in the people of the free States; declaring that while Pennsylvania is on guard at the Federal capital, it is her special duty to look to the fidelity of her sons, and in that view call on the President, as a citizen of this Commonwealth, to see that the public receive no detriment at his hands, and to purge his cabinet of every man known to give aid and comfort to, or in any way countenancing the revolt of, any State against the authority of the Constitution and the laws of the Union."

These events, the robbery of the public treasury and arsenals, seemed to reveal more clearly to the public mind of the North the extent and danger of the Southern conspiracy. Alarm and distrust now became more general, and the people began to fear for the safety of that Union which they had fondly believed to be too greatly endeared to the universal American heart to be in peril from any sectional disaffection. While thus depressed, the news came of the movement of Major Anderson, and that simple act of military duty was hailed as a deed of heroism, and its author as an heroic defender of the Union.

The feeling of patriotic exultation found vent through the press in a burst of ardent rhetoric:

"We must own," exclaimed a writer in the Boston *Courier*, "that the news of the transaction in Charleston harbor was learned by us yesterday with a prouder beating of the heart. *We could not but feel once more that we had a country*—a fact which had been to a certain degree in suspense for some weeks past. What is given up for the moment is of no consequence, provided the one point stands out clear, that *the United States means to maintain its position, where its rights exist, and that its officers, civil and military, intend to discharge their duty.* The concentration of the disposable force in Charleston harbor in a defensible post is thus a bond of union. It is a decisive act, calculated to rally the national heart. * * We are not disposed to allow the Union to be broken up for grievances of South Carolina, which might be settled within the Union; and if there is to be any fighting, we prefer it within, rather than without. The abandonment of Fort Moultrie was obviously a necessary act, in order to carry into effect the purpose contemplated with such an inferior force as that under the command of Major Anderson.

"If anybody ever doubted Major Anderson's eminent military capacity, that doubt must be dispelled by the news that we publish in another column," wrote the editor of the Boston *Atlas*. "Of his own accord, without orders from Washington, but acting on the discretion which an officer in an independent command always possesses,

Major Anderson, commander of the defences of Charleston harbor, transports his troops to the key of his position, Fort Sumter, against which no gun can be laid which is not itself commanded by a 10-inch columbiad in the embrasures of that octagon citadel. This rapid, unexpected manœuvre has disconcerted treason, and received the highest military commendation in the country.

"Brave major of artillery, true servant of your country, soldier of penetrating and far-seeing genius, when the right is endangered by fraud or force, at the proper time the needed man is always provided. The spirit of the age provides him, and he always regards the emergency. WASHINGTON, GARIBALDI, ANDERSON."

Washington, in the mean time, had been no less stirred by the great event. Floyd, the secretary of war, who had been so long pretending to serve the Union, while he had given himself up totally to the demon of rebellion, resigned, and was succeeded by Holt, of Kentucky, a patriot of unquestioned loyalty to the Union. The correspondence between Floyd and the President is a curious memorial of the times when an obvious duty of government was construed into a justifiable cause for disaffection and hostile defiance.

"WAR DEPARTMENT, DEC. 29, 1860.

"SIR: On the morning of the 27th inst. I read the following paper to you in the presence of the cabinet:

'CORNER, CHAMBER, EXECUTIVE MANSION.

'SIR: It is evident now, from the action of the commander of Fort Moultrie, that the solemn pledges of the Government have been violated by Major Anderson. In my judgment, but one remedy is now left us by which to vindicate our honor and prevent civil war. It is in vain now to hope for confidence on the part of the people of South Carolina in any further pledges as to the action of the military. One remedy is left, and that is to withdraw the garrison from the harbor of Charleston. I hope the President will allow me to make that order at once. This order, in my judgment, can alone prevent bloodshed and civil war.

'JOHN B. FLOYD,
'Secretary of War.'

"I then considered the honor of the administration pledged to maintain the troops in the position they occupied, for such had been the assurances given to the gentlemen of South Carolina who had a right to speak for her. South Carolina, on the other hand, gave reciprocal pledges that no force should be brought by them against the troops or against the property of the United States. The sole object of both parties in these reciprocal pledges was to prevent a collision and the effusion of blood, in the hope that some means might be found for a peaceful accommodation of the existing troubles, the two Houses of Congress having both raised committees looking to that object. Thus affairs stood until the action of Major Anderson, taken unfortunately while the commissioners were on their way to this capital on a peaceful mission looking to the avoidance of bloodshed, has complicated matters in the existing manner. Our refusal or even delay to place affairs back as they stood under our agreement invites a collision, and must inevitably inaugurate civil war. I cannot consent to be the agent of such calamity. I deeply regret that I feel myself under the necessity of tendering to you my resignation as secretary of war, because I can no longer hold it under my convictions of patriotism, nor with honor, subjected as I am to a violation of solemn pledges and plighted faith.

"With the highest personal regard,

"I am most truly yours,

"JOHN B. FLOYD.

"To His Excellency the PRESIDENT OF THE UNITED STATES."

THE PRESIDENT'S REPLY.

"WASHINGTON, Dec. 21, 1860.

"MY DEAR SIR: I have received and accepted your resignation of the office of secretary of war; and not wishing to impose upon you the task of performing its mere routine duties, which you have so kindly offered to do, I have authorized Postmaster-General Holt to administer the affairs of the department until your successor shall be appointed.

"Yours, very respectfully,

"JAMES BUCHANAN.

"Hon. JOHN B. FLOYD."

The commissioners appointed by the convention of South Carolina to treat with the President in regard to the delivery of the forts and other Federal property, made the event of Anderson's performance of his duty the occasion for their abrupt departure from Washington, after an insolent demand for satisfaction from the Federal authority, followed by an audacious defiance of its power, and a threat of resistance. The correspondence between the commissioners of South Carolina and the President, is another strange memorial of that period of humiliation for the Union when its chief magistrate was called to account in the capital of the United States by confessed rebels, for not repudiating a simple act of national defence, performed by an officer in the course of his military duties.

THE CORRESPONDENCE BETWEEN THE SOUTH CAROLINA COMMISSIONERS AND THE PRESIDENT OF THE UNITED STATES.

"WASHINGTON, Dec. 29, 1860.

"SIR: We have the honor to transmit to you a copy of the full powers from the convention of the people of South Carolina, under which we are 'authorized and empowered to treat with the Government of the United States for the delivery of the forts, magazines, lighthouses, and other real estate, with their appurtenances, in the limits of South Carolina; and also for an apportionment of the public debt, and for a division of all other property held by the Government of the United States, as agent of the confederated States, of which South Carolina was recently a member, and generally to negotiate as to all other measures and arrangements proper to be made and adopted in the existing relation of the parties, and for the continuance of peace and amity between this Commonwealth and the Government at Washington.'

"In the execution of this trust it is our duty to furnish you, as we now do, with an official copy of the Ordinance of Secession, by which the State of South Carolina has resumed the powers she delegated to the Government of the United States, and has declared her perfect sovereignty and independence.

"It would also have been our duty to have informed you that we were ready to negotiate with you upon all such questions as are necessarily raised by the adoption of this Ordinance, and that we were prepared to enter upon this negotiation with the earnest desire to avoid all unnecessary and hostile collision, and so to inaugurate our new relations as to secure mutual respect, general advantage, and a future of goodwill and harmony, beneficial to all the parties concerned.

"But the events of the last twenty-four hours render such an assurance impossible. We came here the representatives of an authority which could, at any time within the past sixty days, have taken possession of the forts in Charleston harbor, but which, upon pledges given in a manner that we cannot doubt, determined to trust to your honor rather than to its own power. Since our arrival here, an officer of the United States, acting, as we are assured, not only without, but against, your orders, has dismantled one fort and occupied another—thus altering to a most important extent the condition of affairs under which we came.

"Until these circumstances are explained in a manner which relieves us of all doubt as to the spirit in which these negotiations shall be conducted, we are forced to suspend all discussion as to any arrangement by which our mutual interests may be amicably adjusted.

"And, in conclusion, we would urge upon you the immediate withdrawal of the troops from the harbor of Charleston. Under present circumstances, they are a standing menace which renders negotiation impossible, and, as our recent experience shows, threatens speedily to bring to a bloody issue questions which ought to be settled with temperance and judgment. We have the honor to be,

"Very respectfully.
"Your obedient servants,
"R. W. BARNWELL,
"J. H. ADAMS,   } Commissioners.
"JAS. L. ORR,
"To the PRESIDENT OF THE UNITED STATES."

THE PRESIDENT'S REPLY,

"WASHINGTON CITY, *Dec.* 30, 1860.

"GENTLEMEN: I have had the honor to receive your communication of 28th inst., together with a copy of 'your full powers from the convention of the people of South Carolina,' authorizing you to treat with the Government of the United States on various important subjects therein mentioned, and also a copy of the Ordinance, bearing date on the 20th inst., declaring that 'the union now subsisting between South Carolina and other States, under the name of the United States of America, is hereby dissolved.'

"In answer to this communication, I

have to say that my position as President of the United States was clearly defined in the message to Congress on the 3d inst. In that I stated that, 'apart from the execution of the laws, so far as this may be practicable, the Executive has no authority to decide what shall be the relations between the Federal Government and South Carolina. He has been invested with no such discretion. He possesses no power to change the relations hitherto existing between them, much less to acknowledge the independence of that State. This would be to invest a mere executive officer with the power of recognizing the dissolution of the confederacy among our thirty-three sovereign States. It bears no resemblance to the recognition of a foreign *de facto* government— involving no such responsibility. Any attempt to do this would, on his part, be a naked act of usurpation. It is therefore my duty to submit to Congress the whole question in all its bearings.

"Such is my opinion still. I could, therefore, meet you only as private gentlemen of the highest character, and was entirely willing to communicate to Congress any proposition you might have to make to that body upon the subject. Of this you were well aware. It was my earnest desire that such a disposition might be made of the whole subject by Congress, who alone possess the power, as to prevent the inauguration of a civil war between the parties in regard to the possession of the Federal forts in the harbor of Charleston; and I therefore deeply regret that, in your opinion, 'the events of the last twenty-four hours render this impossible.' In conclusion, you urge upon me 'the immediate withdrawal of the troops from the harbor of Charleston,' stating that 'under present circumstances they are a standing menace, which renders negotiation impossible, and, as our recent experience shows, threatens speedily to bring to a bloody issue questions which ought to be settled with temperance and judgment.'

"The reason for this change in your position is, that since your arrival in Washington, 'an officer of the United States, acting, as we [you] are assured, not only without, but against, your [my] orders, has dismantled one fort and occupied another—thus altering to a most important extent the condition of affairs under which we [you] came.' You also allege that you came here, 'the representatives of an authority which could, at any time within the past sixty days, have taken possession of the forts in Charleston harbor, but which, upon pledges given in a manner that we [you] cannot doubt, determined to trust to your [my] honor rather than to its power.'

"This brings me to a consideration of the nature of those alleged pledges, and in what manner they have been observed. In my message of the 3d of December last, I stated, in regard to the property of the United States in South Carolina, that it 'has been purchased for a fair equivalent, by the consent of the Legislature of the State, for the erection of forts, magazines, arsenals, etc., and over these the authority 'to exercise exclusive legislation' has been expressly granted by the Constitution to Congress. It is not believed that any attempt will be made to expel the United States from this property by force; but if in this I should prove to be mistaken, the officer in command of the forts has received orders to act strictly on the defensive. In such a contingency, the responsibility for consequences would rightfully rest upon the heads of the assailants.' This being the condition of the parties, on Saturday, 8th December, four of the representatives from South Carolina called upon me, and requested an interview. We had an earnest conversation on the subject of these forts, and the best means of preventing a collision between the parties, for the purpose of sparing the effusion of blood. I suggested, for prudential reasons, that it would be best to put in writing what they said to me verbally. They did so, accordingly, and on Monday morning, the 10th inst., three of them presented to me a paper signed by all the representatives from South Carolina, with a single exception, of which the following is a copy:

'To His Excellency James Buchanan, President of the United States.

'In compliance with our statement to you yesterday, we now express to you our strong convictions, that neither the constituted authorities, nor any body of the people of the State of South Carolina, will either attack or molest the United States forts in the harbor of Charleston previously to the act of the convention, and we hope and believe not until an offer has been made, through an accredited representative, to negotiate for an amicable arrangement of all matters between the State and the Federal Government, provided that no reinforcements shall be sent into those forts, and their relative military status shall remain as at present.

'John McQueen,
'M. L. Bonham,
'W. W. Boyce,
'Lawrence M. Keitt.

'Washington, Dec. 9, 1860.'

"And here I must, in justice to myself, remark that at the time the paper was presented to me, I objected to the word 'provided,' as it might be construed into an agreement on my part, which I never would make. They said that nothing was further from their intention—they did not so understand it, and I should not so consider it. It is evident they could enter into no reciprocal agreement with me on the subject. They did not profess to have authority to do this, and were acting in their individual character. I considered it as nothing more, in effect, than the promise of highly honorable gentlemen to exert their influence for the purpose expressed. The event has proven that they have faithfully kept this promise, although I have never since received a line from any one of them, or from any member of the convention on the subject. It is well known that it was my determination—and this I freely expressed—not to reinforce the forts in the harbor, and thus produce a collision, until they had been actually attacked, or until I had certain evidence that they were about to be attacked. This paper I received most cordially, and considered it as a happy omen that peace might be still preserved, and that time might be thus given for reflection. This is the whole foundation for the alleged pledge.

"But I acted in the same manner as I would have done had I entered into a positive and formal agreement with parties capable of contracting, although such an agreement would have been on my part, from the nature of my official duties, impossible. The world knows that I have never sent any reinforcements to the forts in Charleston harbor, and I have certainly never authorized any change to be made 'in their relative military status.' Bearing upon this subject, I refer you to an order issued by the secretary of war, on the 11th inst. to Major Anderson, but not brought to my notice until the 21st inst. It is as follows:

'MEMORANDUM OF VERBAL INSTRUCTIONS TO MAJOR ANDERSON, FIRST ARTILLERY, COMMANDING FORT MOULTRIE, S. C.

'You are aware of the great anxiety of the secretary of war that a collision of the troops with the people of this State shall be avoided, and of his studied determination to pursue a course with reference to the military force and forts in this harbor, which shall guard against such a collision. He has therefore carefully abstained from increasing the force at this point, or taking any measures which might add to the present excited state of the public mind, or which would throw any doubt on the confidence he feels that South Carolina will not attempt by violence to obtain possession of the public works, or interfere with their occupancy.

'But as the counsel and acts of rash and impulsive persons may possibly disappoint these expectations of the Government, he deems it proper that you should be prepared with instructions to meet so unhappy a contingency. He has therefore directed me, verbally, to give you such instructions.

'You are carefully to avoid every act which would needlessly tend to provoke aggression, and for that reason you are not, without necessity, to take up any position which could be construed into the assumption of a hostile attitude; but *you are to hold possession of the forts in the harbor, and if attacked, you are to defend yourself to the last extremity.* The smallness of your force will not permit you, perhaps, to occupy more than one of the three forts, but an attack on, or attempt to take possession of, either of them, will be regarded as an act of hostility, and you may then put your command into either of them which you may deem most proper to increase its power of resistance. *You are also authorized to take similar steps whenever you have tangible evidence of a design to proceed to a hostile act.*

"D. P. BUTLER,

'Assistant Adjutant-General.

'FORT MOULTRIE, S. C., *Dec.* 11, 1860.'

'This is in conformity to my instructions to Major Buell.

'JOHN B. FLOYD, Secretary of War.'

"These were the last instructions transmitted to Major Anderson before his removal to Fort Sumter, with a single exception in regard to a particular which does not in any degree affect the present question. Under these circumstances, it is clear that Major Anderson acted upon his own responsibility, and without authority, unless, indeed, he had 'tangible evidence of a design to proceed to a hostile act' on the part of South Carolina, which has not yet been alleged. Still, he is a brave and honorable officer, and justice requires that he should not be condemned without a fair hearing.

"Be this as it may, when I learned that Major Anderson had left Fort Moultrie and proceeded to Fort Sumter, my first promptings were to command him to return to his former position, and there to await the contingencies presented in his instructions. This would only have been done with any degree of safety to the command by the concurrence of the South Carolina authorities. But before any step could possibly have been taken in this direction, we received information that the 'Palmetto flag floated out to the breeze at Castle Pinckney, and a large military force went over last night (the 27th) to Fort Moultrie.' Thus the authorities of South Carolina, without waiting or asking for any explanations, and doubtless believing, as you have expressed it, that the officer had acted not only without, but against, my orders, on the very next day after the night when the removal was made, seized by a military force two of the Federal forts in the harbor of Charleston, and have covered them under their own flag instead of that of the United States.

"At this gloomy period of our history, startling events succeed each other rapidly. On the very day, the 27th instant, that possession of these two forts was taken, the Palmetto flag was raised over the Federal custom-house and post-office in Charleston; and on the same day every officer of the customs—collector, naval officer, surveyor, and appraiser—resigned their offices. And this, although it was well known from the language of my message that, as an executive officer, I felt myself bound to collect the revenue at the port of Charleston under the existing laws. In the harbor of Charleston we now find three forts confronting each other, over all of which the Federal flag floated only four days ago; but now, over two of them, this flag has been supplanted, and the Palmetto flag has been substituted in its stead. It is under all these circumstances that I am urged immediately to withdraw the troops from the harbor of Charleston, and am informed that without this, negotiation is impossible. This I cannot do—this I will not do. Such an idea was never thought of by me in any possible contingency. No such allusion had been made in any communication between myself and any human being. But the inference is that I am bound to withdraw the troops from the only fort remaining in the possession of the United States in the harbor of Charleston, because the officer there in command of all of the forts thought proper, without instructions, to change his position from one of them to another.

"At this point of writing, I have received information by telegraph from Captain Humphreys, in command of the arsenal at Charleston, that 'it has to-day (Sunday, the 30th) been taken by force of arms.' It is estimated that the munitions of war belonging to this arsenal are worth half a million of dollars.

"Comment is needless. After this information, I have only to add, that while it is my duty to defend Fort Sumter, as a portion of the public property of the United States, against hostile attacks, from whatever quarter they may come, by such means as I possess for this purpose, I do not perceive how such a defence can be construed into a menace against the city of Charleston. With great personal regard, I remain yours, very respectfully,
"JAMES BUCHANAN.
"To Hon. ROBERT W. BARNWELL, JAMES H. ADAMS, JAMES L. ORR."

SECOND LETTER OF THE COMMISSIONERS TO THE PRESIDENT.

"WASHINGTON, D. C., *Jan.* 1, 1861.

"SIR: We have the honor to acknowledge the receipt of your letter of the 30th December, in reply to a note addressed by us to you, on the 28th of the same month, as commissioners from South Carolina.

"In reference to the declaration with which your reply commences, that your 'position as President of the United States was already defined in the message to Congress of the 3d instant,' that you possess 'no power to change the relations heretofore existing between South Carolina and the United States,' 'much less to acknowledge the independence of that State,' and that consequently you could meet us only as private gentlemen of the highest character, with an entire willingness to communicate to Congress any proposition we might have to make—we deem it only necessary to say that the State of South Carolina having, in the exercise of that great right of self-government which underlies all our political organizations, declared herself sovereign and independent, we, as her representatives, felt no special solicitude as to the character in which you might recognize us. Satisfied that the State had simply exercised her unquestionable right, we were prepared, in order to reach substantial good, to waive the formal considerations which your constitutional scruples might have prevented you from extending. We came here, therefore, expecting to be received as you did receive us, and perfectly content with that entire willingness, of which you assured us, to submit any proposition to Congress which we might have to make upon the subject of the independence of the State. The willingness was ample recognition of the condition of public affairs which rendered our presence necessary. In this position, however, it is our duty, both to the State which we represent and to ourselves, to correct several important misconceptions of our letter into which you have fallen.

"You say: 'It was my earnest desire that such a disposition might be made of the whole subject by Congress, who alone possess the power, to prevent the inauguration of a civil war between the parties in regard to the possession of the Federal forts in the harbor of Charleston; and I therefore deeply regret that in your opinion the events of the last twenty-four hours render this impossible.' We expressed no such opinion, and the language which you quote as ours, is altered in its sense by the omission of a most important part of the sentence. What we did say was, 'But the events of the last twenty-four hours render such an assurance impossible.' Place that 'assurance' as contained in our letter in the sentence, and we are prepared to repeat it.

"Again; professing to quote our language, you say: 'Thus the authorities of South Carolina, without waiting or asking for any explanation, and doubtless believing, as you have expressed it, that the officer had acted not only without, but against, my orders,' etc. We expressed no such opinion in reference to the belief of the people of South Carolina. The language which you have quoted was applied solely and entirely to our assurances obtained here, and based, as you well know, upon your own declaration—a declaration which, at that time, it was impossible for the authorities of South Carolina to have known. But, without following this letter into all its details, we propose only to meet the chief points of the argument.

"Some weeks ago, the State of South Carolina declared her intention, in the existing condition of public affairs, to secede from the United States. She called a convention of her people to put her declaration in force. The convention met and passed the ordinance of secession. All this you anticipated, and your course of action was thoroughly considered in your annual message. You declared you had no right, and would not attempt, to coerce a seceding State, but that you were bound by your constitutional oath, and would defend the property of the United States within the borders of South Carolina if an attempt was made to take it by force. Seeing very early that this question of property was a difficult and delicate one, you manifested a desire to settle it without collision. You did not reinforce the garrison in the harbor of Charleston. You removed a distinguished and veteran officer from the command of Fort Moultrie because he attempted to increase his supply of ammunition. You refused to send additional troops to the same garrison when applied for by the officer appointed to succeed him. You accepted the resignation of the oldest and most eminent member of your cabinet, rather than allow the garrison to be strengthened. You compelled an officer stationed at Fort Sumter to return immediately to the arsenal forty muskets which he had taken to arm his men. You expressed, not to one, but to many, of the most distinguished of our public characters, whose testimony will be placed upon the record whenever it is necessary, your anxiety for a peaceful termination of this controversy, and your willingness not to disturb the military status of the forts, if commissioners should be sent to the Government, whose communications you promised to submit to Congress. You received and acted on assurances from the highest official authorities of South Carolina, that no attempt would be made to disturb your possession of the forts and property of the United States, if you would not disturb their existing condition until the commissioners had been sent and the attempt to negotiate had failed. You took from the members of the House of Representatives a written memorandum that no such attempt should be made, 'provided that no reinforcements should be sent into those forts, and their relative military status shall remain as at present.' And although you attach no force to the acceptance of such a paper—although you 'considered it as nothing more in effect than the promise of highly honorable gentlemen'—as an obligation on one side, without corresponding obligation on the other—it must be remembered (if we were rightly informed) that you were pledged, if you ever did send reinforcements, to return it to those from whom you had received it, before you executed your resolution. You sent orders to your officers, commanding them strictly to follow a line of conduct in conformity with such an understanding. Besides all this, you had received formal and official notice from the Governor of South Carolina that we had been appointed commissioners, and were on our way to Washington. You knew the implied condition under which we came; our arrival was notified to you, and an hour appointed for an interview. We arrived in Washington on Wednesday, at three o'clock, and you appointed an interview with us at one the next day. Early on that day (Thursday) the news was received here of the movement of Major Anderson. That news was communicated to you immediately, and you postponed our meeting until half-past two o'clock on Friday, in order that you might consult your cabinet. On Friday we saw you, and we called upon you then to redeem your pledge. You could not deny it. With the facts we have stated, and in the face of the crowning and conclusive fact that your secretary of war had resigned his seat in the cabinet, upon the publicly avowed ground that the action of Major Anderson had violated the pledged faith of the Government, and that unless the pledge was instantly redeemed, he was dishonored, denial was impossible; you did not deny it. You do not deny it now, but you seek to escape from its obligations on the grounds, first, that we terminated all negotiation by demanding, as a preliminary, the withdrawal of the United States troops from the harbor of Charleston; and, second, that the authorities of South Carolina, instead of asking explanation, and giving you the opportunity to vindicate yourself, took possession of other property of the United States. We will examine both.

"In the first place, we deny positively that we have ever in any way made any such demand. Our letter is in your possession; it will stand by this on record. In it we informed you of the objects of our mission. We say that it would have been our duty to have assured you of our readiness to commence negotiations, with the most earnest and anxious desire to settle all questions between us amicably and to our mutual advantage, but that events had rendered that assurance impossible. We stated the events, and we said that until some satisfactory explanation of these events was given us, we could not proceed; and then, having made this request for explanation, we added: 'And in conclusion, we would urge upon you the immediate withdrawal of the troops from the harbor of Charleston. Under present circumstances they are a standing menace, which renders negotiation impossible,' etc. 'Under present circumstances!' What circumstances? Why, clearly the occupation of Fort Sumter and the dismantling of Fort Moultrie by Major Anderson, in the face of your pledges, and without explanation or practical disavowal. And there is nothing in the letter which would, or could, have prevented you from declining to withdraw the troops, and offering the restoration of the status to which you were pledged, if such had been you desire. It would have been wiser and better, in our opinion, to have withdrawn the troops; and this opinion we urged upon you; but we demanded nothing but such an explanation of the events of the last twenty-four hours as would restore our confidence in the spirit with which the negotiations should be conducted. In relation to this withdrawal of the troops from the harbor, we are compelled, however, to notice one passage of your letter. Referring to it, you say: 'This I cannot do. This I will not do. Such an idea was never thought of by me in any possible contingency. No allusion to it had ever been made in any communication between myself and any human being.'

"In reply to this statement, we are compelled to say, that your conversation with us left upon our minds the distinct impression, that you did seriously contemplate the withdrawal of the troops from Charleston harbor. And in support of this impression we would add, that we have the positive assurance of gentlemen of the highest possible public reputation and the most unsullied integrity — men whose name and fame, secured by long service and patriotic achievements, place their testimony beyond cavil — that such suggestions had been made to and urged upon you by them, and had formed the subject of more than one earnest discussion with you. And it was this knowledge that induced us to urge upon you a policy, which had to recommend it its own wisdom and the might of such authority. As to the second point, that the authorities of South Carolina, instead of asking explanations, and giving you the opportunity to vindicate yourself, took possession of other property of the United States, we would observe: 1.

That even if this were so, it does not avail you for defence, for the opportunity for decision was afforded you before these facts occurred. We arrived in Washington on Wednesday; the news from Major Anderson reached here early on Thursday, and was immediately communicated to you. All that day men of the highest consideration—men who had striven successfully to lift you to your great office—who had been your tried and true friends through the troubles of your administration, sought you and entreated you to act—to act at once. They told you that every hour complicated your position. They only asked you to give the assurance that if the facts were so—that if the commander had acted without and against your orders, and in violation of your pledges —that you would restore the status you had pledged your honor to maintain. You refused to decide. Your secretary at war, your immediate and proper adviser in this whole matter, waited anxiously for your decision, until he felt that delay was becoming dishonor. More than twelve hours passed, and two cabinet meetings had adjourned, before you knew what the authorities of South Carolina had done; and your prompt decision at any moment of that time would have avoided the subsequent complications. But, if you had known the acts of the authorities of South Carolina, should that have prevented your keeping your faith? What was the condition of things? For the last sixty days you had in Charleston harbor not force enough to hold the forts against an equal enemy. Two of them were empty—one of those two the most important in the harbor. It could have been taken at any time. You ought to know better than any man that it would have been taken, but for the efforts of those who put their trust in your honor. Believing that they were threatened by Fort Sumter especially, the people were with difficulty restrained from securing, without blood, the possession of this important fortress. After many and reiterated assurances, given on your behalf, which we can not believe unauthorized, they determined to forbear, and in good faith sent on their commissioners to negotiate with you. They meant you no harm —wished you no ill. They thought of you kindly, believed you true, and were willing, as far as was consistent with duty, to spare you unnecessary and hostile collision. Scarcely had these commissioners left than Major Anderson waged war. No other words will describe his action. It was not a peaceful change from one fort to another; it was a hostile act in the highest sense, and only justified in the presence of a superior enemy, and in imminent peril. He abandoned his position, spiked his guns, burned his gun-carriages, made preparations for the destruction of his post, and withdrew, under cover of the night, to a safer position. This was war. No man could have believed (without your assurance) that any officer could have taken such a step, 'not only without orders, but against orders.' What the State did was in simple self-defence; for this act, with all its attending circumstances, was as much war as firing a volley; and war being thus begun, until those commencing it explained their action and disavowed their intention, there was no room for delay; and even at this moment while we are writing, it is more than probable, from the tenor of your letter, that reinforcements are hurrying on to the conflict, so that when the first gun shall be fired, there will have been on your part one continuous, consistent series of actions, commencing in a demonstration essentially warlike, supported by regular reinforcements, and terminating in defeat or victory. And all this without the slightest provocation; for, among the many things which you have said, there is one thing you cannot say—you have waited anxiously for news from the seat of war, in hopes that delay would furnish some excuse for this precipitation. But this 'tangible evidence of a design to proceed to a hostile act, on the part of the authorities of South Carolina,' which is the only justification of Major Anderson you are forced to admit, 'has not yet been alleged.' But you have decided, you have resolved to hold, by force, what you have obtained through our misplaced confidence; and by refusing to disavow the action of Major Anderson, have converted his violation of orders into a legitimate act of your executive authority. Be the issue what it may, of this we are assured, that, if Fort Moultrie has been recorded in history as a memorial of Carolina gallantry, Fort Sumter will live upon the succeeding page as an imperishable testimony of Carolina faith.

"By your course, you have probably rendered civil war inevitable. Be it so. If you choose to force this issue upon us, the State of South Carolina will accept it, and, relying upon Him who is the God of Justice as well as the God of Hosts, will endeavor to perform the great duty which lies before her hopefully, bravely, and thoroughly.

"Our mission being one for negotiation and peace, and your note leaving us without hope of a withdrawal of the troops from Fort Sumter, or of the restoration of the *status quo* existing at the time of our arrival, and intimating, as we think, your determination to reinforce the garrison in the harbor of Charleston, we respectfully inform you that we purpose returning to Charleston to-morrow afternoon.

"We have the honor to be, sir, very respectfully, your obedient servants.

"R. W. BARNWELL,
"J. H. ADAMS, } Commissioners.
"JAMES L. ORR,

"To His Excellency the PRESIDENT OF THE UNITED STATES."

The only reply by Mr. Buchanan to this paper was these words endorsed upon it:

"EXECUTIVE MANSION,
"*Half-past three o'clock, Wednesday.*

"This paper, just presented to the President, is of such a character that he declines to receive it."

CHAPTER VII.

Increased Belligerency of South Carolina.—Progress of the Works in the Harbor of Charleston.—Betrayal of a United States Government Vessel.—Fort Sumter Besieged.—Stars and Stripes still Flying.—Offensive Emblem of Union to the Charlestonians.—Plans for Degrading it.—Example of South Carolina followed by other States.—Seizure of Federal Forts in Georgia and North Carolina.—Indications of Hostility.—A more Resolute Tone at Washington.—The Order for Removal of Cannon from Pittsburg Revoked.—A feeble attempt to Reinforce Fort Sumter.—The Sailing of the Star of the West.—A cautious Oiling.—Arrival at Charleston.—A vigilant Enemy.—Fire Opened.—A critical Position.—Return of the Star of the West.—The Demonstration at Fort Sumter.—Correspondence between Major Anderson and Governor Pickens.—The improvement at Washington under the Inspiration of a patriotic Secretary of War.—Correspondence of Holt with the Governor of North Carolina.—The Cotton States not checked by strong words.—Secession of Mississippi.—Secession of Florida and Alabama.—Secession Enthusiasm in Mobile.—Seizure of Fort Barrancas and the Navy Yard at Pensacola.—An insolent Telegram from Florida to Washington.—Secession of Georgia.—Opposition of some leading Politicians.—Popular Demonstrations.—Secession of Louisiana.—Seizure of Federal Property.—More cautious proceedings of Texas.—Secession of Texas.—Departure of the Senators of the Seceding States from Washington.—Farewell Speech of Benjamin, of Louisiana.—Farewell Speech of Davis.—Hand-shaking in the Senate.—The slow Awakening of the North.—Union Meetings.—The Union Sentiment variously Manifested.—Indignation against the Abolitionists.—Alarm about the Safety of Washington.—Scott on Guard.—Peace Convention.

1861.
In South Carolina the people became daily more belligerent in their attitude toward the Federal Government. The works which had been ordered by the convention for the defence of the harbor of Charleston were labored at with great diligence, and soon the South Carolinians boasted that they were able to resist any attempts to reinforce Major Anderson, now in command of Fort Sumter. Batteries of earthwork, palmetto logs, and sand were erected and mounted with cannon on Sullivan's and Morris islands, guarding the approach to the harbor. The South Carolina commander at Castle Pinckney issued an order, forbidding all boats to approach the wharfs without permission, under the severest penalties if disobeyed. The river front of the city was carefully guarded, and mounted patrols paraded the streets night and day. Shipmasters were notified that all vessels must enter and clear at Charleston. The United States revenue cutter the William Aiken, betrayed by her captain into the hands of the insurrectionists, was received into the service of South Carolina, and with her armament and crew increased, was ready, under the Palmetto flag, to turn her guns against the government which her commander had sworn to defend against all enemies.

So great was the ardor and diligence of the South Carolinians, that they soon had their works in such a state of progress that Fort Sumter was completely besieged, and Major Anderson threatened with an attack. The people looked with excessive hostility at the flag of the United States still floating in their harbor, and the prevailing desire was to remove, if possible, that emblem of the Union, so lately the object of their pride, but which they now strove to dishonor. This intense feeling of aversion found expression in a universal cry for the capture of Fort Sumter. Plans of all kinds were devised to effect the purpose. Some proposed to float down rafts, loaded with burning tar-barrels, and thus smoke out the United States garrison; some suggested bribing the soldiers; some thought that a floating battery might be built with breastworks of cotton-bales, behind which sharp-shooters could post themselves and pick off each man in the fort; some hit upon the expedient of filling bomb-shells with prussic acid to throw among the troops and poison them, while others recommended a more protracted, if not more Christian method, of cutting off their supplies and starving them to death.*

In the mean time, the example of South Carolina in taking possession of the Federal property, was being followed by other States. Fort Pulaski was seized by the troops of Georgia, by order of the Governor, and even Governor Ellis, of North Carolina, dispatched the troops of the State to take possession of Fort Macon, at Beaufort, the forts at Wilmington, and the United States arsenal at Fayetteville. At Mobile, too, Fort Morgan and the arsenal, containing six stands of arms, 1,500 barrels of powder, 300,000 rounds of musket cartridges, and other munitions of war, were seized by the secessionists. These acts of undisguised hostility, though they preceded the meeting of the conventions in those States, gave an indication that could not be mistaken of a predetermined purpose to defy and resist the Federal authority.

A more resolute tone had, in the mean while, been assumed by the President. No longer exclusively under the control of traitorous advisers, he ventured to speak more authoritatively. The order for the removal of the cannon from the Alleghany arsenal to Southern forts, which had so greatly stirred the indignation of the citizens of Pittsburg, was revoked, and a feeble attempt* made to sustain Major Anderson and his little garrison at Fort Sumter.

The steamship Star of the West—a merchant vessel chartered by the Government—having taken on board two hundred and fifty artillerists and marines, and a supply of stores and ammunition, sailed at night for Charleston, though she cleared for New Orleans and Havana. She thus stole away in the darkness and under false pretences, with the hope that she might reach her destination and effect her purpose of reinforcing Major Anderson without exciting the suspicion of his besiegers. <small>Jan. 5.</small>

After a prosperous passage, the steamer having previously extinguished all her lights, lest she should be seen, arrived at Charleston Bar at half-past one o'clock in the morning. Here it was necessary to check her speed and grope her way cautiously, for there were no lights in the light-houses to guide her in her dangerous course. She con- <small>Jan. 9.</small>

---

* South Carolina.

* The secretary of the Interior, Thompson, resigned in consequence.

tinued, however, to move on slowly, the lead being thrown at every moment until four o'clock, when a light was seen through the haze of the early dawn. This was supposed to be a signal from Fort Sumter, and the ship having steered in that direction, hove to, to wait for daylight.

As the day broke, a Charleston steamer, the General Clinch, was discovered, which, as soon as she caught sight of the Star of the West, began to burn blue and red lights, as signals to the batteries. Those on guard at Morris Island were at once on the alert and at their posts before the orders could be given them to prepare for action. They expected at every moment a volley from Fort Sumter as they themselves got ready to fire at the approaching steamer. The Star of the West, too, was preparing for a warm reception. The soldiers were thrust below, and none allowed on deck but the crew. She, however, proceeded on her course, following in the wake of the little Charleston steamer, which steamed on, keeping about two miles ahead, and perseveringly sending off rockets and burning blue lights even until after broad daylight.

When the Star of the West had reached within two miles of Fort Moultrie, and about the same distance of Fort Sumter, the battery at Morris Island, from which the Palmetto flag was flying, opened fire. After the first shot the Star of the West hoisted a large American ensign at the fore, in addition to the American flag flying from the flagstaff. She, in spite of the fire, continued her course for ten minutes. In the mean time, the shots from Morris Island came thick and fast. Several passed clear over the steamer, one between the smoke-stack and walking-beam of the engine, one within an ace of the rudder, and another struck the ship just abaft the fore-rigging and stove in the planking.

"At the same time," says McGowan, the captain, in his report, "there was a movement of two steamers from near Fort Moultrie, one of them towing a schooner (I presume an armed schooner), with the intention of cutting us off. Our position now became rather critical, as we had to approach Fort Moultrie within three-quarters of a mile before we could keep away for Fort Sumter. A steamer approaching us, with an armed schooner in tow, and the battery on the island firing at us all the time, and having no cannon to defend ourselves from the attack of the vessels, we concluded that to avoid certain capture or destruction we would endeavor to get to sea. Consequently we wore round and steered down the channel, the battery firing upon us until the shot fell short."

Fort Sumter, in the mean time, had "made no demonstration, except at the port-holes, where the guns were run out, bearing on Morris Island."* Major Anderson, however, at once dispatched a letter to Governor Pickens, which, with the answer and rejoinder, are here given:

"To His Excellency the Governor of South Carolina.

"Sir: Two of your batteries fired

* Charleston Courier.

this morning on an unarmed vessel bearing the flag of my Government. As I have not been notified that war has been declared by South Carolina against the United States, I cannot but think this a hostile act, committed without your sanction or authority. Under that hope, I refrain from opening a fire on your batteries. I have the honor, therefore, respectfully to ask whether the above-mentioned act—one which I believe without parallel in the history of our country or any other civilized government—was committed in obedience to your instructions, and notify you, if it is not disclaimed, that I regard it as an act of war, and I shall not, after reasonable time for the return of my messenger, permit any vessel to pass within the range of the guns of my fort. In order to save, as far as it is in my power, the shedding of blood, I beg you will take due notification of my decision for the good of all concerned. Hoping, however, your answer may justify a further continuance of forbearance on my part, I remain, respectfully,

"ROBERT ANDERSON."

Gov. Pickens, in reply, after describing the position of South Carolina toward the States, said that any attempt to send United States troops into Charleston harbor, to reinforce the forts, would be regarded as an act of hostility; and in conclusion, added, "that any attempt to reinforce the troops at Fort Sumter, or to retake and resume possession of the forts within the waters of South Carolina which Major Anderson abandoned, after spiking the cannon and doing other damage, cannot be regarded by the authorities of the State as indicative of any other purpose than the coercion of the State by the armed force of the Government; special agents, therefore, have been sent off the bar to warn approaching vessels, armed and unarmed, having troops to reinforce Fort Sumter aboard, not to enter the harbor. Special orders have been given the commanders at the forts not to fire on such vessels until a shot across their bows should warn them of the prohibition of the State. Under these circumstances the Star of the West, it is understood, this morning attempted to enter the harbor with troops, after having been notified she could not enter, and consequently she was fired into. This act is perfectly justified by me.

"In regard to your threat about vessels in the harbor, it is only necessary for me to say, you must be the judge of your responsibility. Your position in the harbor has been tolerated by the authorities of the State, and while the act of which you complain is in perfect consistency with the rights and duties of the State, it is not perceived how far the conduct you propose to adopt can find a parallel in the history of any country, or be reconciled with any other purpose than that of your Government imposing on the State the condition of a conquered province.

"F. W. PICKENS."

"To His Excellency GOVERNOR PICKENS.

"SIR: I have the honor to acknowledge the receipt of your communication, and say, that under the circumstances I have deemed it proper to refer the whole matter to my Government, and intend deferring the course I indicated in my note this morning until the arrival from Washington of such instructions as I may receive.

"I have the honor also to express the hope that no obstructions will be placed in the way, and that you will do me the favor of giving every facility for the departure and return of the bearer, Lieutenant T. Talbot, who is directed to make the journey.

"ROBERT ANDERSON."

There were other evidences, besides this well-intentioned, but humble and fruitless attempt to reinforce Major Anderson, of an increased indisposition on the part of the Federal Government to continue to yield unresistingly to the demands and encroachments of the secessionists. Under the patriotic inspiration of the new secretary of war, Holt, a more positive assertion of Federal authority was assumed. Dignified words at least were spoken, if not effective measures taken, in vindication of the Government. To the Governor of North Carolina, who, after restoring the forts of that State to the authorities of the United States, had asked if "it was the purpose of the administration to coerce the Southern States?" the secretary of war had responded somewhat equivocally, but still in words more authoritative than the Government of Buchanan had yet ventured to utter.

"In reply to your inquiry," wrote the secretary, "whether it is the purpose of the President to garrison the forts of North Carolina during his administration, I am directed to say that they, in common with the other forts, arsenals, and other property of the United States, are in the charge of the President, and that if assailed, no matter from what quarter or under what pretext, it is his duty to protect them by all the means which the law has placed at his disposal. It is not his purpose to garrison the forts to which you refer at present, because he considers them entirely safe, as heretofore, under the shelter of that law-abiding sentiment for which the people of North Carolina have ever been distinguished. Should they, however, be attacked or menaced with danger of being seized or taken from the possession of the United States, he could not escape from his constitutional obligation to defend and preserve them. The very satisfactory and patriotic assurance given by your Excellency justifies him, however, in entertaining the confident expectation that no such contingency will arise."

The cotton States, now, had got beyond the influence of words however fitly spoken, and had been so long assured of impunity, that they did not hesitate in their career of insurrection. Mississippi was the first to follow South Carolina in seceding from the Union. The ordinance of secession was opposed only by fifteen members of the convention, and they resisted but a day, when they, too, signed with the rest. Florida and Alabama immediately succeeded. In the former State the secession ordinance

Jan. 9.

Jan. 11.

was carried by a vote of sixty-two to seven. In the latter, though there was the reputable minority of thirty-nine members of the convention to oppose the prevailing number of sixty-one, still the act of secession was hailed with immense enthusiasm. Judge Jones, of the United States District Court, announced with exulting emphasis, from the windows of the court-room at Mobile, that the United States Court for the Southern District of Alabama was "adjourned forever." A prodigal secessionist of the same city gave one hundred cords of wood for the use of the secession garrison in occupation of the Federal Fort Morgan, and proffered twenty negro men to labor on the works to defend the harbor against the United States.

The day was declared to be "the wildest day of excitement in the annals of Mobile." On receiving the news of the simultaneous secession of Florida an immense crowd collected about the "secession pole" to witness the raising of the "Southern flag," which was hoisted to the top amid the "shouts of the multitude and the thunders of cannon." The "Mobile Cadets" paraded the streets all day with the "splendid flag, a most gorgeous banner," which had been presented to them by "sympathetic ladies." At night the houses were illuminated so brilliantly, and tar-barrels burnt so profusely, that "the broad boulevard of Government Street became an avenue of light." To crown this exultant display of secession sentiment, the Federal custom-house was lighted up by "patriotic candles," thus affording "a choice epicureanism of triumph and rejoicing" to those excited citizens as they "piled Ossas of insult on Pelions of injury to Uncle Sam."*

On the passage of the secession ordinance by Florida, her troops, joined by those of Alabama, seized upon Fort Barrancas and the navy-yard at Pensacola, and thus became possessed not only of important posts of defence, but large supplies of ordnance, ammunition, and stores. "Having no means of resistance," said the United States officer in command in his dispatch to the Government, "I surrendered and hauled down my flag." The secessionists of Florida, themselves, telegraphed to their senators in Washington: "This move was in consequence of the Government garrisoning Fort Pickens, which has before remained unoccupied." "You will propose to the administration," they added, with insolent dictation, "to resume the *status quo ante bellum*, and we will immediately evacuate." [Jan. 14.]

Georgia was the next to adopt in convention the secession ordinance by a vote of two hundred and eight against eighty-nine. Some of the leading politicians of the State, as Alexander H. Stephens and Herschel V. Johnson, lately a candidate for Vice-President of the United States, opposed this hasty action, and emphatic manifestations of dislike were exhibited by many of the people at being thus hurried out of the Union. The usual popular demonstrations, however, followed the [Jan. 19.]

* Mobile *Advertiser*.

passage of the ordinance; sky-rockets were let off, torches burned, and mass meetings gathered and were stirred by martial music and jubilant speech.

In a week after, Louisiana followed Georgia, the convention having, by a vote of one hundred and thirteen to seventeen, declared her out of the Union. The seizure of Federal property, forts, arsenals, and treasure succeeded. Texas, checked by the obstinate loyalty of Governor Houston, was less precipitate, but finally passed, in convention, an ordinance of secession. This, however, was on the condition of its approval by the people, to whose suffrage it was to be submitted on the 23d of February, and, if sanctioned, to take effect on the 3d of March. Texas was thus far the only State which had ventured to submit the question of secession to popular vote. The State finally yielded, and declared itself out of the Union on the 4th of March.

Jan. 26.

Feb. 1.

The senators of these various seceding States had lingered at Washington as long as, under the pretence of a desire for conciliation, they could, by intriguing with their confederates at the capital, promote their plans, and by wheedling a feeble Executive, embarrass the action of government.

They now, however, threw off all disguise, and in the Senate of the United States openly confessed their designs and defied all the efforts of the Federal authority to counteract them. Senator Benjamin, of Louisiana, publicly announced his intention of taking farewell of the Senate in a parting "secession" speech. A large crowd gathered to hear him, and as he closed with the declaration that the South could never be subjugated, a shout of applause rose from the galleries, packed with his sympathizing friends.

Jefferson Davis, then United States senator from Mississippi, afterwards Confederate States' President, with an unusual mastery of his impulsive rhetoric, thus with studied deliberation and cool assurance confessed his secession faith, and declared his readiness to fight for it:

Jan. 21.

"I rise for the purpose of announcing to the Senate that I have satisfactory evidence that the State of Mississippi, by solemn ordinance in convention assembled, has declared her separation from the United States. Under these circumstances, of course, my functions terminate here. It has seemed to be proper that I should appear in the Senate and announce that fact, and to say something, though very little, upon it. The occasion does not invite me to go into the argument, and my physical condition will not permit it, yet something would seem to be necessary on the part of the State I here represent, on an occasion like this. It is known to senators who have served here, that I have for many years advocated, as an essential attribute of State sovereignty, the right of a State to secede from the Union. If, therefore, I had not believed there was justifiable cause—if I had thought the State was acting without sufficient provocation—still, under my theory of government, I should have felt bound by her action. I, however, may say I think she had justifiable cause, and I approve of her acts. I conferred with the people before that act was taken, and counselled them that if they could not remain, that they should take the act. I hope none will confound this expression of opinion with the advocacy of the right of a State to remain in the Union, and disregard its constitutional obligations by nullification. Nullification and secession are indeed antagonistic principles. Nullification is the remedy which is to be sought and applied, within the Union, against an agent of the United States, when the agent has violated constitutional obligations, and the State assumes for itself, and appeals to other States to support it. But when the States themselves, and the people of the States, have so acted as to convince us that they will not regard our constitutional rights, then, and then for the first time, arises the question of secession in its practical application. That great man who now reposes with his fathers, who has been so often arraigned for want of fealty to the Union, advocated the doctrine of nullification, because it preserved the Union. It was because of his deep-seated attachment to the Union that Mr. Calhoun advocated the doctrine of nullification, which he claimed would give peace within the limits of the Union, and not disturb it, and only be the means of bringing the agent before the proper tribunal of the States for judgment. Secession belongs to a different class of rights, and is to be justified upon the basis that the States are sovereign. The time has been, and I hope the time will come again, when a better appreciation of our Union will prevent any one denying that each State is a sovereign in its own right. Therefore I say I concur in the act of my State, and feel bound by it. It is by this confounding of nullification and secession that the name of another great man has been invoked to justify the coercion of a seceding State. The phrase 'to execute the law,' as used by General Jackson, was applied to a State refusing to obey the laws and still remaining in the Union. I remember well when Massachusetts was arraigned before the Senate. The record of that occasion will show that I said, if Massachusetts, in pursuing the line of steps, takes the last step which separates her from the Union, the right is hers, and I will neither vote one dollar nor one man to coerce her, but I will say to her, 'God speed!'" Mr. Davis then proceeded to argue that the equality spoken of in the Declaration of Independence was the equality of a class in political rights, referring to the charge against George III. for inciting insurrection, as proof that it had no reference to the slaves. "But we have proclaimed our independence. This is done with no hostility or any desire to injure any section of the country, nor even for our pecuniary benefit, but from the high and solid foundation of defending and protecting the rights we inherited, and transmitting them unshorn to our posterity. I know I feel no hostility to you senators here, and am sure there is not one of you, whatever may have been the sharp discussions between us, to whom I cannot now say, in the presence of my God, I wish you well. And such is the feeling, I am sure, the people I represent feel toward those whom you represent. I, therefore, feel I but express their desire, when I say I hope and they hope for those peaceful relations with you, though we must part, that may be mutually beneficial to us in the future. There will be peace if you so will it, and you may bring disaster on every part of the country, if you thus will have it. And if you will have it thus, we will invoke the God of our fathers, who delivered them from the paw of the lion, to protect us from the ravages of the bear; and thus putting our trust in God, and our own firm hearts and strong arms, we will vindicate and defend the rights we claim. In the course of my long career I have met with a great variety of men here, and there have been points of collision between us. Whatever of offence there has been to me, I leave here. I carry no hostile feelings away. Whatever of offence I have given, which has not been redressed, I am willing to say to senators, in this hour of parting, I offer you my apology for anything I may have done in the Senate; and I go thus released from obligation, remembering no injury I have received, and having discharged what I deem the duty of man, to offer the only reparation at this hour for every injury I have ever inflicted."

As the senators from Florida, Alabama, and Mississippi—all in open rebellion against the United States Government—were about leaving the Senate chamber, most of their fellow-senators, even those of the North, shook hands with them!

The Northern people were slowly awaking to the great dangers which beset the Union, and gradually rising to the efforts necessary to protect it. Prostrated in sympathy with the long inertness of the Government and its still languid action, they might have appeared to a casual observer indifferent to the great issue. There were, however, already indications of that loyalty to the Union which afterwards manifested itself in such a generous outpouring of men and money. Large meetings were held throughout the country to express devotion to its institutions and to offer service in their defence. At a popular gathering at Chicago, in Illinois, **Jan. 6.** resolutions were adopted expressing love for the Union; declaring that every attempt to rend it was the basest treason and most insane folly; that the Constitution of the United States formed a union between the people of the several States, and was intended to be perpetual; that every attempt by a State to secede or annul the laws of the United States was not only a usurpation of the powers of the General Government, but an aggression upon the equal rights of the other States; that peaceable secession, if possible, must necessarily be a matter of agreement between the States, and until such an agreement be made, the existing Government had no choice but to enforce the law and protect the property of the nation; that in view of what was occurring in the Southern States, of threats to prevent the inauguration of a President constitutionally elected, it was incumbent upon the loyal people of the several States to be prepared to render all their aid, military and otherwise, to the enforcement of the Federal laws, and that Major Anderson deserved the thanks of the country for the course pursued by him.

At Cincinnati, a large meeting of workingmen was held, at which resolutions were adopted declaring that the Union must be preserved in its integrity by the enforcement of the laws in every part of the country, through whatever means might be necessary. At Portland, in Maine, also, the people gathered in a "mass meeting," and passed similar resolutions.

Jan. 5.

The legislatures of various Northern States adopted resolutions in favor of the Union, and offered aid to the President to sustain the Government. New York tendered whatever "aid in men or money might be required to enforce the laws and uphold the authority of the Federal Government." Massachusetts did the same, and after declaring that South Carolina had committed an act of war, passed a bill authorizing the increase of the volunteer military of the State.

At the same time, it is true, that there were meetings of Northern citizens, at which there was a disposition to treat the recreant States with more tenderness. These, however, indicated no less the Union sentiment of the country, though they favored more conciliatory treatment. In New Jersey, resolutions were reported deploring the state of the country—advising, as a means of settling differences, the adoption by the people of the Crittenden resolutions, or some other pacific measures, with such modifications as might be deemed expedient; recommending the Legislature of New Jersey to pass a law to take a vote of the people, yes or no, on these; approving of the course of Virginia in appointing a commission to go to Washington, and counselling the Legislature to do the same.

It was the Union sentiment, moreover, however rudely expressed, which prompted some of the citizens of Rochester to break up an abolitionist meeting with noisy shouts for General Scott and Major Anderson, and others to resist with violence the hanging across the streets of a banner bearing the inscription, "No compromise with slavery." It was the same feeling, doubtless, which urged the crowd to overwhelm the disunion declarations of Wendell Phillips at Boston with noisy demonstrations of dissatisfaction, and hustle him in the streets until he was forced to take refuge with a squad of policemen.

In the mean time, some alarm was excited in regard to the safety of Washington, which was known to be filled with secessionists. It was rumored that plots had been laid and military companies organized in Maryland and Virginia, to seize the capital and prevent the inauguration of Lincoln. This call to arms of General Carrington is a memorable illustration of the public fearfulness begotten by the general suspicion.

"TO THE PUBLIC.

"Whereas the militia of the district is not organized, and threats have been made that the President-elect shall not be inaugurated in Washington, and there is reason, therefore, to apprehend that on the 4th of March next our city may be made the scene of riot, violence, and bloodshed; and whereas the undersigned believes that the honor of the nation and our city demands that the President-elect shall be inaugurated in the national metropolis, and that the young men of Washington city are determined not to desert their homes in the hour of danger, but to maintain their ground and defend their families and friends, in the Union and on the side of the Constitution and the laws, therefore the undersigned earnestly invites all who concur with him in opinion, and who are not now connected with some military company, to join with him in forming a temporary military organization, with a view of preserving peace and order in our midst on the 4th of March next, or whenever the emergency requires it—and for that purpose to unite with the volunteer companies of our city, which have, in a spirit of gallantry and patriotism worthy of our imitation, pledged themselves to the cause of the Union, the Constitution, and the laws. It is proper to state that I take this step after consultation with friends in whom I have the greatest confidence. It is not my object to interfere with my brother officers of the militia; the organization proposed is to be purely volunteer, for the purpose above stated, in which I am willing to serve in any capacity. I make the proposition, not as one of the generals of the militia, but as a citizen of Washington, who is prepared to defend his home and his honor at the peril of his life.

"EDWARD C. CARRINGTON."

Lieut. General Scott, however, the venerable custodian of the Union, was on guard, and by his prompt military measures of defence soon relieved the inquietude at the capital.

Even in New York a suspicion of secret plots arose, and excited public anxiety. The entire force at the Brooklyn navy-yard was put under arms, the guns of the frigate North Carolina shotted, and the city militia mustered, in readiness to resist the rumored attack of a band of secession conspirators.

A measure of obvious duty, though perhaps not of technical right, tardily begun and but ineffectively carried out, that of seizing, by the police of New York, arms intended for the seceded States, excited not unnaturally great indignation at the South, and some less expected disfavor even at the North. Jan. The mayor of the city of New York 24. eagerly disclaimed any responsibility for the "outrage," and declared that if he had the power, he "would summarily punish the authors of this illegal and unjustifiable seizure of private property." The Governor of Georgia retaliated by seizing some New York vessels in the harbor of Savannah, which were held until the arms claimed by him were restored.

While the feeling between the unionists and secessionists was thus becoming daily more exasperated, and threatening a collision of arms, a peace convention, suggested by the State of Virginia, had assembled in Washington and been organized, with ex-President Tyler to preside over it.

CHAPTER VIII.

The Meeting of the General Congress of the Seceding States at Montgomery.—Organization.—Formation of Provisional Government and Constitution.—No Conciliation or Compromise.—Nature of the New Constitution.—Its Politic Clauses.—Election of President and Vice-President.—Good Choice.—Extremists and Moderates both suited.—Life of Jefferson Davis.—His Birth.—Parentage.—Military Career.—Resignation.—Cotton Planting.—Political Career.—A Volunteer Officer in the Mexican War.—Turns the Tide of Battle at Buena Vista.—Appointed Brigadier-General.—Scruples of a States Rights Man.—Senator of the United States.—Chairman of Committee on Military Affairs.—Unsuccessful Candidate for Governor.—Electioneering for Pierce.—Secretary of War, and services in that office.—Personal Character and Appearance.—Elected President of the Confederate States.—Inaugural Address.—Biography of Alexander H. Stephens.—A poor Youth.—Educated by Charity.—Rapid eminence as a Lawyer.—Leader of the Whig Party in Congress.—Retirement from Public Life.—Disease.—Stirred by the Secession Movement.—Strong for the Union.—A sudden Conversion.—An earnest Proselyte.—Personal Appearance and Character.—A remarkable Speech.—The Cabinet of President Davis.—Robert Toombs; his Life and Character.—Charles Gustavus Memminger; his Life and Character.—Le Roy Pope Walker; his Life and Character.—Judah P. Benjamin; his Life and Character. Stephen M. Mallory; his Life and Character.—John H. Reagan; his Life and Character.

In accordance with a proposition of Alabama, all the conventions of the seceding States sent delegates to a general congress, which met at Montgomery on the 4th of February. In a few days after its organization, the form of a provisional government and a constitution were unanimously agreed upon, to take effect immediately. No suggestion was made for the restoration of harmony with the Union from which the States represented in the convention had separated. The subjects of conciliation and compromise were waived as totally obsolete. To form an independent nation and provide for its government and defence was the sole object, apparently, of the desire, as it was the motive of the action, of the members of the convention.

1861.

Feb. 8.

The constitution adopted was based on that of the United States, with modifications peculiar to the new government. The preamble dwelt especially on the separate sovereignty of the individual States of the new confederacy, and thus strove to give legal sanction to that heresy which had proved so fatal to the harmony of the Union. It declared:

"We, the deputies of the sovereign and independent States of South Carolina, Georgia, Florida, Alabama, Mississippi, and Louisiana, invoking the favor of Almighty God, do hereby, in behalf of these States, ordain and establish this constitution for the provisional government of the same, to continue one year from the inauguration of the President, or until a permanent constitution or confederation between the said States shall be put in operation, whichsoever shall first occur."

To conciliate the governments of Europe, on whose interposition in behalf of the new confederacy great calculations were made, but whose policy of abolishing the slave-trade seemed fatal to an alliance with any state which might favor that cruel commerce, the following article was adopted:

"The importation of African negroes from any foreign country other than the slaveholding States of the United States, is hereby forbidden, and Congress is required to pass such laws as shall effectually prevent the same."

At the same time, to give full protection to the institution as it existed in the slave States comprising the confederacy, a stringent fugitive law set forth that:

"A slave in one State escaping to another shall be delivered up on the claim of the party to whom said slave may belong, by the executive authority of the State in which such slave may be found; and in case of any abduction or forcible rescue, full compensation, including the value of the slave, and all costs and expenses, shall be made to the party by the State in which such abduction or rescue shall take place."

The following clause was ingeniously introduced as a forcible appeal to Virginia and other border States, still reluctant to leave the Union and try the hazards of the new confederacy.

"Congress shall also have power to prohibit the introduction of slaves from any State not a member of this confederacy."

In the clause relating to the tariff, the favorite Southern doctrine of taxation for revenue, and not for protection, was distinctly enunciated thus:

"The Congress shall have power to lay and collect taxes, duties, imposts, and excises for revenue necessary to pay the debts and carry on the government of the confederacy, and all duties, imposts, and excises shall be uniform throughout the confederacy."

To close up all accounts with the old Union and start the new under the most favorable auspices, an ostentatious profusion of fairness of dealing was made in an article declaring that "the government hereby instituted shall take immediate steps for the settlement of all matters between the States forming it and their late confederates of the United States, in relation to the public property and public debt at the time of their withdrawal from them, these States hereby declaring it to be their wish and earnest desire to adjust everything pertaining to the common property, common liabilities, and common obligations of that union upon principles of right, justice, equity, and good faith."

After the adoption of the Constitution, the Congress proceeded at once to the election of a provisional President and Vice-President. Jefferson Davis, of Mississippi, was chosen the former, and Alexander H. Stephens, of Georgia, the latter. No better appointments could have been made to further the purposes of the new confederacy. Both were experienced statesmen of practised executive talents. Davis, who had been long known as an advocate of State Rights, served to give assurance to the extremists of the South that their special interests were safe in his keeping, while Stephens, whose reluctant secessionism had been equally conspicuous, gave confidence to the moderate men, and encouraged them to give in their adherence to a government of which he was a prominent executive officer.

Jefferson Davis was born on the third of June, 1808, in Christian, now Todd, County, Kentucky. His father, who was a planter and an officer in the army of Revolutionary renown, removed to Mississippi while his son was yet a child. After a sound preliminary academical discipline at school and college, young Davis was admitted a cadet at West Point in 1824. In 1828 he graduated, and entered into active military service. In the Black Hawk war he earned promotion by his gallantry, and being raised to a first lieutenantcy of dragoons, served in that rank in various expeditions against the Indian tribes of the West. In 1835 he resigned his commission and took to cotton planting in Mississippi. He was, however, soon withdrawn from his retirement by the political interests of the country, and in 1844 was chosen a Presidential elector of Mississippi, to vote for Polk and Dallas, the candidates of the Democratic party, for which Davis had early shown his partiality.

In 1845, Davis was chosen a member of Congress, and at once assumed a prominent position, as a debater, on the side of his political friends, the Democrats. The Mexican war having in the mean time broken out, and a Mississippi regiment having elected him its colonel, he left at once his seat in the House of Representatives, and hastened to the scene of hostilities. He was with Taylor at the storming of Monterey, and at the battle of Buena Vista came up, in the nick of time, at the head of his Mississippians, and it is said turned the tide of battle in favor of the American troops. He was wounded while pertinaciously resisting a superior force, but still remained in the saddle until the end of the battle. General Taylor complimented him highly in his dispatch. On the expiration of the term of service of his regiment he returned home, but on his way he was met with a commission of brigadier-general of volunteers from President Polk. This, however, with a scrupulous regard for the "sovereign" rights of his State, he refused to accept, on the ground that the Federal authority, in making such an appointment, was interfering with the prerogative of Mississippi.

In 1847, Davis was appointed by the Governor of Mississippi senator of the United States, to fill a casual vacancy. In the next year, however, he was unanimously elected by the Legislature to complete the term, and again in 1850 was a second time chosen. He was appointed chairman of the committee on military affairs, and took a prominent part in the debates on most important questions, but especially on those which bore upon the interests of the slave States. He proved himself a resolute defender of slavery, and became remarkable for his advocacy of State Rights as supremely sovereign to those of the Union. In 1851 he was nominated candidate for governor expressly as an exponent of these views, but was defeated by the "Union" candidate, Henry S. Foote, who, however, secured his election by the small majority only of nine hundred.

Having resigned his seat in the Senate, on accepting the nomination for governor, he, after his defeat, remained in retirement until the Presidential canvass of 1852, when he electioneered actively for Pierce, and was rewarded, on his accession to the Presidency, by the appointment of secretary of war. In this office Davis proved himself an executive officer of great capacity and energy. He infused a new spirit into the war department, and introduced various effective reforms and improvements. The adoption of the light infantry system of tactics, the manufacture of rifled muskets, pistols and the Minnié ball, and the increase of our coast defences are among the changes he effected.

On the accession of Buchanan to the Presidency, Davis, being deprived of his secretaryship of war, was again elected by the Legislature of Mississippi to the Senate of the United States, and there he remained until the secession of his State, when he took his farewell in the remarkable speech already recorded.

He is described at this time as "of meagre frame and feeble health, but possessed of great energy and powers of endurance. His executive talents no one can question, and being ready of speech, some would claim for him the gift of eloquence. His military education and service, his experience as secretary of the war department of the United States, his familiarity with political intrigue, his dauntless spirit, and his natural capacity are what make Jefferson Davis so effective an ally and so formidable a foe."

On the 18th of February, 1861, Davis was inaugurated provisional President of the "Confederate States of America," when he delivered his inaugural.

INAUGURAL OF JEFFERSON DAVIS.

"GENTLEMEN OF THE CONGRESS OF THE CONFEDERATE STATES OF AMERICA, FRIENDS AND FELLOW-CITIZENS:

"Called to the difficult and responsible station of Chief Executive of the Provisional Government which you have instituted, I approach the discharge of the duties assigned me with an humble distrust of my abilities, but with a sustaining confidence in the wisdom of those who are to guide and aid me in the administration of public affairs, and an abiding faith in the virtue and patriotism of the people. Looking forward to the speedy establishment of a permanent government to take the place of this, and which by its greater moral and physical power will be better able to combat with the many difficulties which arise from the conflicting interests of separate nations, I enter upon the duties of the office to which I have been chosen with the hope that the beginning of our career as a confederacy may not be obstructed by hostile opposition to our enjoyment of the separate existence and independence which we have asserted, and which, with the blessing of Providence, we intend to maintain.

"Our present condition, achieved in a manner unprecedented in the history of nations, illustrates the American idea that governments rest upon the consent of the governed, and that it is the right of the people to alter and abolish governments whenever they become destructive to the ends for which they were established. The declared compact of the Union from which we have withdrawn was to establish justice, insure domestic tranquility, provide for the common defence, promote the general welfare, and secure the blessings of liberty to ourselves and our posterity; and when in the judgment of the sovereign States now composing this confederacy, it has been perverted from the purposes for which it was ordained, and ceased to answer the ends for which it was established, a peaceful appeal to the ballot-box declared that, so far as they were concerned, the government created by that compact should cease to exist. In this they merely asserted the right which the Declaration of Independence of 1776 defined to be inalienable. Of the time and occasion of its exercise they as sovereigns were the final judges, each for itself. The impartial, enlightened verdict of mankind will vindicate the rectitude of our conduct, and He who knows the hearts of men will judge of the sincerity with which we labored to preserve the government of our fathers in its spirit.

"The right solemnly proclaimed at the birth of the States, and which has been affirmed and reaffirmed in the bills of rights of the States subsequently admitted into the Union of 1789, undeniably recognizes in the people the power to resume the authority delegated for the purposes of government. Thus the sovereign States here represented proceeded to form this confederacy, and it is by the abuse of language that their act has been denominated revolution. They formed a new alliance, but within each State its government has remained. The rights of person and property have not been disturbed. The agent through whom they communicated with foreign nations is changed, but this does not necessarily interrupt their international relations. Sustained by the consciousness that the transition from the former Union to the present confederacy has not proceeded from a disregard on our part of our just obligations or any failure to perform every constitutional duty; moved by no interest or passion to invade the rights of others; anxious to cultivate peace and commerce with all nations, if we may not hope to avoid war, we may at least expect that posterity will acquit us of having needlessly engaged in it. Doubly justified by the absence of wrong on our part, and by wanton aggression on the part of others, there can be no cause to doubt that the courage and patriotism of the people of the Confederate States will be found equal to any measure of defence which soon their security may require.

"An agricultural people, whose chief

interest is the export of a commodity required in every manufacturing country, our true policy is peace, and the freest trade which our necessities will permit. It is alike our interest and that of all those to whom we would sell and from whom we would buy, that there should be the fewest practicable restrictions upon the interchange of commodities. There can be but little rivalry between ours and any manufacturing or navigating community, such as the northeastern States of the American Union. It must follow, therefore, that mutual interest would invite good-will and kind offices. If, however, passion or lust of dominion should cloud the judgment or inflame the ambition of those States, we must prepare to meet the emergency and maintain by the final arbitrament of the sword the position which we have assumed among the nations of the earth.

"We have entered upon a career of independence, and it must be inflexibly pursued through many years of controversy with our late associates of the Northern States. We have vainly endeavored to secure tranquility and obtain respect for the rights to which we were entitled. As a necessity, not a choice, we have resorted to the remedy of separation, and henceforth our energies must be directed to the conduct of our own affairs and the perpetuity of the confederacy which we have formed. If a just perception of mutual interest shall permit us peaceably to pursue our separate political career, my most earnest desire will have been fulfilled. But if this be denied us, and the integrity of our territory and jurisdiction be assailed, it will but remain for us with firm resolve to appeal to arms and invoke the blessing of Providence on a just cause.

"As a consequence of our new condition, and with a view to meet anticipated wants, it will be necessary to provide a speedy and efficient organization of the branches of the Executive department having special charge of foreign intercourse, finance, military affairs, and postal service. For purposes of defence the Confederate States may, under ordinary circumstances, rely mainly upon their militia; but it is deemed advisable, in the present condition of affairs, that there should be a well instructed, disciplined army, more numerous than would usually be required on a peace establishment. I also suggest that, for the protection of our harbors and commerce on the high seas, a navy adapted to those objects will be required. These necessities have, doubtless, engaged the attention of Congress.

"With a constitution differing only from that of our fathers in so far as it is explanatory of their well-known intent, freed from sectional conflicts, which have interfered with the pursuits of the general welfare, it is not unreasonable to expect that the States from which we have recently parted may seek to unite their fortunes to ours under the government which we have instituted. For this your constitution makes adequate provision, but beyond this, if I mistake not, the judgment and will of the people are, that union with the States from which they have separated is neither practicable nor desirable. To increase the power, develop the resources, and promote the happiness of the confederacy, it is requisite there should be so much homogeneity that the welfare of every portion would be the aim of the whole. Where this does not exist, antagonisms are engendered which must and should result in separation.

"Actuated solely by a desire to preserve our own rights and to promote our own welfare, the separation of the Confederate States has been marked by no aggression upon others, and followed by no domestic convulsion. Our industrial pursuits have received no check, the cultivation of our fields progresses as heretofore, and even should we be involved in war, there would be no considerable diminution in the production of the staples which have constituted our exports, in which the commercial world has an interest scarcely less than our own. This common interest of producer and consumer can only be intercepted by an exterior force which should obstruct its transmission to foreign markets, a course of conduct which would be detrimental to manufacturing and commercial interests abroad.

"Should reason guide the action of the government from which we have separated, a policy so detrimental to the civilized world, the Northern States included, could not be dictated by even a stronger desire to inflict injury upon us; but if it be otherwise, a terrible responsibility will rest upon it, and the suffering of millions will bear testimony to the folly and wickedness of our aggressors. In the mean time there will remain to us, besides the ordinary remedies before suggested, the well-known resources for retaliation upon the commerce of an enemy.

"Experience in public stations of a subordinate grade to this which your kindness has conferred, has taught me that care and toil and disappointments are the price of official elevation. You will see many errors to forgive, many deficiencies to tolerate, but you shall not find in me either want of zeal or fidelity to the cause that is to me the highest in hope and of most enduring affection. Your generosity has bestowed upon me an undeserved distinction, one which I neither sought nor desired. Upon the continuance of that sentiment, and upon your wisdom and patriotism, I rely to direct and support me in the performance of the duties required at my hands.

"We have changed the constituent parts, but not the system of our government. The Constitution formed by our fathers is that of these Confederate States. In their exposition of it, and in the judicial construction it has received, we have a light which reveals its true meaning. Thus instructed as to the just interpretation of that instrument, and ever remembering that all offices are but trusts held for the people, and that delegated powers are to be strictly construed, I will hope by due diligence in the performance of my duties, though I may disappoint your expectation, yet to retain, when retiring, something of the good will and confidence which will welcome my entrance into office.

"It is joyous in the midst of perilous times to look around upon a people united in heart, when one purpose of high resolve animates and actuates the whole—where the sacrifices to be made are not weighed in the balance against honor, right, liberty, and equality. Obstacles may retard, but they cannot long prevent, the progress of a movement sanctioned by its justice and sustained by a virtuous people. Reverently let us invoke the God of our fathers to guide and protect us in our efforts to perpetuate the principles which by His blessing they were able to vindicate, establish, and transmit to their posterity; and with a continuance of His favor ever gratefully acknowledged, we may hopefully look forward to success, to peace, to prosperity."

Alexander H. Stephens, the Vice-President of the new Confederacy, was born in Georgia on the 11th of February, 1812. His parents were too poor to educate him, but the youth showing an early quickness of parts, attracted the attention of some neighbors, who charitably sent him to school and college and supported him until he was able to make his own livelihood. Choosing the law for his profession, he was admitted to the bar in 1834, and rose rapidly to distinction. In 1843 he was elected by the Whigs a member of Congress, but on the dissolution of their party, he joined the Democrats, and became one of their most prominent leaders. In 1858 he refused to be any longer a candidate for Congress, and retired, apparently forever, to private life. From early youth he had suffered from illness, and now, after the wearing effects of a stirring political career, he seemed incapable of further activity of effort. He was, however, roused by the secession movement in his State, and came forward to resist it. He voted against the secession ordinance passed by the convention of Georgia, and sustained the cause of the Union so manfully in a remarkable speech, that he was hailed by loyal men throughout the country as their great Southern champion. It was even rumored that President Lincoln had offered him a seat in his proposed cabinet. Stephens, however, did not long resist the prevailing sentiment of his State, but giving in his adherence to the secessionists, exhibited the usual zeal of sudden converts by surpassing the veteran apostles of secession in his defence of the doctrine. He is pictured thus: "Wasted to a shadow by a protracted disease, the Vice-President of the Confederacy weighs but ninety-six pounds. He yet seems, in spite of a feeble body, capable of great mental effort. Though his voice, in its shrill and piping tones, gives manifestation of the physical weakness of the invalid, he yet does not hesitate to exercise it in prolonged efforts of oratory, which not seldom rise to the power of true eloquence."

Eager, apparently, to vindicate himself from all suspicion of the sincerity of his conversion, to which his former loyalty to the Union might have exposed him, he manifested an ultraism of opinion in favor of the benefits and rights of slavery, which few even of the most violent secessionists had ventured to assert. He thus held forth to the applause of his fellow-citizens of Savannah, and to the horror of the Christian world, in a speech exposing the objects of the Southern rebellion:

March 21.

"The new Constitution has put at rest forever all the agitating questions relating to our peculiar institutions—African slavery as it exists among us—the proper status of the negro in our form of civilization. This was the immediate cause of the late rupture and present revolution. Jefferson, in his forecast, had anticipated this as the 'rock upon which the old Union would split.' He was right. What was conjecture with him, is now a realized fact. But whether he fully comprehended the great truth upon which that rock stood and stands, may be doubted. The prevailing ideas entertained by him and most of the leading statesmen at the time of the formation of the old Constitution were, that the enslavement of the African was in violation of the laws of nature; that it was wrong in principle, socially, morally, and politically. It was an evil they knew not well how to deal with, but the general opinion of the men of that day was, that somehow or other, in the order of Providence, the institution would be evanescent and pass away. This idea, though not incorporated in the Constitution, was the prevailing idea at the time. The Constitution, it is true, secured every essential guarantee to the institution while it should last, and hence no argument can be justly used against the constitutional guarantees thus secured, because of the common sentiment of the day. Those ideas, however, were fundamentally wrong. They rested upon the assumption of the equality of races. This was an error. It was a sandy foundation, and the idea of a government built upon it; when the 'storm came and the wind blew, it fell.'

"Our new government is founded upon exactly the opposite idea; its foundations are laid, its corner-stone rests, upon the great truth that the negro is not equal to the white man. That slavery—subordination to the superior race—is his natural and moral condition. This, our new government, is the first, in the history of the world, based upon this great physical and moral truth. This truth has been slow in the process of its development, like all other truths in the various departments of science. It has been so even among us. Many who hear me, perhaps, can recollect well, that this truth was not generally admitted, even within their day. The errors of the past generation still clung to many as late as twenty years ago. Those at the North who still cling to these errors, with a zeal above knowledge, we justly denominate fanatics.

* * * * * *

"In the conflict thus far, success has been, on our side, complete throughout the length and breadth of the Confederate States. It is upon this, as I have stated, our actual fabric is firmly planted, and I cannot permit myself to doubt the ultimate success of a full recognition of this principle throughout the civilized and enlightened world.

"As I have stated, the truth of this principle may be slow in development, as all truths are, and ever have been in the various branches of science. It was so with the principles announced by Galileo; it was so with Adam Smith and his principles of political economy; it was so with Harvey and his theory of the circulation of the blood. It is stated that not a single one of the medical profession, living at the time of the announcement of the truths made by him, admitted them. Now they are universally acknowledged. May we not, therefore, look with confidence to the ultimate universal acknowledgment of the truths upon which our system rests. It is the first government ever instituted upon principles of strict conformity to nature, and the ordination of Providence, in furnishing the materials of human society. Many governments have been founded upon the principle of certain classes, but the classes thus enslaved were of the same race, and in violation of the laws of nature. Our system commits no such violation of nature's laws. The negro, by nature, or by the curse against Canaan, is fitted for that condition which he occupies in our system. The architect, in the construction of buildings, lays the foundation with the proper materials, the granite; then comes the brick or the marble. The substratum of our society is made of the materials fitted by nature for it, and by experience we know that it is best, not only for the superior, but for the inferior race, that it should be so. It is, indeed, in conformity with the ordinance of the Creator. It is not for us to inquire into the wisdom of His ordinances, or to question them. For His own purposes he has made one race to differ from another, as He has made 'one star to differ from another star in glory.'

"The great objects of humanity are best attained when conformed to His laws and decrees, in the formation of governments, as well as in all things else. Our confederacy is founded upon principles in strict conformity with those laws. This stone which was rejected by the first builders 'is become the chief stone of the corner' in our new edifice.

"The progress of disintegration in the old Union may be expected to go on with almost absolute certainty. We are now the nucleus of a growing power, which, if we are true to ourselves, our destiny, and high mission, will become the controlling power on this continent. To what extent accessions will go on in the process of time, or where it will end, the future will determine."

With President Davis and Vice-President Stephens were associated in the executive department of the confederacy Robert Toombs, of Georgia, as secretary of state; C. S. Memminger, of South Carolina, as secretary of the treasury; Leroy Pope Walker, of Alabama, as secretary of war; Judah P. Benjamin, of Louisiana, as attorney-general; Stephen M. Mallory, of Florida, as secretary of the navy; and John H. Reagan as postmaster-general.

Toombs was born in Wilkes County, Georgia, on the 2d of July, 1810. His early education was received in his native State, but after a short collegiate career at the University of Georgia, he was transferred to Union College, at Schenectady, in New York, where he graduated. After studying for the bar, his restless hankering for adventure induced him to volunteer to serve in the Creek war, and he was chosen captain. On his return home he was elected to the Legislature, and subsequently a member of the United States House of Representatives and of the United States Senate. He was conspicuous always as an intemperate advocate of slavery and of the sovereign rights of the Southern States. It was he who boasted that he would call the roll of his slaves at the base of the Bunker Hill Monument in Boston. He was among the first to move in behalf of secession, and while still a senator of the United States, did not cease to conspire and stir up his fellow-citizens in rebellion against the Union. Possessed of an impulsive temper, and unscrupulous in the use of means to gratify his desire, he was one of the most audacious and active, if not the most capable, of the confederate leaders.

Charles Gustavus Memminger was born in Wurtemburg, Germany, on the 7th of January, 1803. At the age of two years he was brought to Charleston by his mother, a poor widow, who soon after died and left him destitute. Found a vagrant child in the streets, he was sent to the orphan asylum of the city, where he remained until he was nine years old. His lively parts attracted the notice of Governor Thomas Bennett, who received him into his family and sent him to Columbia College, the university of the State, where he graduated in 1820. He now studied law, and was admitted to practice in 1825.

His first political action was as an opponent of South Carolina nullification, which he resisted strenuously and so conspicuously, that he was recognized a leader of the Union party. He aided the cause with pen as well as speech, and not only wrote against nullification in the political journals, but ridiculed it in a work entitled, "The Book of Nullification," written in Scriptural style.

In 1836 he was first elected to the Legislature, and continued to serve unremittingly until 1852. Being appointed chairman of the committee on finance—a position he retained for many years—he made that subject an especial study. He opposed the suspension of specie payment by the banks of South Carolina in 1839, and on the question coming before the courts, was employed to assist the attorney-general in the prosecution of a case. Though opposed by the ablest counsel of the State, he gained his cause, and the banks were declared to have forfeited their charters. While in the Legislature, he advocated the adoption of the Sub-treasury scheme, and abandoning his early opinions, sustained the peculiar political views of Calhoun.

In 1852 he retired from public life, but again in 1854 sought and obtained his election to the Legislature, with the view of effecting a reform in the system of public schools, in which he finally succeeded, in spite of an obstinate opposition.

In 1859 he was appointed a commissioner of South Carolina to the State of Virginia, to induce co-operation, on the part of the slave States, in resistance to the abolitionists of the North, a fear of whom had been awakened by the insurrectionary attempt of John Brown at Harper's Ferry. Previously he had always borne the character of an upright man in private life, though for a long time his political integrity was suspected by the constant disunionists, as they recalled his early efforts in favor of the Union and his tardy conversion to the doctrine of State Rights. His active interest in the Episcopal Church, to whose general convention he was frequently a delegate, and his earnest efforts to advance the public education and improve the charitable institutions of his city and State, had given him a character for piety and benevolence which few were disposed to question. His practised capacity as a financier, and his general accomplishments, made him one of the most efficient of President Davis' cabinet.

Leroy Pope Walker was born in Alabama in the year 1816. His family is one of note; his father was a man of wealth and some military distinction; one of his brothers was a member of Congress, another a judge, both being prominent men in the late confederacy. Prominent as a politician, he was always known as a Southern Democrat, especially devoted to the interests of the slave States. He stood high as a lawyer, and man of eloquence and capacity in business, and was among the first and most ardent to espouse the cause of secession in his State.

The attorney-general, Judah P. Benjamin, attained to great eminence as a jurist and an advocate in Louisiana. While a senator of the United States, he was a professed Whig, but always a State Rights' partisan. Being a brilliant rhetorician, a subtle lawyer, a man skilled in political intrigue, and unscrupulous in the use of means to effect the objects of party or to reach the aim of his personal ambition, he proved an able adviser.

Stephen M. Mallory was for a long period a United States senator from Florida, and though unobtrusive, bore the character of a useful member of the upper house of Congress. He was always considered a conservative man in his political views, and supposed to be strongly attached to the Union. He is thought to have linked his fortunes to secession rather from the force of circumstances, than from any personal predilections for the cause. He was probably appointed secretary of the navy of the Confederate States in consequence of his presumed experience obtained as chairman of the committee of the United States Senate on naval affairs.

John H. Reagan, the postmaster of the Confederate States, was but little known beyond the boundaries of his own State, although he had served several terms in the national Congress.

CHAPTER IX.

Abraham Lincoln and Hannibal Hamlin declared duly elected President and Vice-President of the United States.—Opening of Electoral Votes.—The reading of the Vote of South Carolina.—Concentration of public attention upon Lincoln.—The Siege of Springfield.—Throng of Visitors.—Insatiable Curiosity.—Lincoln Photographed.—House and Furniture minutely described.—Habits and Personal Appearance of the new President taken off.—Social Freedom and Political Reticence.—A Newspaper Interpreter.—Lincoln speaking for himself.—A grave Farewell.—Commencement of a triumphal Journey.—Speeches.—Homely Oratory.—A clever Illustration.—A Night Surprise.—An unexpected Visitor.—Portentous Intelligence.—A Tragic Plot.—Who were the Conspirators?—The effect of the intelligence upon Lincoln and his Friends.—A sudden and mysterious Movement.—Lincoln safe in Washington.—Indignation at Baltimore.—Exposition of the Plot, and how it was ferreted out.—Congressional Debates.—Crittenden Compromise.—Adjournment of Peace Conference.—The Product.—Hopefulness of the North.—Speculations in regard to Lincoln's Policy.—The Inauguration.—The Ceremonies.—Novel Additions.—Thirty-four young Ladies in loving Union.—A strong Military Force in Ambush.—Reading of the Message.—The Notables.—The Crowd.—The Message of Lincoln.

1861. On the 14th of February, Abraham Lincoln, of Illinois, and Hannibal Hamlin, of Maine, were declared "duly elected" President and Vice-President of the United States for the four years commencing on the 4th of March, 1861. The senators and members of Congress having been assembled in the House of Representatives, and Vice-President Breckinridge having taken his seat at the right of the speaker, he, in accordance with the Constitution, opened the packages containing the electoral votes of the several States, and the result was announced. The reading of the vote of South Carolina was received with an exhibition of good-humored hilarity.

Immediately after the election of Lincoln, and before it was constitutionally announced, all the attention of the public was concentrated upon the future President. Eager office-seekers, newspaper gossip-mongers, insatiate photographers, aspiring politicians, and civic deputations thronged the little town of Springfield, in Illinois, and beset Mr. Lincoln in his humble home. With his usual readiness of welcome, he had a hand to shake with all comers, and none went away without a good-natured word and an impression of the unpretending amiability and simple honesty of the new President. His visitors, with a desire to satisfy the insatiable curiosity of the public, concentrated their powers of observation upon him, and took care to describe with photographic minuteness his every feature, word, movement, and local surrounding. Through his wicket gate, open to every comer, they walked, unbidden, into his residence, noting each clap-board of its shingly structure, and reproduced in print and picture the "good-sized house of wood, simply but tastefully furnished, surrounded by trees and flowers." Having a free run from kitchen to garret, they strolled into the library, cataloguing his law-books, and inspecting his accounts, informed the world that "he owes no man a dollar;" they lounged in the parlor and took an inventory of Brussels carpet, sofa, piano, and of Mrs. Lincoln, in her newest silk. They dogged Mr. Lincoln everywhere, from his breakfast, through the town to his daily round of business, and back again to his dining-table, duly reporting that "he loves a good dinner, and eats with the appetite which goes with a great brain, but his food is plain and nutritious; he never drinks intoxicating liquors of any sort."

Meanwhile, they had fixed every line and tint, every light and shadow, of the man upon their memorandum-books and photographic plates. Thus his fellow-citizens throughout the country could see at a glance that "his features, though they are those of a man of mark, are not such as belong to a handsome man; that his eyes are "dark grey, and fine when lighted up;" his hair black and, though thin, wiry; "his head sits well on his shoulders, but beyond that, defies description;" that his "head is unlike either Webster or Clay's, but is very large and phrenologically well proportioned, betokening power in all its developments;" that he has "a slightly Roman nose, a wide-cut mouth, and a dark complexion, with the appearance of having been weather-beaten."

There was, however, notwithstanding the free exposition of Mr. Lincoln to his inquisitive visiters on most points, a resolute reticence in regard to his future action toward the secession States of the South. To the "hundreds of people" who had flocked to Springfield and met him at a public reception in the town-hall, he frankly declared that the time had not come for a definition of the policy of his administration, and that they must be satisfied for the present with a hearty greeting, which he proceeded to give by "shaking hands with most of the attendants."*

Public curiosity was aroused to the highest pitch, and although Lincoln resolutely kept silence, some of the newspapers, unable to resist the universal eagerness for an oracular response, spoke for him: "I will suffer," said his newspaper interpreter in behalf of Lincoln, "death before I will consent, or will advise my friends to consent, to any concession or compromise which looks like buying the privilege of taking possession of this government, to which we have a constitutional right, because whatever I might think of the merit of the various propositions before Congress, I should regard any concession in the face of menace the destruction of the Government itself, and a consent on all hands that our system shall be brought down to a level with the existing disorganized state of affairs in Mexico. But this thing will hereafter be as it is now, in the hands of the people; and if they desire to call a convention to remove any grievances complained of, or to give new guarantees for the permanence of vested rights, it is not mine to oppose."

When his election was, however, duly declared, Mr. Lincoln ventured to speak for himself. On the 11th of February

* New York Times, Feb. 4th, 1861.

he bade farewell to his fellow-citizens at Springfield in these grave words:

"MY FRIENDS: No one not in my position can appreciate the sadness I feel at this parting. To this people I owe all that I am. Here I have lived more than a quarter of a century, here my children were born, and here one of them lies buried. I know not how soon I shall see you again. A duty devolves upon me which is, perhaps, greater than that which has devolved upon any other man since the days of Washington. He never would have succeeded except for the aid of Divine Providence, upon which he at all times relied. I feel that I cannot succeed without the same Divine aid which sustained him; and in the same Almighty Being I place my reliance for support, and I hope you, my friends, will all pray that I may receive that Divine assistance, without which I cannot succeed, but with which success is certain. Again I bid you all an affectionate farewell."

This solemn leave-taking brought tears into his eyes and those of his fellow-citizens. He now commenced a triumphant journey toward Washington. Crowds of people, with civic deputations at their head, met and welcomed him on his passage through the large cities. His speeches, which were frequent, showed an amiable desire, though not always gracefully expressed, to conciliate his political opponents by yielding his partisanship to the general interests of the country, but evinced a resolute determination to uphold the Federal authority against the attacks of its enemies. His homely oratory was taken generally in good part by those who listened to it, and it occasionally, by an apt illustration, struck a chord of popular sympathy. "In their [the secessionists] view," he said happily at Indianapolis, "the Union, as a family relation, would seem to be no regular marriage, but rather a sort of free-love arrangement, to be maintained on passional attraction."

After passing through Cincinnati, Indianapolis, Columbus, Pittsburg, New York, and Trenton, he finally reached Philadelphia. Here, to the usual programme of military parade, public reception, speech-making, and shaking of hands, was added that of raising the American flag upon Independence Hall, the ancient seat of Congress, on Friday, the 22d of February, the anniversary of Washington's birthday.

On the night previous, Mr. Lincoln, after having gone to bed in the hotel, was aroused and informed that a visitor desired to see him on "a matter of life and death." He was refused admission, unless he gave his name, which he did, and as it was one that carried with it an authority* that Mr. Lincoln was not disposed to pass unheeded, he, while "yet disrobed," received the visitor.

The object of this mysterious, nocturnal visit was to inform Mr. Lincoln of the organization of a body of men who had determined that he should not be inaugurated President, and to effect their purpose, were ready to capture

---

* The visitor was, it is believed, the son of Mr. Lincoln's secretary of state.

him or to take his life on his way to Washington. Some influential persons in the interests of the secessionists were supposed to be implicated in the plot. The morning's telegram came with this startling announcement:

"Statesmen laid the plan, bankers indorsed it, and adventurers were to carry it into effect. As they understood Mr. Lincoln was to leave Harrisburg at nine o'clock this morning by special train, the idea was, if possible, to throw the cars from the road at some point where they would rush down a steep embankment and destroy in a moment the lives of all on board. In case of the failure of this project, their plan was to surround the carriage on the way from depot to depot in Baltimore, and assassinate him with dagger or pistol-shot."

Whatever may have been the exact nature of the revelation, it was sufficiently serious to induce his wife and friends to persuade the reluctant Mr. Lincoln to forego the continuance of his triumphal progress of public reception, flag-raising, speech-making, and hand-shaking.

"Mr. Lincoln did not want to yield," says the telegraph reporter, "and Col. Sumner actually cried with indignation; but Mrs. Lincoln, seconded by Mr. Judd, and Mr. Lincoln's original informant, insisted upon it, and *at nine o'clock* Mr. Lincoln *left on a special train.* He wore a Scotch plaid cap and a very long military cloak, so that he was entirely unrecognizable. Accompanied by Superintendent Lewis and one friend, he started, while all the town, with the exception of Mrs. Lincoln, Col. Sumner, Mr. Judd, and two reporters, who were sworn to secresy, supposed him to be asleep.

"The telegraph wires were put beyond the reach of any one who might desire to use them."

At the same moment that the world was excited by this alarming intelligence, its agitation was composed by the welcome statement that Mr. Lincoln had arrived safe at Willard's Hotel, in Washington, and on the same day, "accompanied by Mr. Seward, had paid his respects to President Buchanan" at the White House.

The press and people of Baltimore supposed to be friendly to secession expressed great disappointment and indignation that Lincoln and his friends should have manifested any distrust of their hospitality. Those, however, who were unquestionably loyal to the Union, confessed to a riotous intent on the part of some of the people of Baltimore, and declared that Lincoln's proceeding was "a simple and practical avoidance of what might have been an occasion of disorder and of mortification to all interested in the preservation of the good name of the city."*

A detailed, and apparently authentic exposition of the formation of the plot, the agents employed, and the means used to thwart it, appeared in one of the Northern journals.†

"Some of Mr. Lincoln's friends having heard that a conspiracy existed to assassinate him on his way to Washington,

---

* Baltimore American. † Albany Evening Journal.

set on foot an investigation of the matter. For this purpose they employed a detective of great experience, who was engaged at Baltimore in the business some three weeks prior to Mr. Lincoln's expected arrival there, employing both men and women to assist him. Shortly after his coming to Baltimore, the detective discovered a combination of men banded together under a most solemn oath to assassinate the President-elect. The leader of the conspirators was an Italian refugee, a barber, well-known in Baltimore, who assumed the name of *Orsini*, as indicative of the part he was to perform. The assistants employed by the detective, who, like himself, were strangers in Baltimore city, by assuming to be secessionists from Louisiana and other seceding States, gained the confidence of some of the conspirators, and were intrusted with their plans. It was arranged in case Mr. Lincoln should pass safely over the railroad to Baltimore, that the conspirators should mingle with the crowd which might surround his carriage, and by pretending to be his friends, be enabled to approach his person, when, upon a signal from their leader, some of them would shoot at Mr. Lincoln with their pistols, and others would throw into his carriage hand-grenades filled with detonating powder, similar to those used in the attempted assassination of the Emperor Louis Napoleon. It was intended that in the confusion which should result from this attack, the assailants should escape to a vessel which was waiting in the harbor to receive them, and be carried to Mobile, in the seceding State of Alabama.

"Upon Mr. Lincoln's arrival in Philadelphia upon Thursday, the 21st of February, the detective visited Philadelphia, and submitted to certain friends of the President-elect the information he had collected as to the conspirators and their plans. An interview was immediately arranged between Mr. Lincoln and the detective. The interview took place in Mr. Lincoln's room, in the Continental Hotel, where he was staying during his visit in Philadelphia.

"Mr. Lincoln, having heard the officer's statement, informed him that he had promised to raise the American flag on Independence Hall on the next morning —the morning of the anniversary of Washington's birthday—and that he had accepted the invitation of the Pennsylvania Legislature to be publicly received by that body in the afternoon of the same day. 'Both of these engagements,' said he, with emphasis, 'I will keep if it costs me my life. If, however, after I shall have concluded these engagements, you can take me in safety to Washington, I will place myself at your disposal, and authorize you to make such arrangements as you may deem proper for that purpose.

"On the next day, in the morning, Mr. Lincoln performed the ceremony of raising the American flag on Independence Hall, in Philadelphia, according to his promise, and arrived at Harrisburg on the afternoon of the same day, where he was formally welcomed by the Pennsylvania Legislature. After the reception, he retired to his hotel, the Jones House, and withdrew with a few confidential friends to a private apartment. Here he remained until nearly six o'clock in the evening, when, in company with Colonel Lamon, he quietly entered a carriage without observation, and was driven to the Pennsylvania Railroad, where a special train for Philadelphia was waiting for him. Simultaneously with his departure from Harrisburg, the telegraph wires were cut, so that his departure, if it should become known, might not be communicated at a distance.

"The special train arrived in Philadelphia at a quarter to eleven at night. Here he was met by the detective, who had a carriage in readiness into which the party entered, and were driven to the dépôt of the Philadelphia, Wilmington, and Baltimore Railroad.

"They did not reach the dépôt until a quarter past eleven; but, fortunately for them, the regular train, the hour of which for starting was eleven, had been delayed. The party then took berths in the sleeping car, and without change of cars passed directly through to Washington, where they arrived at the usual hour, half-past six o'clock, on the morning of Saturday the 23d. Mr. Lincoln wore no disguise whatever, but journeyed in an ordinary traveling dress.

"It is proper to state here that, prior to Mr. Lincoln's arrival in Philadelphia, General Scott and Senator Seward, in Washington, had been apprised, from independent sources, that imminent danger threatened Mr. Lincoln in case he should publicly pass through Baltimore; and accordingly a special messenger, Mr. Frederick W. Seward, a son of Senator Seward, was dispatched to Philadelphia, to urge Mr. Lincoln to come direct to Washington, in a quiet manner. The messenger arrived in Philadelphia late on Thursday night, and had an interview with the President-elect, immediately subsequent to his interview with the detective. He was informed that Mr. Lincoln would arrive by the early train on Saturday morning, and, in accordance with this information, Mr. Washburn, member of Congress from Illinois, awaited the President-elect at the dépôt in Washington, whence he was taken in a carriage to Willard's Hotel, where Senator Seward stood ready to receive him.

"The detective traveled with Mr. Lincoln under the name of E. J. Allen, which name was registered with the President-elect's on the book at Willard's Hotel. Being a well-known individual, he was speedily recognized, and suspicion naturally arose that he had been instrumental in exposing the plot which caused Mr. Lincoln's hurried journey. It was deemed prudent that he should leave Washington two days after his arrival, although he had intended to remain and witness the ceremonies of inauguration.

"The friends of Mr. Lincoln do not question the loyalty and hospitality of the people of Maryland, but they were aware that a few disaffected citizens who sympathized warmly with the secessionists, were determined to frustrate, at all hazards, the inauguration of the President-elect, even at the cost of his life.

"The characters and pursuits of the conspirators were various. Some of them were impelled by a fanatical zeal which they termed patriotism, and they justified their acts by the example of Brutus, in ridding his country of a tyrant. One of them was accustomed to recite passages put into the mouth of the character of Brutus, in Shakspeare's play of "Julius Cæsar." Others were stimulated by the offer of pecuniary reward. These, it was observed, staid away from their usual places of work for several weeks prior to the intended assault. Although their circumstances had previously rendered them dependent on their daily labor for support, they were during this time abundantly supplied with money, which they squandered in bar-rooms and disreputable places.

"After the discovery of the plot, a strict watch was kept by the agents of detection over the movements of the conspirators, and efficient measures were adopted to guard against any attack which they might meditate upon the President-elect until he was installed in office.

"Mr. Lincoln's family left Harrisburg for Baltimore, on their way to Washington, in the special train intended for him. And as, before starting, a message announcing Mr. Lincoln's departure and arrival at Washington had been telegraphed to Baltimore over the wires, which had been repaired that morning, the passage through Baltimore was safely effected.

"The remark of Mr. Lincoln, during the ceremony of raising the flag on Independence Hall on Friday morning, that he would assert his principles on his inauguration, although he were to be assassinated on the spot, had evident reference to the communication made to him by the detective on the night preceding.

"The names of the conspirators will not at present be divulged; but they are in possession of responsible parties, including the President.

"The number originally ascertained to be banded together for the assassination of Mr. Lincoln was twenty; but the number of those who were fully apprised of the details of the plot became daily smaller as the time for executing it drew near.

"Some of the women employed by the detective went to serve as waiters, seamstresses, etc., in the families of the conspirators, and a record was regularly kept of what was said and done to further their enterprise. A record was also kept by the detective of their deliberations in secret conclave, but, for sufficient reasons, it is withheld for the present from publication. The detective and his agents regularly contributed money to pay the expenses of the conspiracy."

In the mean time, while the triumphal progress of Mr. Lincoln was brought to so inglorious a close by his forced flight to the capital, and the country was rejoicing at his escape from his enemies, the Senate was busily at work striving, by excited debate and discordant motions, to compose the country. The "Crittenden Compromise" continued to be the main subject of discussion, which promised to be indefinitely protracted by the perplexing amendments of the secessionists on the one hand, and the Republicans on the other. The "Peace Conference," too, was in constant session, and after a long labor finally adjourned *sine die*, after having brought forth a proposition of compromise which was destined to prove, like the rest, but an abortive attempt to conciliate discordant factions. The more important points of this plan were embraced in these two sections of the thirteenth article:

Feb. 27.

"*Sec.* 1. In all the present territory of the United States north of the parallel of 36 degrees 30 minutes of north latitude, involuntary servitude, except as punishment of crime, is prohibited. In all the present territory south of that line the status of persons held to service or labor, as it now exists, shall not be changed. Nor shall any law be passed by Congress or the territorial legislature to hinder or prevent the taking of such persons from any of the States of the Union to said territory, nor to impair the rights arising from said relation. But the same shall be subject to judicial cognizance in the Federal courts, according to the course of the common law. When any territory, north or south of said line, with such boundary as Congress may prescribe, shall contain a population equal to that required for a member of Congress, it shall, if its form of government be republican, be admitted into the Union on an equal footing with the original States, with or without involuntary servitude, as the constitution of such State may provide.

"*Sec.* 2. Territory shall not be acquired by the United States, unless by treaty; nor, except for naval and commercial stations and dépôts, unless such treaty shall be ratified by four-fifths of all the members of the Senate."

The other articles prohibited Congress from abolishing slavery in the District of Columbia without the consent of Maryland and of the owners, and without making due compensation; from abolishing slavery in the United States dock-yards; and from taxing slaves higher than land. One article prohibited the slave-trade forever; and another aimed at a more thorough execution of the Fugitive Slave law.

These propositions of the peace conference seemed to meet with no more favor than the other attempts to harmonize the discordant opinions of the Senate. The people of the North, however, were still hopeful, though they despaired of the efficacy of congressional action. It was to the future President that the universal attention was directed. Various speculations were indulged in, in regard to his policy; but while some believed that it would be conciliatory or conservative, as they termed it, and others, that it would while I do not choose now to specify particular acts of Congress as proper to be enforced, I do suggest that it will be much safer for all, both in official and private stations, to conform to and abide by all those acts which stand unrepealed, than to violate any of them, trusting to find impunity in having them held to be unconstitutional.

"It is seventy-two years since the first inauguration of a President under our national Constitution. During that period fifteen different and very distinguished citizens have in succession administered the executive branch of the Government. They have conducted it through many perils, and generally with great success. Yet, with all this scope for precedent, I now enter upon the same task, for the brief constitutional term of four years, under great and peculiar difficulties.

"A disruption of the Federal Union, heretofore only menaced, is now formidably attempted. I hold that in the contemplation of universal law and of the Constitution, the union of these States is perpetual. Perpetuity is implied, if not expressed, in the fundamental law of all national governments. It is safe to assert that no government proper ever had a provision in its organic law for its own termination. Continue to execute all the express provisions of our national Constitution, and the Union will endure forever, it being impossible to destroy it except by some action not provided for in the instrument itself.

"Again: if the United States be not a government proper, but an association of States in the nature of a contract merely, can it, as a contract, be peaceably unmade by less than all the parties who made it? One party to a contract may violate it—break it, so to speak; but does it not require all to lawfully rescind it? Descending from these general principles, we find the proposition that in legal contemplation the Union is perpetual, confirmed by the history of the Union itself.

"The Union is much older than the Constitution. It was formed, in fact, by the Articles of Association in 1774. It was matured and continued in the Declaration of Independence in 1776. It was further matured, and the faith of all the then thirteen States expressly plighted and engaged that it should be perpetual, by the Articles of Confederation, in 1778; and, finally, in 1787, one of the declared objects for ordaining and establishing the Constitution was to form a more perfect Union. But if the destruction of the Union by one or by a part only of the States be lawfully possible, the Union is less than before, the Constitution having lost the vital element of perpetuity.

"It follows from these views that no State, upon its own mere motion, can lawfully get out of the Union; that resolves and ordinances to that effect are legally void; and that acts of violence within any State or States against the authority of the United States, are insurrectionary or revolutionary, according to circumstances.

"I therefore consider that in view of the Constitution and the laws, the Union is unbroken, and, to the extent of my ability, I shall take care, as the Constitution itself expressly enjoins upon me, that the laws of the Union shall be faithfully executed in all the States. Doing this, which I deem to be only a simple duty on my part, I shall perfectly perform it, so far as is practicable, unless my rightful masters, the American people, shall withhold the requisition, or in some authoritative manner direct the contrary.

"I trust this will not be regarded as a menace, but only as the declared purpose of the Union that it will constitutionally defend and maintain itself.

"In doing this there need be no bloodshed nor violence, and there shall be none, unless it is forced upon the national authority.

"The power confided to me *will be used to hold, occupy, and possess the property and places belonging to the Government,* and collect the duties and imposts; but beyond what may be necessary for these objects, there will be no invasion, no using of force against or among the people anywhere.

"Where hostility to the United States shall be so great and so universal as to prevent competent resident citizens from holding the Federal offices, there will be no attempt to force obnoxious strangers among the people that object. While the strict legal right may exist of the Government to enforce the exercise of these offices, the attempt to do so would be so irritating, and so nearly impracticable withal, that I deem it better to forego for the time the uses of such offices.

"The mails, unless repelled, will continue to be furnished in all parts of the Union.

"So far as possible, the people everywhere shall have that sense of perfect security which is most favorable to calm thought and reflection.

"The course here indicated will be followed, unless current events and experience shall show a modification or change to be proper; and in every case and exigency my best discretion will be exercised according to the circumstances actually existing, and with a view and hope of a peaceful solution of the national troubles, and the restoration of fraternal sympathies and affections.

"That there are persons, in one section or another, who seek to destroy the Union at all events, and are glad of any pretext to do it, I will neither affirm nor deny. But if there be such, I need address no word to them.

"To those, however, who really love the Union, may I not speak, before entering upon so grave a matter as the destruction of our national fabric, with all its benefits, its memories, and its hopes? Would it not be well to ascertain why we do it? Will you hazard so desperate a step while any portion of the ills you fly from have no real existence? Will you—while the certain ills you fly to are greater than all the real ones you fly from—will you risk the commission of so fearful a mistake? All profess to be content in the Union if all constitutional rights can be maintained. Is it true, then, that any right, plainly written in the Constitution, has

been denied? I think not. Happily the human mind is so constituted, that no party can reach to the audacity of doing this.

"Think, if you can, of a single instance in which a plainly written provision of the Constitution has ever been denied. If, by the mere force of numbers, a majority should deprive a minority of any clearly written constitutional right, it might, in a moral point of view, justify revolution; it certainly would if such right were a vital one. But such is not our case.

"All the vital rights of minorities and of individuals are so plainly assured to them by affirmations and negations, guarantees and prohibitions in the Constitution, that controversies never arise concerning them. But no organic law can ever be framed with a provision specifically applicable to every question which may occur in practical administration. No foresight can anticipate, nor any document of reasonable length contain, express provisions for all possible questions. Shall fugitives from labor be surrendered by national or by State authorities? The Constitution does not expressly say. Must Congress protect slavery in the Territories? The Constitution does not expressly say. From questions of this class spring all our constitutional controversies, and we divide upon them into majorities and minorities.

"If the minority will not acquiesce, the majority must, or the Government must cease. There is no alternative for continuing the Government but acquiescence on the one side or the other. If a minority in such a case will secede rather than acquiesce, they make a precedent which in turn will ruin and divide them, for a minority of their own will secede from them whenever a majority refuses to be controlled by such a minority. For instance, why not any portion of a new confederacy, a year or two hence, arbitrarily secede again, precisely as portions of the present Union now claim to secede from it? All who cherish disunion sentiments are now being educated to the exact temper of doing this. Is there such perfect identity of interests among the States to compose a new Union as to produce harmony only, and prevent renewed secession? Plainly the central idea of secession is the essence of anarchy.

"A majority held in restraint by constitutional check and limitation, and always changing easily with deliberate changes of popular opinions and sentiments, is the only true sovereign of a free people. Whoever rejects it, does, of necessity, fly to anarchy or to despotism. Unanimity is impossible; the rule of a majority, as a permanent arrangement, is wholly inadmissible. So that, rejecting the majority principle, anarchy or despotism in some form is all that is left.

"I do not forget the position assumed by some, that constitutional questions are to be decided by the Supreme Court, nor do I deny that such decisions must be binding in any case upon the parties to a suit as to the object of that suit, while they are also entitled to very high respect and consideration in all parallel

IMPOSSIBILITY OF SEPARATION.

cases by all other departments of the Government; and while it is obviously possible that such decision may be erroneous in any given case, still the evil effect following it, being limited to that particular case, with the chance that it may be overruled and never become a precedent for other cases, can better be borne than could the evils of a different practice.

"At the same time the candid citizen must confess that if the policy of the Government upon the vital questions affecting the whole people is to be irrevocably fixed by the decisions of the Supreme Court, the instant they are made, as in ordinary litigation between parties in personal actions, the people will have ceased to be their own masters, unless having to that extent practically resigned their government into the hands of that eminent tribunal.

"Nor is there in this view any assault upon the court or the judges. It is a duty from which they may not shrink, to decide cases properly brought before them; and it is no fault of theirs if others seek to turn their decisions to political purposes. One section of our country believes slavery is right and ought to be extended, while the other believes it is wrong and ought not to be extended; and this is the only substantial dispute; and the fugitive slave clause of the Constitution, and the law for the suppression of the foreign slave-trade, are each as well enforced, perhaps, as any law can ever be in a community where the moral sense of the people imperfectly supports the law itself. The great body of the people abide by the dry legal obligation in both cases, and a few break over in each. This, I think, cannot be perfectly cured, and it would be worse in both cases after the separation of the sections than before. The foreign slave trade, now imperfectly suppressed, would be ultimately revived, without restriction, in one section; while fugitive slaves, now only partially surrendered, would not be surrendered at all by the other.

"Physically speaking, we cannot separate—we cannot remove our respective sections from each other, nor build an impassable wall between them. A husband and wife may be divorced, and go out of the presence and beyond the reach of each other, but the different parts of our country cannot do this. They cannot but remain face to face; and intercourse, either amicable or hostile, must continue between them. Is it possible, then, to make that intercourse more advantageous or more satisfactory after separation than before? Can aliens make treaties easier than friends can make laws? Can treaties be more faithfully enforced between aliens than laws can among friends? Suppose you go to war, you cannot fight always; and when, after much loss on both sides and no gain on either, you cease fighting, the identical questions as to terms of intercourse are again upon you.

"This country, with its institutions, belongs to the people who inhabit it. Whenever they shall grow weary of the existing government, they can exercise their constitutional right of amending, or their revolutionary right to dismember or overthrow it. I cannot be ignorant of the fact that many worthy and patriotic citizens are desirous of having the national Constitution amended. While I make no recommendation of amendment, I fully recognize the full authority of the people over the whole subject, to be exercised in either of the modes prescribed in the instrument itself; and I should, under existing circumstances, favor, rather than oppose, a fair opportunity being afforded the people to act upon it.

"I will venture to add, that to me the convention mode seems preferable, in that it allows amendments to originate with the people themselves, instead of only permitting them to take or reject propositions originated by others not especially chosen for the purpose, and which might not be precisely such as they would wish either to accept or refuse. I understand that a proposed amendment to the Constitution (which amendment, however, I have not seen) has passed Congress, to the effect that the Federal Government shall never interfere with the domestic institutions of States, including that of persons held to service. To avoid misconstruction of what I have said, I depart from my purpose not to speak of particular amendments, so far as to say that, holding such a provision to now be implied constitutional law, I have no objection to its being made express and irrevocable.

"The chief magistrate derives all his authority from the people, and they have conferred none upon him to fix the terms for the separation of the States. The people themselves, also, can do this if they choose, but the Executive, as such, has nothing to do with it. His duty is to administer the present Government as it came to his hands, and to transmit it unimpaired by him to his successor. Why should there not be a patient confidence in the ultimate justice of the people? Is there any better or equal hope in the world? In our present differences, is either party without faith of being in the right? If the Almighty Ruler of nations, with his eternal truth and justice, be on your side of the North, or on yours of the South, that truth and that justice will surely prevail by the judgment of this great tribunal, the American people. By the frame of the Government under which we live, this same people have wisely given their public servants but little power for mischief, and have with equal wisdom provided for the return of that little to their own hands at very short intervals. While the people retain their virtue and vigilance, no administration, by any extreme wickedness or folly, can very seriously injure the Government in the short space of four years.

"My countrymen, one and all, think calmly and well upon this whole subject. Nothing valuable can be lost by taking time.

"If there be an object to hurry any of you, in hot haste, to a step which you would never take deliberately, that object will be frustrated by taking time;

but no good object can be frustrated by it.

"Such of you as are now dissatisfied still have the old Constitution unimpaired, and on the sensitive point, the laws of your own framing under it; while the new administration will have no immediate power, if it would, to change either.

"If it were admitted that you who are dissatisfied hold the right side in the dispute, there is still no single reason for precipitate action. Intelligence, patriotism, Christianity, and a firm reliance on Him who has never yet forsaken this favored land, are still competent to adjust, in the best way, all our present difficulties.

"In your hands, my dissatisfied fellow-countrymen, and not in mine, is the momentous issue of civil war. The Government will not assail you.

"You can have no conflict without being yourselves the aggressors. You have no oath registered in heaven to destroy the Government, while I shall have the most solemn one to "preserve, protect, and defend" it.

"I am loth to close. We are not enemies, but friends. We must not be enemies. Though passion may have strained, it must not break our bonds of affection.

"The mystic cords of memory, stretching from every battle-field and patriot grave to every living heart and hearth-stone all over this broad land, will yet swell the chorus of the Union, when again touched, as surely they will be, by the better angels of our nature."

CHAPTER X.

The opinion of the Secessionists on the Message.—The opinion of the Unionists.—Unanimous satisfaction at the exit of Buchanan.—The fate of Buchanan.—A Nation's Reprovals.—Difficulty of forming a Judgment.—What were the Motives of his conduct.—A fatal Administration.—Life of Buchanan.—Birth.—Origin.—Early Education.—Political Career.—Member of the Legislature.—Minister to Russia.—United States Senator.—Adherent of General Jackson.—Opposed to Nullification. Political friend of Van Buren.—Supporter of his Policy.—Rallies to the support of Tyler.—In favor of the Recognition of Texas.—An advocate of the War with Mexico.—Secretary of State under Polk.—Retirement to Private Life.—Opposed to the Wilmot Proviso.—Advocates Compromises.—Ambassador to Great Britain.—The famous Ostend Conference.—Its Manifesto.—Return to the United States.—Candidate for President—Elected President.—Public Confidence.—His conduct in regard to Kansas.—Charged with Partisanship.—Secession of Six States from the Union.—Historic Importance of Buchanan.—Could Buchanan have checked the Rebellion?—Why he did not.—Last act of his Administration.—Opinion of Free Traders of his signing the Morrill Tariff.—The two Patriots in his Cabinet.—Lincoln's Cabinet.—Its party character.—William H. Seward.—His Life.—Education.—Political Career.—Character and Personal Appearance.—Salmon Portland Chase.—His Birth. Education.—Professional success.—Opinions on Slavery. Political Career.—Character. Simon Cameron. His Origin.—Influence in Pennsylvania.—His Character.—Gideon Welles: his Career and Character.—Montgomery Blair: his Career and Character.—Edward Bates: his Career and Character.—Caleb B. Smith: his Career and Character.

WHILE the secessionists pronounced the message of President Lincoln warlike, and affected great indignation, and even in Baltimore some of the daily journals declared it "sectional and mischievous," the unionists accepted the document as firm, but conservative. Those in North Carolina who were still clear of the heresy of secession, welcomed it as a hopeful indication of the peace policy of the administration; and while in Missouri the exponent of one party declared that it "met the highest expectations of the country, both in point of statesmanship and patriotism," that of another expressed its disappointment at not having "a more conservative and conciliatory expression of sentiments."

Whatever may have been the difference of opinion in regard to Lincoln, there was a unanimous feeling of satisfaction, among all who continued loyal to the Union, that Buchanan was no longer President. It was said of him at this time that "whatever may be his hope of justification by posterity, he must resign himself for the present to the reproach of an afflicted people. With his administration will always be associated those complicated ills of factious and corrupt government, vacillating and contemned authority, to which are owing the present civil strife and the arrested progress of the country. It would be difficult in the heat of war and under the pressure of national suffering to assume that equanimity of temper or reach that elevated height necessary to a broad and dispassionate judgment of the degree of responsibility to be attached to the head of an administration which has proved so fatal to the country.

"Whether his conduct is to be attributed to habitual partisanship, evil counsel, corrupt motive, or senile weakness, cannot be easily determined. To the direful results of his administration, however, President Buchanan can triumphantly oppose a previous career of prosperous statesmanship and a private life of unquestioned purity."

James Buchanan, the fifteenth President of the United States, was born at Stony Batter, in Franklin County, Pennsylvania, on the 22d of April, 1791. His father was an Irishman who emigrated to America in 1783. His mother, however, Elizabeth Spear, was the daughter of a Pennsylvania farmer. In spite of the poverty of his parents, their son was sent to Dickinson College, where he graduated with the honors of his class. In 1812 he began to practice law at Lancaster, and with such success, that he retired, at the age of forty, with a fair competence. At twenty-three years of age he was elected a member of the Legislature. In 1820 he first entered Congress, and continued to serve until 1831, when he resigned, and was appointed minister to Russia by President Jackson, to whom he was a faithful adherent. In 1833 he returned, and was elected United States senator from Pennsylvania, and continued a firm supporter of Jackson's policy. He stood firmly by the President in his successful conflicts with the United States Bank and the nullification of South Carolina. During the agitation in 1835 of the question of the abolition of slavery in the District of Columbia, he advocated the reception by Congress of petitions in its favor, but strove to resist their effect by the introduction of an act declaring that Congress had no power to legislate upon the subject. Buchanan gave to President Van Buren the same uncompromising political support that he had given to his predecessor.

On the change of policy effected by President Tyler, after the death of Harrison, Buchanan rallied to the support of the administration; he advocated the recognition of the independence of Texas, as he subsequently did its admission into the Union and the consequent war with Mexico. Under President Polk he became secretary of state, and at the expiration of the Presidential term retired to private life. He, however, used his great political influence in opposition to the Wilmot proviso, and in favor of an extension to the Pacific Ocean of the Missouri Compromise line of latitude 36 degrees 30 minutes north. On the accession of Pierce to the Presidency, Buchanan was appointed ambassador to Great Britain. It was while thus serving that he joined with the United States minister to Paris, and Pierre Soulé, the minister to Madrid, in forming the notable Ostend Conference, the object of which was to induce Spain to sell Cuba.

A memorandum of the proceedings of the conference was published, and has been dignified with the title of a protocol. This set forth the importance of Cuba, commercially and defensively, to the United States; the advantage to Spain in consenting to receive compensation for a possession the prolonged tenure of which was so uncertain, and the necessity—in case the island should fall under the control, like St. Domingo, of its African population—of the interference of the United States to secure the Southern slave States from so dangerous a neighborhood of free negroes.

Mr. Buchanan returned to the United States in the spring of 1856, and in the following June was unanimously nominated, by the Democratic Convention at Cincinnati, candidate for President. In November he was elected by the electoral vote of nineteen States. Upon his accession to office there was a general willingness to concede to him a disposition to repress sectional differences and to administer the Government with a national spirit. His administration, however, served only to reinvigorate factious dispute, and the Republican party attacked him with great animosity for his partisan efforts to secure the admission of Kansas as a slave State.

The most momentous event, however, during Buchanan's administration, was the secession of six States from the Union. This will always give him an historic importance, and serve to make his character and conduct subjects of the deepest interest to the investigator of the causes of the civil war initiated during his Presidency.

"That Buchanan could have checked the fatal movement [the rebellion], no one can affirm; but that it was his duty to make the effort, few will deny. That he did not do so, is attributed by some to corrupt connivance with the conspirators who shared his counsels; by some, to the timidity of enfeebled age; and by others, to the conviction that neither right nor expediency would justify an attempt to repress the rising rebellion. His irreproachable personal character, his previous career of reputable statesmanship, and his honored position as President, forbid the imputation of treasonable design or corrupt motive. It is more reasonable to attribute his conduct to the influence of unworthy but unsuspected counsellors acting upon an infirm judgment and unsteady moral courage."*

The last act of President Buchanan's administration was the signing of the Morrill tariff. This sanction of high protective custom dues was contrary to his professed opinion that duties should be levied only for revenue. The advocates of free trade, both in the United States and Europe, condemn this act as one of the most unworthy of his administration, while the protectionists doubtless commend it as the best.

Within a few weeks of the close of his term of office, Buchanan had called to his aid in the cabinet two statesmen whose energetic action, inspired by the truest patriotism, had served to redeem, to some degree, an administration which had proved so fatal to the country. These men were Joseph H. Holt, of Kentucky, and John A. Dix, of New York, the former the secretary of war, and the latter secretary of the treasury. It was hoped that Lincoln would have waived so far his party predilections as to have retained these statesmen, who had won the confidence of the nation by their loyal firmness in sustaining the dignity and power of the Federal authority against the menace of disaffection and the attack of treason.

The new President, however, in accordance with traditional practice, chose his cabinet from that party to which he was indebted for his own elevation. Wm. H. Seward, of New York, was appointed secretary of state; Salmon P. Chase, of Ohio, secretary of the treasury; Simon Cameron, of Pennsylvania, secretary of war; Gideon Welles, of Connecticut, secretary of the navy; Montgomery Blair, of Maryland, postmaster-general; Edward Bates, of Missouri, attorney-general; and Caleb B. Smith, of Indiana, secretary of the interior.

Some of these were known to the country as prominent statesmen; others, possessed only of local fame, were comparatively obscure, but all had been active promoters of the "Republican" cause. The most distinguished was the secretary of state.

William H. Seward was born in the village of Florida, Orange County, in the State of New York, on the 16th day of May, 1801. After a good elementary schooling he was sent to Union College, at Schenectady, where he received his academic degree with the honors of his class. In 1820 he became a student at law in the office of John Anthon, Esq., an eminent counsellor of the city of New York, but completed his studies under the guidance of Ogden Hoffman, then district attorney. In 1822 he was admitted to the bar at Goshen, in Orange County, but soon after removed to Auburn, where he formed a partnership with Judge Miller, whose daughter he

---

* Manuscript work, by the author.

subsequently married. His success as a lawyer was rapid and well assured, and he soon ranked among the most honored members of the profession.

His first political step was as a warm partisan of the anti-masonic cause, but in 1828 he appeared as a youthful leader in the canvass for the re-election of John Quincy Adams to the Presidency. Elected senator of his State in 1830, he soon became prominent as an advocate of measures of reform.

After four years' service in the Senate of New York, he was nominated the Whig candidate for Governor, but was defeated by his veteran Democratic opponent, William L. Marcy. Again a candidate at the succeeding election, he triumphed over his old competitor, and was elected Governor by the large majority of ten thousand. In 1840 he was a third time a candidate and once more successful, being chosen as a representative of the party which had triumphantly carried the election of President Harrison, of whom he had proved himself in the canvass an energetic supporter. In 1848 he advocated the nomination of General Zachary Taylor, and strove zealously in behalf of his election. The successful Whig party of the New York State Legislature soon after elected Seward senator of the United States. On the death of Taylor and the accession of Fillmore, Seward was suddenly deprived of that leadership upon which he had not unnaturally presumed. His supposed extreme opinions on the subject of slavery were undoubtedly averse to his being accepted, by Fillmore, as an exponent of the policy of his conciliatory administration. Seward opposed emphatically the compromise measures of 1850.

"I feel assured," said he, in his speech on the question, "that slavery must give way, and will give way to the salutary instructions of economy and to the ripening influences of humanity; that emancipation is inevitable and is near; that it may be hastened or hindered; that all measures which fortify slavery or extend it tend to the consummation of violence; all that check its extension and abate its strength tend to its peaceful extirpation. But I will adopt none but lawful, constitutional, and peaceful means to secure even that end; and none such can I or will I forego."

In 1852, Seward was an advocate for the election of General Scott as President, though he did not concur with the concessions made to the slave interests of the South in the manifesto of his party. In the Senate he at the same time continued his persistent opposition to the extension of slavery, and emphatically denounced the Kansas-Nebraska bill.

After the dissolution of the Whig party, and the formation of the new Republican combination, of which he was one of the prominent founders and leaders, he was a candidate for nomination as President. He, however, was forced to yield to the superior "availability" of Colonel Fremont, for whose election, notwithstanding, he canvassed vigorously.

During the summer of 1859, Mr. Seward visited Europe, and extended his tour to Syria and Egypt. His reception was everywhere studiously courteous in deference to his recognized position as a distinguished and leading statesman in his own country.

In 1860, Seward was forced again to yield his presumed claims to a comparatively obscure man. At the Republican Convention which met at Chicago, Seward was the leading candidate for nomination as President, but after several obstinate ballots gave way to Mr. Lincoln, who was chosen, and whose subsequent triumphant election to office was greatly due to the zealous efforts of his late rival.

Notwithstanding his previous persistent resistance to the encroachments of, and his apparent readiness for, the "irrepressible conflict" with slavery, Seward is considered to have been the most conciliatory of Lincoln's cabinet. Though some doubted his possession of that moral grandeur which was so necessary to the important office he had to administer, none questioned the secretary's mental capacity to master the ordinary technical difficulties of his office. A man of refined culture and tact, his speeches and writings possess a dignity of tone and a completeness of literary finish which are rarely to be discovered in the effusions of our extemporized speakers and writers.

Judging him from the rapid flashes of speech, struck off in the course of a heated political canvass, there are some, especially in Europe, who affect to think that Seward is more eager to captivate the undiscerning many than to convince the judicious few.

In appearance, Mr. Seward, with his slight figure of medium size, his heavy features, and his worn expression, is not imposing. His eyes, however, brighten with excitement, and his face not seldom assumes an attractive vivacity.

The secretary of the treasury, Salmon Portland Chase, was born at Cornish, in New Hampshire, on the 13th of January, 1808. Two years after the death of his father, and at the age of twelve, he was placed under the charge of his uncle, Bishop Chase, of Ohio, with whom he removed from Worthington to Cincinnati, and there entered the college of which the bishop had been appointed president. Here, however, he remained but a year, when he returned to his mother's home in Keene, New Hampshire. In 1824 he was admitted a student of Dartmouth College, where he received his degree after two years' study. After graduating, he opened a school at Washington, and numbered among his pupils the sons of Henry Clay, William Wirt, and Samuel L. Southard. In the mean time, he studied law under the direction of Wirt, and in 1829, quitting his school, he was admitted to the bar at Washington.

In 1830, Mr. Chase removed to Cincinnati, where he strove to establish himself as a lawyer. While waiting for practice, he published an edition of the Statutes of Ohio, with original notes, and a prefatory sketch of the history of the State. This work served to bring him into notice, and add to his legal business. He now became a thriving practitioner, and was appointed solicitor of two of the banks.

Being employed in 1837 in behalf of a negro woman who was claimed to be a fugitive slave, Mr. Chase argued that Congress had not the right to impose upon State magistrates any duty or confer any power in such cases.

Again, soon after, while defending James E. Birny, who had been arrested for harboring a negro slave, he held that slavery is local, and dependent for its legality upon State law, and that therefore a slave who made his escape into Ohio became free, and might be harbored with impunity.

In 1846, Mr. Chase, together with William H. Seward, was defendant's counsel in the Van Zandt case, before the Supreme Court of the United States. In an elaborate argument, he contended that, by the ordinance of 1787, no fugitive from service could be reclaimed from Ohio unless there had been an escape from one of the original States; that it was the clear understanding of the framers of the Constitution, and of the people who adopted it, that slavery was to be left exclusively to the disposal of the several States, without sanction or support from the National Government; and that the clause in the Constitution relating to persons held to service was one of compact, and conferred no power of legislation on Congress.

Other cases ensued in which Mr. Chase defended the same positions, and thus became identified with those who resisted all national recognition of slavery.

Devoted to his professional pursuits, Mr. Chase avoided for a long time all positive alliances with political parties, but had voted sometimes with the Democrats, and at other times and more frequently with the Whigs. In 1841, however, he became one of the originators of the "Liberty" party of Ohio, and was the author of their address to the people. In 1843 he was a member of the convention of this party which met at Buffalo. While one of a committee nominated by said convention, he opposed the resolution, "to regard and treat the third clause of the Constitution, whenever applied to the case of a fugitive slave, as utterly null and void, and consequently as forming no part of the Constitution of the United States, whenever we are called upon or sworn to support it." This resolution was accordingly rejected by the committee, and not reported, although it was afterward renewed by its original mover, and adopted by the convention. When twitted in the United States Senate by Senator Butler, of South Carolina, for the mental reservation seemingly sanctioned by this resolution, Chase responded: "I have only to say, I never proposed the resolution; I never would propose or vote for such a resolution. I hold no doctrine of mental reservation. Every man, in my judgment, should speak just as he thinks, keeping nothing back, here or elsewhere."*

* The New American Cyclopedia. New York: D. Appleton & Co.

In 1845, a convention, at the suggestion of Mr. Chase, met in Cincinnati, of "all who, believing that whatever is worth preserving in republicanism can be maintained only by uncompromising war against the usurpations of the slave power, and are therefore resolved to use all constitutional and honorable means to effect the extinction of slavery within their respective States, and its reduction to its constitutional limits in the United States." The gathering was large, consisting of two thousand delegates and four thousand interested visitors. The address—the main burden of which was opposition to the extension of slavery— was written by Mr. Chase, and was widely circulated. When the second convention met, in 1847, Mr. Chase opposed the making of Federal nominations, believing that the general agitation throughout the country in regard to the Wilmot proviso would extend the basis of the movement against slavery extension, and afford a less restricted foundation for a party.

In 1848, however, distrusting the Whig and Democratic parties, Mr. Chase again called a convention in favor of free territory. It was largely attended, but it merged itself in the National Convention, which met at Buffalo in August of the same year, and nominated Martin Van Buren for President. The Democratic party of Ohio having now adopted the free-soil views of Mr. Chase, he accepted their nomination for the United States Senate, and in 1849 was elected. He continued to act with the Democrats of his State until 1852, when, upon the nomination of Pierce, they accepted the platform of the Baltimore Convention, approving of the compromise acts of 1850, and denouncing the further agitation of the question of slavery extension. Having abandoned his old allies, he gave in his adherence to the Independent Democratic Convention, assembled at Pittsburg in 1852, which adopted a manifesto mainly prepared by Mr. Chase.

When the Nebraska bill agitated the country, and induced the formation of the Republican party, Mr. Chase, finding its principles in consonance with his long established views, eagerly joined it, and became one of its leaders.

In 1855, Mr. Chase was nominated as Governor of Ohio, and being elected, was inaugurated in January of the succeeding year. He gave proof, in his new office, of a moderation and discretion which many were disposed to question, in consequence of his supposed extreme opinions on slavery. At the close of his first term he was disposed to retire, but was so urgently pressed to accept a re-nomination, that he was prevailed upon and re-elected Governor.

After the expiration of his second term he was again elected senator of the United States, but resigned his seat to accept the office of secretary of the treasury in the cabinet of Mr. Lincoln, of which he was considered not only one of the ablest, but firmest members.

Simon Cameron, a man of humble origin, successively a printer's apprentice, printer, journalist, a local politician, a United States senator, and afterward secretary of war, was born in Pennsylvania. He has been for a long time one of the most influential men in that State, and the success of the Republican party there was greatly indebted to his efforts. Wielding a large capital actively employed in railroads, mining operations, and other active enterprises in Pennsylvania, he was enabled to exercise a wide influence, which was owing not less to his financial than to his political ability. His executive talents, thoroughly exercised by his extensive business relations, were calculated to make him an effective officer in the busy department of which he was the chief.

Gideon Welles was originally a printer, and subsequently editor of the Hartford *Times*, in the skilful conduct of which he has acquired all his political fame. His reputation had, however, hardly extended beyond the limits of his native State of Connecticut, when he was called to a position in Lincoln's cabinet, at the earnest solicitation, it is believed, of his brother-in-law, Vice-President Hamlin. As the editor of the Hartford *Times*, he was considered one of the most forcible exponents of the Democratic policy. Warmly espousing the doctrine of non-extension of slavery, he soon identified himself with the Republican party, of which he was an ardent supporter. He has frequently represented his State in its own Legislature and Senate, but never in the Federal councils. It may be doubted whether, with his reflective habits as a political thinker and writer, and his restricted experience of the business of state, he had the scope of view and energy of action necessary to the chief of the naval department during a great war.

Montgomery Blair, a son of the vigorous Democratic journalist, Francis Preston Blair, the founder and editor of the Washington *Globe*, was born in Kentucky. Like his father, he is a valiant defender of the Republican cause, and is supposed to have been one of the most emphatic of the cabinet to urge the full exercise of the Federal authority in checking treason, as he was among the most resolute in favor of vigorously waging war against rebellion. His energy of will and sanguineness of temperament rendered him a spirited coadjutor of the executive in the stir of conflict; but in the quiet of peace, his fitness for office, and especially that practical one which he holds, might be more questionable.

Edward Bates, the attorney-general, was born in Goochland County, in Virginia, in 1791. Having been carefully educated by a relative of high culture, he emigrated with a brother to Missouri, where he began to practice law. He soon acquired eminence as a jurist. Although he served in the Legislature of Missouri, and represented that State in Congress, his life had been mostly devoted to the pursuits of his profession. In 1847, however, he was a member of the convention which met at Chicago for the advancement of internal improvements, where he commanded attention by a brilliant speech and his impressive character. Efforts were made to induce him to give to the State the benefit of his acknowledged powers, but he refused office in Missouri and resisted the offer of a place in the cabinet of President Fillmore. His early political bias was shown by his support of Henry Clay and John Quincy Adams, with whose views of public policy he generally accorded. At a later period he opposed the repeal of the Missouri Compromise act, and the admission of Kansas as a State under the Lecompton Constitution, and otherwise exhibited his sympathy with the free-soil party. An accomplished jurist, he filled satisfactorily the office of attorney-general, and a man of dignified personal character, he gave increased weight to Mr. Lincoln's cabinet.

Caleb B. Smith, of Indiana, the secretary of the interior, had brought with him from his own State a high reputation for ability and integrity, and he was also considered an effective member of the Government.

CHAPTER XI.

Action of the Confederate States.—Organization of an Army.—Its composition.—Officers.—Resignations in the United States Army.—Buchanan's sanction of Treason.—A change of conduct under Secretary Holt.—The Treason of Twiggs.—His Expulsion from the Army.—His Surrender of Government Property to the Authorities of Texas.—Its Character and Value.—Military Career of General Twiggs.—His motives for Seceding.—Treachery.—Encouragement of the Confederate States.—Defiant Tone and Attitude.—Commissioners to Washington.—Their Letter to the Secretary of State.—A polite Rebuff.—The Commissioners linger in Washington.—Career of Independent Government of the Confederate States.—A new Flag.—A Political Blunder.—The Influence of a bit of Bunting.—The motive for adopting a new Flag.—The Confederate Flag described.—Active preparation for War.—General Beauregard sent to Charleston.—Call upon the Confederate States for Militia.—Progress of the Works in the Harbor of Charleston.—Soldiers and Negroes.—Floating Battery.—Ardent Gentlemen as Privates.—Statesmen in the Ranks.—Rumored Evacuation of Fort Sumter.—Courteous relations between Major Anderson and Citizens of Charleston.—Messengers from the Federal Government.—Vigilance of the Batteries.—An Eastern Schooner driven out of the Harbor.—Perplexities of Lincoln and his Cabinet.—A Decision at Last.—A Demonstration to be made in favor of Major Anderson.—Preparations.—A Special Messenger sent to the Authorities of Charleston.—The purport of his Message.—The effect upon the Southern Confederacy.—Excitement at Charleston.—Appeal to Arms.—Departure of the Confederate Commissioners from Washington.—Their parting Defiance.—Correspondence between Beauregard and the Secretary of War of the Confederates.—Correspondence between Beauregard and Anderson.

1861. The "Confederate States" having organized a government, proceeded to prepare to sustain it by the formation of a military establishment. This was composed of one corps of engineers, one corps of artillery, six regiments of infantry, one regiment of cavalry, and of a staff department, making in all ten thousand seven hundred and forty-five officers and men. Those who had abandoned the United States for the Confederate service gave the new army a large supply of highly educated and experienced officers. This number was daily increasing.

The government of Buchanan had at first sanctioned the disloyalty of many of our officers by accepting their resignations, though their purpose in giving up their commissions could not be doubted. Inspired, however, by the patriotic counsels of his new secretary of war, Holt, Buchanan had become less considerate toward treason. When, Feb. 18. therefore, General Twiggs, a veteran officer of the army of the United States, surrendered the posts which he commanded to the commissioners of Texas, the President, with unusual impatience and severity, did not wait for a resignation, but expelled the disloyal officer from the army.

By this action of General Twiggs, the State authorities of Texas, which was on the eve of its secession from the United States, became possessed of an immense supply of arms and military stores of all kinds, to be added, as none could doubt, to the resources of the Confederate States. In San Antonio, the arsenal contained forty-four cannon and howitzers of different calibres, one thousand nine hundred muskets, rifles, and Sharp's carbines, four hundred Colt's pistols, two magazines full of ammunition, containing one million five hundred thousand ball-cartridges, and five thousand five hundred pounds of powder.

At Forts Brown, Duncan, and Clark there were large numbers of cannon and magazines filled with ammunition. At the various posts there were several thousand mules and horses, many hundred wagons, abundant clothing and stores, and a great variety of valuable implements. The whole of the Federal property thus traitorously disposed of amounted in value to nearly a million and a half of dollars.

General Daniel E. Twiggs was one of the oldest officers in the United States army, which he had entered in 1812, at the age of twenty-two years. He had served under our flag with a fair reputation. He was a captain during the war with Great Britain; served as a major under Generals Gaines and Jackson in the Florida campaign; took part in the Black Hawk war; was in command of the arsenal at Augusta during the nullification excitement, and in the Mexican war received the rank of brevet brigadier-general for his services at Palo Alto and Resaca de la Palma; commanded a division at Monterey, and shared with General Scott in the triumphs of our army from Vera Cruz to the capital of Mexico. He was in command of the department of Texas, with his headquarters at San Antonio, when he brought to so dishonorable a close his long career of reputable military service. He ranked next to Lieutenant-General Scott, and would have been entitled, if he had remained loyal to his country, to have succeeded him in the chief command of our army. A Georgian by birth, and a large owner of land and slaves, his adherence to his own State was not unexpected, but few thought that one of the most honored officers of the Federal army would have been guilty of adding treachery to treason.

Encouraged by the addition of Texas to the confederacy, and an unconcealed sympathy on the part of some of the other slave States, which gave promise of further acquisitions, the new government at Montgomery, Alabama, assumed a more independent tone and defiant attitude. Commissioners Messrs. John Forsyth and Martin J. Crawford were appointed to negotiate with the United States. On their arrival at Washington they presented themselves as the representatives of an independent power. "Seven States," they said, "of the late Federal Union having, in the exercise of the inherent right of every free people to change or reform their political institutions, and through conventions of their people, withdrawn from the United States and reassumed the attributes of sovereign power delegated to it, have formed a government of their own. The Confederate States constitute an independent nation *de facto* and *de jure*, and possess a government perfect in all its parts and endowed with all the means of self-support." With this assumption of independence, the commissioners proceeded to declare their purpose. "With a view to a speedy adjustment of all questions growing out of this political separation upon such terms of amity and good-will as the respective interests, geographical contiguity, and future welfare of the two nations may render necessary," they said that they were instructed to "make to the Government of the United States overtures for the opening of negotiations, assuring the Government of the United States that the President, Congress, and people of the Confederate States earnestly desire a peaceful solution of those great questions; that it is neither their interest nor their wish to make any demand which is not founded in strictest justice, nor to do any act to injure their late confederates."

March 12.

The secretary of state, Mr. Seward, had already declined the request of the commissioners for an unofficial interview with him, and now refused their demand for an official presentation to the President. It is curious, however, at this period, to note with what studied courtesy a high state officer is constrained to address, and with what diplomatic consideration to argue the question of rebellion with its confessed representatives. "The secretary of state," wrote Mr. Seward, "frankly confesses that he understands the events which have recently occurred, and the condition of political affairs which actually exists in the part of the Union to which his attention has thus been directed, very differently from the aspect in which they are presented by Messrs. Forsyth and Crawford. He sees in them, not a rightful and accomplished revolution and an independent nation, with an established government, but rather a perversion of a temporary and partisan excitement to the inconsiderate purposes of an unjustifiable and unconstitutional aggression upon the rights and the authority vested in the Federal Government, and hitherto benignly exercised, as from their very nature they always so must be exercised, for the maintenance of the Union, the preservation of liberty, and the society, peace, welfare, happiness, and aggrandizement of the

American people. The secretary of state, therefore, avows to Messrs. Forsyth and Crawford that he looks patiently but confidently for the cure of evils which have resulted from proceedings so unnecessary, so unwise, so unusual, and so unnatural, not to irregular negotiations, having in view new and untried relations with agencies unknown to and acting in derogation of the Constitution and laws, but to regular and considerate action of the people in those States, in co-operation with their brethren in the other States, through the Congress of the United States, and such extraordinary conventions, if there shall be need thereof, as the Federal Constitution contemplates and authorizes to be assembled.

"It is, however, the purpose of the secretary of state, on this occasion, not to invite, or engage in, any discussion of these subjects, but simply to set forth his reasons for declining to comply with the request of Messrs. Forsyth and Crawford.

"On the 4th of March inst., the newly elected President of the United States, in view of all the facts bearing on the present question, assumed the executive administration of the Government, first delivering, in accordance with an early, honored custom, an inaugural address to the people of the United States. The secretary of state respectfully submits a copy of this address to Messrs. Forsyth and Crawford.

"A simple reference to it will be sufficient to satisfy those gentlemen that the secretary of state, guided by the principles therein announced, is prevented altogether from admitting or assuming that the States referred to by them have, in law or in fact, withdrawn from the Federal Union, or that they could do so in the manner described by Messrs. Forsyth and Crawford, or in any other manner than with the consent and concert of the people of the United States, to be given through a national convention, to be assembled in conformity with the provisions of the Constitution of the United States. Of course the secretary of state cannot act upon the assumption, or in any way admit that the so-called Confederate States constitute a foreign power, with whom diplomatic relations ought to be established."

The commissioners, in spite of this rebuff, or encouraged probably by the courteous style in which it was conveyed, still lingered at the capital awaiting the issue of events.

The Confederate States continued to pursue with vigor their career of independent government. Having set up a constitution and an administration of their own, they now adopted a flag. In this respect they acted with less than their usual discretion. Presuming, as they still did undoubtedly, however justly or unjustly, upon a strong sympathy in the border and middle States with their movement, it was not politic in them to disregard the revered symbol of the united glory of the country. They thought, doubtless, that it was merely a matter of a bit of bunting with more or less colored stripes and stars, but they forgot how such trifles are endeared to the heart of a nation when they have once become associated with its history.

The committee to whom was referred the subject of the Confederate flag, seemed not altogether unconscious of the influence of the stars and stripes upon the national sentiment, and in their report thus ingeniously strove to weaken it: "Whatever attachment may be felt, from association, for the 'stars and stripes' (an attachment which, your committee may be permitted to say, they do not all share), it is manifest that in inaugurating a new government, we cannot," said the committee, "retain the flag of the government from which we have withdrawn, with any propriety, or without encountering very obvious practical difficulties. There is no propriety in retaining the ensign of a government which, in the opinion of the States composing this confederacy, had become so oppressive and injurious to their interests as to require their separation from it. It is idle to talk of 'keeping' the flag of the United States when we have voluntarily seceded from them. It is superfluous to dwell upon the practical difficulties which would flow from the fact of two distinct and probably hostile governments, both employing the same or very similar flags. It would be a political and military solecism. It would produce endless confusion and mistakes. It would lead to perpetual disputes. As to 'the glories of the old flag,' we must bear in mind that the battles of the Revolution, about which our fondest and proudest memories cluster, were not fought beneath its folds; and although in more recent times—in the war of 1812 and in the war with Mexico —the South did win her fair share of glory, and shed her full measure of blood under its guidance and in its defence, we think the impartial page of history will preserve and commemorate the fact more imperishably than a mere piece of striped bunting. When the colonies achieved their independence of the 'mother country' (which up to the last they fondly called her), they did not desire to retain the British flag or anything at all similar to it. Yet under that flag they had been planted, and nurtured, and fostered. Under that flag they had fought in their infancy for their very existence against more than one determined foe. Under it they had repelled and driven back the relentless savage, and carried it farther and farther into the decreasing wilderness as the standard of civilization and religion. Under it the youthful Washington won his spurs, in the memorable and unfortunate expedition of Braddock, and Americans helped to plant it on the Heights of Abraham, where the immortal Wolfe fell, covered with glory, in the arms of victory. But our forefathers, when they separated themselves from Great Britain—a separation not on account of their hatred of the English constitution or of English institutions, but in consequence of the tyrannical and unconstitutional rule of Lord North's administration, and because their destiny beckoned them on to independent expansion and achievement—cast no lingering, regretful looks behind. They were proud of their race and lineage, proud of their heritage in the glories, and genius, and language of Old England, but they were influenced by the spirit of the motto of the great Hampden, '*Vestigia nulla retrorsum.*' They were determined to build up a new power among the nations of the world. They therefore did not attempt 'to keep the old flag.' We think it good to imitate them in this comparatively little matter, as well as to emulate them in greater and more important ones."

The committee (of which it may not be impertinent to say that a South Carolinian was chairman, who, from the traditional disloyalty of his native State, was less likely to sympathize with the reverence of the nation for the symbol of its union) therefore recommended a new flag for the Confederate States, which was adopted, "consisting of a red field with a white space extending horizontally through the centre and equal in width to one third the width of the flag, the red spaces above and below being of the same width as the white; the union blue extends down through the white space, but terminates at the lower red one. In the blue are stars corresponding in number to the States of the confederacy. The three colors, red, white, and blue, are the true republican colors. In heraldry they are emblematic of the three great virtues, of valor, purity, and truth," reported the committee, while they added, "the colors constrast admirably, and are lasting."

The Confederate Government began to prepare actively for war. The governors of the several States having been ordered by President Davis, issued proclamations, calling upon the militia to muster. General Beauregard, formerly a major in the United States engineer corps, was dispatched to take command of the works and forces at Charleston. In the mean time the South Carolinians had made great progress in strengthening and manning their defences. The people of Charleston were becoming each day more excited as they contemplated the flag of the Union persistingly raised in their harbor. "The fate of the Southern Confederacy hangs," they said, "by the ensign halliards of Fort Sumter." The Governor of South Carolina made repeated calls for troops, until seven thousand men had been gathered, and immense gangs of negro slaves brought from the plantations in the interior and set to work upon the fortifications. The floating batteries, which had been in course of construction for months, were now finished, mounted, manned, and anchored in the harbor. Ardent gentlemen of South Carolina volunteered as privates, among whom there was a large number of the members of the convention, which had lately adjourned. Senators and members of Congress from Carolina and other seceded States had offered their services, and while some, like Senator Wigfall, of Texas, received appointments on General

March 3.

Beauregard's staff, others were constrained to take their places in the ranks.

In the mean time, however, there were still rumors that a conflict would be avoided by the evacuation of Fort Sumter by Major Anderson, with whom there continued to be preserved a courteous relation by the citizens of Charleston, who not unfrequently had him to dinner, or supplied him with delicacies from their tables and madeira from their cellars. Messengers traveling by land passed between the Federal Government and the fort, with the concurrence of the authorities of South Carolina. The batteries in the harbor, however, abated not a jot of their vigilance, and were determined not to let a vessel enter under the flag of the United States. A trading schooner of Boston, laden with ice, having drifted in a dense fog over the Charleston bar, close to the fort on Morris Island, was fired at. The captain hoisted the stars and stripes, but this only increased the intensity of the attack; and he was glad finally to make his escape to sea, after having received several thirty-two-pounder shots in his rigging.

At Washington, the President and cabinet were supposed to be a long time perplexed how to act in regard to Fort Sumter, but finally came to a decision. It was determined to make a demonstration at least of sustaining Major Anderson. A fleet was hurriedly fitted out for the purpose, and prepared to sail, the destination of which it was not doubted was Charleston, although not publicly announced. At the same time a special messenger was sent by the United States Government to the authorities at Charleston, bearing the message that a peaceable effort would be made to supply the garrison of Fort Sumter with provisions, and that if this were not permitted, force would be tried.

The Southern Confederacy accepted this as a menace of hostility. The people of Charleston were roused to a high degree of excitement. "We have patiently submitted," they said, "to the insolent military domination of a handful of men in our bay for over three months after the declaration of our independence of the United States. The object of that self-humiliation has been to avoid the effusion of blood while such preparation was making as to render it causeless and useless.

"It seems we have been unable, by discretion, forbearance, and preparation, to effect the desired object, and that now the issue of battle is to be forced upon us. The gage is thrown down, and we accept the challenge. We will meet the invader, and the God of battles must decide the issue between the hostile hirelings of Abolition hate and Northern tyranny, and the people of South Carolina defending their freedom and their homes. We hope such a blow will be struck in behalf of the South, that Sumter and Charleston harbor will be remembered at the North as long as they exist as a people."[a]

The commissioners of the Confederate States now left Washing- April 9.

* Charleston Mercury.

ton, after sending a defiant missive to the secretary of state: "It is proper, however, to advise you," they said in their dispatch to Mr. Seward, "that it were well to dismiss the hopes you seem to entertain, that, by any of the modes indicated, the people of the Confederate States will ever be brought to submit to the authority of the Government of the United States. You are dealing with delusions, too, when you seek to separate our people from our Government, and to characterize the deliberate, sovereign act of the people as a 'perversion of a temporary and partisan excitement.' If you cherish these dreams, you will be awakened from them, and find them as unreal and unsubstantial as others in which you have recently indulged. The undersigned would omit the performance of an obvious duty were they to fail to make known to the Government of the United States, that the people of the Confederate States have declared their independence with a full knowledge of all the responsibilities of that act, and with as firm a determination to maintain it by all the means with which nature has endowed them, as that which sustained their fathers when they threw off the authority of the British crown."

As soon as it was suspected at Charleston that there was an intention on the part of the Federal authorities to make an effort to sustain Major Anderson and his garrison, all communication between the people and the fort was at once stopped. Upon the arrival of the Federal messenger, Beauregard announced the fact by telegraph to the secretary of war of the Confederate States, Leroy P. Walker.

"An authorized messenger from President Lincoln just informed Governor Pickens and myself," wrote Beauregard, "that provisions will be sent to Fort Sumter peaceably, or otherwise by force." [April 8.]

To this the secretary answered:

"If you have no doubt of the authorized character of the agent who communicated to you the intention of the Washington Government, to supply Fort Sumter by force, you will at once demand its evacuation, and if this is refused, proceed in such a manner as you may determine to reduce it. Answer." [April 10.]

Beauregard briefly responded: "The demand will be made at twelve o'clock." [April 10.]

The secretary, in his impatience, again replied: "Unless there are especial reasons connected with your own condition, it is considered proper that you should make the demand at an early hour."

"The reasons are special for twelve o'clock," was the positive response of the General. [April 10.]

Accordingly Beauregard made his demand on the 11th of April, which led to the following correspondence:

"HEADQUARTERS, PROVISIONAL ARMY, C.S.A.
CHARLESTON, S. C., *April* 11, 1861—2 P.M.

"SIR: The Government of the Confederate States has hitherto forborne from any hostile demonstration against Fort Sumter, in the hope that the Government of the United States, with a view to the amicable adjustment of all questions between the two governments, and to avert the calamities of war, would voluntarily evacuate it. There was reason at one time to believe that such would be the course pursued by the Government of the United States; and under that impression, my Government has refrained from making any demand for the surrender of the fort.

"But the Confederate States can no longer delay assuming actual possession of a fortification commanding the entrance of one of their harbors, and necessary to its defence and security.

"I am ordered by the Government of the Confederate States to demand the evacuation of Fort Sumter. My aids, Colonel Chesnut and Captain Lee, are authoized to make such demand of you. All proper facilities will be afforded for the removal of yourself and command, together with company arms and property, and all private property, to any post in the United States which you may elect. The flag which you have upheld so long and with so much fortitude, under the most trying circumstances, may be saluted by you on taking it down.

"Colonel Chesnut and Captain Lee will, for a reasonable time, await your answer.

"I am, sir, very respectfully,
"Your obedient servant,
"G. T. BEAUREGARD,
"Brigadier-General Commanding."

"Major ROBERT ANDERSON, commanding at Fort Sumter, Charleston Harbor, S. C."

"HEADQUARTERS, FORT SUMTER, S. C.,
April 11, 1861.

"GENERAL: I have the honor to acknowledge the receipt of your communication demanding the evacuation of this fort; and to say in reply thereto, that it is a demand with which I regret that my sense of honor and of my obligations to my Government prevent my compliance.

"Thanking you for the fair, manly, and courteous terms proposed, and for the high compliment paid me,

"I am, General, very respectfully,
"Your obedient servant,
"ROBERT ANDERSON,
"Major U. S. Army, Commanding.

"To Brigadier-General G. T. BEAUREGARD, commanding Provisional Army, C. S. A."

"MONTGOMERY, April 11.
"Gen. BEAUREGARD, Charleston:

"We do not desire needlessly to bombard Fort Sumter, if Major Anderson will state the time at which, as indicated by him, he will evacuate, and agree that, in the mean time, he will not use his guns against us, unless ours should be employed against Fort Sumter. You are thus to avoid the effusion of blood. If this or its equivalent be refused, reduce the fort as your judgment decides to be most practicable.

"L. P. WALKER, Sec. of War."

"HEADQUARTERS, PROVISIONAL ARMY, C.S.A.
CHARLESTON, April 11, 1861—11 P.M.

"MAJOR: In consequence of the verbal observations made by you to my aids, Messrs. Chesnut and Lee, in relation to the conditon of your supplies, and that you would in a few days be starved out if our guns did not batter you to pieces—or words to that effect—and desiring no useless effusion of blood, I communicated both the verbal observation and your written answer to my communication to my Government.

"If you will state the time at which you will evacuate Fort Sumter, and agree that in the mean time you will not use your guns against us, unless ours shall be employed against Fort Sumter, we will abstain from opening fire upon you. Colonel Chesnut and Captain Lee are authorized by me to enter into such an agreement with you. You are therefore requested to communicate to them an open answer.

"I remain, Major, very respectfully,
    "Your obedient servant,
        "G. T. BEAUREGARD,
        "Brigadier-General Commanding.

"Major ROBERT ANDERSON, commanding at Fort Sumter, Charleston Harbor, S. C."

    "HEADQUARTERS, FORT SUMTER, S. C.,
       2.30 A.M., *April* 12, 1861.

"GENERAL: I have the honor to acknowledge the receipt of your second communication of the 11th inst., by Colonel Chesnut, and to state, in reply, that cordially uniting with you in the desire to avoid the useless effusion of blood, I will, if provided with the proper and necessary means of transportation, evacuate Fort Sumter by noon on the 15th instant, should I not receive, prior to that time, controlling instructions from my Government, or additional supplies; and that I will not, in the mean time, open my fire upon your forces, unless compelled to do so by some hostile act against this fort or the flag of my Government, by the forces under your command, or by some portion of them, or by the perpetration of some act showing a hostile intention on your part against this fort, or the flag it bears.

"I have the honor to be, General,
    "Your obedient servant,
        "ROBERT ANDERSON,
        "Major U. S. A. Commanding.

"To Brigadier-General G. T. BEAUREGARD, commanding Provisional Army, C. S. A."

    "FORT SUMTER, S. C.,
      April 12, 1861, 3.20 A.M.

"SIR: By authority of Brigadier-General Beauregard, commanding the Provisional forces of the Confederate States, we have the honor to notify you that he will open the fire of his batteries on Fort Sumter in one hour from this time.

"We have the honor to be, very respectfully,
    "Your obedient servants,
        "JAMES CHESNUT, Jr.,
            "Aid-de-Camp.
        "STEPHEN D. LEE,
"Captain S. C. Army and Aid-de-Camp.

"Major ROBERT ANDERSON, United States Army, commanding Fort Sumter."

CHAPTER XII.

Excitement in the North in regard to Fort Sumter.—Precarious position of Major Anderson and his Garrison.—Opinion of General Scott.—No effort to sustain Fort Sumter reported.—Effect of the Intelligence.—Government at last resolved to make an Attempt.—Change of Feeling at the North.—Preparations of the Federal Government.—A Fleet got Ready.—Its Composition and Force.—The proposed destination uncertain.—Arrival at the Rendezvous at Charleston.—Non-arrival of the Tug-boats.—Defeat of purpose.—Schemes concocted.—Failure.—Fort Sumter.—The Artificial Island.—Construction and Cost.—The Fortress.—Its Character.—Strength and number of Guns.—Its incompleteness.—Its Position and Distances.—Its meagre Garrison.—Activity of the Enemy.—Skilful Engineering of Beauregard.—Description of Fort Moultrie.—Its Strength and Armament.—The Iron Battery at Point Cummings.—The Floating Battery.—Its Construction and Efficiency.—The Batteries at Fort Johnson.—Their Strength and Construction.—The Force of the Enemy.—Defences of Charleston.—Skill of Beauregard.—Life of Beauregard.—Birth.—A Cadet at West Point.—Curious change of Name.—His Father.—Ducal descent of his Mother.—Graduation of Beauregard.—His Services in the War with Mexico.—Differs in opinion with his superior.—Beauregard's Judgment Triumphant.—Rewards of Gallantry.—Another illustration of superior Judgment and another Triumph.—Return to Louisiana.—Honor to the young Hero.—Government appointments.—Personal appearance and character.—Becomes a Secessionist.—Correspondence between Beauregard and Anderson.—Opening of the Fire upon Fort Sumter.—Extent of Fire surprising.—Tardy Response of Major Anderson.—Division of his Garrison.—Who fired the first Gun?—Enthusiasm of the Men.—Effect of the Fire.—The Enemy's Vigor.—The Parapet of Fort Sumter dreadfully damaged.—Danger to Life.—Havoc among the *Guns en barbette*.—The effect of the Enemy's Rifled Cannon.—On guard.—"Shot or Shell."—The Laborers at the Guns.—A Hit in the Centre.—The Barracks on Fire.—Danger of the Magazine.—Continued Conflagration.—The descent of the Flag.—Only a Salute.—A genuine Shot.—The Flag still flying.—"Knocked down temporarily."—Cessation of the Fire of Fort Sumter during the Night.—The Enemy still firing.—Attempt to rig new Halyards for the Flag.—Expecting Aid or an Assault.—Saturday Morning.—The Conflagration of the Barracks continuing.—Its Effect.—Terrific Scene.—Danger of an Explosion.—Powder thrown overboard.—Scarcity of Cartridges.—An Explosion.—The Crash.—Breaking of the Flagstaff.—Flag nailed to its Place.—Arrival of a Stranger through an Embrasure.—The agitated Wigfall.—His purpose.—Displays his white Handkerchief.—An uncomfortable Post.—An Interview with the Major.—"I am General Wigfall."—Departure of Wigfall.—An unauthorized Messenger.—Commissioners from Beauregard.—Interview with Major Anderson.—Hoisting of the White Flag.—Terms of Surrender agreed upon.—Departure of Major Anderson and his Garrison.—Firing of Salute to the United States Flag.—Accident.—Major Anderson sails for New York.

THE public mind at the North had been greatly excited in regard to Fort Sumter. The position of Major Anderson with his meagre garrison was known to be very precarious, besieged as he was by the powerful works in Charleston harbor, with an infuriated mob of seven thousand men to defend them, and cut off from all communication by land or sea. The highest military authority of the Union, Lieutenant-General Scott, was reported to have given it as his opinion that it was impracticable, without such a military and naval force as the Government at that time could not command, to reinforce Fort Sumter. Anderson's masterly movement, in quitting Fort Moultrie, and his resolute and protracted support of the flag of the United States, while surrounded by those who with intense hostility were resolutely bent upon dishonoring it, had won for him the sympathy of the whole country. When, therefore, it was authoritatively declared again and again that no effort could or would be made to sustain him, an anguish of despair wrung every

1861.

patriotic heart. A sudden change, however, came with the rumor that the Government had at last determined at all hazards to make the attempt, and the desponding nation was once more cheered with hope.

The Federal authorities were evidently preparing for some momentous movement. Orders had been issued to have the vessels of war at the various navy yards immediately detailed for service. A number of large merchant steamers and sailing vessels had been chartered. The garrisons of the various forts in the Northern harbors had been got ready to embark. The recruiting in the large cities for sailors and soldiers had been stimulated to an unusual degree. Finally, a fleet was got ready and sailed, and although the Government strove to keep its destination a secret, all suspected, as they hoped, that it was Charleston. The vessels sailed from the various ports where they happened to be, to meet at a certain rendezvous determined upon. The steam sloop of war Pawnee, Captain S. C. Rowan, of ten guns, and with two hundred men, sailed from Washington with sealed orders on the morning of Saturday, April April 6th. On the afternoon of 6th. the same day, the steam sloop of war Powhatan, of eleven guns, and with two hundred and seventy-five men, left the Brooklyn navy yard.

On the following Monday, the revenue April cutter Harriet Lane, after having 8. exchanged her revenue flag for that of the United States, sailed from the harbor of New York with an armament of five guns and a crew of ninety-six men.

Three of the largest and swiftest of the merchant steamers hitherto engaged in peaceful commerce had been chartered, and now laden with armed men and munitions of war joined the expedition. The Atlantic, with three hundred and fifty-eight troops, com- April posed of Companies A and M of 7. the Second Artillery, Companies C and H of the Second Infantry, and Company A of Sappers and Miners, from West Point, steamed out of the harbor of New York on the morning of Sunday, April 7th. Two days after, the Baltic followed, with a hundred and sixty April troops, Companies C and D, which 9. had been lately recruited and stationed at Governor's Island, in New York bay. On the same day the Illinois put to sea with three hundred troops, made April up of Companies B, E, F, G, and H, 9. of a detachment of Company D, and two companies of the Second Infantry gathered from the recruits at Governor's Island, Bedloe's Island, and Fort Hamilton.

Two steam-tugs—the Yankee, which sailed on Monday, the 8th of April, April and the Uncle Ben, which followed 8. on the day after—completed this hurriedly gathered but not unimposing naval force.

Thirty launches were also distributed among the larger steamers, to be used for the purpose of landing the troops through the surf under the cover of the fire of the armed vessels, or, being protected with sand-bags, and armed with swivel guns and riflemen, to aid in the attack of batteries.*

Of this force, though the whole was supposed by the people to be destined for Charleston, only the Powhatan, the Pawnee, the Harriet Lane, the Baltic, and the steam-tugs sailed for that port. The rest took their course for the Gulf of Mexico, to reinforce the garrisons of the Federal forts on the coasts of Alabama and Florida.

April 12. The Pawnee, the Harriet Lane, and the Baltic reached the rendezvous off Charleston on the 12th of April, but the Yankee and Uncle Ben had failed to arrive, having been detained by unfavorable weather. The orders of the fleet were, that unarmed boats should first be sent in with stores; but if they were fired upon, an effort was to be made to relieve the fort by force. Without the tug-boats, the proposed object of the expedition could not be effectually accomplished, as the only unarmed steamer, the Baltic, was of too great a draught of water to pass the bar of Charleston, and the steam-tugs were alone capable of approaching the fort through the shallow water. The naval commanders, however, after a council, determined to make an effort for the relief of Major Anderson, who was already under shot, for as soon as the first rockets had been sent up to signalize the concentration of the fleet, the enemy had opened fire. The plan agreed upon was to hoist out the small boats and launches, load them with men and stores, and to tow them as far as possible, and then, while covering them with the guns of the steamers, to send them in alone. This, however, failed in consequence of the Baltic having got aground during the night, while preparations were being made to disembark her stores and troops. Other schemes were devised, but before they could be put into execution, the time for action had past. Fort Sumter had fallen.

Fort Sumter had been considered one of the strongest works in the United States. The island upon which it is built was artificially constructed by placing upon the original sand and mud a large quantity of refuse granite, brought from Northern quarries, and pressing it deeply down until an unyielding foundation was laid. This alone cost the labor of ten years and an expense of five hundred thousand dollars, to which another half million was added before the completion of the whole fort. The walls of the fortification, composed of brick and compact concrete, are sixty feet in height and from eight to twelve feet in thickness. The fort is pentagonal, and is pierced for three tiers of guns, on all sides but the southern, where are the sally-ports and docks, which had been left unpro-

---

* The whole force may be thus recapitulated:

Vessels.	Guns.	Men.
Sloop of war Pawnee	10	200
Sloop of war Powhatan	11	275
Cutter Harriet Lane	5	96
Steam transport Atlantic	—	353
Steam transport Baltic	—	100
Steam transport Illinois	—	300
Steam-tug Yankee	Ordinary crew.	
Steam-tug Uncle Ben	Ordinary crew.	
Total number of vessels		8
Total number of guns (for marine service)		26
Total number of men and troops		1,384

tected, as it looks toward the land, and the work had been mainly intended as a defence against attack from the sea.

Although it was originally designed to have armed the fort with one hundred and forty cannon of various calibres, there were but seventy-five in position when the enemy opened fire. Of these, eleven were Paixhans, and a number, thirty-two pounders, four of which were *en barbette*, and uncovered, and being on pivots could be made to take a wide range. Fort Moultrie was within command of nine of the Paixhans, and the two others pointed toward Castle Pinckney, too far distant, however, to be within range. Most of the large columbiads in the fort were not yet mounted. The magazines were well supplied with ammunition, sufficient it was thought for a year, and artificial wells had been constructed capable of holding a supply of water for the same period.

The distance from Fort Sumter to Charleston is three miles and three eighths of a mile. Together with Fort Moultrie, which had been abandoned by Anderson, Sumter was surrounded by Cumming's Point and Fort Johnson, where strong works had been constructed and mounted, and a floating battery. From Fort Moultrie, Fort Sumter is distant one and one-eighth of a mile; from Cumming's Point three-fourths of a mile; from Fort Johnson one and one fourth of a mile; while the floating battery had been anchored about half a mile from the weak side of Sumter. The greatest range of the guns of Fort Sumter was estimated at three miles, which placed the city of Charleston beyond reach of its fire.

Six hundred men would have been required fully to garrison the fort and work the guns; but Major Anderson could only muster one hundred and nine,* of whom thirty were laborers, and fifteen composed the band.

The enemy had diligently improved every moment in strengthening the Federal forts they had taken possession of, and in adding new works, under the skilful direction of General Beauregard, once esteemed as among the ablest officers of engineers in the United States service.

Fort Moultrie, on Sullivan's Island, had been repaired, its dismantled guns unspiked and mounted again, and the lateral spaces between the cannon protected by sand-bags, to secure them against a flank fire. Though a weak work, in comparison with Fort Sumter, its walls, built of brick, capped with stone and filled in with earth, presented a solid enclosure of nearly sixteen feet in thickness. Its original armament

---

* The garrison was thus composed:

Officers.	Rank.	Regimental Corps.	Original Entry into Service.	Born in
R. Anderson	Major	1st Artillery	July 1, 1825	Ky.
S. W. Crawford	Ass't Surgeon	Medical Staff	March 10, 1851	Penn.
A. Doubleday	Captain	1st Artillery	July 1, 1842	N. Y.
T. Seymour	Captain	1st Artillery	July 1, 1846	Vt.
T. Talbot	1st Lieut.	1st Artillery	May 22, 1847	S. C.
Jeff. C. Davis	1st Lieut.	1st Artillery	June 17, 1848	Ind.
J. N. Hall	2d Lieut.	1st Artillery	July 1, 1849	N. Y.
J. G. Foster	Captain	Engineers	July 1, 1846	N. H.
G. W. Snyder	1st Lieut.	Engineers	July 1, 1856	N. Y.
R. K. Meade	2d Lieut.	Engineers	July 1, 1857	Va.
Officers				9
Band				15
Artillerists				55
Laborers				30
Total				109

was composed of eleven guns of heavy calibre and several powerful mortars.

On Cumming's Point the enemy had erected a battery made of thick logs of yellow pine. This was covered with a slanting roof of the same material, which had been rendered ball-proof by railroad iron dovetailed and riveted together. The port-holes were supplied with iron shutters, which opened as the guns were thrust out to fire, and fell as they recoiled after a shot, and thus shut in the artillerists within an iron-bound and impenetrable cover. This novel battery was mounted with three columbiads, which bore directly on the southern and weakest side of Fort Sumter.

The most curious, and not the least effective, perhaps, of the enemy's works, was the floating battery, which in the course of its construction had given rise to much speculation and not a little ridicule. This, too, was constructed of heavy pine logs and faced with a double layer of railroad iron. It was about a hundred feet in length and twenty-five in width. Its face presented an angle horizontally disposed, formed by its retreating roof and the front wall inclining backward as it descended to the water. It was mounted with four guns of the heaviest calibre, which were said to require sixty men to work them. A magazine for ammunition was built in the hold, below the water-line, and lined with sand-bags, laid seven feet thick, not only to protect it from shot, but to act as ballast necessary to counterpoise the heavy armament above. To the stern of this strange structure was attached a floating hospital, to provide for the ordinary emergencies of war.

At Fort Johnson—so called from its being the site of an old work no longer existing—on James' Island, two long batteries were erected of sand, and mounted with heavy cannon and mortars. Other temporary structures were raised, some of palmetto logs, and others of earth and sand, on Morris and Stono islands, Hadril's Point, and other parts of the harbor, which bore on its approaches, or upon Fort Sumter.

A large force, said to have amounted to over seven thousand men, had been mustered to the defence of Charleston. Four thousand of these were manning the works in the harbor, while the rest were held in reserve on Sullivan and Morris islands and in Charleston, to be ready to repel any attack by land.

The city itself was immediately defended by the fort at Castle Pinckney, and cannon on the Battery in front of Charleston. These, however, could only be of service in case the above works had failed to keep out any intruder. Castle Pinckney is situated at the southern extremity of Shute's Folly Island. Its armament consists of some thirty-two pounders, columbiads, and mortars, amounting in all to about twenty-five pieces. Its walls are six feet in thickness, and are pierced for one row of guns, while there is another *en barbette*. The work is small, and of little importance in an attack from the sea. All the old defences had been greatly improved, and new ones constructed, by the skilful engineering of General Beauregard, the officer who had been sent by the government of the Confederate States to take command at Charleston.

Peter Gustavus Toutant Beauregard had already, while in the service of the United States, won a distinguished reputation as an engineer. He was born on his father's plantation, near New Orleans. The family name is said to be Toutant, and that of the estate Beauregard, which, by a curious accident, was originally attached to the patronymic, and assumed by the present bearer, in this wise: The youth, when admitted a cadet at West Point, was presented as Toutant de Beauregard, signifying merely that he was a Toutant of the plantation of Beauregard, and thus entered upon the records of the institution. This, however, was supposed to be his surname, and he was so called. Not averse, probably, to the dignified sounding of the appellation, the youth did not care to correct the error, and subsequently assumed the name of Beauregard as his own.

His father was a wealthy creole, with extensive estates in Louisiana, and a descendant of a reputable French family. His mother's name was Reggio, for whom has been claimed a descent from the Italian ducal house of the Reggios of Italy. In 1834, young Beauregard entered the military academy at West Point, where he graduated in 1838, ranking the second of a class of forty-five cadets. On his graduation, he received the commission of a second lieutenant in the First Regiment of Artillery, but in a week after was transferred to the Corps of Engineers. In June, 1839, he was promoted a first lieutenant, and was serving in this grade when the war with Mexico broke out. He accompanied the army to Vera Cruz, and continued with it during its career of conquest to the capital of Mexico.

At the very first moment he gave indications of that surety of eye, precision of foresight, and carefulness of judgment which are his distinguishing qualities. Before Vera Cruz, he was sent out at the head of a party of sappers and miners to dig and prepare a trench, in accordance with the directions of his colonel. Upon examining the ground, however, he appeared to find serious obstacles to the proposed plan. To assure himself, he climbed a tree, and with the aid of his glass took a careful survey, which resulted in confirming the objections to his colonel's plan. He discovered that the trench, if made as proposed, would be enfiladed by the enemy's guns. It was a difficult position for a young subaltern thus to find himself at variance with the judgment of his superior. He, however, did not hesitate, but returned to his colonel without having turned a sod. The officer, surprised to see him so soon, asked if he had done the work already. Beauregard replied that he had not touched it, and gave his reasons. The colonel was still more startled by the presumption of the youthful subaltern who had ventured to dispute the judgment of his superior, instead of submissively obeying his orders. He accordingly, with the characteristic peremptoriness of the military commander, reminded him of duties of obedience, and at the same time impatiently declared that "the ground had been thoroughly examined, a perfect reconnoisance had been made, and that a mistake was impossible." Notwithstanding this, he was impressed by the judgment of Beauregard, and took another survey of the ground, when he found reason to concur with the view of his young lieutenant.

For his gallant conduct at Contreras and Cherubusco, Beauregard was brevetted captain, to date from 20th of August, 1847, and again for his services at Chapultepec, he was promoted to the brevet rank of major, to date from the 13th of September of the same year.

At the assault of the Belen gate of the city of Mexico, Beauregard was wounded, and throughout the whole campaign he was not only among the most brave, but ranked among the ablest and most useful of the officers. General Scott, in his dispatch from the capital of Mexico, into which he had just entered as conqueror, spoke of Beauregard as one of "our distinguished engineers," by the aid of whose efficient and daring reconnoissances, he was enabled to follow up the victory of El Molino del Rey with the triumphal capture of the city of Mexico. Again, in his official report, Scott alluded to Beauregard as one of the five lieutenants of engineers "who were the admiration of all" during the storming of the fortress of Chapultepec, the struggle at the gates, and the entrance into the capital.

Another illustration of the correctness of his judgment is given in the following incident, said to have occurred before the city of Mexico:

A night or two before the attack, a council of war was held. There were assembled all the officers, from the Lieutenant-General, including Major-General Worth and others, down to Beauregard, the youngest in the room. The council sat many hours. All the officers, but one, had spoken, and unanimously maintained a plan of operations at variance with that of Scott. The officer who had not tendered his opinion was Beauregard. At last General Pierce crossed over and said: "You have not expressed an opinion." "I have not been called on," said Beauregard. Pierce, soon resuming his seat, announced that Lieutenant Beauregard had not given his views. Being then called upon, he remarked, that if the plan which had received the consent of all but the commanding general was carried into effect, it would prove disastrous. It would be another Cherubusco affair. He then detailed the objections to it at length; and taking up the other, urged the reasons in its favor with equal earnestness. The council reversed their decision. The city of Mexico was entered according to the plan urged by the young lieutenant, and it would seem that his reasons influenced the decision. A few days afterward, General Scott, in the presence of a number of general officers, alluded to Lieutenant Beauregard's opinion at the council, and the consequences which had followed from it.

On his return to Louisiana, the young

STANDARD ILLUSTRATED BOOKS.

BENSON J. LOSSING'S "LIFE OF WASHINGTON"
"BATTLES OF AMERICA BY SEA AND LAND."
"THE WAR WITH THE SOUTH," by Robt. Tomes, M
Illustrated by F. O. C. DARLEY, and other Eminent Artists.

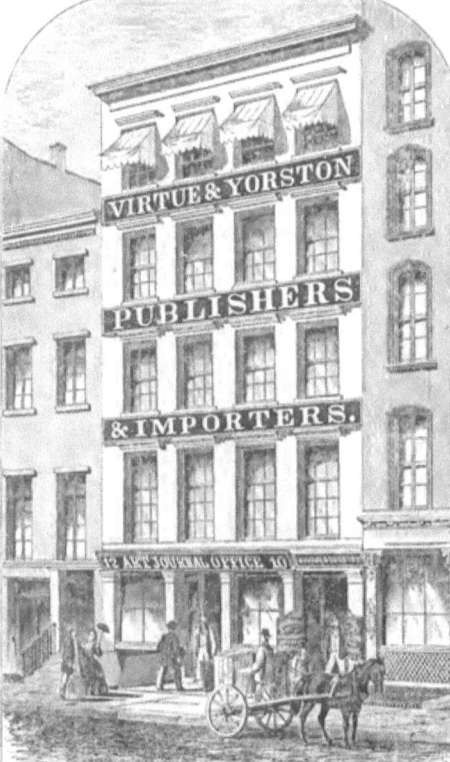

OFFICE OF
WEALE'S SERIES
OF
RUDIMENTARY,
SCIENTIFIC,
Educational
AND
CLASSICAL
WORKS

REISSUE
OF
Punch,
&c., &c.

ILLUSTRATED
WORKS
ON THE SCENERY
The United States
CANADA
ITALY
SWITZERLAND
THE
BOSPHORUS
The DANUBE
&c., &c.

THE
TURNER GALLERY
Vernon Gallery
WILKIE GALLERY
Sculpture Gallery
&c., &c.

12 DEY ST., and 544 BROADWAY
NEW YORK.

VIRTUE & YORSTON,

FIRE OPENED ON SUMTER.

hero was presented with a costly sword. The Government of the United States appointed him the chief engineer to superintend the construction of the Mint and Custom-house at New Orleans, and of the fortifications at the mouth of the Mississippi.

Beauregard at this time was forty-three years of age, and with his healthful manhood, his vigorous and concentrated frame, his promptitude of movement and power of endurance, had all the bodily qualifications for a hardy campaigner. His abilities and thorough culture as an engineer are unquestioned, and his admirers claim for him great capacity as a strategist and leader of armies.

Born in Louisiana, and bound to it by the strong ties of family and property, he had not unnaturally joined his destiny to the fate of his native State. He is, moreover, supposed to have been early involved in the Southern conspiracy, through the influence of his brother-in-law, John Slidell, the former senator of the United States from Louisiana, and one of the main instigators of the late rebellion.

"By authority of Brigadier-General Beauregard, commanding the provisional forces of the Confederate States, we have the honor to notify you that he will open the fire of his batteries on Fort Sumter in one hour from this time." This was the communication addressed by the aids-de-camp of Beauregard to Major Anderson at twenty minutes past three o'clock on the morning of Friday, the 12th of April. At twenty minutes past four o'clock, accordingly,

April 12.

the batteries surrounding Fort Sumter opened fire. Major Anderson waited until full daylight, as he did not care to waste any of his ammunition before replying. He, however, immediately ordered the sentinels away from the parapets, the posterns closed, the flag drawn up, and forbid his men to leave the bomb-proofs until summoned by the drum.

The extent of the enemy's fire greatly surprised the garrison, which, however, was now explained by the revelation, for the first time, of a battery of which there had been hitherto no suspicion. This was a battery on Sullivan's Island, masked by a cover of brush-wood and other materials. Skilfully constructed, heavily mounted, and artfully protected, its fire was very effective. It showed seventeen mortars, throwing ten-inch shells, and thirty-three heavy cannons, most of which were columbiads. The shots from these powerful guns struck against the walls of Fort Sumter with a "terrific crash," as the defenders declared, and several of the shells burst inside the fort.

Major Anderson, however, did not respond, and as late as half-past six o'clock had not fired a shot, the men at that hour being at breakfast, which they ate "leisurely and calmly." Immediately after, however, everything was got ready for work. The garrison was so few in number and so worn out by the harassing labors of a long siege, that it was found necessary to husband its strength. The whole was accordingly divided into three reliefs or parties, which were to work the batteries in turns each during four hours.

The first relief was under the command of Captain Doubleday, of the Artillery, and Lieutenant Snyder, of the Engineer Corps. Upon this party accordingly devolved the duty of opening the fire, and at seven o'clock in the morning the first gun was fired by Doubleday. The fire was directed against the batteries at Cumming's Point, sixteen hundred yards distant; the iron floating battery, anchored about two thousand yards away, and Fort Moultrie and the additional batteries on Sullivan's Island. The cannonade was kept up with great spirit for four hours; and such was the enthusiasm of the garrison, that it was impossible to prevent the reliefs off duty from taking part in the work. The fire told apparently with good effect upon the walls of Fort Moultrie, the embrasures of which were considerably damaged. The battery on Cumming's Point, however, seemed invulnerable, shot and shell glancing harmlessly off from its mail of iron.

The enemy's fire was constant and effective. Their shells burst in rapid succession against all parts of the fort, scattering the loosened brick and stone in every direction, breaking the windows and setting fire to whatever wood-work they touched. The gorge in the rear of the fort was already so pierced with balls that it looked like a sieve.

The enemy poured their heaviest fire on the parapet of the fort, and it became impossible to go there without the certainty of death. Their shot, aimed principally at the guns *en barbette*, soon made great havoc among them, disabling one ten-inch columbiad, one eight-inch columbiad, one forty-two pounder, and two eight-inch howitzers. At the same time, a large portion of the parapet, upon which these guns were placed, was carried away, and Major Anderson was obliged to forbid his men to expose themselves there any longer in manning the *barbette*, or uncovered, cannons. The garrison was thus limited to the use of the two lower tiers of guns, which were protected by casemates.

An English rifle cannon, which had been presented to Charleston by an enthusiastic friend of secession at Liverpool, was fired with great accuracy. Its balls frequently entered the embrasures of Fort Sumter, and on one occasion slightly wounded four men. More mischief would have been done, had not a man been kept constantly on the lookout to cry, whenever the enemy fired, "shot" or "shell," as it happened to be, so that our men could seek safety under cover. Our soldiers never faltered at their work, and even the laborers, though at the beginning reluctant to handle the guns, finally took hold and vied with the others in the dangerous service.

"We had to abandon one gun," wrote one of the officers, "on account of the close fire made upon it. Hearing the fire renewed, I went to the spot. I there found a party of workmen engaged in serving it. I saw one of them stooping over, with his hands on his knees, convulsed with joy, while the tears rolled down his powder-begrimed cheeks."

FIRST DAY OF THE SIEGE. 147

'What are you doing here with that gun?' I asked. 'Hit it right in the centre,' was the reply; the man meaning that his shot had taken effect in the centre of the floating battery."

The shot of the enemy was particularly destructive to the barracks where the officers had their quarters. Most of the brick work was demolished, and the interior, of wood, was in flames several times. As the day advanced, the fire was continued with more vigor by the enemy than ever, while Major Anderson soon found his ability to respond greatly diminished. His cartridges became exhausted about noon, and he was forced to set his men to work in the magazine, making them of blankets and shirts.

The frequent conflagration of the officers' barracks was now a source of increased annoyance and danger. Three times they had caught, and three times been put out. While extinguishing the flames, the men were obliged to go out upon the parapet, where, though directly exposed to the thickest of the shower of balls, they could not resist the temptation of discharging clandestinely the cannon which had been loaded and pointed on the day before, ready to fire.

The soldiers throughout exhibited great daring. On Friday, when some of our vessels outside having saluted the fort, Major Anderson ordered his flag to be lowered and raised in response, Sergeant Hart, catching a glance at it just as it was descending, and thinking it had been cut away by a shot, rushed out into the open parade in the thickest of the fire, in order to raise it. As it rose, a ball really did come which divided the halyards, but the rope caught by the wind twisted around the staff and held the flag in its place.

A veteran sergeant, of the name of Kearnan, who had served in the Mexican campaigns, was struck on the head by a portion of masonry shivered by a shot, and felled to the ground. On rising, he was asked if he were badly hurt. "No," said he, "I was only knocked down temporarily." The men were now obliged to keep so close to their work, that their meals were served to them while at their guns. The fire of the enemy became more brisk and accurate as the day was closing. Their iron battery at Cumming's Point, with its rifled cannon, was making great havoc, striking the embrasures at every shot. During Friday night some of our men strove to climb the flagstaff and rig new halyards in place of those which had been cut away, but could not succeed. The flag, however, still was flying. At night, Major Anderson ordered the port-holes to be closed, and ceased active operations, but the enemy continued their fire. A shot or shell struck against the walls, within which the little garrison was cooped up, about every fifteen minutes during the whole night. Major Anderson stationed until next morning a non-commissioned officer and four men at each salient embrasure, to be in readiness for any boats that might come, whether from friend or foe, as relief from the fleet outside or an assault from the enemy was not improbable.

On Saturday morning the officers' quarters again caught fire from the bursting of a ten-inch shell discharged by the enemy. It was now found impossible even to make the attempt to put out the conflagration, as red-hot shot were pouring constantly into the fort, and from the general ruin the exposure was so great. The main gates were already destroyed, so that five hundred men could have readily formed in the gorge and marched in without opposition. The walls, too, were so weakened, it was feared that each shot might pierce or prostrate them. The fire of the barracks spread rapidly, and was soon sweeping up all the wood-work of the fortress.

<small>April 13.</small>

Great fears were now entertained for the safety of the magazine. Every man who could be spared was put to work in removing the powder. Ninety-six barrels were rolled out through the flames, at the imminent hazard of life, and most of them flung into the sea. Two hundred were left behind, as it was found impossible to make any further effort, in consequence of the excessive heat, to remove them. The doors of the magazine were now closed and locked, but there was a constant dread of an explosion as the flames gathered about the whole structure.

The direction of the wind was such that it blew the smoke into the fort, and so filled it that the men could no longer see each other, and the air became so hot and stifling that it was almost impossible to breathe. They were finally forced to cover their faces with wet cloths, and often thus to lie prostrate on the ground. Some, however, managed to grope their way to the cannon. A gun was occasionally fired, to give the fleet and the enemy notice that the garrison still held out, but the cannoneers could not see to aim, and the cartridges had become so scarce that there was hardly a cannon wad left. As the sparks flew thick in every direction, it was impossible to attempt to make fresh cartridges. The men at the same time had become prostrate, as much in consequence of their constant working at the guns as for want of proper food. They had eaten their last biscuit thirty-six hours previous.

In the mean time the enemy increased their fire, which, added to the conflagration, the heat and the smoke, the crash and the ruin, produced a scene of indescribable awe and confusion. "The crashing of the shot, the bursting of the shells, the falling of walls, and the roar of the flames made," reported an eye-witness, "a pandemonium of the fort."

Now, to add to the horror of the scene, the shells and ammunition in the upper service-magazines exploded, scattering the tower and upper portions of the structure in every direction. "The crash of the beams, the roar of the flames, the rapid explosion of the shells, and the shower of fragments of the fort, with the blackness of the smoke, made the scene," wrote one who was present, "indescribably terrific and grand."

The conflagration continued to spread, and having reached the men's quarters, soon enveloped them in flames. The barrels of powder which had been taken out of the magazine and retained for use, were now in danger of explosion. All but four were accordingly thrown through the embrasures into the water, and those which were left were wrapped in many thicknesses of wetted woollen blankets. The garrison was now reduced to its last three cartridges, and those were already in the guns.

The flagstaff, which seemed to have been the constant aim of the enemy, had been struck already eight times, when it received a ninth shot, which broke it at about fifty feet from the truck and brought down the flag. "The flag is down—it has been shot away!" was the cry, when Lieutenant Hall rushed out and brought it in safely. It was found impossible, from the entanglement of the halyards, to hoist it again, and it was accordingly nailed to the broken staff and planted upon the ramparts in the midst of a shower of shot and shell from the enemy's busy batteries. Soon after the flag had fallen, and toward the close of day, a man presented himself at one of the embrasures of the fort in a boat, with a white handkerchief tied to a sword, asking to see Major Anderson. In his impatience, however, to get under cover, he climbed up, and was crawling through the embrasure when he was told that Major Anderson was at the main gate. He, however, did not heed what was said, but continued to make his way into the fort, where, on landing, he said, hurriedly:

"I wish to see Major Anderson; I am General Wigfall, and come from General Beauregard;" while he added, with great agitation, "let us stop this firing. You are on fire, and your flag is down. Let us quit."

Lieutenant Davis replied:

"No, sir—our flag is not down. Step out here and you will see it waving over the ramparts."

"Let us quit this," exclaimed the agitated Wigfall. "Here's a white flag [handing his handkerchief]—will anybody wave it out of the embrasure?"

"That is for you to do, if you choose," was the reply; to which Wigfall rejoined:

"If there's no one else to do it, I will;" and jumping into the embrasure through which he had just crawled, he waved his white handkerchief toward Fort Moultrie. The firing, however, of the enemy still continued, to the evident disappointment of Wigfall, who, after repeated requests on his part, was relieved from his hazardous position by a corporal who took his place and waved the flag. The enemy, however, still gave it no heed, and the corporal, finding the shot falling thick and fast about him, leaped down from the embrasure, exclaiming: "Damn it! they don't respect this flag—they are firing at it."

"They fired at me two or three times, and I stood it," answered Wigfall, "and I should think you might stand it once."

As he spoke, he turned toward the officers and added: "If you will show a white flag from your ramparts, they will cease firing." Lieutenant Davis replied: "If you request that a flag shall be shown there while you hold a conference with Major Anderson, and for that purpose alone, it may be done."

At this moment Major Anderson came up, and Wigfall said to him: "I am General Wigfall, and come from General Beauregard, who wishes to stop this."

The Major, rising on his toes, and coming down firmly on his heels, exclaimed, "Well, sir!"

"Major Anderson," resumed Wigfall, "you have defended your flag nobly, sir. You have done all that is possible for man to do, and General Beauregard wishes to stop the fight. On what terms, Major Anderson, will you evacuate this fort?"

"General Beauregard is already acquainted with my only terms," replied the Major.

"Do I understand that you will evacuate upon the terms proposed the other day?"

"Yes, sir, and on those conditions only."

"Then, sir," said Wigfall, "I understand that the fort is to be ours?"

"On those conditions only, I repeat," firmly declared Anderson.

"Very well—that's all I have to do. You military men will arrange everything else on your own terms," said the modest Wigfall, and retired.

He now left in his boat, his white handkerchief waving from the rampart where it had been placed at his request, but the United States flag nailed to the broken staff was no longer standing.

Shortly after his departure, Major Lee, the Honorable Porcher Miles, Senator Chesnut, and the Honorable Roger A. Pryor, the staff of General Beauregard, approached the fort with a white flag, and said they came from General Beauregard, who had observed that the flag had been down and raised again a few minutes afterward. The General had sent over, desiring to know if he could render any assistance, as he had observed that the fort was on fire. Major Anderson, in replying, requested them to thank General Beauregard for the offer, but it was too late, as he had just agreed with General Beauregard for an evacuation. The three, comprising the deputy, looked at each other blankly, and asked with whom? Major Anderson, observing that there was something wrong, remarked that General Wigfall, who had just left, had represented himself to be the Aid of General Beauregard, and that he had come over to make the proposition.

After some conversation among themselves, they said to Major Anderson that Wigfall had not seen General Beauregard for two days. Major Anderson replied that General Wigfall's offer and its acceptance had placed him in a peculiar position, and ordered the United States flag to be raised again. They then requested him to place in writing what General Wigfall had said to him, and they would lay it before General Beauregard, and at the same time urged him to leave the flag down in the meanwhile, with which request Anderson complied.

After the note reached General Beauregard, he sent his adjutant-general and other members of his staff, including the Honorable Roger A. Pryor and Governor Manning, proposing the same conditions which Major Anderson had offered to go out upon, with the exception only of not saluting his flag. Major Anderson said that he had already informed General Beauregard that he was going out. They asked him if he would not accept of the terms without the salute. Major Anderson told them, No; but that it should be an open point.

General Beauregard soon after sent word that Major Anderson's terms had been accepted, and that he would send the Isabel, or any other vessel at his command, to convey him and his men to any port in the United States he should choose.

The terms of evacuation were, that the garrison should take all their individual and company's property with them; that they should march out with their side and other arms, with all the honors in their own way and in their own time, and that they should salute their flag and bear it away with them. It was late on Saturday night when the terms demanded were finally agreed to by General Beauregard. Next morning, on Sunday, the Isabel came down from Charleston and anchored near Fort Sumter, and the little steamer Clinch lay alongside the wharf to transport Major Anderson and his men to the larger vessel.

April 14.

When the baggage had been all put on board the Clinch, the soldiers being inside of the fort under arms, a number were detailed to salute the United States flag. At the fiftieth gun, the flag was lowered and the men set up a loud cheer. In firing, however, this last discharge, a premature explosion took place which killed one man instantaneously, seriously wounded another, and injured less seriously two other men. These were the only casualties of moment during the whole conflict.

The troops, now being formed, were marched out, while the band played "Yankee Doodle" and "Hail to the Chief." Remaining on board the Isabel during the night, in consequence of the state of the tide, Major Anderson and his command were transferred next morning to the Baltic, and during the evening of the day after sailed for New York.

bed. Our limited time prevented us from visiting the battery to the north of Fort Moultrie. We learn, however, that though many of the buildings around it had been struck several times, and fences, trees, etc., cut away, the battery sustained no injury. Providentially, no hot shot was thrown from Sumter—probably from the fact that the garrison had no fuel.

The battery on Cumming's Point had escaped without damage, beyond six indentations in its iron armor, showing the accuracy of the firing of Fort Sumter, as well as proving the invulnerability of the novel structure.

The greatest interest had been naturally displayed by the people of Charleston at the approach of and during the bombardment of Fort Sumter. The enthusiasm was described as "intense, and the eagerness for the conflict, if it must come, as unbounded." For days before the attack, the citizens of Charleston were alert with expectation. Thus, at midnight, on one occasion, a discharge of the signal guns of Citadel Square being fired, the whole city was aroused. Hundreds of men left their beds, hurrying to and from their respective posts. In the absence of sufficient armories, the armed citizens gathered at the corners of the streets, in the public squares, and other convenient places, and all night long the roll of the drum, the steady tramp of the military, and the gallop of the cavalry resounding through the city betokened, apparently, the approach of the long-expected hostilities. The Home-Guard corps of old men, who from their age were exempt from the ordinary military duties, rode through the city, arousing the soldiers to arms, and doing other duty required by the emergency. Numbers of citizens were up all night. The Seventeenth Regiment, eight hundred strong, mustered in an hour, and left for the fortifications. The Rutledge Mounted Riflemen, the Charleston Dragoons, the German Hussars, and Phenix Sharpshooters, composed of the citizens of Charleston, followed, and in a short space several thousand homes were bereft for a time of all their male members capable of bearing arms.

The guards of the city were trebled. One hundred "beat men," armed with muskets and revolvers, who, at the first sound of the "bell of St. Michael's," would be reinforced by eight hundred more, patrolled the streets, in addition to the usual horse and foot police. A flotilla of small boats, with flaming torches, guarded the bar every night. A veteran Southern politician, well known as a secession agitator throughout the South, the Honorable Edmund Ruffin, of Virginia, a man over sixty years of age, shouldered his rifle and marched to the works as a private;[*] and even boys, hardly in their teens, volunteered to serve in the ranks, and bore part in the conflict.

From the firing of the first gun at Fort Sumter until its surrender, the intensity of interest continued unabated. Day and night the streets were thronged with people, "full of excitement and enthusiasm." The housetops, the Bat-

[*] He fired the first gun against Fort Sumter.

tery, the wharves, the shipping, and every place from which a view could be had of the scene, were thronged by an eager multitude. When at last, after thirty-three hours of impatient watching of the struggle, the Confederate flag rose upon the ruined walls of Fort Sumter, the bells of all the churches in the city of Charleston rang out "a merry peal," and the citizens became "wild with joy."*

General Beauregard announced the fall of Sumter in a general order, studiously flattering to his troops:

April 14.

HEADQUARTERS PROVISIONAL ARMY, C. S. A.,
CHARLESTON, S. C., *April* 14.

GENERAL ORDERS, No. 20.

"The Brigadier-General commanding is happy to congratulate the troops under his command on the brilliant success which has crowned their gallantry, privations, and hardships, by the reduction of the stronghold in the harbor of Charleston. This feat of arms has been accomplished after a severe cannonading of about thirty-three hours, in which all the troops have indicated, by their daring and bravery, that our cause must and shall triumph.

"Fort Sumter, which surrendered yesterday about 1.45 P.M., will be evacuated at 9 o'clock, A.M., to-day, and to show our magnanimity to the gallant defenders, who were only executing the orders of their government, they will be allowed to evacuate upon the same terms which were offered to them before the bombardment commenced. Our success should not lull us into a false security, but should encourage us in the necessary preparations to meet a powerful enemy, who may at any time attempt to avenge this, their first check in the present contest.

"The commandants of batteries will promptly send in their reports through the proper channels, giving a journal of the firing of their batteries against Fort Sumter, and of the fire of Fort Sumter against their batteries; furnishing the names of those who particularly distinguished themselves, and other incidents relative thereto, in order that the General commanding may be able to make known to the Confederate States Government, in a proper manner, their bravery and gallantry.

"The General is highly gratified to state that the troops, by their labor, privations, and endurance at the batteries, and at their posts, have exhibited the highest characteristics of tried soldiers, and he takes the occasion to thank all, his staff, the regulars, the volunteers, the militia, the naval forces, and the numerous individuals who have contributed to the surrender of Fort Sumter.

"By order of Brigadier-General Beauregard,

"D. R. JONES, Ass't. Adj.-General."

The authorities at Montgomery, the seat of the Confederate Government, were honored on the occasion by a serenade, when the secretary of war,

---

* A newspaper correspondent wrote:

"The scene in the city, after the raising of the flag of truce and the surrender, is indescribable; the people were perfectly wild. Men on horseback rode through the streets proclaiming the news, amidst the greatest enthusiasm.

"On the arrival of the officers from the fort they were marched through the streets, followed by an immense crowd, hurrahing, shouting, and yelling with excitement."

Walker, after exulting in the success at Charleston, prophesied "that the flag which now flaunts the breeze here [Montgomery], would float over the dome of the old Capitol before the first of May." "Let them try," he added, "Southern chivalry, and test the extent of Southern resources, and it might float eventually over Faneuil Hall itself."

Throughout all the States which had already seceded, great delight was manifested at the fall of Sumter. Even in Virginia, which still affected to be loyal, but whose convention was on the eve of passing an ordinance of secession, a "wild shout" of delight went up from the crowds which had gathered about the newspaper offices, eager for the news, when the telegram was announced: "Sumter is taken, and the Confederate flag waves over it!"

At the North, the progress of the bombardment, as it was briefly told in the hourly telegrams, was watched with painful anxiety. Many doubted, it is true, the ability of Major Anderson to hold out, although generally the hope was entertained of a successful issue to the attempt of the Government to reinforce him. When, therefore, the daily newspaper, so eagerly clutched and read, gave out with spasmodic emphasis its meagre revelations, the public mind was tortured with doubt and fear. First came the brief announcement: "The cannonading is going on fiercely from all points." Then followed immediately the ominous intelligence: "Fort Sumter is on fire!" relieved, however, by the cheering news: "The Federal flag still waves." Again the telegram declared: "Major Anderson is hemmed in by ruins and fire. Every building in Fort Sumter is burning." This alarming intelligence was, however, mitigated by the encouraging assurance, "This does not in anywise diminish his strength." "The destruction of Fort Sumter is inevitable," was the next disheartening word; but in a succeeding paragraph hope smiled once more with the declaration, that "Two ships are making in toward Morris Island, with a view to land troops and silence the batteries there." "The flames have nearly subsided in Fort Sumter," was again a hopeful gleam of sunshine, blotted out, however, by the dark line which closed the paragraph: "but Major Anderson does not fire any guns." Finally came the announcement of the last scene of the exciting drama:

"CHARLESTON, via AUGUSTA,
April 13, 1861.

"FORT SUMTER HAS SURRENDERED!

"The Confederate flag floats over its walls!

"None of the garrison or Confederate troops are hurt.

"The bombarding has closed.

"*Major Anderson has drawn down the stripes and stars, and displays a white flag, which has been answered from the city, and a boat is on the way to Sumter.*"

The conduct of Major Anderson was freely discussed; but though there were some to question his military capacity, and even to doubt his loyalty, the country finally settled into the conviction that he had acted bravely and prudently, and resolutely persisted in claiming him as one of its heroes who had gallantly sustained the honor of the United States flag.

Robert Anderson was born in Kentucky. In 1821 he was admitted a cadet at the military academy of West Point. After completing the usual four years' course of study, he graduated on the 1st of July, 1825, and entered the army as second lieutenant of the Second, but was soon after transferred to the Third, Artillery. During the Black Hawk war, in 1832, he served as acting inspector-general of the Illinois volunteers, of which Mr. Lincoln, late President, was captain.

In June, 1833, Anderson was promoted to a first lieutenancy, and in 1835 he became assistant instructor of artillery in the military academy at West Point. After serving for three or four months in the subordinate position, he was appointed instructor-in-chief of this branch of study, and held the place until 1837. In 1838, he was selected by General Scott as one of his aids-de-camp, and served in the campaign against the Indians in Florida. He was rewarded for his gallant conduct by promotion, in 1838, to the brevet rank of captain. In the same year he served as adjutant-general, but resigned in 1841, on being promoted to the captaincy of his own regiment.

During the Mexican war, Captain Anderson served under General Scott, whom he accompanied in all his triumphs, from the siege of Vera Cruz to the capture of the Mexican capital. He greatly distinguished himself at El Molino del Rey, one of the hardest fought battles of the whole campaign. Here, while acting field officer, he was severely wounded, but continued at the head of his column, "regardless of pain and self-preservation, and setting a handsome example"—wrote Captain Blake in his report—"to his men, of coolness, energy, and courage." His services on that day won for him his brevet as major. His conduct of the battery he commanded at Chapultepec elicited the praise of Scott, who mentioned him in his dispatches with an emphatic declaration of his great services.

On the 18th of November, 1860, Major Anderson was ordered to Fort Moultrie, in the harbor of Charleston, to relieve Colonel Gardiner, sent to Texas. His judicious movement in abandoning this post, as well as his defence and final surrender of Fort Sumter, have been already described.

The want of concert of action between Major Anderson and the fleet has been the source of perplexity. Some have attributed it to the fact that the message to him, conveying the intention of his government, had been studiously withheld by the authorities at Charleston. Others, however, have surmised that it was never seriously designed to expose the armed vessels to the fire of the Charleston forts, and that Major Anderson, made aware of this circumstance through his private dispatches, had acted accordingly. It has been also suggested that the administration at Washington had intended only to make a demonstration of force, without contemplating the exercise of it, either for the purpose of intimidating the people of Charleston, or precipitating them, if war was their purpose, into the first act of hostility, while the Government was performing an obvious act of duty in making an attempt to supply a starving garrison with provisions. Whatever may have been the real or pretended object, the first gun fired by the Charleston forts was considered an act of war against the Union, and rallied all its friends to its defence.

Anderson's report of the surrender of Fort Sumter was brief, and to the point:

"Having defended," he wrote to the secretary of war, Cameron, "Fort Sumter for thirty-four hours, until the quarters were entirely burned, the main gates destroyed by fire, the gorge wall seriously injured, the magazine surrounded by flames, and its door closed from the effects of the heat, four barrels and three cartridges of powder only being available, and no provisions but pork remaining, I accepted terms of evacuation offered by General Beauregard, being the same offered by him on the 11th instant [April], prior to the commencement of hostilities, and marched out of the fort Sunday afternoon, the 14th instant [April], with colors flying and drums beating, bringing away company and private property, and saluting my flag with fifty guns."

The secretary of war responded with a complimentary tribute:

"I am directed," he wrote, "by the President of the United States, to communicate to you, and through you to the officers and men under your command at forts Moultrie and Sumter, the approbation of the Government of your and their judicious and gallant conduct there, and to tender to you and them the thanks of the Government for the same."

Major Anderson, as an adopted hero of the country, became at once an object of universal curiosity. His portrait was displayed in every shop-window, and his name was soon familiar to every ear. Personally there is nothing very impressive about the "hero of Fort Sumter." A man of small stature and shrunken frame, he would easily pass unnoticed. The general expression of his face is that of quiet amiability, yet in the keenness of his concentrated eyes and in the firm closure of his thin lips there are signs of a resoluteness equal to the severest trials of a soldier's profession.

There is a simple earnestness, to which a certain puritanical fervor of piety gives zest, that marks all his words and writings, and commends him to the sympathy of the unsophisticated multitude.

His raising of the flag he had brought with him from Fort Moultrie, as he took possession of Fort Sumter, was accompanied by a ceremony characteristic of Major Anderson's devotional tendencies. Having gathered all his men about the staff, he himself took the halyards in his hand, and kneeling down, directed the chaplain to offer a prayer. At its close, having fervently uttered the "Amen," in which he was joined by the rest, he slowly raised the flag, as the band struck up "Hail, Columbia!"

When the United States Government had resolved upon an attempt to send provisions to Fort Sumter, it also determined to reinforce Fort Pickens, which was the only one of the several public works in the harbor of Pensacola which remained in the possession of the Federal Government. The insurgents of Florida had seized all the rest early in January, and now held them with a strong force under the command of General Bragg, of the Confederate army, more honorably known as Captain Bragg, the commander of the battery which did such good service in the battle of Buena Vista, and to whom General Taylor addressed his famous command : "A little more grape, Captain Bragg."

Pensacola being one of the largest and safest harbors on the Southern coast, had been chosen as the principal naval station of the South. Here, accordingly, a large navy-yard and arsenal had been established, and strong works of defence constructed. The principal of these was Fort Pickens, built upon the island of Santa Rosa, a long stretch of low land which intervenes between the harbor and the sea. The fortress rises upon the extreme western point of the island, and commands both the harbor and approaches. It is a bastioned work of great strength and extent, requiring a garrison of one thousand two hundred and sixty soldiers. The walls are of granite — forty-five feet high and twelve feet thick, pierced for three tiers of guns, two of which are concreted, and the third *en barbette*. Its whole armament, when complete, consists of sixty-three forty-two pounders, seventeen thirty-two pounders, forty-nine twenty-four pounders, five eighteens, thirteen twelves, six brass field-pieces, twenty-six brass flank howitzers, thirteen heavy eight-inch howitzers, one thirteen-inch mortar, four heavy ten-inch mortars, four light eight-inch mortars, four sixteen-inch stone mortars, and five cohorns—making in all two hundred and ten guns. Fort Pickens was begun in 1828, and completed in 1853, at a cost of one million of dollars.

Directly opposite, on the mainland, stands Fort McRae, also a bastioned work of considerable strength, with walls of brick, twelve feet thick, and mounting one hundred and fifty cannon, in three tiers—two under casemates, and the third *en barbette*. When properly garrisoned, it contains six hundred and fifty men. The guns, like those of Fort Pickens, have a wide range, and, together with the water-battery of eight guns toward the south, Forts Pickens and McRae defend the harbor of Pensacola from every approach in the direction of the Gulf of Mexico.

On the mainland, directly north of Fort Pickens, is another strong bastioned work, called Fort St. Carlos de Barrancas, from the ancient Spanish fortress originally standing upon the same site. It is mounted with forty-nine guns, and requires a garrison of two hundred and fifty men. A strong redoubt is built in its rear to give it additional support. Forts McRae and Barrancas, together with the navy-yard and arsenal, having been seized by the Confederates, there seemed imminent danger of their getting possession also of Fort Pickens, but they were thwarted in their design by Lieutenant Slemmer, the United States commander. This young officer being on the alert, no sooner discovered their purpose, than he concentrated his little garrison of eighty men within the fort, and kept the enemy at bay until the 12th of April, when the first successful attempt was made to reinforce him. This was effected by the United States man-of-war Brooklyn, and is thus described by one* who shared in the enterprise:

"On Friday, April 12th," says he, "our captain received orders to prepare for landing the troops (Company A, First Artillery) which we brought from Fort Monroe. After sunset, all the boats were hoisted out and dropped astern. Volunteers were called for to man them, and every man in the ship volunteered. After selecting the crews, they were armed to the teeth for covering the landing of the troops. As the enemy threatened to prevent the landing, having stationed coast-guards along shore for that purpose, it was necessary to send a considerable force; so the Sabine and St. Louis' boats were sent to assist our men. After the moon had set, all deck lights were extinguished, to prevent the enemy discovering our movements. Strange to say, the light-house on shore, whose powerful light would make the position of our ships visible, was put out about the same time. Between ten and eleven o'clock the ship got under way, creeping slowly toward the shore and sounding all the way, anchoring in seven fathoms of water, which indicated close proximity to the shore. The boats were then got alongside, and the men disembarked. At this time the ship's deck presented an interesting and lively spectacle, though all was done very quietly, reflecting great credit upon the officers in command. After all was ready, Lieutenant Albert N. Smith, who had command of the boat expedition, shoved off, and the other boats followed in line. He intended landing on the beach near the ship and marching to the fort, a distance of about three miles; but finding the surf too heavy, he determined to pull into the harbor and land in front of Pickens. He was successful; the doors of the fort were opened, and the troops entered. In the mean while the Wyandotte carried all the Sabine's marines and put them on the Brooklyn, which, together with the Brooklyn's marines, were to go also. The boats made a second trip, being successful in getting the marines into the fort; but day broke before the boats got out of the harbor, making the sleepy sentinels on McRea and Barrancas rub their eyes in astonishment, not daring to molest the returning party."

This landing of marines was, however, but a temporary provision. The regular reinforcements soon arrived and took their place. The transport steamer Atlantic was the first to arrive, with four

* Correspondent "Harper's Weekly."

hundred and fifty men, sixty-nine horses, and large supplies of food and munitions. She sailed from New York on the 7th of April, and having stopped on her way at Key West to take on board additional men and supplies, arrived on the evening of the 16th off the island of Santa Rosa, and anchored four miles from the shore, close to the frigate Sabine. The Sabine, 50 guns, was the flag-ship under Captain Adams, the commander of the squadron, which was composed in addition of the steam-corvette Brooklyn, 14 guns, the corvette St. Louis, 22 guns, the Water-Witch, Crusader, the Wyandotte and Mohawk, each 10 guns, for some time stationed off Pensacola. Immediately after the arrival of the Atlantic, the operation of landing her reinforcements began. Taking in tow the small boats of the fleet, some twenty in number, and the night having closed in and all lights being put out, the steamer stood in toward the shore and anchored within a mile of Fort Pickens. The guns of Fort McRae and of the water batteries, in command of the rebels, were in direct range, and signal rockets were firing from Fort Pickens, indicating the expectation of an attack. The first boat from the Atlantic pushed off at half-past nine o'clock, containing Colonel Brown, the commander, who was to supersede the intrepid subaltern, Lieutenant Slemmer. The other boats containing the troops soon followed, and before midnight the most of the officers and troops had reached the fort in safety. On the next morning, at an early hour, the rest of the men were landed, with the exception of the artillerists of Barry's Flying Artillery. To land these with their horses, the Atlantic weighed anchor and moved to a point three and a half miles distant from Fort Pickens, but within half a mile of the beach of the island of Santa Rosa. The troublesome work of landing the horses did not commence before noon, and continuing all night, was not completed until next morning.

The steamer Powhatan, Commander David D. Porter, had in the mean time arrived, and in two days after was followed by the transport steamer Illinois, which had been detained by long-continued severe weather. The reinforcements brought by the Illinois consisted of three hundred men and a number of horses, besides five hundred muskets and a large quantity of munitions of war and provisions. The troops were landed in safety during the next morning, but three days passed before the horses, forage, the ordnance, provisions, and general stores were conveyed to the shore. Four of the horses on board the Illinois had perished during the stormy passage, one was drowned alongside the ship, another had his neck broken while landing through the surf, and a third died from exhaustion. During the debarkation, the steamers Powhatan and Brooklyn took such a position that they could at the same time shield the transports under the cover of their guns, and prevent the enemy on the mainland from attempting to invade the island, and thus obstruct the landing. Colonel Brown now being the senior officer, assumed the command of Fort Pickens. He succeeded, with additional men and defences, in keeping at bay the large forces of the Confederates gathered on the mainland opposite. The rebel General Bragg was reported to have had under his command, at various times, no less than ten thousand men, who were kept busily strengthening the works in the harbor and entrenching their camp.

CHAPTER XIV.

Divided Opinion of the North in regard to the Political Causes of the Civil Quarrel.—Uniformity of Sentiment in regard to the Attack on Fort Sumter.—The National Dignity insulted.—Necessity of Striking in behalf of the National Honor.—The cry of the Masses.—Their faith in the indissolubility of the Union.—The Flag to be again raised all over the United States.—The Opinions of the Press.—War pronounced to be inevitable.—Change of Sentiment.—Union Sentiment of a Journal once threatened by the Mob for its Sympathy with the South.—The Tirades of the Ultra-Republicans.—An Ultra-Republican Paper on the Unity of Feeling.—The Proclamation of President Lincoln.—Its effect at the North.—Enthusiasm of the People.—A sudden and universal blazing of the "Stars and Stripes."—Scarcity of Bunting.—Patriotic Waistcoats and Bodices.—Patriotic Neckerchiefs and Mantillas.—Patriotic Shopkeepers and Patriotic Customers.—Patriotic fervor of the Newspapers.—Flowers of Rhetoric.—A fervid Leader.—Exceptional cases of protest at the North against the President's Proclamation.—Bold dissent in New England.—An Appeal in behalf of the Secessionists from Maine.—An Opposition to the War from Connecticut.—A vigorous word for the Union from Kentucky.—Call for Militia.—Circular of the Secretary of War.—Quotas of Militia of each State.—The Patriotic Response from the North.—The Refusal and bold Defiance of the Slave States.—The Answer of the Governor of Virginia.—Answer of the Governor of Missouri.—Answer of the Governor of North Carolina.—Answer of the Governor of Kentucky.—Answer of the Governor of Tennessee.—Poetical Response from President Jefferson Davis.—His Privateering Proclamation.—His Call for Soldiers.—The effect of his Proclamation at the North.—Opinion of Privateering, which is pronounced Piracy.—President Lincoln's Proclamation.—A Blockade announced.—Southern Privateers to be dealt with as Pirates.

1861. Although opinion at the North, in regard to the political causes of the civil quarrel, was still widely divided, there was little diversity of sentiment concerning the blow which had been struck by the rebellious South at Fort Sumter. It was universally felt that in this violence to its flag, a gross indignity had been offered to the nation, and that it had become necessary, in order to vindicate the national honor, as well as to preserve the national existence, to meet force with force. The few who were less sanguine as to the issue even acknowledged that an appeal to arms was absolutely obligatory, were it only to assert the idea of government, and thus save the country from anarchy and social disorder. The more hopeful, however, who formed the great mass of the people, were eager not only to avenge the insulted flag, but to restore it to its former proud position throughout the wide domain of the United States. With their traditional reverence for the Union, and faith in its power, they could not contemplate the possibility of its disruption; and doubting the persistency of secession, and presuming on its weakness, they fondly believed that with a single effort of the Federal might, rebellion could be suppressed, and the flag raised once more over a united land.

Though the expression of opinion by the press was toned somewhat by its various shades of partisanship, there was hardly a journal which ventured to dispute the necessity of war. They indulged, it is true, in mutual recriminations, charging each other with having caused an event which they all now acknowledged to be inevitable. One journal, which had before so warmly and perseveringly advocated the cause of secession as to bring upon itself the anger of a Northern mob, now declared : " In a conflict of this sort, there can be but two parties—a Northern and a Southern party; for all other parties will cease to exist. The political principles, organizations, and issues which have divided our country and our people, in various shapes and forms, since the treaty of our independence with England, will all be very soon overwhelmed in the sweeping changes of a civil war. It would be folly now to argue what might, could, would, or should have been done by Southern fire-eaters and Northern disorganizers in 1854, 1860, or by Mr. Buchanan, or by Mr. Lincoln, or by the late session of Congress. Civil war is upon us, and the questions which now supersede all others are : What are the consequences now before us? Where is this war to end, and how, and when? What is our duty under this warlike condition of things? and what are the movements and the conditions necessary to change this state of war to a state of peace?"

An ultra Republican journal, after giving vent to a tirade against " our journals lately parading the pranks of the secessionists with scarcely disguised exultation," declares, " Democrat as well as Republican, Conservative, and Radical, instinctively feel that the guns fired at Sumter were aimed at the heart of the American Republic. Not even in the lowest groggery of our city [New York] would it be safe to propose cheers for Beauregard and Governor Pickens. The Tories of the Revolution were relatively ten times as numerous here as are the open sympathizers with the Palmetto rebels. It is hard to lose Sumter ; it is a consolation to know that in losing it we have gained a united people. Henceforth, the loyal States are a unit in uncompromising hostility to treason, wherever plotted, however justified. Fort Sumter is temporarily lost, but the country is saved. Live the Republic !"

The proclamation of the President, giving an authoritative sanction to the national sentiment, served still more to arouse the spirit of union.

PROCLAMATION OF THE PRESIDENT.

"Whereas the laws of the United States have been for some time past, and now are, opposed, and the execution thereof obstructed in the States of South Carolina, Georgia, Alabama, Florida, Mississippi, Louisiana, and Texas, by combinations too powerful to be suppressed by the ordinary course of judicial proceedings, or by the powers vested in the marshals by law ; now, therefore, I, Abraham Lincoln, President of the United States, in virtue of the power in me vested by the Constitution and the laws, have thought fit to call forth, and hereby do call forth, the militia of the several States of the Union to the aggregate number of 75,000, in order to suppress said combinations, and to cause the laws to be duly executed.

"The details for this object will be immediately communicated to the State authorities through the War Department. I appeal to all loyal citizens to favor, facilitate, and aid this effort to maintain the honor, the integrity, and existence of our national Union, and the perpetuity of popular government, and to redress wrongs already long enough endured. I deem it proper to say that the first service assigned to the forces hereby called forth will probably be to repossess the forts, places, and property which have been seized from the Union; and in every event the utmost care will be observed, consistently with the objects aforesaid, to avoid any devastation, any destruction of or interference with property, or any disturbance of peaceful citizens in any part of the country ; and I hereby command the persons composing the combinations aforesaid to disperse, and retire peaceably to their respective abodes within twenty days from this date.

"Deeming that the present condition of public affairs presents an extraordinary occasion, I do hereby, in virtue of the power in me vested by the Constitution, convene both Houses of Congress. The senators and representatives are therefore summoned to assemble at their respective chambers at twelve o'clock, noon, on Thursday, the fourth day of July next, then and there to consider and determine such measures as, in their wisdom, the public safety and interest may seem to demand.

"In witness whereof, I have hereunto set my hand, and caused the seal of the United States to be affixed.

"Done at the city of Washington, this fifteenth day of April, in the year of our Lord one thousand eight hundred and sixty-one, and of the independence of the United States the eighty-fifth.

"ABRAHAM LINCOLN.

"By the President.

"WM. H. SEWARD, Secretary of State."

Throughout the North the effect of this proclamation was to excite the people to an intense enthusiasm. The population of the large cities became suddenly so absorbed in the excitement of the hour, that all the ordinary transactions of business were suspended. Flags floated from every public building, church steeple, and private house. Such was the demand for bunting, that the ordinary supply was soon exhausted, and the ardent gathered every chance-colored rag or ribbon that fell in their way, to fashion into the "stars and stripes" of their patriotic desire. Union devices and badges were sold at the corners of every street, and flaunted upon each patriotic waistcoat and boddice.

Shop windows patriotically glowed with the national colors, and a display of bonnets and mantillas, not less abundant than neckerchiefs and shirt bosoms, profusely studded with stars and variegated with red and white stripes, revealed the enthusiasm of patriotic dealers, and awakened the longing of patriotic wearers.

The newspapers forgot their factious contentions and joined in a fervid expression of Union sentiments. Their leading articles burst forth into unusual flowers of patriotic rhetoric. The language of one* may serve to show the spirit pervading all: "The incidents of the last two days will live in history. Not for fifty years has such a spectacle been seen, as that glorious uprising of American loyalty which greeted the news that open war had been commenced upon the Constitution and Government of the United States. The great heart of the American people beat with one high pulsation of courage, and of fervid love and devotion to the great Republic. Party dissensions were instantly hushed; political differences disappeared, and were as thoroughly forgotten as if they had never existed; party bonds flashed into nothingness in the glowing flame of patriotism; men ceased to think of themselves or their parties, they thought only of their country and of the dangers which menace its existence. Nothing for years has brought the hearts of all the people so close together—or so inspired them all with common hopes, and common fears, and a common aim, as the bombardment and surrender of an American fortress.

"We look upon this sublime outburst of public sentiment as the most perfect vindication of popular institutions—the most conclusive reply to the impugners of American loyalty, the country has ever seen. It has been quite common to say that such a Republic as ours could never be permanent, because it lacked the conditions of a profound and abiding loyalty. The Government could never inspire a patriotic instinct, fervid enough to melt the bonds of party, or powerful enough to override the selfishness which free institutions so rapidly develop. The hearts of our own people had begun to sink within them, at the apparent insensibility of the public to the dangers which menaced the Government. The public mind seemed to have been demoralized—the public heart seemed insensible to perils which threatened utter extinction to our great Republic. The secession movement, infinitely the most formidable danger which has ever menaced our Government, was regarded with indifference and treated as merely a novel form of our usual political contentions. The best among us began to despair of a country which seemed incompetent to understand its dangers, and indifferent to its own destruction.

"But all this is changed. The cannon which bombarded Sumter awoke strange echoes, and touched forgotten chords in the American heart. American loyalty leaped into instant life, and stood radiant and ready for the fierce

---
* New York *Times*, April 16th.

encounter. From one end of the land to the other—in the crowded streets of cities, and in the solitude of the country —wherever the splendor of the stars and stripes, the glittering emblems of our country's glory, meets the eye, come forth shouts of devotion and pledges of aid, which give sure guarantees for the perpetuity of American freedom. War can inflict no scars on such a people. It can do them no damage which time cannot repair. It cannot shake the solid foundations of their material prosperity, while it will strengthen the manly and heroic virtues which defy its fierce and frowning front."

Although the prevailing tone of the North was one of enthusiasm in behalf of waging war against those who had insulted the flag of the Union, there were still some of the Northern papers which ventured to protest against the President's proclamation. From New England, by a strange contrast with its general feeling, came some of the boldest dissent from the predominating sentiment of the nation.

"Democrats of Maine!" was the daring appeal of an audacious Northern editor,* "the loyal sons of the South have gathered around Charleston as your fathers of old gathered about Boston in defence of the same sacred principles of liberty—principles which *you* have ever upheld and defended with your vote, your voice, and your strong right arm. Your sympathies are with the defenders of the truth and the right. Those who have inaugurated this unholy and unjustifiable war are no friends of yours, no friends of Democratic liberty. Will you aid them in their work of subjugation and tyranny?

"When the Government at Washington calls for volunteers or recruits to carry on the work of subjugation and tyranny under the specious phrase of 'enforcing the laws,' 'retaking and protecting the public property,' and 'collecting the revenue,' let every Democrat fold his arms and bid the minions of Tory despotism do a Tory despot's work. Say to them, fearlessly and boldly—in the language of England's great lord, the Earl of Chatham, whose bold words in behalf of the struggling Colonies of America, in the dark hours of the Revolution, have enshrined his name in the heart of every friend of freedom and immortalized his fame wherever the name of liberty is known—say in his thrilling language: 'If I were a Southerner, as I am a Northerner, while a foreign troop was landed in my country, I would never lay down my arms— *never, never, never!*'"

Another,* more calmly, but not less decidedly, opposed the war:

"The President has issued his proclamation, calling Congress to meet on the 4th of July. Also calling for 75,000 volunteers to aid in carrying on a conflict with the South. The news already received from the border States indicates that they will leave the Union, and that the war will be between nineteen free and fifteen slave States.

"Could this war policy possibly save

---

* Bangor (Me.) *Union.*   * Hartford (Ct.) *Times.*

the Union and promote the welfare of the people, we could look upon it with more complacency. But as it must inevitably more completely divide the Union and injure the interests of the whole country, we believe it to be an unwise and unsafe policy. To march soldiers into the Southern country to contend with armies and yellow fever, and to end in no good, but much evil, does not seem to be a discreet or a righteous policy.

"A bloody conflict may be continued with the South for weeks, for months, or for years. At its close a compromise must be made no more favorable to the North than was the Crittenden compromise. But the evils of the unnecessary strife will continue into the long years of the future, and be felt by millions. No good whatever can come out of the shocking conflict.

"War has been commenced. Its origin is the negro agitation. Let the friends of the agitation point out the spot where a slave has been benefited, if they can. Great evils have come. Where are the benefits?"

As a set-off, however, to this expression of Southern opinion at the North, there was a vigorous word uttered for union in the slave State of Kentucky:

"The secession leaders," wrote the editor of the Louisville *Journal*, "are relying very largely upon the first shock of battle for the promotion of a general secession feeling in the Southern States. They ought, however, to consider that the sympathies of honest and sensible men are not likely to go with the wrong-doers. If the General Government commit any wrong or outrage upon South Carolina or Florida, it will be condemned; but if a United States vessel shall be fired into and her men slain for a mere attempt to take food to the Government's troops in the Government's own forts, and if war shall grow out of the collision, no spirit of secession or rebellion will be created thereby this side the cotton line. Such, at least, is our opinion, founded upon our conviction that the great mass of our fellow-citizens are sensible, and patriotic, and just. Who that loves his country would see it humiliated and its honor trampled on?"

With the proclamation by the President came the call upon the several States for their quotas of militia to make up the required number of troops to be mustered for the suppression of the rebellion and the defence of the Union. The following circular was addressed by the secretary of war to the governors not only of the free States, but of those slave States whose loyalty might be suspected, but which yet nominally continued to acknowledge the Federal authority:

"SIR: Under the act of Congress for calling out the militia to execute the laws of the Union to suppress insurrection, to repel invasion, etc., approved February 28, 1795, I have the honor to request your Excellency to cause to be immediately detailed from the militia of your State the quota designated in the table below, to serve as infantry or riflemen for a period of three months, unless sooner discharged. Your Excellency will please communicate to me the time at about which your quota will be expected at its rendezvous, as it will be met as soon as practicable by an officer or officers to muster it into the service and pay of the United States. At the same time the oath of fidelity to the United States will be administered to every officer and man. The mustering officers will be instructed to receive no man under the rank of commissioned officer who is in years apparently over forty-five or under eighteen, or who is not in physical strength and vigor. The quota for each State is as follows:

Maine	1	Virginia	3
New Hampshire	1	North Carolina	2
Vermont	1	Kentucky	4
Massachusetts	2	Arkansas	1
Rhode Island	1	Missouri	4
Connecticut	1	Ohio	13
New York	17	Indiana	6
New Jersey	4	Illinois	6
Pennsylvania	16	Michigan	1
Delaware	1	Iowa	1
Tennessee	2	Minnesota	1
Maryland	4	Wisconsin	1

"It is ordered that each regiment shall consist, on an aggregate of officers and men, of 780. The total thus to be called out is 73,391. The remainder, to constitute the 75,000 men under the President's proclamation, will be composed of troops in the District of Columbia."

In response to this call, there came from all the free States, without an exception, an ardent expression of patriotic sympathy with the President's proclamation, and an immediate effort to meet its requirements. Proclamations were at once addressed by the governors to the people of the several Northern States, appealing to their loyalty, and invoking them to manifest it by taking up arms in defence of the Union.

The slave States, with the exception of Maryland and Delaware, answered with a resolute refusal, expressed in a tone of bold defiance of the Federal authority. The Governor of Virginia, John Letcher, wrote: "I have only to say, that the militia of Virginia will not be furnished to the powers at Washington for any such use or purpose as they have in view. Your object is to subjugate the Southern States, and a requisition made upon me for such an object—an object, in my judgment, not within the purview of the Constitution or the act of 1795—will not be complied with. You have chosen to inaugurate civil war, and having done so, we will meet it in a spirit as determined as the administration has exhibited toward the South."

C. F. Jackson, Governor of Missouri, wrote: "Your requisition, in my judgment, is illegal, unconstitutional, and revolutionary in its objects, inhuman and diabolical, and cannot be complied with. Not one man will the State of Missouri furnish to carry on such an unholy crusade."

John W. Ellis, Governor of North Carolina, wrote: "I have to say in reply, that I regard the levy of troops made by the administration for the purpose of subjugating the States of the South, as in violation of the Constitution, and a usurpation of power. I can be no party to this wicked violation of the laws of the country, and to this war upon the liberties of a free people. You can get no troops from North Carolina."

Magoffin, the Governor of Kentucky, wrote: "I say emphatically that Kentucky will furnish no troops for the wicked purpose of subduing her sister Southern States."

Governor Harris, of Tennessee, replied: "Tennessee will not furnish a single man for coercion, but fifty thousand, if necessary, for the defence of our rights, or those of our Southern brethren."

Governor Reeder, of Arkansas, answered with equal resoluteness of refusal, but less courtesy:

"In answer to your demand for troops from Arkansas to subjugate the Southern States, I have to say that none will be furnished. The demand is only adding insult to injury.

"The people of this Commonwealth are freemen, not slaves, and will defend to the last extremity their honor, lives, and property against Northern mendacity and usurpation."

President Davis, of the Confederate States, after venting this exulting *jeu d'esprit*,

"With mortar, Paixhan, and petard
We sent the foe our Beauregard,"

met the proclamation of President Lincoln with this menacing document:

"Whereas Abraham Lincoln, President of the United States, has, by proclamation, announced his intention of invading the Confederacy with an armed force, for the purpose of capturing its fortresses, and thereby subverting its independence and subjecting the free people thereof to the dominion of a foreign power; and whereas it has thus become the duty of this Government to repel the threatened invasion, and defend the rights and liberties of the people by all the means which the laws of nations and usages of civilized warfare place at its disposal;

"Now, therefore, I, Jefferson Davis, President of the Confederate States of America, do issue this, my proclamation, inviting all those who may desire, by service in private armed vessels on the high seas, to aid this Government in resisting so wanton and wicked an aggression, to make application for commissions or letters of marque and reprisal, to be issued under the seal of these Confederate States; and I do further notify all persons applying for letters of marque, to make a statement in writing, giving the name and suitable description of the character, tonnage, and force of the vessel, name of the place of residence of each owner concerned therein, and the intended number of crew, and to sign each statement, and deliver the same to the secretary of state or collector of the port of entry of these Confederate States, to be by him transmitted to the secretary of state; and I do further notify all applicants aforesaid, before any commission or letter of marque is issued to any vessel, or the owner or the owners thereof, and the commander for the time being, they will be required to give bond to the Confederate States, with, at least, two responsible sureties not interested in such vessel, in the penal sum of five thousand dollars; or if such vessel be provided with more than one hundred and fifty men, then in the penal sum of ten thousand dollars, with the condition that the owners, officers, and crew who shall be employed on board such commissioned vessel shall observe the laws of these Confederate States, and the instructions given them for the regulation of their conduct, that shall satisfy all damages done contrary to the tenor thereof by such vessel during her commission, and deliver up the same when revoked by the President of the Confederate States.

"And I do further specially enjoin on all persons holding offices, civil and military, under the authority of the Confederate States, that they be vigilant and zealous in the discharge of the duties incident thereto; and I do, moreover, exhort the good people of these Confederate States, as they love their country—as they prize the blessings of free government—as they feel the wrongs of the past, and those now threatened in an aggravated form by those whose enmity is more implacable, because unprovoked—to exert themselves in preserving order, in promoting concord, in maintaining the authority and efficacy of the laws, and in supporting and invigorating all the measures which may be adopted for a common defence, and by which, under the blessings of Divine Providence, we may hope for a speedy, just, and honorable peace.

"In witness whereof, I have set my hand and have caused the seal of the Confederate States of America to be attached this seventeenth day of April, in the year of our Lord one thousand eight hundred and sixty-one.

"JEFFERSON DAVIS.
"ROBERT TOOMBS, Secretary of State."

At the same time that President Davis thus threatened Northern commerce with a fleet of privateers, he called upon the Confederacy for a hundred and fifty thousand men, in addition to the thirty-two thousand already demanded. A loan of five millions of dollars had been issued, and subscriptions were reported to be rapidly coming in under the stimulus of approaching war.

Davis' invitation to applications for letters of marque created great alarm, and was received by the North with a universal burst of indignation. Privateering was pronounced an infamous weapon of warfare. The destruction of private property in the course of a conflict between two hostile parties was declared to be a relic of barbarism. Davis was reminded of the treaties of the United States with certain European powers, which prohibited citizens of either nation from accepting letters of marque from any authority hostile to the agreeing parties. This, they declared, would prevent his obtaining privateers from Europe, and destroy any hope of toleration from them from that quarter. It was declared that there was not one foreign port where, if Davis' privateers should venture to enter, they would not be seized as pirates, and dealt with accordingly. If any man, in this country, or in any other, dared to accept a letter of marque from the Confederacy and act upon it, he would, it was threatened, be hung as a pirate. The proclamation was, in a word, branded as a formal sanction of piracy, and it was met not only with the menace of the yard-arm, but its author was reminded that the most terrific retaliation awaited him if he should carry out his purpose. "The first seizure of an American vessel by one of his privateers will let loose," said a journalist,* "upon the South more John Browns than he can hire pirates in a year."

The commercial cities of the North were greatly fluttered by the prospect of a swoop by the rebellious birds of prey upon their fleets which were winging their way over every sea and ocean. The Chamber of Commerce of New York met and resolved, "That the proposition of Mr. Jefferson Davis to issue letters of marque to whomsoever may apply for them, emanating from no recognized government, is not only without the sanction of public law, but piratical in its tendencies, and therefore deserving the stern condemnation of the civilized world." To this was added the further resolution, that "it is the duty of our Government to issue at once a proclamation warning all persons that privateering under the commissions proposed will be dealt with as simple piracy."

The President promptly responded by establishing a blockade of the ports of the seceding States, and did not hesitate to warn all privateers sailing under the flag of the Confederates that they would be treated as pirates:

"Whereas an insurrection against the Government of the United States has broken out in the States of South Carolina, Georgia, Alabama, Florida, Mississippi, Louisiana, and Texas, and the laws of the United States for the collection of the revenue can not be efficiently executed therein conformably to that provision of the Constitution which requires duties to be uniform throughout the United States;

"And whereas a combination of persons, engaged in such insurrection, have threatened to grant pretended letters of marque to authorize the bearers thereof to commit assaults on the lives, vessels, and property of good citizens of the country lawfully engaged in commerce on the high seas, and in waters of the United States;

"And whereas an Executive Proclamation has been already issued, requiring the persons engaged in these disorderly proceedings to desist therefrom, calling out a militia force for the purpose of repressing the same, and convening Congress in extraordinary session to deliberate and determine thereon;

"Now, therefore, I, Abraham Lincoln, President of the United States, with a view to the same purposes before mentioned, and to the protection of the public peace, and the lives and property of quiet and orderly citizens pursuing their lawful occupations, until Congress shall have assembled and deliberated on the said unlawful proceedings, or until the same shall have ceased, have further

---

* New York *Times*.

deemed it advisable to set on foot a blockade of the ports within the States aforesaid, in pursuance of the laws of the United States and of the laws of nations in such cases provided. For this purpose a competent force will be posted so as to prevent entrance and exit of vessels from the ports aforesaid. If, therefore, with a view to violate such blockade, a vessel shall approach, or shall attempt to leave any of the said ports, she will be duly warned by the commander of one of the blockading vessels, who will endorse on her register the fact and date of such warning; and if the same vessel shall again attempt to enter or leave the blockaded port, she will be captured and sent to the nearest convenient port, for such proceedings against her and her cargo as prize as may be deemed advisable.

"And I hereby proclaim and declare, that if any person, under the pretended authority of said States, or under any other pretence, shall molest a vessel of the United States, or the persons or cargo on board of her, such person will be held amenable to the laws of the United States for the prevention and punishment of piracy.

"ABRAHAM LINCOLN.

"By the President.

"WILLIAM H. SEWARD, Secretary of State.

"WASHINGTON, *April* 19, 1861."

CHAPTER XV.

Inquietude about the Border States.—The Convention of Virginia.—Committee appointed to wait upon the President.—Its Message.—President Lincoln's Answer.—Its effect.—Virginia Convention passes an Act of Secession.—Impatience of the Secessionists.—Proclamation of Governor Letcher.—Recognition of the Southern Confederacy.—Preparations for War.—The Harbor of Norfolk Obstructed.—Attempt on Harper's Ferry.—Description of the place.—Its picturesque beauty.—Its Resources.—Unhappy Associations.—Virginia Troops Mustering for an Attack upon Harper's Ferry.—A Force Marches.—Description of the March.—The Federal Commander and his little Garrison.—Anticipated Attack.—Preparations to thwart its object.—Preparing for a Conflagration.—Positive Information.—The Torch applied.—Retreat of the Federal Commander and his Men.—An excited Populace.—Held at Bay.—Continued Flight of the Federal Commander.—Safe arrival in Pennsylvania.—Rewards of Gallantry.—Another Destruction of Public Property.—Hemming in of the Gosport Navy Yard.—Exulting Dispatch.—Description of the Navy Yard.—The Ships.—Resolution of Commodore Macaulay.—The Demand of the Insurgents.—Arrival of the Pawnee.—Her Sail from Fortress Monroe to Norfolk.—Boisterous Welcome.—The Marines set to work.—Securing the Papers.—Destruction of Arms.—The Firing of the Barracks.—Laying of the Trains.—Departure of the Pawnee.—A Signal.—The Conflagration of Ships and Navy Yard.—The Burning of the old Pennsylvania.—The People of Norfolk bursting through the Gates of the Navy Yard.—The Havoc.—Incomplete Destruction.—Curious Reasons for it.—Details of the Property destroyed.—The Feeling at the North.—The Destruction pronounced unnecessary.—Quick work of the Insurgents.—Erection of defiant Batteries.

1861.

THE greatest inquietude had long existed at the North in regard to the action of the border States, and more especially of Maryland and Virginia. In the latter State a convention had been for some time in secret session, and the result was awaited with intense anxiety. A committee, consisting of

Messrs. Preston, Stuart, and Randolph, had been appointed to wait upon the President at Washington, and to present to him the following preamble and resolution passed by the Convention of Virginia:

"Whereas, in the opinion of this Convention, the uncertainty which prevails in the public mind as to the policy which the Federal Executive intends to pursue toward the seceded States is extremely injurious to the industrial and commercial interests of the country, tends to keep up an excitement which is unfavorable to the adjustment of the pending difficulties, and threatens a disturbance of the public peace, therefore,

"*Resolved*, That a committee of three delegates be appointed to wait on the President of the United States, present to him this preamble, and respectfully ask him to communicate to this Convention the policy which the Federal Executive intends to pursue in regard to the Confederate States."

The bearers of this demand, courteous in form but insolent in substance, were duly presented at the White House, and received from Mr. Lincoln a response in which he characteristically rather discussed the question amiably with his interlocutors, than firmly asserted his Executive authority.

April 13.

"In answer, I," said the President, "have to say that having, at the beginning of my official term, expressed my intended policy as plainly as I was able, it is with deep regret and mortification I now learn there is great and injurious uncertainty in the public mind as to what course I intend to pursue. Not having as yet seen occasion to change, it is now my purpose to pursue the course marked out in the inaugural address. I commend a careful consideration of the whole document as the best expression I can give to my purposes. As I then and therein said, I now repeat: 'The power confided in me will be used to hold and possess property and places belonging to the Government, and to collect the duties and imports; but beyond what is necessary for these objects there will be no invasion, no using of force against and among the people anywhere.' By the words 'property and places belonging to the Government,' I chiefly allude to the military posts and property which were in possession of the Government when it came into my hands. But if, as now appears to be true, in pursuit of a purpose to drive the United States authority from these places, an unprovoked assault has been made upon Fort Sumter, I shall hold myself at liberty to repossess it, if I can, and like places which had been seized before the Government was devolved upon me; and in any event I shall, to the best of my ability, repel force by force. In case it proves true that Fort Sumter has been assaulted, as is reported, I shall, perhaps, cause the United States mails to be withdrawn from all the States which claim to have seceded, believing that the commencement of actual war against the Government justifies and possibly demands it. I scarcely need to say that I consider the military posts and property situated within the States which claim to have seceded, as yet belonging to the Government of the United States, as much as they did before the supposed secession. Whatever else I may do for the purpose, I shall not attempt to collect the duties and imposts by any armed invasion of any part of the country; not meaning by this, however, that I may not land a force deemed necessary to relieve a fort upon the border of the country. From the fact that I have quoted a part of the inaugural address, it must not be inferred that I repudiate any other part, the whole of which I reaffirm, except so far as what I now say of the mails may be regarded as a modification."

This answer, however, was sufficiently firm to convince the Virginian commissioners that the President had determined to exercise his proper authority in the suppression of rebellion. Their return to Richmond with this response served to precipitate the action of the Convention, and accordingly it passed, in secret session, on the 17th of April, an ordinance of secession, conditional, however, upon its ratification by a majority of the votes of the people of the State on the fourth Thursday in the ensuing month of May. The secession leaders of Virginia, however, in their impatience to rebel, could not await the deliberate course of law, and began at once a series of hostile acts, soon to result in open war against the Federal authority.

Letcher, the Governor of Virginia, issued a proclamation in which he recognized the independence of the seceded States, declaring that they have, " by authority of their people, solemnly resumed the powers granted by them to the United States, and have framed a constitution and organized a government for themselves, to which the people of those States are yielding willing obedience, and have so notified the President of the United States by all the formalities incident to such action, and thereby become to the United States a separate, independent, and foreign power." At the same time he thought proper "to order all armed volunteer regiments or companies within the State forthwith to hold themselves in readiness for immediate orders."

Before the people of the State, however, had an opportunity of expressing their will as legally provided by the acts of the Virginia Legislature and Convention, Governor Letcher commenced to wage war against the United States. He ordered the main entrance of the harbor of Norfolk to be obstructed by the sinking of small boats, to prevent communication with the Federal navy-yard at that port, which he had evidently determined to seize on the first occasion favorable to his purpose, as will be developed in the course of this narrative.

His first attempt, however, was to capture the United States arsenal and armory at Harper's Ferry. This town, now so memorable, is in Jefferson Co., Virginia. It is situated on the Potomac River, just where the Shenandoah enters, and the two streams united pass through the Blue Ridge. The town originally clustered about the base of a hill, but is gradually rising up its steep sides, and some scattered hamlets and houses have already reached the table-land on the summit, nearly four hundred feet above the water. The ridge on either side of the gap through which the Potomac, united with the Shenandoah, forces its way, rises in steep and bare cliffs to an elevation of twelve hundred feet or more, the simple grandeur of which, contrasting with the picturesque beauty of the lesser and cultivated heights, gives to the surrounding scenery of Harper's Ferry the most impressive effect. Thomas Jefferson said that it was "one of the most stupendous scenes in nature, and well worth a voyage across the Atlantic to witness."

The town is described as at this time "containing a population of 10,000, and of considerable trading importance as the point of junction of the Baltimore and Ohio and the Winchester and Potomac railways. A bridge of nine hundred feet in length connects it with the opposite shore of Maryland. The main business of the place is manufacturing. It has one of the largest mills in the United States for grinding flour." Additional importance was given to the town by the establishment there of the Federal arsenal and armory. Ninety thousand stand of arms were ordinarily stored in the dépôts, and the work-shops were capable of producing twenty-five thousand annually.

The place had already acquired an unhappy association with our sectional quarrels, by the invasion of John Brown, who, at the head of twenty-two men, had taken possession of the town and strove to excite the negroes of Virginia to insurrection. It has again repeatedly become a scene of commotion and conflict during this civil war.

The Governor of Virginia was eager to possess himself of the arsenal and armory, and thus supply his secession allies with the means of carrying on the war against the United States, which he contemplated. He accordingly sent secret orders to Charlestown, the county seat of Jefferson, to muster a force for the purpose of seizing the Federal property at Harper's Ferry. Some three thousand men had been summoned, but only two hundred and fifty, in consequence of the suddenness of the call, mustered at Halltown, the rendezvous half way between the county town and Harper's Ferry, and about four miles from each place. Here they remained until night, that they might have the cover of darkness for their intended act of violence against the laws of the United States.

The force having been formed, consisting of a small body of infantry, termed the Jefferson Battalion, commanded by a Captain Allen, one piece of artillery, and a squad of "Fauquier" cavalry, under a Captain Ashby, marched, at about eight o'clock in the night of the very day on which the order had been received from Richmond.

"The troops marched," says one who was with them, "in silence, and about a mile from the starting-point the column was challenged by sentries posted

April 18.

April 18.

in the road. They halted, loaded with ball-cartridge, and advanced with fixed bayonets until they reached the brow of the hill overlooking the town and at the outskirts of the village of Bolivar. Here the advance was again challenged, and the column halted. As these sentries were known to be employes of the armories, and as it was thought probable from the temper manifested during the day that the whole body of workmen had united with the Government troops, thus giving them four hundred effective men, with full preparation and choice of position, it was thought proper to send a flag into the town to ascertain how matters stood. An influential gentleman accompanying the troops, offered his services to execute this delicate duty, and to dissuade the citizens, if possible, from taking part in the contest. From after-knowledge it was ascertained that this precaution was unnecessary, as the mass of the inhabitants were loyal to the soil where they lived, and such as might have entertained different sentiments were silenced by the reports of the imposing force which was supposed to be at hand.

"While the Virginia officers were in consultation, there was seen in the direction of the armory a flash, accompanied by a report like the discharge of a cannon, followed by a number of other flashes in quick succession, and then the sky and surrounding mountains were lighted with the steady glare of ascending flames. Captain Ashby, with his squad, immediately rode down into the town, and in a short time returned with the report that the troops had fired the public buildings and retreated across the Potomac bridge, taking the mountain road toward Carlisle Barracks, in Pennsylvania.

"On our way down we met a long line of men, women, and boys, carrying loads of muskets, bayonets, and other military equipments. The streets at the confluence of the two rivers were brilliantly illuminated by the flames from the old arsenal, which burned like a furnace. The inclosure around these buildings was covered with splintered glass, which had been blown out by the explosion of the powder-train. A few arm-boxes, open and empty, lay near the entrance; but nearly all the muskets in this building, fifteen thousand, as stated, were destroyed.

"Of the armory buildings on Potomac Street, one large work-shop was in a light blaze, and two others on fire. Alarmed by the first explosions, the citizens hesitated to approach the work-shops, and warned the Virginia troops not to do so, supposing them to be mined; but presently becoming reassured on that subject, they went to work with the engines, extinguished some of the fires, and prevented their extension to the town and railroad bridges."

The plans of the secessionists had been anticipated and their designs thwarted by the Federal commander and his little force at Harper's Ferry. The Federal garrison consisted of a detachment of United States Rifles, amounting to about forty in number, under the command of Lieutenant Roger Jones. This officer had been notified some days previously by the Government at Washington of the danger which **April** threatened his post. On the 17th **17.** of April, before the march of the Virginians, he learned from various sources that the attack was to be made on the succeeding day. The militia of the town of Harper's Ferry, although they professed loyalty, were either alarmed at the rumors of an approaching force, or unwilling to oppose it, and consequently disbanded. The workmen employed at the arsenal and armory showed symptoms, if not of disaffection, at least of great uneasiness. Every hour brought with it fresh rumors, more or less exaggerated, of the advancing secessionists. The railroad was in their power, and a special train, bearing armed men, was known to be hurrying forward. Troops, amounting to two thousand in number, were reported to have gathered from Winchester, Charleston, and other neighboring points, and to be marching to Harper's Ferry.

Lieutenant Jones, conscious of the purpose of this movement, and unable, with his meagre garrison of forty men in a country believed to be hostile, to defend his post, determined to destroy the arsenal and armory, lest their important works and valuable supplies of arms should fall into the possession of those who were undoubtedly determined to use them in waging war against the Federal Government.

Early in the evening of the 17th of April, accordingly, the Lieutenant set his men to work in making prepara- **April** tions for the destruction of the **17.** public property, should it prove necessary. With swords the soldiers cut up the planks and other timber to supply wood for firing the buildings. The mattresses were ripped up, their contents emptied out, and then filled with powder. This was all done inside of the arsenals and armories, to conceal the purpose from the people of the town, whose loyalty was suspected, and who, if they should discover it, might rise and prevent it. The arms, some fifteen thousand stand, were now collected and piled together, and the chipped wood and mattresses filled with powder were so placed that the guns and the buildings might all be destroyed together in one common explosion and conflagration. On the next night, having received **April** "positive and reliable information **18.** that twenty-five hundred or three thousand State troops would reach Harper's Ferry in two hours from Winchester, and that the troops from Halltown, increased to three hundred, were advancing, and even at that time—a few minutes after ten o'clock—within twenty minutes' march of the Ferry," Lieutenant Jones gave the order to apply the torch. The windows and doors of the buildings had been opened so that the flames could have free sway, and when all was ready, the fires were started in the carpenter's shop, and the trains leading to the powder ignited. This done, the Lieutenant marched out his men and began a rapid retreat. In three minutes after, the buildings of the arsenal and the carpenter's shop were in a "complete blaze."

The fire alarmed the town, and its excited populace pursued Lieutenant Jones and his men, coming upon them just as they had reached the bridge, for the purpose of escaping across. The crowd pressed forward, crying vengeance upon them for having set fire to the buildings. Jones wheeled his men, and facing the multitude declared, unless they dispersed, he would fire upon them. The intimidated throng shrunk back, and Jones took the occasion to continue his retreat and take to the woods, followed, however, by several shots, which fortunately were without effect. He now hurried northward, his way being lighted up by the blazing buildings. The explosion took place almost as soon as he got beyond the town, and he flattered himself that the destruction of the arsenal and armory had been complete. Hurriedly marching all night across streams and bogs, he reached Hagerstown in safety on the next morning, at seven o'clock, and thence pursued his way to Chambersburg, in Pennsylvania, where, confident of being among a loyal people, he could stop to refresh his wayworn men, who had marched all night and eaten nothing since they left Harper's Ferry. Four of his little garrison, however, were missing, and it was feared that they had been captured, or perhaps slain.

April 19.

From Chambersburg Lieutenant Jones proceeded with his men to Carlisle Barracks, a Federal post, whence he dispatched a report of his proceedings to the United States Government.

April 20.

His conduct met with the approbation of the President, who, in consideration of "his skilful and gallant conduct at Harper's Ferry," gave him the commission of assistant-quarter-master-general with the rank of captain, and sent to him through the secretary this flattering tribute:

"WAR DEPARTMENT, WASHINGTON, *April 22d*, 1861.

"LIEUTENANT ROGER JONES:

"MY DEAR SIR: I am directed by the President of the United States to communicate to you, and through you to the officers and men under your command at Harper's Ferry armory, the approbation of the Government of your and their judicious conduct there, and to tender to you and them the thanks of the Government for the same.

"I am, sir, very respectfully,

"SIMON CAMERON,

"Secretary of War."

This was soon followed by another more important, but less justifiable destruction of public property in Virginia. It will be recollected that Governor Letcher had already ordered the main entrance of the harbor of Norfolk to be obstructed by the sinking of small boats. Seven vessels had been sunk at the mouth of the Elizabeth River, the only channel of communication between the sea and the Gosport navy-yard. The obvious object of this was to hem in that important naval station, so that by preventing the egress of the United States vessels there, or the ingress of any force that might be sent to their aid, the navy-yard with its ships and its stores should be at the mercy of the State of Virginia. The dispatch which announced the execution of the Governor's order exultingly declared: "Thus have we secured for Virginia three of the best ships of the navy," alluding to the Cumberland, Merrimac, and Pennsylvania, then among the vessels in the Gosport navy-yard at Norfolk. The inhabitants had, moreover, shown their hostile intentions by seizing the United States magazine, situated below the city, and containing four thousand kegs of powder.

April 19.

The navy-yard was in command of Commodore Charles S. Macaulay, a veteran naval officer. The establishment, one of the largest in the United States, contained not only stores of naval and military munitions of war and ships, but arsenals, foundries, workshops, and docks—a mass of public property which had cost the United States over fifty millions of dollars.

There were twelve vessels of war stationed at the yard, with an aggregate tonnage of about thirty-five thousand tons, and an armament of six hundred and fifty guns. These were the Pennsylvania, a sailing vessel, the largest line-of-battle-ship ever built in the United States. Her tonnage was three thousand three hundred and forty-one tons, and she was built to carry a hundred and twenty guns, to work which and the ship would have required a crew of a thousand men. Launched in 1837, at Philadelphia, she remained there as the wonder of all sight-seers, until she sailed to Norfolk, many years after, where she remained a useless hulk, too unwieldly and too expensive for service.

The Delaware, also a sailing line-of-battle-ship, was of two thousand six hundred and thirty-three tons, carrying an armament of eighty-four guns, and a crew of eight hundred men. She, however, was rotten, and had been long condemned as unfit for service.

The Columbus, a line-of-battle-ship, of two thousand four hundred and eighty tons burthen, and rated for eighty guns and eight hundred men, was also useless as a sailing vessel, but was thought capable of being converted into a steamer. The Raritan, a frigate of one thousand seven hundred and twenty-six tons, and fifty guns, was another vessel which had been condemned as unfit for service.

The Plymouth, a first-class sloop-of-war, of nine hundred and eighty-nine tons, and twenty-two guns, was undergoing repairs, and was a vessel of little value.

There was the New York, the keel of which was laid forty-five years ago, still on the stocks, and was hardly thought to be available. To these vessels of little value, may be added the old United States, built in 1797.

There were, however, the four sailing ships, the fine frigate Cumberland, the Germantown, the Columbia, and the brig Dolphin, which were for the most part in good condition and capable of the best service. In addition was the first-class steam frigate the Merrimac, of three thousand two hundred tons, and forty guns. Built at the Charlestown navy-yard, near Boston, in 1855, she had proved herself ever since to be one of the most powerful and valuable steamers in the United States navy.

Commodore Macaulay, supposed to be acting with the concurrence of the authorities at Washington, now determined to save what little he could of this valuable Government property, and destroy the remainder in order to prevent its falling into the possession of the Virginians. The commander of the insurgents at Norfolk, General Taliafero, had already demanded the surrender of the navy-yard, and after a conference with the Commodore, at noon, declared that he had his assurance that "none of the vessels should be removed, nor a shot fired, except in self-defence." However this may be, the Commodore doubtless was so persuaded of the hostile intent of the force assembled in Norfolk, as to believe that the most decided measures had become necessary to thwart it.

April 20.

In the evening the United States steamer the Pawnee arrived from Washington with two hundred volunteers and a hundred marines, in addition to her own crew, and after stopping at Fortress Monroe and taking on board a reinforcement of men, proceeded at once to co-operate with Commodore Macaulay, and aid him in whatever action he had determined upon.

April 20.

It was about seven o'clock, on a clear moonlight night, that the Pawnee, Captain Paulding, flying at her peak the commodore's pennant, moved from the dock of Fort Monroe cheered by the shouts of the garrison gathered on the parapet of the fortress, and steamed off for Norfolk. Notwithstanding the sunken vessels in the channel, the steamer passed without difficulty up Hampton Roads, past Norfolk, to Gosport navy-yard, where she arrived at half-past eight o'clock. The people of Norfolk and Portsmouth were greatly disturbed by her approach, as they believed she had come to aid in bombarding their towns. Overcome with fright, and unprepared for resistance, they made no show of opposition, but every inhabitant took care to keep at a discreet distance.

April 20.

Our people at the navy-yard, expecting the coming of the Pawnee, were on the alert, and as she came alongside the dock, the sailors on board the Cumberland and Pennsylvania, crowding into the shrouds and manning the yards, heartily cheered her. Cut off as they had been for so long a time from all communication with the town, insulted and threatened daily and hourly by the infuriated insurgents of Virginia, they saw, in the arrival of the Pawnee, a means of relief, if not an opportunity of vindicating the national dignity, and exulted greatly.

As soon as the steamer had made fast to the dock, Colonel Wardrop, the military commander, marched out his men and stationed them at the gates of the navy-yard, to prevent the entrance of the insurgents, should they make the attempt. The marines of the different vessels were now mustered and set busily to work. Some collected the records, papers, and archives from the offices and placed them on board the Pawnee, and some gathered whatever was valuable, important, and easily transferable from the various ships, and stored it in the Cumberland. After thus having secured what could be readily carried away, the marines were ordered to begin the work of destruction. Many thousand stands of arms, and a large quantity of pistols and revolvers, were broken by severing the barrels from the stocks, and thrown into the river. Thousands of shot and shell followed, and everything on the ships that might be of service to the insurgents met with the same fate. The cannon which were still left unspiked were now spiked and dismounted, and some fifteen hundred, of which several were Dahlgrens and columbiads, were thus rendered useless. The men persevered in this work of destruction from nine o'clock in the evening until midnight, when the moon sunk below the horizon. The barracks, situated within the yard, were then set on fire, in order that the marines might, by the glare of the flames, be enabled to continue their labors, which they renewed with increased spirit, as if enlivened by the crackling and blaze of the conflagration. The day, however, was approaching, and it was feared that the insurgents, gathering in force, might obstruct the escape of the Pawnee and the Cumberland. Gunpowder trains were now laid upon the decks of the doomed ships and the ship-houses. The crews of the various ships and all who belonged to the navy-yard, with the exception of two left behind to fire the trains, now hurried on board of the Pawnee and Cumberland. The former left the dock on Sunday morning, at four o'clock, on her return. As she cast off her moorings she sent up a signal rocket, and as it burst, the torch was applied, and in a moment the whole yard seemed to be wrapped in a common flame. Ships and ship-houses caught simultaneously, and the old New York, the keel of which had been laid forty-five years before, and was still on the stocks, burned, with its huge wooden cover, like tinder. The Pennsylvania, the Merrimac, the Germantown, the Plymouth, the Raritan, the Columbia, and the brig Dolphin caught at the same time, and were left in flames. Some of the guns were loaded, though not charged with shot, and when the fire reached them they exploded and added to the effect of this scene of destruction. "The Pennsylvania burned like a volcano for five hours and a half before her mainmast fell. I stood watching," says an eye-witness.[*] "the proud but perishing old leviathan, as this sign of her manhood was about to come down. At precisely half-past nine o'clock by my watch, the tall tree that stood in her centre tottered and fell, and crushed deep into her burning sides, while a stream of sparks flooded the sky."

April 21.

Two of the ships—the Delaware and Columbus—had been already scuttled and sunk on the day before the arrival

[*] New York Times, April 26.

of the Pawnee. The rest, with the exception of the old hulk, the United States, left untouched, had been fired. The only vessel thus which was saved was the fine man-of-war Cumberland, which, in tow of the Yankee tug-boat, followed the Pawnee down the river.

No sooner had the Pawnee steamed away, than the people of Norfolk and Portsmouth broke through the gates and filled the navy-yard. Soon after, a military company raised the flag of Virginia and took formal possession of the place in the name of that State. The insurgents, though grieved at the loss of the Cumberland, which they had hoped to secure, were surprised that the destruction, when once begun, had not been more thorough. A hopeful writer, whose sanguine speculations it is curious now to read, gave, at the time of the act, this reason for its incompleteness. "Long before," he says, "the workshops and armories, the foundries, and ship-wood left unharmed, can bring forth new weapons of offence, this war will be ended. And may be, as of yore, the stars and stripes will float over Gosport navy-yard. All that is now spared will then be so much gained!"

A Norfolk editor reported, after a cursory visit, that "the property destroyed embraced, besides the ship-houses and contents, the range of buildings on the north line of the yard (except the commodore's and commander's residences, which are unhurt), the old marine barracks and one or two work-shops, the immense lifting shears, the ships Pennsylvania, Merrimac, Raritan, Columbus, and brig Dolphin—burned to the water's edge ; the sloop Germantown, broken and sunk ; the Plymouth, scuttled and sunk even with her deck ; and a vast amount of small arms, chronometers, and valuable engines and machinery in the ordnance and other shops, broken up and rendered utterly useless."

The feeling at the North, on the destruction of this valuable public property, was one of national humiliation, not unmixed with anger at the Government for not having avoided it by timely precaution. Every one spoke of it as a great loss and a national disgrace. By proper foresight, steam-tugs could have been provided, it was believed, to tow every vessel away from the navy-yard in safety. Even when by delay it had become too late to make such means available, it was thought that a more resolute commander would have been able to keep the insurgents at Norfolk at bay. With a fleet of ships heavily armed at his command, it was urged that he might have turned his guns upon the towns of Norfolk and Portsmouth, and have successfully repelled every attack.

The insurgents, on the very day of the departure of the Pawnee, had begun to unspike the cannon and remove them below Norfolk to mount the sand batteries which they had raised in defence of their harbor and in defiance of the Federal authorities.

The Cumberland was towed from the navy-yard by the steam-tug Yankee, which followed in the wake of the Pawnee. The three vessels proceeded down the river until nine o'clock in the morning when they came to anchor at the point where the channel had been obstructed with sunken vessels. Boats were sent out to sound, with the view of discovering another passage. This, however, proving without avail, the fleet weighed anchor and forced its way directly through the obstructions. The Cumberland got entangled with one of the sunken vessels and carried it along with her, and for a time there seemed danger of her drifting on the shore, where the enemy had their batteries. Another steamer, the Keystone State, however, arriving from Washington, went to her aid, and, in conjunction with the tug Yankee, succeeded in freeing her from the wreck and towing her safely under the guns of Fort Monroe.

CHAPTER XVI.

Increased War Spirit of the North.—Unity of Sentiment.—Great Meetings.—Great Meeting at New York.—The Patriotic Enthusiasm of the Citizens.—The display of Union Colors and Symbols.—The immense Gathering at Union Square.—A dozen "Monster Meetings."—Officers and Orators.—The supposed effect of the New York Demonstration upon the Southern Rebellion.—No passing Effervescence of Popular Emotion.—Generous Largesses of Men and Money.—Rapid Military Organization.—March to the Capital.—Dangers of Washington.—Precautions for its Safety.—Disaffection of Maryland.—An anxious Proclamation.—The Agitation of Baltimore.—Continued Anxiety about Washington.—Rumored Approach of Jefferson Davis.—The effect at the North. Military Aspect of the Northern Cities.—March of the Sixth Massachusetts Regiment.—Triumphal Ovations on its route.—Arrival in Baltimore.—Anxieties about its reception.—The Mob of Baltimore.—The Cars Attacked.—Obstruction of the Track.—The March of the Massachusetts Men through the Streets of Baltimore.—The Attack on them by the Mob.—The First Shot.—The Soldiers return the Fire.—A continued Struggle.—The tragic Result.—The Massachusetts Men Fight their way and reach Washington.—The Philadelphia Men turned back.—The Killed and Wounded.—Indignation at the North.—A pathetic Dispatch from the Governor of Massachusetts.—An Official Statement.—Determined Hostility of Maryland.—The impotent Authorities of Maryland.—Vague Response of the Mayor of Baltimore to the Governor of Massachusetts.—A decided Rejoinder.—The Governor of Maryland perplexed.—A Message to the President.—Commissioners sent.—The President's Answer.—Continued Alarm of the Governor of Maryland.—A strange Proposition.—A dignified Rebuke from the Secretary of State.

1861. THE war spirit which had been aroused at the North by the fall of Fort Sumter continued to increase in intensity. Immense meetings were held in the free States, at which leading politicians of all parties vied in their expressions of devotion to the Union, and willingness to sustain it at all hazards to life and property. Stirring resolutions were passed and committees appointed to collect money and organize troops for the defence of the Union and vindication of an insulted government.

The most memorable of these great gatherings was that which was called by "leading citizens, without distinction of party," and assembled around Union Square, New York. On the day appointed, the business of the city was by common consent arrested. Commerce, trade, and wealth all deserted their usual resorts, and sought to **April 20.**

"The people of this State will, in a short time, have the opportunity afforded them, in a special election of members of Congress of the United States, to express their devotion to the Union, or their desire to have it broken up. T. H. HICKS.
"BALTIMORE, *April* 18, 1861."

Baltimore especially, never renowned for its respect for public order, was suspected of a disposition to combine with the insurgents of Virginia, in a violent disruption of the Union.

The Virginians openly in arms, were thus threatening the capital of the United States on one side; the disaffected of Maryland on the other, were scarcely restrained from violence, while secret conspirators, and a suspected population in Washington itself, aroused the fears of the whole Northern people for its safety and quickened them to effort in its defence. An additional stimulus came in the rumor that Jefferson Davis, the President of the Confederate States, was hurrying to the North, at the head of a considerable force which was rapidly increasing on the way. The militia from the nearest points pushed forward at once, and the volunteers of all the Northern States organized with great rapidity. The large cities assumed a warlike air. Men in uniform filled the streets; the public parks were turned into parade grounds; public buildings were appropriated and rude structures of wood raised for barracks; and troops were constantly marching in and out on their way to Washington.

The Sixth Regiment of Massachusetts militia was the first to march, and passed through a succession of triumphal ovations from town to town, greeted on their arrival with the cheers of immense multitudes of enthusiastic people, and urged forward on their patriotic mission with inspiriting shouts of encouragement. After having thus triumphantly passed through New York and Philadelphia, this noble regiment arrived in Baltimore, where a different reception awaited it. It was half-past ten o'clock in the morning when the Massachusetts men reached the city. Here horses were attached to the cars to convey them from one end to the other of the city to reach the dépôt of the Baltimore and Washington Railroad. The regiment filled eleven cars. Meeting with no opposition on their arrival, or indication even of an unfriendly spirit, the regiment started in the most cheerful mood. Fears, it is true, had been expressed by some anxious inhabitants of the danger of an attack, but these were now deemed only the alarms of the timid. The cars, however, had only proceeded the length of two blocks, or squares of houses, when it became clear that the anxiety of the Baltimoreans was not unfounded. A great mass of excited people so obstructed the streets that the horses could hardly push through it. This mob at the same time began with hootings, yells, and threatening cries, to try to provoke the Massachusetts men. The soldiers, however, neither showed themselves nor responded to the insults they were receiving. Stones, brickbats, and

April 17.

April 19.

bits of pavement torn from the sidewalks were now thrown by the infuriated mob against the cars, smashing the windows and bruising some of the troops. In spite, however, of this attack, nine of the cars moved steadily on, and deposited their inmates in safety at the dépôt. Two cars, with the rest of the Massachusetts men, were yet behind.

In the mean time, the Baltimore mob had succeeded in obstructing the track by means of large and heavy iron anchors, lying near by, which they dragged into the street and placed across the rails. The mob having accomplished this work, began to exult with loud shouts for "the South," "Jefferson Davis," "South Carolina," and "secession," to give vent to their hatred of the North by groans for "Lincoln" and "Massachusetts," and to attack the soldiers, from some of whom they succeeded in snatching the muskets.

It was now determined to abandon the cars, and march through the streets to the dépôt. The one hundred men, accordingly, who were all that were left behind of the regiment, alighted, and forming, prepared to push forward. Just as they began to move they were met by a large throng crowding down the street, with a secession flag borne at their head. As they approached they saluted the little band of Massachusetts men with a volley of stones, and cried out to them that they could not proceed through the city, and that if they attempted it, "not a white nigger of them would be left alive."

Nothing daunted, the soldiers continued their march, when the missiles from the mob began to fly thick and fast. The crowd increased at every step and became more violent each moment, hurling paving stones and brickbats at the soldiers continually. Two of them had been struck and knocked down by stones, when there came a shot from either pistol or gun. The captain in command of the Massachusetts men now ordered them to prime their guns, which had been hitherto loaded though not capped, and to protect themselves. The soldiers accordingly fired into the people, who, with renewed fury, returned the shot by an increased volley of missiles and the discharge of revolvers. The Mayor of Baltimore at last came forward, and occasionally putting himself at the head of the troops, made a show of protection, which proved, however, of little effect. The Massachusetts men were forced to fight their way through the streets to the dépôt, a mile distant. The route was a continued scene of struggle between the mob and the soldiers—the one hurling missiles of all kinds, and occasionally discharging revolvers and guns, and the other returning the attack with a regular musket fire from their ranks. Many, both soldiers and citizens, fell dead by the wayside, some of whom were borne away by their comrades, while others were carried into the nearest apothecary shops. Reaching the dépôt, the little band of soldiers, who had thus cut their way through the infuriated mob, once

more joined their fellows who awaited them, and the whole regiment prepared to start for Washington. The mob, however, had followed, and still beset them.

"The scene while the troops were changing cars," wrote an eye-witness, "was indescribably fearful. Taunts, clothed in the most fearful language, were hurled at them by the panting crowd, who, almost breathless with running, passed up to the car windows, presenting knives and revolvers, and cursed up into the faces of the soldiers. The police were thrown in between the cars, and forming a barrier, the troops changed cars, many of them cocking their muskets as they stepped on the platform.

"After embarking, the assemblage expected to see the train move off, but its departure was evidently delayed in the vain hope that the crowd would disperse; but no, it swelled; and the troops expressed to the officers of the road their determination to go at once, or they would leave the cars and make their way to Washington.

"While the delay was increasing the excitement, a wild cry was raised on the platform, and a dense crowd ran down the platform, and along the railroad toward the Spring Gardens, until the track for a mile was black with an excited, rushing mass. The crowd, as it went, placed obstructions of every description on the track. Great logs and telegraph poles, requiring a dozen or more men to move them, were laid across the rails, and stones rolled from the embankment.

"A body of police followed after the crowd, both in a full run, and removed the obstructions as fast as they were placed on the track. Various attempts were made to tear up the track with logs of wood and pieces of timber, and there was a great outcry for pickaxes and handspikes, but only one or two could be found. The police interfered on every occasion, but the crowd growing larger and more excited, would dash off at a break-neck run for another position farther on, until the county line was reached. The police followed, running, until forced to stop from fatigue. At this point many of the throng gave it up from exhaustion; but a crowd, longer-winded, dashed on for nearly a mile farther, now and then pausing to attempt to force the rails, or place some obstruction upon them. They could be distinctly seen for a mile along the track, where it makes a bend at the Washington road bridge. When the train went out, the mass of people had almost returned to the depot."

In the same railroad train by which the Massachusetts regiment had come from Philadelphia, there were some Pennsylvania troops. These formed one half of the Washington Brigade, and consisted of six companies of the First Regiment, under the command of Lieutenant-Colonel Berry, and four companies of the Second Regiment, under Lieutenant-Colonel Schoenleber and Major Gullman. Being, however, unarmed, they did not venture an attempt to force their way, and remained in the cars at the depot where they had at first arrived.

They, too, were assailed by the insulting cries of the mob, and some of them were bruised severely by missiles hurled against the cars, which broke the windows and penetrated inside. After remaining for two hours thus exposed, they were finally protected by the police of Baltimore, but were obliged to retrace their way back to the North.

The total number of killed and wounded, in the street conflict between the Massachusetts regiment and Baltimore mob, amounted to twenty-two. Of these, nine citizens and two soldiers were killed, and three citizens and eight soldiers wounded. This tragic event excited great indignation throughout the North, and especially in Massachusetts, where the victims of the Baltimore riot were considered as martyrs who had been sacrificed in a holy cause. The Governor of the State expressed his reverence for their memory in this patriotic dispatch to the Mayor of Baltimore:

"I pray you cause the bodies of our Massachusetts soldiers, dead in battle, to be immediately laid out, preserved in ice, and tenderly sent forward by express to me. All expenses will be paid by this Commonwealth.

"JOHN A. ANDREW,
"Governor of Massachusetts."

The occurrence,* however, presented a graver aspect than it showed merely in its sentimental bearings. The com-

without uniforms or arms, they intending to get them here. After we arrived, the cars were taken, two at a time, and drawn to the dépôt, at the lower part of the city, a mob assaulting them all the way. The Lowell Mechanic Phalanx car was the ninth, and we waited till after the rest had left for our turn, till two men came to me and informed me that I had better take my command and march to the other dépôt, as the mob had taken up the track to prevent the passage of the cars. I immediately informed Captain Pickering, of the Lawrence Light Infantry, and we filed out of the cars in regular order. Captain Hart's company, of Lowell, and Captain Dike's, of Stoneham, did the same, and formed in a line on the sidewalk. The captains consulted together, and decided that the command should devolve upon me. I immediately took my position at the right, wheeled into column of sections, and requested them to march in close order. Before we had started, the mob was upon us, with a secession flag attached to a pole, and told us we never could march through that city. They would kill every white nigger of us before we could reach the other dépôt. I paid no attention to them, but after I had wheeled the battalion, gave the order to march.

"As soon as the order was given, the brickbats began to fly into our ranks from the mob. I called a policeman, and requested him to lead the way to the other dépôt. He did so. After we had marched about a hundred yards, we came to a bridge. The rebels had torn up most of the planks. We had to play 'Scotch hop' to get over it. As soon as we had crossed the bridge they commenced to fire upon us from the streets and houses. We were loaded, but not capped. I ordered the men to cap their rifles and protect themselves, and then we returned their fire, and told a great many of them away. I saw four fall on the sidewalk at one time. They followed us up, and we fought our way to the other dépôt, about one mile. They kept at us till the cars started. Quite a number of the rascals were shot after we entered the cars. We went very slowly, for we expected the rails were torn up along the road.

"I do not know how much damage we did. Report says about forty were killed, but I think that is exaggerated. Still, it may be so. There is any quantity of them wounded. Quite a number of horses were killed. The mayor of the city met us almost half way. He said that there would be no more trouble, and that we could get through, and kept with me for about a hundred yards; but the stones and balls whistled too near his head, and he left, took a gun from one of my company, fired, and brought his man down. That was the last I saw of him. We fought our way to the cars, and joined Colonel Jones and the seven companies that left us at the other end of the city; and now we are here, every man of

---

* The following report by Captain Follansbee, who commanded the Massachusetts men who fought their way through Baltimore, though not in every respect accurate, is interesting:

"We arrived in Baltimore about ten o'clock A. M. The cars are drawn through the city by horses. There were about thirty cars in our train, there being, in addition to Colonel Jones' command, 1,200 troops from Philadelphia,

President Lincoln's answer was tenderly considerate of the nervous agitation of the Maryland officials, and indicated as well by its complacent concessions how at that early period the Government was embarrassed by the manœuvres of its enemies.

"WASHINGTON, *April* 20, 1861.
"GOVERNOR HICKS AND MAYOR BROWN:

"GENTLEMEN: Your letter, by Messrs. Bond, Dobbin, and Brune, is received. I tender you both my sincere thanks for your efforts to keep the peace in the trying situation in which you are placed. For the future, troops *must* be brought here, but I make no point of bringing them *through* Baltimore.

"Without any military knowledge myself, of course I must leave details to General Scott. He hastily said this morning, in the presence of these gentlemen, 'March them *around* Baltimore, and not through it.'

"I sincerely hope the General, on fuller reflection, will consider this practicable and proper, and that you will not object to it.

"By this a collision of the people of Baltimore with the troops will be avoided, unless they go out of their way to seek it. I hope you will exert your influence to prevent this.

"Now and ever I shall do all in my power for peace, consistently with the maintenance of the Government.

"Your obedient servant,
"ABRAHAM LINCOLN."

The Governor's agitation was not calmed, however, by the good-natured sympathy of President Lincoln and his readiness of concession. On the contrary, each day the disaffected people of Maryland became more threatening and their Governor more alarmed. He now begged that no more troops should be sent not only through Baltimore, but through Maryland, while he proposed, with a strange disregard of the dignity of the Government to which he claimed to be loyal, that the English ambassador at Washington should be invited to mediate between the United States and its rebellious citizens!

"EXECUTIVE CHAMBER, ANNAPOLIS,
April 22, 1861.
"TO HIS EXCELLENCY A. LINCOLN, PRESIDENT OF THE UNITED STATES:

"SIR: I feel it my duty, most respectfully, to advise you that no more troops be ordered or allowed to pass through Maryland, and that the troops now off Annapolis be sent elsewhere, and I most respectfully urge that a truce be offered by you, so that the effusion of blood may be prevented. I respectfully suggest that Lord Lyons be requested to act as mediator between the contending parties of our country.

"I have the honor to be, very respectfully, your obedient servant,
"THOS. H. HICKS."

The President, on receiving this remarkable missive, no longer trusted to his own amiable and informal mode of dealing with his adversaries, but submitted the Governor's dispatch to the secretary of state, to be dealt with according to that distinguished statesman's more official and dignified manner:

NEW NATIONAL WORK ON THE LATE REBELLION.

Now Publishing, in Parts at 50 cents, and Divisions at $1.

THE GREAT CIVIL WAR:

A HISTORY OF

THE LATE REBELLION;

Being a complete Narrative of the Events connected with the Origin, Progress, and Conclusion of the War, with Biographical Sketches of Leading Statesmen and Distinguished Military and Naval Commanders, etc., etc.

By ROBERT TOMES, M.D.

Continued from the beginning of the year 1864 to the end of the War.

By BENJ. G. SMITH, Esq.

Illustrated by numerous highly finished Steel Engravings, Colored Maps, Plans, etc., from Drawings by F. O. C. Darley and other eminent Artists.

The four years' war, now happily ended—so remarkable for its sudden outbreak, its unexpected duration, and its entire termination—not only absorbed universal attention at home, but had, during its continuance, a paramount interest for the nations of Europe, and was the subject of constant comment and prophecy on the part of both the friends and enemies of national self-government. It not only displayed the astonishing resources of the country, and exhibited, even while the struggle continued, in the vast armies raised and the persistent spirit of the people, a capacity for war that entitles the United States to the first rank among military nations, but also demonstrated the enduring character of the government and institutions, which have proved themselves able to withstand even the fearful shocks of a gigantic civil war.

A history of this great war will be a necessity to every loyal American. To be without a knowledge of the causes and events of the great struggle for the preservation of the Union would be as inexcusable as to be ignorant of the events which led to its formation.

The present work will be a complete history of the war and of its immediate causes, from the election of Mr. Lincoln and the commencement of actual hostilities by the attack on Fort Sumter, to the evacuation of Richmond and the surrender of the armies of Lee, Johnston, and Kirby Smith. It will contain detailed accounts of the great battles, sieges, marches, and naval operations, a record of political events, remarks on foreign relations, statistical facts with regard to the resources of both the Northern and Southern States, descriptions of fortresses and battle-fields, and a large number of biographical sketches of distinguished commanders and statesmen, to which will be appended a copious and elaborate Index.

Not the least attractive feature of the work will be the large number of beautiful and costly steel engravings, comprising portraits of statesmen and military and naval commanders, Northern and Southern, who have become famous in the course of the war.

Among the illustrations are also splendid bird's-eye views of Fortress Monroe and vicinity, Charleston, Richmond, and New Orleans; representations of battle-scenes, views of forts and battle-fields, sea views, and a number of carefully prepared colored maps and plans, highly useful in making clear the movements and positions of armies.

CONDITIONS OF PUBLICATION.

The work will be printed in a clear, bold type, on superfine, calendered paper, and issued in Parts at Fifty Cents, and Divisions at $1 each.

The illustrations will comprise fifty-four portraits and thirty-six battle-scenes, plans, maps, bird's-eye views, etc.

A Part will be published every two weeks and a Division every month until completed, the whole not to exceed forty-five Parts, at Fifty Cents each.

No subscriber's name received for less than the whole work; and each Part or Division will be payable on delivery, the carrier not being allowed to give credit or receive payment in advance.

VIRTUE & YORSTON, 12 DEY STREET, & 544 BROADWAY, NEW YORK.
And Sold by their Agents in all the Principal Cities of the United States and Canadas.

New National Work on the Late Rebellion.

To be Completed in Forty-five Parts, at Fifty Cents each.

"DEPARTMENT OF STATE,
April 22, 1861.

"HIS EXCELLENCY THOS. H. HICKS, GOVERNOR OF MARYLAND:

"SIR: I have had the honor to receive your communication of this morning, in which you inform me that you have felt it to be your duty to advise the President of the United States to order elsewhere the troops then off Annapolis, and also that no more may be sent through Maryland; and that you have further suggested that Lord Lyons be requested to act as mediator between the contending parties in our country, to prevent the effusion of blood.

"The President directs me to acknowledge the receipt of that communication, and to assure you that he has weighed the counsels which it contains with the respect which he habitually cherishes for the Chief Magistrates of the several States, and especially for yourself. He regrets, as deeply as any magistrate or citizen of the country can, that demonstrations against the safety of the United States, with very extensive preparations for the effusion of blood, have made it his duty to call out the force to which you allude.

"The force now sought to be brought through Maryland is intended for nothing but the defence of this capital. The President has necessarily confided the choice of the national highway, which that force shall take in coming to this city, to the Lieutenant-General commanding the army of the United States, who, like his only predecessor, is not less distinguished for his humanity than for his loyalty, patriotism, and distinguished public service.

"The President instructs me to add, that the national highway thus selected by the Lieutenant-General has been chosen by him, upon consultation with prominent magistrates and citizens of Maryland, as the one which, while a route is absolutely necessary, is furthest removed from the populous cities of the State, and with the expectation that it would, therefore, be the least objectionable one.

"The President cannot but remember that there has been a time in the history of our country when a General of the American Union, with forces designed for the defence of its capital, was not unwelcome anywhere in the State of Maryland, and certainly not at Annapolis, then, as now, the capital of that patriotic State, and then, also, one of the capitals of the Union.

"If eighty years could have obliterated all the other noble sentiments of that age in Maryland, the President would be hopeful, nevertheless, that there is one that would forever remain there and everywhere. That sentiment is, that no domestic contention whatever that may arise among the parties of this Republic ought in any case to be referred to any foreign arbitrament, least of all to the arbitrament of a European monarchy.

"I have the honor to be, with distinguished consideration, your Excellency's most obedient servant,

"WILLIAM H. SEWARD."

CHAPTER XVII.

Indignation against Maryland in the North.—To Washington through Baltimore.—An energetic Citizen of New York addresses the President.—An Editorial Re-echo.—Increased Martial Ardor.—The Seventh Regiment.—Its composition.—Anticipatory Heroes.—Their Departure from New York. Enthusiasm of the People. March of the Seventh.—Its Glorification.—An Account by an Historiographer from the Ranks.—The Eighth Massachusetts.—Obstructions to their March to the Capitol.—General Butler in command.—His Promptitude and Energy.—Seizure of the Ferry-boat Maryland.—Arrival at Annapolis.—Rescue of "Old Ironsides."—The difficulty of the Achievement.—Honor to Butler.—His Biography.—Birth and Descent.—Education.—Professional Career.—Prominence as a Lawyer.—His Legal Characteristics.—First Appearance in Public Life.—A Delegate to the Democratic Convention at Charleston.—A Breckenridge Elector.—A Candidate for Governor of Massachusetts.—Suspiciously regarded.—A proof of Loyalty.—Welcomed as a Defender of the Union.—Appointed to Command by his Political Opponent.—His Energy and Success. National Gratitude.—Personal Description and Character of Butler.—His Coolness in Danger Illustrated.—Other proofs in the course of this History.

THE attack of the mob of Baltimore upon the Massachusetts troops, and the apparent determination of the secessionists of Maryland, by obstructing the railroads, tearing up the tracks, and burning the bridges, to cut off all communication through their State between Washington and the North, greatly angered the Northern people. The universal cry was now, "To Washington *through* Baltimore!" and the determination was expressed that the way must be cleared at all hazards. An energetic citizen* of New York addressed the President in an emphatic letter, in which he said: "It is demanded of Government that they at once take measures to open and establish those lines of communication, and that they protect and preserve them from any further interruption. Unless this is done, the people will be compelled to take it into their own hands, let the consequences be what it may and let them fall where they will." The press echoed these resolute sentiments of a private citizen with emphatic sympathy, and declared: "If any man of position as a military leader or as a strong, resolute commander, would offer to lead a force through Baltimore, with or without orders, he could have fifty thousand followers as soon as they could rush to his standard." To this, an editor added, alluding to the energetic private citizen already referred to, that he "could raise in three days volunteers enough to clear the track, even if it should leave Baltimore an ash-heap." The doom of that city was foreshadowed as a second Sodom which must be destroyed, "if it is necessary first to destroy the Government at Washington that now defends it."

In the mean time, the martial ardor of the country was daily intensifying. The choice military corps of the large cities hurried forward to the endangered capital. The Seventh Militia Reg-

1861.

* Mr. George Law.

ment of the city was the first to move of the large force rapidly mustering everywhere in New York. This corps, composed of young men belonging more or less to the wealthier classes, and long admired for the precision of their drill and the elegance of their *tenue*, was the pet regiment of the city. When, therefore, it was announced that these youthful soldiers, who had been hitherto the mere ornaments of a gala parade, had determined to come forward to assume the serious work of fighting for their country, the population of the city applauded their spirited resolution, and, confident of their good conduct, anticipated its rewards by bestowing upon them the honors of an accomplished heroism. On the day of their departure for Washington the city was unusually excited. "Never before," said a daily paper, "were the people moved to such a pitch of enthusiastic patriotism. There have been gala days, and funeral pageants, and military shows, and complimentary receptions, and triumphal processions that filled the streets with crowds of curious, wondering, sympathetic people, but never has there been developed such a universal, heartfelt, deep-rooted, genuine enthusiasm. The American colors were prominent everywhere—on housetops, on flagstaffs, on horses attached to all kinds of vehicles, on ropes stretched across the streets, on the masts of shipping in the harbor, on breastpins, on the lappets of coats, on the fronts of men's hats; on all sides the glorious old red, white, and blue waved in the joyous breeze and every eye was dazzled with bright colors. The awful solemnity of civil war came pressing home to our people who had sons, and brothers, and fathers just departing, perhaps never to return. The news of the difficulties in Baltimore, the struggle of the troops with the rabble, the reported death of many, the rumors of an attack on the capital, the tearing up of railroad tracks, and all the attendant horrors of internecine warfare, struck terror into many a stout heart, while the tears of kind-hearted women flowed copiously as a rain-storm."

April 19.

"It was many Fourths-of-July rolled into one," was the comprehensive climax arrived at by a writer* who had in vain attempted an adequate description of the scene.

The story of the journey of the Seventh to Philadelphia; its prudent dodging of the rioters at Baltimore, by passing down the Delaware and up the Chesapeake; its arrival and encampment at Annapolis, and its famous march to Washington were told again and again in daily newspapers, in pictorial weeklies, and in grave monthlies.

The regiment did not want for historiographers, as in its gallant ranks there were those who were not unknown to fame for their skill in the literary art. One† who recorded the eventful progress of the Seventh to Washington, gave an animating account, from which the following extracts are made:

"Swift through New Jersey. * * *

---

* New York *Times*, April 20.
† Captain Fitz-James O'Brien, in the New York *Times*.

All along the track shouting crowds, hoarse and valorous, sent to us, as we passed, their hopes and wishes. When we stopped at the different stations, rough hands came in through the windows, apparently unconnected with any one in particular until you shook them, and then the subtle magnetic thrill told that there were bold hearts beating at the end. This continued until night closed, and, indeed, until after midnight.

"Within the cars the sight was strange. A thousand young men, the flower of the North, in whose welfare a million of friends and relatives were interested, were rushing along to conjectured hostilities with the same smiling faces that they would wear going to a 'German' party in Fifth Avenue. It was more like a festivity than a march. Those fine old songs, the chorusses of which were familiar to all, were sung with sweet voice. * * *

"Our arrival at Philadelphia took place at four o'clock. We slept in the cars, awaiting orders from our Colonel, but, at daylight, hunger—and it may be thirst—becoming imperious, we sallied out and roamed about that cheerless neighborhood that surrounds the dépôt. * * * Finding that we were likely to remain for some time in the city—although under the impression that we were to go straight through to Baltimore—we wandered away from the desert of the dépôt and descended on civilized quarters. The superintendent of the Deaf and Dumb Asylum was a man for the emergency. He provided a handsome breakfast for all such members of the Seventh as chose to partake of it, and we commanded beefsteak on our fingers, and ordered tea by sign-manual. Great numbers of our regiment, being luxurious dogs, went down to the Continental and Girard hotels, where they campaigned on marble floors, and bivouacked on velvet couches; they are such delicate fellows, the Seventh Regiment! * *

"We, of course, were entirely ignorant of our route, or how we were going. The general feeling of the regiment was in favor of pushing our way *coute qui coute* straight through Baltimore. Rumors came along that the city was in arms. The Massachusetts troops had to fight their way through, killing eighteen, and losing two men. This seemed only to stimulate our boys, and the universal word was Baltimore! But, as it turned out afterward, we were under a wise direction, and the policy of our Colonel, to whom we perhaps are altogether indebted for bringing us safe here, was, I presume, to avoid all unnecessary collision, and bring his regiment intact into Washington. The rails were reported to have been torn up for forty miles about Baltimore, and as we were summoned for the defence of the capital, it follows, according to reason, that if we could get there without loss we would better fulfil our duty. As it happened afterward, we had to run through more peril than Baltimore could have offered.

"There seemed but little enthusiasm in Philadelphia. * * I understand that the people were out in large numbers to see us enter, but our delay disappointed them, and they went home. * * We came and went without a reception or demonstration.

"There was one peculiar difference that I noticed existing between the Massachusetts regiments that we met in Philadelphia and our men. The Massachusetts men—to whom all honor be given for the splendid manner in which they afterward acted in a most trying situation—presented a singular moral contrast to the members of the Seventh. They were earnest, grim, determined. Badly equipped, haggard, unshorn, they yet had a manhood in their look that hardships could not kill. They were evidently thinking all the time of the contest into which they were about to enter. Their grey, eager eyes seemed to be looking for the heights of Virginia. With us it was somewhat different. Our men were gay and careless, confident of being at any moment capable of performing, and more than performing, their duty. They looked battle in the face with a smile, and were ready to hob-nob with an enemy and kill him afterward. The one was courage in the rough; the other was courage burnished. The steel was the same in both, but the last was a little more polished.

"On April 20, at 4.20 P.M., we left the Philadelphia dock, on board the steamer Boston. The regiment was in entire ignorance of its destination. Some said we were going back to New York, at which suggestion there was a howl of indignation. Others presumed that we were going to steam up the Potomac—a course which was not much approved of, inasmuch that we were cooped up in a kind of river steamer that a shot from the fort at Alexandria might sink at any moment. * * *

"The first evening, April 20, on board the Boston, passed delightfully. We were all in first-rate spirits, and the calm, sweet evenings that stole on us as we approached the South, diffused a soft and gentle influence over us. The scene on board the ship was exceedingly picturesque. Fellows fumbling in haversacks for rations, or extracting sandwiches from reluctant canteens; guards pacing up and down with drawn bayonets; knapsacks piled in corners; bristling heaps of muskets, with sharp, shining teeth, crowded into every available nook; picturesque groups of men lolling on deck, pipe or cigar in mouth, indulged in the *dolce far niente*, as if they were on the blue shores of Capri rather than on their way to battle; unbuttoned jackets, crossed legs, heads leaning on knapsacks, blue uniforms everywhere, with here and there a glint of officers' red enlivening the foreground —all formed a scene that such painters as the English Warren would have revelled in.

"I regret to say that all was not rose-colored. The steamer that the Colonel chartered had to get ready at three or four hours' notice, he having changed his plans, in consequence of the tearing up of the rails around Baltimore. The result was that she was imperfectly provisioned. As the appetites of the men began to develop the resources of the vessel began to appear. In the first place, she was far too small to accommodate a thousand men, and we were obliged to sleep in all sorts of impossible attitudes. There is an ingenious device known to carpenters as 'dove-tailing,' and we were so thick that we had positively to dove-tail, only that there was very little of the dove about it; for when perambulating soldiers stepped on the faces and stomachs of the sleepers, as they lay on deck, the greeting that they received had but little flavor of the olive-branch.

"Notwithstanding that we found very soon that the commissariat was in a bad way, the men were as jolly as sandboys. I never saw a more good-humored set of men in my life. Fellows who would at Delmonico's have sent back a *turban de volaille aux truffes* because the truffles were tough, here cheerfully took their places in file between decks, tin plates and tin cups in hand, in order to get an insufficient piece of beef and a vision of coffee. But it was all merrily done. The scant fare was seasoned with hilarity; and here I say to those people in New York who have sneered at the Seventh Regiment as being dandies, and guilty of the unpardonable crimes of cleanliness and kid gloves, that they would cease to scoff and remain to bless had they beheld the square, honest, genial way in which these military Brummells roughed it. Farther on you will see what they did in the way of endurance and activity.

"April 21st was Sunday. A glorious cloudless day. We had steamed all night, and about ten o'clock were in the vicinity of Chesapeake Bay. At eleven o'clock A.M. we had service read by our chaplain, and at one P.M. we were seven miles from the coast. The day was calm and delicious. In spite of our troubles with regard to food—troubles, be it understood, entirely unavoidable—we drank in with delight the serenity of the scene. A hazy tent of blue hung over our heads. On one side the dim thread of shore hemmed in the sea. Flights of loons and ducks skimmed along the ocean, rising lazily, and spattering the waves with their wings as they flew against the wind, until they rose into air, and, wheeling, swept into calmer feeding grounds. Now and then the calm of the hour was broken with the heavy tramp of men and the metallic voice of the corporal of the guard relieving his comrades. At five o'clock P.M. we passed a light-ship and hailed her, our object being to discover whether any United States vessels were in the neighborhood waiting to convoy us up the Potomac River. We had heard that the forts at Alexandria were ready to open upon us if we attempted to pass up, and our steamer was of such a build that, had a shell or shot struck it, we would have been burned or drowned. It therefore behooved us to be cautious. The answers we got from the light-ship and other vessels that we hailed in this spot were unsatisfactory, and although the feelings of the men were unanimous in wishing to force the Potomac, wiser counsels, as it proved, were behind us.

and we kept on. * * * All this time we were entirely ignorant of where we were going. The officers kept all secret, and our conjectures drifted like a drifting boat. On the morning of the 22d we were in sight of Annapolis, off which the Constitution was lying, and there found the Eighth Regiment of Massachusetts volunteers, on board the Maryland. They were aground, owing, it is supposed, to the treachery of the captain, whom they put in irons, and wanted to hang. I regret to say that they did not do it. During the greater portion of that forenoon we were occupied in trying to get the Maryland off the sand-bar on which she was grounded. From our decks we could see the men in file trying to rock her, so as to facilitate our tugging. These men were without water and without food, were well conducted and uncomplaining, and behaved, in all respects, like heroes. They were under the command of Colonel Butler. * * *

"On the afternoon of the 22d we landed at the Annapolis dock, after having spent hours in trying to relieve the Maryland. For the first time in his life your correspondent was put to work to roll flour barrels. He was intrusted with the honorable and onerous duty of transporting stores from the steamer to the dock. Later still he descended to the position of mess servant, when, in company with gentlemen well-known in Broadway for immaculate kids, he had the honor of attending on his company with buckets of cooked meat and crackers, the only difference between him and Co. and the ordinary waiter being, that the former were civil.

"After this I had the pleasing duty of performing three hours of guard duty on the dock with a view to protect the baggage and stores. It was monotonous —being my first guard—but not unpleasant. The moon rose calm and white. A long dock next to the one on which I was stationed stretched away into the bay, resting on its numerous piles, until it looked in the clear moonlight like a centipede. All was still and calm, until at certain periods the guard challenged persons attempting to pass. There was a holy influence in the hour, and somehow the hot fever of anxiety that had been over us for days, seemed to pass away under the touch of the magnetic fingers of the night.

"We were quartered in the buildings belonging to the Naval School at Annapolis. I had a bunking-place in what is there called a fort, which is a rickety structure that a lucifer match would set on fire, but furnished with imposing guns. I suppose it was merely built to practice the cadets, because as a defence it is worthless. The same evening, boats were sent off from the yard, and toward nightfall the Massachusetts men landed, fagged, hungry, thirsty, but indomitable. At an early hour there was a universal snore through the Naval School of Annapolis.

"The two days that we remained at Annapolis were welcome. We had been without a fair night's sleep since we left New York, and even the hard quarters we had there were luxury compared to the dirty decks of the Boston. Besides, there were natural attractions. The grounds are very prettily laid out, and in the course of my experience I never saw a handsomer or better bred set of young men than the cadets; and they have proved loyal, only twenty having left the school owing to political conviction. The remainder are sound Union fellows, eager to prove their devotion to the flag. After spending a delightful time in the Navy School, resting and amusing ourselves, our repose was disturbed, at 9 P. M., April 23d, by rockets being thrown up in the bay. The men were scattered all over the grounds; some in bed, others walking or smoking, all more or less undressed. The rockets being of a suspicious character, it was conjectured that a Southern fleet was outside, and our drummer beat the roll-call to arms. From the stroke of the drum until the time that every man, fully equipped and in fighting order, was in the ranks, was exactly, by watch, *seven minutes.* It is needless to say anything about such celerity—it speaks for itself. The alarm, however, proved to be false, the vessels in the offing proving to be laden with the Seventy-first and other New York regiments; so that, after an unpremeditated trial of our readiness for action, we were permitted to retire to our virtuous couches, which means, permit me to say, a blanket on the floor, with a military overcoat over you, and a nasal concert all around you that, in noise and number, outvies Musard's celebrated *concerts monstres.*

"On the morning of the 24th of April we started on what afterward proved to be one of the hardest marches on record. The secessionists of Annapolis and the surrounding district had threatened to cut us off in our march, and even went so far as to say that they would attack our quarters. This, of course, was the drunken Southern ebullition. A civilian told me that he met in the streets of Annapolis two cavalry soldiers who came to cut our throats without delay, but as each brave warrior was endeavoring to hold the other up, my friend did not apprehend much danger.

"A curious revulsion of feeling took place at Annapolis, and indeed all through Maryland, after our arrival.

"The admirable good conduct which characterizes the regiment, the open liberality which it displays in all pecuniary transactions, and the courteous demeanor which it exhibits to all classes, took the narrow-minded population of this excessively wretched town by surprise. They were prepared for pillage. They thought we were going to sack the place. They found, instead, that we were prepared and willing to pay liberal prices for everything, and that even patriotic presentations were steadily refused. While we were in the Navy School, of course all sorts of rumors as to our operations were floating about. It surprised me that no one suggested that we were to go off in a balloon; however, all surmises were put to an end by our receiving orders, the evening of the 23d, to assemble in marching order next morning. The dawn saw us up. Knapsacks, with our blankets and overcoats strapped on them, were piled on the green. A brief and insufficient breakfast was taken, our canteens filled with vinegar and water, cartridges distributed to each man, and after mustering and loading, we started on our first march through a hostile country.

"General Scott has stated, as I have been informed, that the march that we performed from Annapolis to the Junction is one of the most remarkable on record. I know that I felt it the most fatiguing, and some of our officers have told me that it was the most perilous. We marched the first eight miles under a burning sun, in heavy marching order, in less than three hours; and it is well-known that, placing all elementary considerations out of the way, marching on a railroad track is the most harassing. We started at about eight o'clock A. M., and for the first time saw the town of Annapolis, which, without any disrespect to that place, I may say, looked very much as if some celestial schoolboy, with a box of toys under his arm, had dropped a few houses and men as he was going home from school, and that the accidental settlement was called Annapolis. Through the town we marched, the people unsympathizing, but afraid. They saw the Seventh for the first time, and for the first time they realized the men that they had threatened.

"The tracks had been torn up between Annapolis and the Junction, and here it was that the wonderful qualities of the Massachusetts Eighth Regiment came out. The locomotives had been taken to pieces by the inhabitants, in order to prevent our travel. In steps a Massachusetts volunteer, looks at the piece-meal engine, takes up a flange, and says coolly, 'I made this engine, and I can put it together again.' Engineers were wanted when the engine was ready. Nineteen stepped out of the ranks. The rails were torn up. Practical railroad makers out of the regiment laid them again, and all this, mind you, without care or food. These brave boys, I say, were starving while they were doing this good work. What their Colonel was doing I can't say. As we marched along the track that they had laid, they greeted us with ranks of smiling but hungry faces. One boy told me, with a laugh on his young lips, that he had not eaten anything for thirty hours. There was not, thank God, a haversack in our regiment that was not emptied into the hands of these ill-treated heroes, nor a flask that was not at their disposal.

"Our march lay through an arid, sandy, tobacco-growing country. The sun poured on our heads like hot lava. The Sixth and Second companies were sent on for skirmishing duty, under the command of Captains Clarke and Nevers, the latter commanding as senior officer. A car, on which was placed a howitzer, loaded with grape and canister, headed the column, manned by the engineer and artillery corps, commanded by Lieutenant Bunting. This was the rallying point of the skirmishing party, on which, in case of difficulty, they could fall back. In the centre of the column came the cars laden with medical stores, and bearing our sick and wounded, while the extreme rear was brought up with a second howitzer, loaded also with grape and canister. The engineer corps, of course, had to do the forwarding work. New York dandies, sir!—but they built bridges, laid rails, and headed the regiment through that terrible march. After marching about eight miles, during which time several men caved in from exhaustion, and one young gentleman was sun-struck and sent back to New York, we halted, and instantly, with the divine instinct which characterizes the hungry soldier, proceeded to forage. The worst of it was, there was no foraging to be done. The only house within reach was inhabited by a lethargic person, who, like most Southern men, had no idea of gaining money by labor. We offered him extravagant prices to get us fresh water, and it was with the utmost reluctance we could get him to obtain us a few pailfuls. Over the mantle-piece of his miserable shanty I saw—a curious coincidence—the portrait of Colonel Duryea, of our regiment.

"After a brief rest of about an hour, we again commenced our march; a march which lasted until the next morning—a march than which, in history, nothing but those marches in which defeated troops have fled from the enemy, can equal. Our Colonel, it seems, determined to march by railroad, in preference to the common road, inasmuch as he had obtained such secret information as led him to suppose that we were waited for on the latter route. Events justified his judgment. There were cavalry troops posted in defiles to cut us off. They could not have done it, of course, but they could have harassed us severely. As we went along the railroad we threw out skirmishing parties from the Second and Sixth companies, to keep the road clear. I know not if I can describe that night's march. I have dim recollections of deep cuts through which we passed, gloomy and treacherous-looking, with the moon shining full on our muskets, while the banks were wrapped in shade, and each moment expecting to see the flash and hear the crack of the rifle of the Southern guerrilla. The tree frogs and lizards made a mournful music as we passed. The soil on which we traveled was soft and heavy. The sleepers lying at intervals across the track made the march terribly fatiguing. On all sides dark, lonely pine woods stretched away, and high over the hooting of owls or the plaintive petition of the whip-poor-will rose the bass commands of Halt! Forward! March!—and when we came to any ticklish spot, the word would run from the head of the column along the line, 'Holes,' 'Bridge, pass it along,' etc.

"As the night wore on, the monotony of the march became oppressive. Owing to our having to explore every inch of the way, we did not make more than a mile, or a mile and a half an hour. We ran out of stimulants, and almost out of water. Most of us had not slept for four nights, and as the night advanced, our march was almost a stagger. This was not so much fatigue as want of excitement. Our fellows were spoiling for a fight, and when a dropping shot was heard in the distance, it was wonderful to see how the languid legs straightened and the column braced itself for action. If we had had even the smallest kind of a skirmish, the men would have been able to walk to Washington. As it was, we went sleepily on. I myself fell asleep walking in the ranks. Numbers, I find, followed my example; but never before was there shown such indomitable pluck and perseverance as the Seventh showed in that march of twenty miles. The country that we passed through seemed to have been entirely deserted. The inhabitants, who were going to kill us when they thought we daren't come through, now vamosed their respective ranches, and we saw them not. Houses were empty. The population retired into the interior, burying their money and carrying their families along with them. They, it seems, were under the impression that we came to ravage and pillage, and they fled as the Gauls must have fled when Attila and his Huns came down on them from the North. As we did at Annapolis, we did in Maryland State. We left an impression that can not be forgotten. Everything was paid for. No discourtesy was offered to any inhabitant, and the sobriety of the regiment should be an example to others. * * *

"The secret of this forced march, as well as our unexpected descent on Annapolis, was the result of Col. Lefferts' judgment, which has since been sustained by events. Finding that the line along the Potomac was closed, and the route to Washington by Baltimore equally impracticable, he came to the conclusion that Annapolis, commanding, as it did, the route to the capital, must of necessity be made the basis of military operations. It was important to the Government to have a free channel through which to transport troops, and this post presented the readiest means. The fact that since then all the Northern troops have passed through the line that we thus opened, is a sufficient comment on the admirable judgment that decided on the movement. It secured the integrity of the regiment, and saved lives the loss of which would have plunged New York into mourning. Too much importance can not be attached to this strategy."

The Eighth Massachusetts Regiment, which had passed through New York on the day of the departure of the Seventh Regiment, had, after reaching Philadelphia, pushed forward by the railway as far as the Susquehanna River. Here it was found impossible to continue the route through Maryland, in consequence of the destruction of the bridges by the secessionists. Brigadier-General Butler, of Massachusetts, had accompanied the Eighth on his way to Washington to assume the general command of the militia force of his State, sent to aid in the defence of the capital. He accordingly assumed the command and directed the movements of the Massachusetts soldiers when thus obstructed on their march. It was by his energy and promptitude of action that

April 19.

a way was finally cleared to the capital. General Butler seized the steam ferryboat the Maryland, on the Susquehanna, and embarking his troops sailed down the river into Chesapeake Bay and took possession of the city of Annapolis. Here his first act was to save the ship Constitution—used by the cadets of the Naval School as an exercise ship, and familiarly known as "Old Ironsides," one of the most revered of our national relics—from the clutch of some insurgents who were about pouncing upon her. The General learning of the helpless condition, from want of a crew, of the old ship, mustered his men and declared "if there are any men in the ranks who understand how to manage a ship, let them step forward." Fifty-three presented themselves, and they were immediately put on board. The Maryland then took her in tow, and she was safely borne out of harm's way. The General's announcement of the event in his order of the day was characteristic:

April 22.

"The purpose which could only be hinted at in the orders of yesterday has been accomplished. The frigate Constitution has lain for a long time at this port, substantially at the mercy of the armed mob which sometimes paralyzes the otherwise loyal State of Maryland. Deeds of daring, successful contests, and glorious victories had rendered Old Ironsides so conspicuous in the naval history of the country, that she was fitly chosen as the school in which to train the future officers of the navy to like heroic acts. It was given to Massachusetts and Essex counties first to man her; it was reserved to Massachusetts to have the honor to retain her for the service of the Union and the laws. This is a sufficient triumph of right—a sufficient triumph for us. By this the blood of our friends, shed by the Baltimore mob, is so far avenged. The Eighth Regiment may hereafter cheer lustily upon all proper occasions, but never without orders. The old Constitution, by their efforts, aided untiringly by the United States officers having her in charge, is now 'possessed, occupied, and enjoyed' by the Government of the United States, and is safe from all her enemies."

The revered Constitution had been thus rescued with much difficulty from imminent danger. For four days and nights, previous to the arrival of General Butler, her crew had been at quarters with the guns shotted. The insurgents of Maryland were plotting her destruction or capture. It may easily be imagined that it was a work of no little difficulty to move her, threatened as she was by the people on shore. She had four anchors and seven chains out when the Maryland was ordered by General Butler alongside. One anchor alone was hove up, the rest were slipped, and finally by lighting and careening, and by dint of hard labor, she was dragged over the bar. The crew of the Maryland were only kept to their work and duty by placing a guard over them armed with revolvers. After dragging her over the bar, the vessel grounded on the Outer Spit. About ten

P. M., information having been brought off that the channel outside the ship would be obstructed, kedges were laid out, and it was endeavored to warp the ship over the Spit, part of the men being at the guns. The Maryland having been run aground by her officers during the warping, a squall came up and drove the ship ashore again. At daylight a steam-tug from Havre de Grace came in sight, and was taken to tow the ship out. She was then taken in tow by the R. R. Cuyler, and brought to New York. Subsequently she was sent to Newport, Rhode Island, whither the Naval School formerly at Annapolis was removed.

The General's next operation was to re-establish the railroad between Annapolis and Washington. His own ranks supplied skilled mechanics to reconstruct the broken engines, and the hardy men of Massachusetts, aided by the tender hands of the gentlemen of New York, performed the rude labor of laying the iron rails.

These timely services of General Butler won for him the gratitude of the whole Northern people who fondly cherished his rising military repute, and hailed him in advance as one of their future heroes.

Benjamin F. Butler was born in Deerfield, Rockingham County, New Hampshire, in 1818. He claims relationship with the Cilleys, a family of Revolutionary renown, from which sprang the Honorable Jonathan Cilley, who was killed in a duel with his associate in Congress, Graves, of Kentucky. Young Butler was educated at a Baptist college in Waterville, Maine. He subsequently studied law, and removing to Massachusetts commenced its practice at Lowell. Here he soon acquired prominence as a successful advocate in jury cases. He was remarkable for his devotion to the interests of his clients, and the oratorical vehemence with which he defended their cause. With an impulsive nature, and great flexibility and readiness of speech, restrained by no over-fastidiousness of rhetoric, his eloquence is distinguished rather by its force than its refinement.

Though long prominent as an active politician of the Democratic party, his first appearance in public life was in 1853, when he became a member of the Legislature of Massachusetts. In the same year he was elected to the Constitutional Convention, and in 1859–60 was senator of the State. In May, 1860, he was chosen a delegate to the Democratic Convention, which first met at Charleston. In the rupture which ensued in the party, he sided with the Southern faction, and was a member of the subsequent convention at Baltimore which nominated Breckenridge for President. He was appointed one of the Presidential electors for Massachusetts, and headed the electoral list on the Breckenridge ticket. He was also nominated as the candidate for Governor of Massachusetts, by that portion of the Democratic party supposed to be favorable to the policy of the slave States.

Though suspiciously regarded in the anti-slavery State of Massachusetts as a political ally of the "States Rights" men of the South, he, on the first overt act of Southern rebellion, proved his loyalty to the Union by coming forward among the earliest to offer his services in its defence. Governor Andrew, of Massachusetts, though always his political opponent, was glad to welcome so spirited and able a co-operator in the common cause of national unity, and appointed him commander of the Eighth Massachusetts Regiment. Leading this corps to the defence of the capital, he found his progress suddenly obstructed; and an occasion offering for the exercise of those energies which characterize him, he exerted them with a spirit and a success which won for him the gratitude of the whole nation. His picture was thus forcibly drawn at this time as "in the prime of life, being forty-three years of age. Though somewhat unwieldly in appearance, he is possessed of great physical activity. His expression, disfigured by a cast in his left eye, might be thought severe and even sinister by the casual observer, but by his friends he is esteemed as an amiable companion, and by his subordinates readily obeyed as a popular commander.

"With his acknowledged energy in action, fertility of resource, and coolness in danger, there is reason to believe when his natural impulsiveness of character has been duly tempered by military experience, that he will become one of the most efficient leaders in the present war."

As proof of his coolness and intrepidity in danger, the following incident is told. It occurred in Lowell, Massachusetts, in 1856.

"It was during the Presidential contest, and Hon. Rufus Choate had been invited to address the conservative citizens. The largest hall of the city was crowded to excess; the audience was wild with enthusiasm, as the brilliant orator swayed them by his eloquence; but in the midst of the applause a jar was felt, a crash was heard, and every face save one turned pale as the cry went forth, 'The floor is sinking!' The man whose cheek knew no pallor was General Butler. He sprang up and calmed the fears of the multitude by telling them that he did not apprehend the least danger; that the architect was present; but to allay any misgiving, he would go with the architect and examine the building. An immediate investigation showed that the edifice was in the greatest possible danger, and a sudden movement, a rush on the part of the assembly, would result in the slaughter of thousands. Forgetful of himself, he bravely pushed through the dense crowd. He did not shriek—he showed no marks of trepidation—but with a bland countenance whispered a few apparently pleasant and assuring words to Mr. Choate. Mr. Butler then turned to the audience, and in a calm, clear voice remarked: 'My friends, there is no present danger; but as the house is overcrowded, it will be better to quietly adjourn to the open air; and I therefore invite you to the front of the Merrimack House.' The whole thing was accomplished in a few moments. It was only by Mr. Butler's self-possession that the catastrophe was avoided. On this occasion he showed more cool courage than any battle will ever call into requisition. In the life of Mr. Choate we find what the words were that blandly fell, *sotto voce*, from Mr. Butler, viz., 'Mr. Choate, I must clear this house, or we shall all be in h—ll in five minutes!'"* Before the close of this history, there will be found other more memorable incidents recorded, in which Butler has given ample proof of his characteristic energy and courage.

CHAPTER XVIII.

Perplexities of President Lincoln and his Cabinet.—Humiliating Expedients.—The Governor of Maryland and the Mayor of Baltimore summoned to Washington.—The Conference with the President.—Opinion of General Scott.—The Federal Authority agrees not to bring Troops through Baltimore.—End of the Conference.—Another Interview.—Troops Recalled from Cockeysville.—The continued Movement of Troops to Washington.—The Route by Annapolis kept open by General Butler.—Opposition from Maryland.—A Protest from the Governor.—Response of Butler.—Another Letter from Butler.—A pertinent Question as to the Loyalty of Maryland.—A Rebuke to the Governor.—Another Protest from Governor Hicks.—The Legislature of Maryland convened.—A Home-thrust from Butler.—Factious regard for Maryland.—Offer to suppress a Slave Insurrection.—The offer declined.—The Legislature of Maryland meets at Frederick.—The Message of the Governor.—Amiable Rhetoric.—Gentleness, Peace, and Neutrality.—The Secession tendencies of the Legislature. Hesitation.—Union Meetings.—A forcible Appeal to Loyalty.—Movement of Butler to the Relay House.—Indirect Action of the Legislature.—The "Board of Public Safety."—Its purpose.—Defeated by the Conservatives.—Animosity of the Legislature.—Expression of Opinion in regard to the Re-opening of Communications.—A *quasi* Justification of the violence of the Maryland Rioters.—Guarantees demanded from the Federal Government.—Commissioners sent to the President.—Their Report.—Sympathy with Secession manifested.

THE President and his cabinet, beset by a rebellion the extent of which it was impossible to measure, and unprepared to meet it with the scattered resources of a government they were so suddenly called to administer, were naturally perplexed. Surrounded with dangers, the greater as they were undefined, and prevented from the exercise of powers which, however great, were yet beyond their control, the Federal authorities were obliged to resort to the humiliating expedient of temporizing with the insurgents of Maryland. The President accordingly summoned the Governor of Maryland and the Mayor of Baltimore to Washington to "consult" with them for "the preservation of the peace of Maryland."

1861.

April 21.

"Governor Hicks not being at hand, Mayor Brown, with several notable citizens, proceeded without him to the capital in obedience to the summons of the President. An audience was immediately granted by President Lincoln, accompanied by all the members of his cabinet and Lieutenant-General Scott. A long conversation and discussion† en-

* *Harper's Weekly.*
† The occurrences at this interview are related as reported in the "statement" of Mayor Brown, *National Intelligencer*, April 22.

sued. The President recognized the good faith of the city and State authorities of Maryland, and insisted upon his own. He admitted the excited state of feeling in Baltimore, and his desire and duty to avoid the fatal consequences of a collision with the people. He urged, on the other hand, the absolute, irresistible necessity of having a transit through the State for such troops as might be necessary for the protection of the Federal capital. The protection of Washington, he asseverated with great earnestness, was the sole object of concentrating troops there, and he protested that none of the troops brought through Maryland were intended for any purposes hostile to the State or aggressive as against the Southern States. Being now unable to bring them up the Potomac in security, the Government must either bring them through Maryland or abandon the capital.

"General Scott being called upon for his opinion, said that troops might be brought through Maryland, without passing through Baltimore, by either carrying them from Perryville to Annapolis and thence by rail to Washington, or by bringing them to the Relay House, on the Northern Central Railroad, and marching them to the Relay House, on the Washington Railroad, and thence transporting them by rail to the capital. If the people of Maryland would permit the troops to go by either of these routes uninterruptedly, the necessity of their passing through Baltimore might be avoided. If, however, the General declared, the people would not allow them to take this circuitous route, the soldiers would be obliged to select their own best course, and, if need be, fight their own way through Baltimore, a result which he most earnestly deprecated.

"The President expressed his hearty concurrence with the desire of the General to avoid a collision, and said that no more troops should be ordered to pass through Baltimore, if they were permitted to go uninterruptedly by either of the routes suggested by General Scott. The secretary of war, Cameron, gave his assent to the decision of Mr. Lincoln.

"Mayor Brown assured the President that the city authorities would use all lawful means to prevent their citizens from leaving Baltimore to attack the troops in passing at a distance; but he urged at the same time the impossibility of their being able to promise anything more than their best efforts in that direction. The excitement was great, he told the President; the people of all classes were fully aroused, and it was impossible for any one to answer for the consequences of the presence of Northern troops anywhere within the borders of Maryland. He reminded the President, also, that the jurisdiction of the city authorities was confined to their own population, and that he could give no promises for the people elsewhere, because he would be unable to keep them if given. The President frankly acknowledged this difficulty, and said that the Government would only ask the city authorities to use their best efforts with respect to those under their jurisdiction.

"The interview terminated with the distinct assurance on the part of the President, that no more troops would be sent through Baltimore, unless obstructed in their transit in other directions, and with the understanding that the city authorities should do their best to restrain their own people.

"The Mayor and his companions, before departing, urged upon the President in the most earnest manner a course of policy which would give peace to the country, and especially the withdrawal of all orders contemplating the passage of troops through any part of Maryland."

The Mayor had, however, just as he was about leaving the capital, received a dispatch informing him of the march of Pennsylvania troops to Cockeysville, in Maryland, only distant fifteen miles from Baltimore. This appeared to him as a threatening approach, and he hurried with his dispatch to the President, who expressed great surprise at its purport, and immediately summoned General Scott and the secretary of war, who at once appeared, in company with the other members of the cabinet. The dispatch containing intelligence of the movement of the Pennsylvania troops was now submitted to the whole conclave. Mr. Lincoln having declared that he had no idea that a force was to move on that day to Cockeysville, urged emphatically the immediate recall of the troops, to avoid the slightest suspicion of bad faith on his part in summoning the Mayor of Baltimore to Washington, and allowing troops to advance toward the city during his absence. The President then expressed his desire that the troops might, if practicable, be sent back at once to York or Harrisburg.

General Scott warmly concurred, and immediately issued an order to that effect and delivered it to an aid-de-camp, who departed on the instant. At the same time assurances were given that the troops at Cockeysville were not intended to march through Baltimore, but to the Relay House, on the Baltimore and Ohio Railroad.

The military activity, however, of the free States was quickly relieving the Government from its position of perplexity and humiliation. The militia regiments already organized, and the volunteer corps forming with wonderful rapidity, kept daily moving on toward the capital. Some reached Annapolis by the way of Philadelphia, while others were transported directly thither from Northern ports on steamers chartered by the Government for the purpose. The route from Annapolis to Washington, through a disaffected State, was kept clear by the energetic action of General Butler, who continued to hold the chief command in that quarter.

This spirited officer met with great opposition in Maryland from the authorities of that State, either intimidated by the rebellious, or disposed to sympathize with their disloyalty. Governor Hicks had repaired to Annapolis, the capital of Maryland, and remonstrated against Butler's landing of the troops:

April 20. "I would most earnestly advise," he wrote, "that you do not land your men at Annapolis. The excitement here is very great, and I think that you should take your men elsewhere. I have telegraphed to the secretary of war, advising against your landing your men here."

To this communication Butler merely answered, in the first place, that the arrival of his command at Annapolis was the result of circumstances beyond his control, and that their landing was a necessary part of the performance of his duty to the Federal Government. Receiving no reply, he wrote another communication to the Governor, demanding a direct answer to a question very pertinent to the loyalty of the State of Maryland: "I desire of your Excellency an immediate reply," wrote Butler, "whether I have the permission of the State authorities of Maryland to land the men under my command, and of passing quietly through the State on my way to Washington, respecting private property, and paying for what I receive, and outraging the rights of none—a duty which I am bound to do in obedience to the requisitions of the United States." At the same time General Butler took occasion to object to the sectional character the Governor had attributed to the State troops, summoned to the defence of the Union: "I beg leave," he said, "to call your Excellency's attention to what I hope I may be pardoned for deeming an ill-advised designation of the men under my command. They are not Northern

April 22.

troops; they are a part of the whole militia of the United States, obeying the call of the President."

Governor Hicks withheld his consent to the landing of the troops, but contented himself with a protest against the movement, declaring, that "in view of the excited condition" of Maryland, he considered it an "unwise step on the part of the Government."

In the mean time, Governor Hicks, though hitherto he had firmly refused, summoned the Legislature to meet at Annapolis. This was a timid concession to the secessionists, who were believed to control that body. Butler having, in spite of protests and threatened resistance, landed his troops, had, in order to secure their transit, taken possession of the Annapolis and Elk Ridge Railroad. The Governor protested against this seizure of the railroad, declaring that its military possession would prevent the members of the Legislature from assembling at Annapolis, the capital. He, however, thus exposed his secession proclivities, if not his complicity with the rebellious, which he had vainly attempted to conceal, but which had caused his ready compliance with their demands. Butler, in his answer to the Governor's protest, thrust this charge of prevarication home to him:

April 26.

"HEADQUARTERS, THIRD BRIGADE, U. S. MIL.,
ANNAPOLIS, MD., *April* 23, 1861.

"To His EXCELLENCY THOS. H. HICKS, Governor OF MARYLAND:

"You are credibly informed that I have taken possession of the Annapolis and Elk Ridge Railroad. It might have escaped your memory, but at the official meeting between your Excellency and the Mayor of Annapolis, and the authorities of the Government and myself, it was expressly stated as the reason why I should not land, and that my troops could not land, because the company had taken up the rails, and they were private property. It is difficult to see how it could be that if my troops could not pass over the railroad one way, the members of the Legislature could pass the other way. I have taken possession for the purpose of preventing the carrying out of the threats of the mob, as officially represented to me by the master of transportation of this city, 'that if my troops passed over the railroad, the railroad should be destroyed.'

"If the government of the State had taken possession of the railroad in any emergency, I should have long waited before I entered upon it. But, as I had the honor to inform your Excellency in regard to insurrection against the laws of Maryland, I am here armed to maintain those laws, if your Excellency desires, and the peace of the United States, against all disorderly persons whatever. I am endeavoring to save, and not to destroy, to obtain means of transportation, so I can vacate the capital prior to the sitting of the Legislature, and not be under the painful necessity of occupying your beautiful city while the Legislature is in session. I have the honor to be your Excellency's obedient servant, Br.-Gen. B. F. BUTLER."

While thus resolute, however, in the performance of his duty to the General Government, Butler was not less solicitous to uphold the institutions and support the laws of Maryland. His fastidious regard for the State was manifest on the occasion of a threatened rising of the negroes. Butler offered the aid of his troops in suppressing the rumored insurrection.

"HEADQUARTERS THIRD BRIG. MASS. V. MIL.,
ANNAPOLIS, *April 23*, 1861.

"To HIS EXCELLENCY THOMAS H. HICKS, GOVERNOR OF THE STATE OF MARYLAND:

"I did myself the honor, in my communication of yesterday, wherein I asked permission to land the portion of the militia of the United States under my command, to state that they were armed only against the disturbers of the peace of the State of Maryland and of the United States.

"I have understood within the last hour that some apprehensions are entertained of an insurrection of the negro population of this neighborhood. I am anxious to convince all classes of persons that the forces under my command are not here in any way to interfere with or countenance any interference with the laws of the State. I am therefore ready to co-operate with your Excellency in suppressing most promptly and effectively any insurrection against the laws of Maryland.

"I beg, therefore, that you announce publicly that any portion of the forces under my command is at your Excellency's disposal, to act immediately for the preservation and quietness of the peace of this community.

"And I have the honor to be your Excellency's obedient servant,

"BENJAMIN F. BUTLER,
"General of Third Brigade."

The Governor gratefully acknowledged this tender of service, but, confident in the ability of the citizens themselves to suppress any insurrection of the slave population of Maryland, declined General Butler's conciliatory but officious offer.

The Legislature of Maryland, under the pretence that it was not safe to meet in Annapolis, the capital, while in the military possession of General Butler with Northern troops, convened at Frederick. The Governor, in his message, April 27, gave a resumé of his action, and after bewailing the angry disposition of the State, strove, in a strain of amiable rhetoric, to compose it by counseling gentleness, peace, and neutrality.

"It is my duty," he said, "to advise you of my own convictions of the proper course to be pursued by Maryland in the emergency which is upon us. It is of no consequence now to discuss the causes which have induced our troubles. Let us look to our distressing present and to our portentous future. The fate of Maryland, and perhaps of her sister border slave States, will undoubtedly be seriously affected by the action of your honorable body. Therefore should every good citizen bend all his energies to the task before us, and therefore should the animosities and bickerings of the past be forgotten, and all strike hands in the bold cause of restoring peace to our State and to our country. I honestly and most earnestly entertain the conviction, that the only safety of Maryland lies in preserving a neutral position between our brethren of the North and of the South. We have violated no right of either section. We have been loyal to the Union. The unhappy contest between the two sections has not been commenced or encouraged by us, although we have suffered from it in the past. The impending war has not come by any act or any wish of ours. We have done all we could to avert it. We have hoped that Maryland and other border slave States, by their conservative position and love for the Union, might have acted as mediators between the extremes of both sections, and thus have prevented the terrible evils of a prolonged civil war. Entertaining these views, I cannot counsel Maryland to take sides against the General Government until it shall commit outrages on us which would justify us in resisting its authority. As a consequence, I can give no other counsel than that we shall array ourselves for union and peace, and thus preserve our soil from being polluted with the blood of brethren. Thus, if war must be between the North and South, we may force the contending parties to transfer the field of battle from our soil, so that our lives and property may be secure."

There was a strong disposition on the part of a majority of the Legislature of Maryland to precipitate the State into secession. Checked, however, by the increased manifestation of loyalty to the

Union, on the part of some of their fellow-citizens, and awed by the rapid accumulation of United States troops in Maryland and in Washington, they hesitated. Meetings had, in the mean time, gathered in Baltimore and other parts of the State, and passed resolutions of loyalty to the Union. The United States flag began to be unfurled, and secession badges and colors to disappear. There was, however, in the rapid mustering of the Northern militia, a more forcible appeal in behalf of the Union. The concentration at Annapolis of a large force, and the movement of General Butler to the Relay House, at the junction of the Baltimore and Ohio and Baltimore and Washington railways, only seven miles south of Baltimore, and commanding its most important communications, caused even the most headstrong of the Maryland Legislature to pause before taking the dangerous step of secession to which they had been otherwise so inclined. Finding the Federal Government prepared to vindicate its authority, and fearful of bringing upon their State its armed vengeance, the secessionists gave up all hope of the direct accomplishment of their purpose,* but strove to secure its fulfilment by indirect action. Not venturing to pass an act of immediate secession, they made an effort to bring it about sooner or later through the establishment of a "Board of Public Safety," to be officered and controlled by their own friends. This board was intended to assume the executive power of the State in place of the regularly constituted authorities, whose supposed fidelity to the Union was an obstacle to the designs of the secessionists. Thus they hoped to accomplish indirectly their fixed purpose of wresting Maryland from the Union. Their intention, however, being obvious, was at once opposed and defeated by the timely interposition of the conservatives of the State. At a convention which met at Baltimore, the following resolutions were passed:

May 5.

"*Resolved*, That the Convention, in the name of the order-loving people of Baltimore, do solemnly protest against the attempt now making in the Legislature of Maryland to inaugurate a military despotism, by the enactment of a bill to create a Committee of Public Safety, which, under a profession of providing for the protection, safety, peace, and defence of the State, would, if enacted into a law, confer on an irresponsible body powers which are unconstitutional and tyrannical in principle, and which, by withdrawing from the citizen all guarantees now enjoyed for his individual security, must endanger the public peace; and in the event of the enactment of that bill, we shall esteem it our duty to avail ourselves of all constitutional remedies for defeating its execution and vindicating public liberty.

"*Resolved*, secondly, That the measures enacted and enacting by the Legislature are indicative of a purpose on the part of the majority thereof, to precipitate Maryland into a struggle with the

---

* A vote, however, was taken, which resulted in fifty-three against and thirteen for secession from the Union.

constitutional authorities of the Union, and to effect, by indirect action, a result which they acknowledge they are unable to accomplish by direct legislation on the subject, and that we deprecate any efforts to change the relations at present existing between the Union and this State, by any authority whatsoever."

The secessionists of the Legislature, though thwarted in their plans of hostility, did not conceal their animosity to the Northern States and the Federal Government. When called upon by the Mayor of Baltimore for action in regard to the restoration of the communications between that city and other parts of the country, which had been closed by the destruction of railroad bridges, and the hostile attitude of the people of Maryland, a committee was appointed to consider the subject. In their report, while they confessed that "the almost total interruption of direct communication between Baltimore and the North, by destruction of bridges upon the Northern, Central, and Philadelphia railroads, is an evil very aggravated in its character, not only in itself but in its manifest bearings upon the prosperity of the State and its commercial metropolis," they could not refrain from a *quasi* justification of the violence which had caused it. The committee declared that "in the face of a danger which would seem inevitable, if facilities for invasion were offered to the fanatical and excited multitudes of the Northern cities, where animosity to Baltimore and Maryland is measured by no standard, and who publicly threaten our destruction, without subordination even to the Federal authority, it could hardly be consistent with the commonest prudence to reopen the avenues which would bring them to our very doors." Adding, "that the channels of intercourse with the Northern States cannot be effectually re-established without a guarantee from some quarter of the safety and peace of Maryland," the committee recommended that this should be sought from the Federal Government.

Three commissioners were accordingly appointed to communicate with the President of the United States "in regard to the present and any proposed military use or occupation of the soil and property of the State by the General Government." Having proceeded to the capital and communicated with Mr. Lincoln and his cabinet, the commissioners duly reported the result. The report is a cautiously worded document, but the sympathy of its authors with secession is manifest, in spite of their technical adherence to the legal obligations of loyalty.

"To the Honorable General Assembly of Maryland:

"The undersigned commissioners have the honor to report to the General Assembly of Maryland that they waited in person on the President of the United States on the 4th inst., and presented him with a copy of the joint resolutions adopted by your honorable body on the 2d inst. They were received by the President with respectful courtesy, and made such representations as were necessary to convey to him the sense of

May 6.

the General Assembly of Maryland, in relation to the occupation of the capital of the State by Federal troops, and the forcible seizure of property of the State, and of private citizens on the Annapolis Railroad, and on the Washington Branch of the Baltimore and Ohio Railroad; and in this connection his attention was called to the suspension of intercourse between Baltimore and Washington, and other parts of the State with Annapolis, and the indignity put upon the State while still in the Federal Union, by such an interference with the private rights of its citizens, and by such an occupation of its soil and ways of communication by the Federal Government. Full explanations were exchanged between the undersigned and the secretary of war and secretary of state, who were present and participated in the discussion, as to the facts and circumstances rendered necessary by the extraordinary incidents accompanying the passage of the Federal troops through Maryland *en route* to the city of Washington, and especially in reference to those acts of the authorities of the city of Baltimore, which arrested the progress of the troops by the railroads leading from Pennsylvania and Delaware into Maryland, and of the opposition to the landing of the troops subsequently at Annapolis by the Governor of the State, and in conjunction with the action of the authorities of the State. The hostile feeling manifested by the people to the passage of these troops through Maryland was considered and treated with entire frankness by the undersigned, who, while acknowledging all the legal obligations of the State to the Federal Government, set forth fully the strength of the sympathy felt by a large portion of our people for our Southern brethren in the present crisis. Although many of the instances and circumstances referred to were regarded in different lights by the undersigned and the Federal Government, even to the extent of a difference of opinion as to some of the facts involved, yet in regard to the general principle at issue a concurrence of opinion was reached. The President concurred with the undersigned in the opinion that so long as Maryland has not taken, and was not about taking, a hostile attitude to the Federal Government, that the executive military occupation of her ways of communication, and the seizure of the property of her citizens, would be without justification; and what has been referred to in this connection, so far as it occurred, was treated by the Government as an act of necessity and self-preservation. The undersigned did not feel themselves authorized to enter into any engagement with the Federal Government to induce it to change its relations to the State of Maryland, considering it proper under the circumstances to leave the entire discretion and responsibility of the existing state of things to that Government, making such representations as they deem proper to vindicate the moral and legal aspects of the question, and especially insisting on its obligation to relieve the State promptly from restraint and indignity, and to abstain from all action in the transportation of troops that can be regarded as intended for chastisement or prompted by resentment. The undersigned are not able to indicate to what extent or to what degree the executive discretion will be exercised in modifying the relations which now exist between the State of Maryland and the Federal Government, and in the particular matter of the commercial communication between the city of Baltimore and the other part of the country, brought to the attention of the General Assembly by the Mayor and City Council of Baltimore; but they feel authorized to express the opinion that some modification may be expected. The undersigned feel painfully confident that a war is to be waged to reduce all the seceding States to allegiance to the Federal Government, and that the whole military power of the Federal Government will be exerted to accomplish that purpose; and though the expression of this opinion is not called for by the resolution of your honorable bodies, yet, having had the opportunity to ascertain its entire accuracy, and because it will explain much of the military preparations and movements of the troops through the State of Maryland, it is proper to bring it to your attention.

"Otho Scott,
"Robert M. McLane,
"Wm. J. Ross."

CHAPTER XIX.

The rapid Response to the President's Call for Troops.—The Capital pronounced safe.—Maryland Awed.—Virginia kept in check.—Increased Resources of the Government.—Reinforcement of Fortress Monroe.—Description of Fortress Monroe.—The importance of its Position.—Its Construction.—Site.—Communications with the Mainland.—The Outer Walls.—The form of the Fort.—The Armament.—Late Additions.—The Moat.—The Water Battery.—The Gates.—The Redoubt.—How Commanded.—Its Approaches.—How Defended.—The Defects of the Fort.—The Exterior.—The Hygeia Hotel.—Old Point Comfort.—Importance of the Post.—Danger of losing it.—Anxiety of the North.—Reinforcements from Massachusetts.—Increased Authority and Vigor of the Federal Government.—New Military Departments.—Another Call from the President for Troops.—His Proclamation.—The swift Answer of the North.—Virginia and North Carolina included in the Blockade.—Increase of the Fleet.—Purchase of Merchant Steamers.—General Butler's Fortifications at the Relay House.—Command of the Baltimore and Ohio Railroad.—Reconstruction of Bridges and Opening of Communications.—Fort McHenry Reinforced.—Its effect upon Baltimore.—Description of the Fortress.—The good conduct of its Commander.—Position of the Fort.—Revulsion of Sentiment in Maryland.—Union Feeling claimed to be predominant.—Union Meetings and Union Orators.—Speech of Beverdy Johnson.—Presentation of Flag to the Home Guard of Frederick.—Great Crowds of Unionists.—Remarkable display of Union Emblems.—Manly Rhetoric of Johnson.—Sensible Advice to Marylanders.—A fervid Appeal in behalf of the United States Flag.—The Secessionists awed to Silence.—Secret efforts to advance Secession.—The City of Baltimore tranquilized.—Disbandment of the City Soldiery.—Butler Marches into the City.—His Reception.—Encampment on Federal Hill.—Proclamation of Butler.—Seizure of Arms.—Arrest of prominent Citizens.—Good effects of Decision.—The Governor of Maryland takes Courage.—He responds to the President's call for Troops.—A Proclamation Modified to suit Equivocal Loyalty.—Comparative Propriety of the Legislature.—A Spirit of Disaffection finds vent.—The last Act of the Legislature.—The Route through Baltimore opened.—The first great Victory for the Union.

1861. Such had been the **promptitude with which** the North had **responded to** the proclamation, of **the 15th of April,** of the President calling forth the militia, that in less than ten days after, more than twenty thousand troops had marched. The capital, which was supposed to have been in imminent danger from Virginia and Maryland, was now pronounced safe. The insurgents of the former State in arms against the Federal Government, and who had mustered to the number of several thousands, and encamped on the banks of the Potomac opposite to Washington, were kept in awe by the militia which had rapidly accumulated at the capital. Maryland, dominated by a considerable Federal force in possession of the channels of communication, also feared any longer to make violent demonstration of its disaffection, and appeared suddenly to be converted to loyalty.

The Federal Government strengthened thus by the military ardor and promptitude of the loyal States, was enabled not only to provide for the immediate defence of the capital, and to check the rebellious tendencies of Maryland, but to reinforce a post of the greatest importance in the future conduct of the war. This was Fortress Monroe, the most extensive work of defence in the United States. Situated at the mouth of the Chesapeake, it commands the only approaches from the sea to Maryland and Virginia, and to the various rivers, the Susquehannah, the Potomac, Rappahannock, York, James, and the numerous small streams and creeks which empty into the bay, and thus find their outlet to the Atlantic Ocean.

Fortress Monroe was designed by the celebrated French engineer General Barnard, in 1819, then in the service of the United States. Fort Wool, on the Rip Raps, intended to cross fire with it, is yet incomplete. Fortress Monroe is built upon a peninsula connected with the mainland by a narrow strip of sand beach, not more than forty rods in width. In addition to this communication, there has been constructed a causeway with a bridge toward its end which leads from the fort to the road on the mainland which passes to Hampton. This passage is so narrow and so completely commanded by some of the heaviest guns of the fort, as to render any approach in that direction almost impracticable. The waters of the bay which flow in between the peninsula and the mainland, enclosed, as it were, like a lake, between the natural neck of sand and the artificial causeway, vary in width from one to three miles.

The outer walls of Fortress Monroe embrace an area of nearly sixty-five acres, of which twenty-five regularly laid out and shaded by a fine growth of live oak form the parade ground. The work is bastioned, and is of an irregular heptagon form. The walls, constructed of granite and embanked with thick mounds of sand and clay, rise to a height of thirty-five feet. On the ramparts are mounted heavy guns, some of which are forty-two pounders and others columbiads. These being *en barbette* are uncovered. There are about seventy large casemates, which are bomb and shot proof. Some of these are appropriated for officers' quarters, and others for guard-houses and general barracks. The embrasures, though intended originally for forty-two pounders, are sufficiently large for columbiads of the greatest size.

The armament of the fortress as originally recorded in the official statement was composed of forty-two forty-two pounders, a hundred and thirty-nine thirty-two pounders, ten twenty-four pounders, fourteen eighteen pounders, twenty-five twelve pounders, twelve field pieces, sixteen flank howitzers, twenty heavy eight-inch howitzers, five light eight-inch howitzers, three thirteen-inch mortars, seven heavy ten-inch mortars, three light ten-inch mortars, five light eight-inch mortars, five sixteen-inch stone mortars, and fifteen cohorns, making in all three hundred and seventy-one guns.

This armament, however, has been much modified and considerably augmented since. Columbiads of various calibres have been liberally supplied, and mortars of various construction and other cannon added, so that its ramparts now frown with the most formidable enginery of war yet constructed.

A broad and deep moat surrounds the whole work. This is faced with dressed granite, and when flooded by the opening of the gates, is supplied with water, varying from eight to fifteen feet in depth, and from seventy-five to a hundred and fifty feet in breadth, presenting a formidable obstacle to be overcome in an attempted assault.

As the fort was chiefly intended to protect the approaches from sea, the chief labor and expense were concentrated upon the work in that direction.

Here is what is termed the Water Battery, which is constructed of stone, of a thickness so great, and of a masonry so solid, that it is supposed to be proof against any weight of metal. It has forty-two embrasures, originally mounted with that number of forty-two pounders. Presenting a formidable front to the sea, this defence would seem impregnable to a naval attack from without. The slope of the battery is laid with green turf, like the ramparts of the rest of the fortress, and in times of peace was a favorite promenade for the fashionable frequenters of the peninsula seeking the fresh breezes of the ocean.

On the north side of the fort there is a postern gate, which leads to a redoubt or outerwork, built to protect the land side, which, as the work was never intended except as a protection against a foreign enemy, was left, as in all our coast defences, comparatively weak. Since, however, the commencement of this civil war, great efforts have been made to give additional strength to this portion of the works. Heavy guns and mortars have been mounted to command the artificial causeway and the strip of beach which join the peninsula with the mainland. The surface of the country in the immediate neighborhood, moreover, being generally level, there is hardly a favorable point for commencing the operations of a siege. The only rising ground for many miles is a slight elevation with trees on either side, at the extremity of the neck of land. This, however, is so commanded by the guns of the fort as to be untenable.

On the beach outside of the walls there is a fifteen-inch columbiad placed there for practice, and for additional defence against an attack from the sea. It, however, also commands the neck of land, and would seem to check the approach of the most venturesome in that direction. The whole cost of the extensive works of Fortress Monroe has been estimated at nearly three millions. The greatest deficiency of the fort is the precariousness of its supply of water. An attempt was made some fifteen years ago to bore an Artesian well, but the effort was abandoned, and the only dependence at present is upon large cisterns, which are supplied by the rains.

Outside of the fort are the numerous foundries and work and machine shops, where large quantities of munitions of war can be rapidly fabricated. There is a wharf on the southern side of the peninsula, three hundred yards distant from the fort, where vessels of the greatest draft of water can lie. About a quarter of a mile distant, and on the western side of the walls, stood the "Hygeia Hotel," a famous resort in past summers for the planters of the South in search of the sea breeze at "Old Point Comfort," as the peninsula is called. Within the fort itself there is a group of nearly fifty houses of brick and wood, forming quite a village, and on one side of the parade ground is a seemly Episcopal chapel.

To secure this important post became at once a matter of the greatest moment. Placed as it was within the boundaries of a State already in open rebellion, and threatened by a force gathered apparently for the purpose of attempting to wrest it from the meagre garrison which held it, there was great danger of its loss. Massachusetts, however, which had been foremost in pouring out her resources of men and money in defence of the Union, came to the rescue, and promptly sent one of her regiments of militia to aid in its defence. Embarking on board of the steamer Maine, at Boston, the Fourth Regiment of Massachusetts militia sailed directly to the Chesapeake, and landed in safety at Fortress Monroe on the 20th of April. *April 20.*

The Government, encouraged by the enthusiasm of loyalty of the people, and fortified by their generosity of service, began to assert with more confidence, and to vindicate with more firmness, its contemned authority. New military departments were organized. The District of Columbia, Fort Washington and the adjacent country, and the State of Maryland as far as Bladensburgh, were erected into the Department of Washington, and placed under the command of Colonel J. K. F. Mansfield, inspector-general, with his headquarters at the capital. That part of Maryland including the country for twenty miles on each side of the railroad from Annapolis to the city of Washington, as far as Bladensburgh, was formed into a new military department, entitled the Department of Annapolis, and Butler, with the rank of brigadier-general of Massachusetts volunteers, assigned to the command, with his headquarters at An- *April 27.*

napolis. To these was added a third, the Department of Pennsylvania, including that State, the State of Delaware, and all of Maryland not within the other departments, and the command given to Major-General Patterson, with his headquarters at Philadelphia, or any other point which he might be temporarily occupying.

This was soon after followed by this proclamation of the President calling for volunteers for three years, and an increase of the regular army and navy:

May 3.

"Whereas existing exigencies demand immediate and adequate measures for the protection of the national Constitution and the preservation of the national Union, by the suppression of the insurrectionary combinations now existing in several States for opposing the laws of the Union and obstructing the execution thereof, to which end a military force in addition to that called forth by my proclamation of the fifteenth day of April in the present year appears to be indispensably necessary, now, therefore, I, Abraham Lincoln, President of the United States, and Commander-in-chief of the Army and Navy thereof, and of the militia of the several States, when called into actual service, do hereby call into the service of the United States forty-two thousand and thirty-four volunteers, to serve for a period of three years, unless sooner discharged, and to be mustered into service as infantry and cavalry. The proportions of each arm and the details of enrolment and organization will be made known through the department of war; and I also direct that the regular army of the United States be increased by the addition of eight regiments of infantry, one regiment of cavalry, and one regiment of artillery, making altogether a maximum aggregate increase of 22,714 officers and enlisted men, the details of which increase will also be made known through the department of war; and I further direct the enlistment, for not less than one nor more than three years, of 18,000 seamen, in addition to the present force, for the naval service of the United States. The details of the enlistment and organization will be made known through the department of the navy. The call for volunteers, hereby made, and the direction of the increase of the regular army, and for the enlistment of seamen hereby given, together with the plan of organization adopted for the volunteers and for the regular forces hereby authorized, will be submitted to Congress as soon as assembled.

"In the mean time I earnestly invoke the co-operation of all good citizens in the measures hereby adopted for the effectual suppression of unlawful violence, for the impartial enforcement of constitutional laws, and for the speediest possible restoration of peace and order, and with those of happiness and prosperity throughout our country.

"In testimony whereof, I have hereunto set my hand, and caused the seal of the United States to be affixed.

"Done at the city of Washington this third day of May, in the year of our Lord one thousand eight hundred and sixty-one, and of the Independence of the United States the eighty-fifth.

"ABRAHAM LINCOLN.
"By the President.
"WILLIAM H. SEWARD, Secretary of State."

All the Northern States began to respond rapidly to this call of the President for additional troops, and the Government was judiciously availing itself of its increased naval and military resources. Virginia and North Carolina were included in the blockade already declared, of South Carolina, Georgia, Florida, Alabama, Louisiana, Mississippi, and Texas. Merchant steamers were purchased or chartered to strengthen the naval arm, quite inadequate to the duty of watching so extensive a line of sea-coast. The various ports on the Chesapeake and the Potomac were especially guarded by the Government cruisers, and the communications of Virginia with the sea thus effectually cut off.

April 27.

As before stated, General Butler, with a large force, took possession of the Relay House, at the junction of the Baltimore and Ohio Railroad, only seven miles from Baltimore. Here he planted eight howitzers on the viaduct over the Patapsco River and threw up entrenchments. He thus could overawe the rebellious tendencies of that disaffected city, and, by commanding the Baltimore and Ohio Railroad, prevent the sending of supplies to the insurgents of Virginia in force at Harper's Ferry, by their sympathizers in Maryland. At the same time the communications between Baltimore and the North were being opened

May 5.

by the reconstruction of the railroad bridges, destroyed by the rioters of Maryland, and troops from Pennsylvania were preparing to advance.

Fort McHenry, too, which had been fortunately preserved to the Government by the resolute conduct of its Federal commander, Captain Robinson, was reinforced, and, with its guns threatening the destruction of their city, kept the people of Baltimore discreetly quiet. When the Northern troops were attacked on their passage through Baltimore, Fort McHenry had been threatened by the mob; but Captain Robinson made it so manifest that he was determined to defend his post to the last extremity, that the most violently disposed forbore to attack him. Fort McHenry is an old-fashioned work, built many years ago. Though never of great strength, it succeeded during the war of 1812 in resisting a bombardment by the British fleet. Its guns were all on the parapet, without any protection from casemates, and its armament, principally composed of forty-two pounders, ten-inch mortars, and eight-inch howitzers, though originally deemed formidable enough, would prove of little effect against the improved cannon of more modern times. Situated, however, on a point of land between the harbor of Baltimore and the Patapsco River which empties into it, its position is favorable for defending the approaches, while it commands at the same time a portion of the city. Several artillery companies were thrown in to reinforce the garrison, and Major

Morris assumed the command, while Robinson was transferred to other service.

The union sentiment of Maryland was now claimed to be predominant. Large meetings were held and addressed in strains of loyal rhetoric by leading politicians of Maryland, who, although their fidelity to the Federal Government had never been questioned, had hitherto been prevented from openly manifesting it. Reverdy Johnson, an eminent lawyer and statesman of Maryland, took the occasion of the presentation of a United States flag by the ladies of Frederick, to the Home Guard of that place, to deliver a glowing eulogy upon the Union. There was a large audience gathered to listen to his ardent rhetoric. The population of the city was swelled by the influx of a large number of friends of the Union, from the neighboring towns and villages, some in troops on horseback, some in long trains of country vehicles of every kind, and others in groups afoot. All came in their holiday costume, and with blooming manifestations of their loyalty. "Union cockades and badges were displayed in profusion upon the coats of the jubilant Union men, numbers of whom were decidedly ambitious in their ideas of patriotic personal adornment, wearing cockades as large as sunflowers. The stars and stripes fluttered from about forty different points, and altogether," says an exultant newspaper reporter, "Frederick may be said to have donned her holiday suit for the occasion."

Reverdy Johnson's speech was a manly defence of the Government, and a sensible exposition of the advantages of the Union to all the States, and especially to Maryland:

"I hope," he said, "you will consider the occasion as justifying a few thoughts as to the duty and interest of our State in the present emergency. In the original causes which have produced it, she, thank God, had no share. Among the foremost and bravest in winning our independence ; among the truest and wisest in forming our Government, and among the first in adopting it, her sons have uniformly given it a faithful and zealous support. No treasonable thought, so far as we know, ever entered the mind of one of them ; certainly no threat of treason was ever whispered by them. They ever felt the immense advantage of the Union ; they saw evidenced by everything around them the blessings it conferred upon Maryland and upon all ; prosperity unexampled, a national power increasing every year with a rapidity and to a degree never before witnessed in a nation's history, and winning for us a name challenging the respect and admiration of the world. They saw in the extent of the country, and the differences of climate and habits, elements of strength rather than of weakness, and apprehended therefore no parricidal efforts in any quarter to destroy the Government. If occasionally murmurs of dissatisfaction were heard elsewhere, they were attributed to the whining disposition of some and the disappointed ambition of others. They were ridiculed, subjected to no other punishment, but left to stand as 'monuments of the safety with which error of opinion may be tolerated where reason is left free to combat it.' No 'whisky insurrection' ever occurred within our borders; no ordinance of nullification was ever threatened by us; and, if we continue true to patriotic duty, no ordinance of secession, direct or indirect, open or covert, will ever be adopted by those in authority, or, if madly adopted, be tolerated by the people.

"To this steadfast attachment to the Union we are not only bound by gratitude to the noble ancestry by whose patriotic wisdom it was bequeathed to us, and by the unappreciable blessings the bequest has conferred upon us, but by the assurance, which the most stolid intellect can hardly fail to feel, that its destruction would not only and at once deprive us of all these, but precipitate us into irreparable ruin. In this ruin all would more or less participate, but our geographical position would make it to us immediate and total. A peaceable disseverance the good and great men who have heretofore guided our public councils ever predicted to be impossible. The proclamations now trumpeted through the land, the marshaling of hosts by thousands and tens of thousands, the whitening of our waters with an immense naval marine, the blockade of ports, the prostration of commerce, the destruction of almost all civil employment, the heated tone of the public press of all sections, belching forth the most bitter enmity—all, all testify to the truth of the prediction. How this is to result, Heaven alone knows.

"But to my mind one thing is certain: the Government by no single act of its own has given cause for resistance to its rightful authority. The powers which it was exercising at the moment when rebellion began to muster its 'armies of pestilence,' were clearly conferred upon it by the Constitution. And if the Executive, then just legally chosen, had meditated any illegal policy, the friends of constitutional rights were numerous enough in Congress, had they remained at their posts, as they were bound to do by their oaths and their duty to the holy cause of constitutional government, successfully and peacefully to have thwarted it.

"The professed especial friends of Southern rights, instead of this, rudely shot from their spheres, and, under the utterly ridiculous claim of constitutional right, advised State secession. Madmen—if not worse—they desecrated, too, in support of this dogma, the name of Calhoun. He may have committed political errors—who has not? His doctrine of nullification was certainly one, in the judgment of all his great compeers, sanctioned by almost the entire country, but he never maintained the nonsensical heresy of rightful secession. On the contrary, long after that of the short-lived nullification, in February, 1844, writing to his 'political friends and supporters' refusing to permit his name to be presented before the then approaching Baltimore Convention, he said:

"'That each State has the right to act as it pleases in whatever relates to itself exclusively, no one will deny ; but it is a perfectly novel doctrine that any State has such a right when she comes to act in concert with others in reference to what concerns the whole. In such cases it is the plainest dictate of common sense, that whatever affects the whole should be regulated by the *mutual consent of all, and not by the discretion of each.*'

"That great philosophical statesman understood, as in another letter of the 3d of July, 1843, he invites his countrymen to understand, 'in all its great and beautiful proportions, the noble political structure reared by the wisdom and patriotism of our ancestors, and to have the virtue and the sense to preserve and protect it,' and declared it the 'duty of the Federal Government, under the guarantees of the Constitution, *promptly to suppress physical force as an element of change,* and to keep wide open the door for the free and full action of all the moral elements in its power.'

"The truth is—and I regret sincerely to believe it—that fear of a violation of Southern rights was with the prompters of the rebellion but a pretence.

"What they have done and are still doing at the sacrifice of the nation's welfare, and of the welfare of their own section, exerting every nerve to accomplish, was and is but to retain official power, which they fancied was passing from them. Look at the usurped government at Montgomery. The mention of names is unnecessary ; they are destined to an unhappy immortality. Those who plotted the seizure of forts, arsenals, mints, navy-yards, custom-houses, the admitted property of the United States, seducing soldiers and sailors from their sworn allegiance—using the very Senate chamber, dedicated and sacred to duty, as a spot from which to issue their treacherous telegrams—are there to be seen all in power, actual or prospective. The fact too clearly tells the revolting story. Men long enjoying public honors, earning through many years of service a national fame—owning their renown because of the world-wide fame of a glorious government, are striving, day and night, to reduce it to dishonor and destruction. Thank God, our consolation is that the effort, however pregnant with the present calamity, will fall short of its horrid aim. They may ' as well strike at the heavens with their arms' as lift them against the ' American Union.'

"That the end must fail, who can doubt ? The recent census furnishes pregnant proof of this. It shows that the free States have a population of males, between eighteen and forty-five, of 3,778,000, and all the slave States only 1,655,000, and the seceding States, excluding Virginia, but 531,000 ; and if to this vast difference of men is added that of wealth, inventive skill, habits of industry, and the absence of any element of domestic danger, the disparity is infinitely greater. In a struggle between such hosts—which may God in his mercy avert—who can fail to see what must be the end?

"But to our State these facts teach a lesson that all can understand. If mad and wicked enough to attempt it, what could we do to resist this immense power on our borders? Call on the South? Make our State the battle-field? How long could the entire South, if flying to our succor, remain with and aid us? They might assist in drenching our land with blood; they might witness with us the desolation that in such a contest would be our doom. They would be compelled to retire within their own limits, and we left alone in our calamity, to be rendered the more acute when we awoke'—as we should—to the insanity and crime which occasioned it. Looking, therefore, to interest alone, adherence to the Government is our clear policy."

The orator closed with a fervid appeal to the reverence of his listeners for the national flag.

"Though not especially impulsive, I cannot," he said, "imagine how an American eye can look upon that standard without emotion. The twenty stars added to the first constellation tell its proud history, its mighty influence, and its unequalled career. Are these now to be forgotten and lost? Tell me not that this is sentiment. Sentiment, to be sure it is, but it is one that purifies, and animates, and strengthens the national heart. God may be worshipped (I make the comparison with all proper reverence) in the open field, in the stable —but is there no virtue in the cathedral? Does not the soul turn its thoughts heavenwards the moment its sacred threshold is crossed? This, too, is sentiment, but it is one that honors our nature, and proves our loyalty to the Almighty.

"So it is with our national emblem. The man who is dead to its influence is in mind a fool or in heart a traitor. It is this emblem I am the honored organ now to present to you. I need not commend it to your constant, vigilant care; that, I am sure, it will ever be your pride to give it. When, if ever your hearts shall despond—when, if ever you shall desire your patriotism to be specially animated, throw it to the winds, gaze on its beautiful folds, remember the years and the fields over which, from '76 to the present time, it has been triumphantly borne; remember how it has consoled the dying and animated the survivor; remember that it served to kindle even to a brighter flame the patriotic ardor of Washington—went with him through all the struggles of the Revolution, consoled him in defeat, gave to victory an additional charm, and that his dying moments were consoled and cheered by the hope that it would forever float over a perpetual union, and you at once feel its almost holy influence and swear to stand by and maintain it till life itself shall be no more."

With this increased demonstration of Federal power, and this bolder manifestation of loyalty on the part of the unionists of Maryland, the secessionists no longer ventured upon an open display of their sentiments. They, however, still continued secretly to aid the insurgents of Virginia with supplies of men and means, and to promote their cause by concealed efforts to involve the State in the Southern insurrection.

The city of Baltimore had suddenly become wondrously tranquilized, and May 6. submitted almost without a murmur to the disbandment of its citizen soldiery. A few days subsequently, General Butler, who marched May 13. into the city with a force of two thousand men, of whom the Sixth Regiment of Massachusetts, before so cruelly treated, formed a part, was welcomed with apparent enthusiasm. "The streets were crowded with applauding people, Union flags flung to the breeze, and in some instances the private dwellings were illuminated."* Butler immediately encamped upon Federal Hill, an elevation commanding the city, and proceeded at once, with characteristic energy, to secure the military occupation of Baltimore. On the next day he issued this proclamation:

"DEPARTMENT OF ANNAPOLIS, FEDERAL HILL, BALTIMORE, *May* 14, 1861.

"A detachment of the forces of the Federal Government under my command have occupied the city of Baltimore for the purpose, among other things, of enforcing respect and obedience to the laws as well of the State, if requested thereto by the civil authorities, as of the United States, which are being violated within its limits by some malignant and traitorous men; and in order to testify the acceptance, by the Federal Government, of the fact that the city and all the well-intentioned portion of its inhabitants are loyal to the Union and the Constitution, and are to be so regarded and treated by all. To the end, therefore, that all misunderstanding of the purposes of the Government may be prevented, and to set at rest all unfounded, false, and seditious rumors, to relieve all apprehensions, if any are felt by the well-disposed portion of the community, and to make it thoroughly understood by all traitors, their aiders or abettors, that their rebellious acts must cease, I hereby, by the authority vested in me, as commander of the department of Annapolis, of which the city of Baltimore forms a part, do now command and make known that no loyal and well-disposed citizen will be disturbed in his lawful occupation or business, that private property will not be interfered with by the men under my command, or allowed to be interfered with by others, except in so far as it may be used to afford aid and comfort to those in rebellion against the Government, whether here or elsewhere, all of which property, munitions of war, and that fitted to aid and support the rebellion, will be seized and held subject to confiscation; and, therefore, all manufacturers of arms and munitions of war are hereby requested to report to me forthwith, so that the lawfulness of their occupation may be known and understood, and all misconstruction of their doings be avoided. No transportation from the city to the rebels of articles fitted to aid and support troops in the field will be permitted, and the fact of such transportation after the publication

* New York *Times*, May 15.

of this proclamation will be taken and received as proof of illegal intention on the part of the consignees, and will render the goods liable to seizure and confiscation.

"The Government being ready to receive all such stores and supplies, arrangements will be made to contract for them immediately; and the owners and manufacturers of such articles of equipment, and clothing, and munitions of war, and provisions are desired to put themselves in communication with the commanding General, in order that their workshops may be employed for loyal purposes, and the artisans of the city resume and carry on their wonted profitable occupations.

"The acting assistant-quarter-master and commissary of subsistence of the United States here stationed, has been instructed to procure and furnish at fair prices 40,000 rations for the use of the army of the United States, and further supplies will be drawn from the city to the full extent of its capacity if the patriotic and loyal men choose so to furnish supplies.

"All assemblages, except the ordinary police of armed bodies of men, other than those regularly organized and commissioned by the State of Maryland and acting under the orders of the Governor thereof, for drill and other purposes, are forbidden within the department.

"All officers of the militia of Maryland having command within the limits of the department, are requested to report through their officers forthwith to the General in command, so that he may be able to know and distinguish the regularly commissioned and loyal troops of Maryland from armed bodies who may claim to be such.

"The ordinary operations of the corporate government of the city of Baltimore and of the civil authorities will not be interfered with, but, on the contrary, will be aided by all the power at the command of the General upon proper call being made; and all such authorities are cordially invited to co-operate with the General in command to carry out the purposes set forth in the proclamation, so that the city of Baltimore may be shown to the country to be, what she is in fact, patriotic and loyal to the Union, the Constitution, and the laws." No flag, banner, ensign, or device of the so-called Confederate States, or of any of them, will be permitted to be raised or shown in this department, and the exhibition of either of them by evil-disposed persons will be deemed, and taken to be, evidence of a design to afford aid and comfort to the enemies of the country. To make it the more apparent that the Government of the United States by far more relies upon the loyalty, patriotism, and zeal of the good citizens of Baltimore and vicinity than upon any exhibition of force calculated to intimidate them into that obedience to the laws which the Government doubts not will be paid from inherent respect and love of order, the commanding General has brought to the city with him, of the many thousand troops in the immediate neighborhood, which might be at once concentrated here, scarcely more than an ordinary guard, and, until it fails him, he will continue to rely upon that loyalty and patriotism of the citizens of Maryland which have never yet been found wanting to the Government in time of need. The General in command desires to greet and treat in this part of his department all the citizens thereof as friends and brothers, having a common purpose, a common loyalty, and a common country. Any infractions of the laws by the troops under his command, or any disorderly, unsoldierlike conduct, or any interferences with private property, he desires to have immediately reported to him, and he pledges himself that if any soldier so far forgets himself as to break those laws that he has sworn to defend and enforce, he shall be most rigorously punished.

"The General believes that if the suggestions and requests contained in this proclamation are carried out by the co-operation of all good and Union-loving citizens, and peace, and quiet, and certainty of future peace and quiet are thus restored, business will resume its accustomed channels, trade take the place of dulness and inactivity, efficient labor displace idleness, and Baltimore will be, in fact, what she is entitled to be—in the front rank of the commercial cities of the nation.

"Given at Baltimore, the day and year herein first above written.

"BENJ. F. BUTLER,

"B.-G. Com. Depart. of Annapolis."

This was soon followed by the seizure of a large quantity of arms, amounting to "fifteen dray-loads," which had been secreted by the secessionists of Baltimore, and the arrest of some leading citizens suspected of conniving at the overthrow of the Federal authority. These decided measures produced an immediate effect. The Governor of Maryland, who had been so intimidated by the disaffected of his State that he had not hitherto ventured to pay full allegiance to that government to which he claimed to be loyal, now, after a delay of a month, responded favorably to the President's call for troops. He yet, however, was constrained to deal tenderly with the uncertain temper of his fellow-citizens, and to qualify his appeal to arms in defence of the Union, by a condition to suit their equivocal loyalty.

May 14.

"Whereas the President of the United States, by his proclamation of April 15, 1861, has called upon me, the Governor of Maryland, for four regiments of infantry or riflemen, to serve for a period of three months, the said requisition being made in the spirit and in pursuance of the law; and

"Whereas to the said requisition has been added the written assurance of the secretary of war, that said four regiments shall be detailed to serve within the limits of the State of Maryland, or for the defence of the capital of the United States, and not to serve beyond the limits aforesaid;

"Now, therefore, I, Thomas Holliday Hicks, Governor of Maryland, do, by this my proclamation, call upon loyal citizens of Maryland to volunteer their services to the extent of four regiments, as aforesaid, to serve during a period of three months within the limits of Maryland, or for the defence of the capital of the United States, to be subject under the conditions aforesaid, to the orders of the Commander-in-chief of the army of the United States.

"Given under my hand and the great seal of the State of Maryland, at the city of Frederick, this 14th day of May, 1861.
"THOS. H. HICKS."

The Legislature, too, was frightened into comparative propriety, and brought May 11. its refractory proceedings to a close by a sudden adjournment. The spirit of disaffection, however, which May 10. prevailed, was made manifest by the adoption, a few days before, of these resolutions:

"Whereas the war against the Confederate States is unconstitutional and repuguant to civilization, and will result in a bloody and shameful overthrow of our institutions; and while recognizing the obligations of Maryland to the Union, we sympathize with the South in the struggle for their rights—for the sake of humanity, we are for peace and reconciliation, and solemnly protest against this war, and will take no part in it; therefore,

"*Resolved*, That Maryland implores the President, in the name of God, to cease this unholy war, at least until Congress assembles; that Maryland desires and consents to the recognition of the independence of the Confederate States. The military occupation of Maryland is unconstitutional, and she protests against it, though the violent interference with the transit of Federal troops is discountenanced; that the vindication of her rights be left to time and reason, and that a convention, under existing circumstances, is inexpedient."

The last act of the Legislature of Maryland was to appoint two commissioners to visit President Jefferson Davis, two to visit President Lincoln, two to visit Richmond, and two to visit Pennsylvania.

The route through Baltimore to the capital was now secured, and the Federal Government could claim its first great victory in the struggle for the assertion of its authority.

CHAPTER XX.

Increased Energy of the Government.—Augmenting force of Secession.—Progress of North Carolina to Secession.—Seizure of United States Mint and Arsenal.—Action of the Governor.—Convening of the Legislature.—Denunciation of the President's Proclamation.—Ordinance of Secession.—Union with the Confederate States.—Action of Arkansas.—Seizure of Federal Property.—Act of Secession.—Sanguine hopes entertained of Tennessee.—Union Sentiment in Tennessee.—A Vote against a Convention.—Disregarded by the Governor.—Legislature Convened.—Military League with the Southern Confederacy.—Ratification of League.—Opposition in the Legislature.—Question submitted to the People.—Strange Contrast.—Arbitrary Action.—Pretended Submission to the Will of the People.—Apology of the Tennessee Legislature.—The strong Union Sentiment in Eastern Tennessee.—Description of East Tennessee.—Character of the Population.—Opposition to the Action of the Legislature.—A Convention called at Knoxville.—Its object.—The unavailing resistance in East Tennessee.—Ratification by the People of the State of the Ordinance of Secession.—Great Encouragement for the Union in Western Virginia.—Description of Western Virginia.—Geographical and Social Characteristics.—Whites and Blacks.—Free Labor.—Sympathy with the North.—Enterprise and Thrift.—Immense Resources.—Future Prospects.—Disputes with Eastern Virginia.—Difference of Interests.—Unequal Taxation.—Opposition to Secession.—Union Meetings.—Convention in Western Virginia.—"New Virginia."—Action of the Convention.—An ardent Appeal for the Union.—Rallying to Arms.—Union Enthusiasm.—Union Military Companies.—Union Preachers.—The first Encounter in Western Virginia.—A bloodless beginning of a Bloody War.

1861.

WHILE the Federal Government was asserting its authority with increased energy and power, and the Union sentiment of the North was daily strengthening, the Southern rebellion was augmenting with even greater force and rapidity. North Carolina was passing through the various phases of defiance and spoliation of the General Government which had marked the career of the other slave States in their progress to secession. Her Governor had resolutely and contemptuously refused the call of the President for the State's quota of troops for the defence of the Union. April 21. The United States Branch Mint had been seized and held by a military force under his command, and April 22. on the next day the Federal arsenal at Fayetteville, filled with munitions of war belonging to the United States, was forced to surrender to the State authorities. At the same time the Governor of North Carolina called for thirty thousand volunteers, in addition to the regular militia, and ordered them to be ready at a moment's notice.

These acts, the purport of which was obvious, were followed by April 26. the Governor's proclamation convening the Legislature. In this document he denounced President Lincoln's proclamation and Secretary Cameron's requisition for seventy-five thousand troops, the "high-handed act of tyrannical outrage," the object of which was "the violent subversion of the liberties of a free people constituting a large part of the whole population of the United States; it is not only," the Governor added, "in violation of all constitutional law, utter disregard of every sentiment of humanity and Christian civilization, and conceived in a spirit of aggression unparalleled by any act of recorded history, but is a direct step toward the subjugation of the whole South, and the conversion of a free republic, inherited from our fathers, into a military despotism, to be established by worse than foreign enemies on the ruins of our once glorious Constitution of equal rights." He closed by an appeal to the fidelity of the people of North Carolina, to the "sovereign" authority of their State. "I furthermore exhort," he said, "all good citizens throughout the State to be mindful that their first allegiance is due to the sovereignty. which protects their homes and dearest interests, as their first service is due for the sacred defence of their hearths, and of the soil which holds the graves of our glorious dead. United action in defence of the sovereignty of North Carolina, and of the rights of the South, becomes now the duty of all."

May 20. In three weeks after, a convention "declared and ordained that the ordinance adopted by the State of North Carolina, in the Convention of 1789, whereby the Constitution of the United States was ratified and adopted, and also all acts and parts of acts of the General Assembly ratifying and adopting amendments to the said Constitution, are hereby repealed, rescinded, and abrogated."

It was then "declared and ordained" that, the union with the United States being dissolved, and North Carolina in full possession of the "rights of sovereignty, the State accepts the Constitution of the 'Confederate States of America,' and will enter into federal association with them, when admitted in due form. North Carolina thus gave in her adherence to the new confederacy, and joined in the armed combination to dissolve the old Union.

Arkansas was the next to follow. She began, too, with spoliation. At Napoleon, the Federal dépôt was seized by order of the Governor, and military supplies belonging to the United States, consisting of one hundred and fifty thousand ball cartridges, a hundred Maynard rifles, two hundred cavalry saddles, and five hundred sabres, were appropriated by the State. Fort Smith, too, which had cost the Federal Government over three hundred thousand dollars, was forced to surrender. The State troops upon taking possession raised the Confederate flag amid the firing of cannon and the exulting cheers of the people, who gave shouts of applause for the citizen soldiery of Arkansas, its Governor, and for Jefferson Davis. April 22. April 25.

These usual preliminaries of disruption were soon followed by the act of secession from the Federal Union, the adoption of the Constitution of the Confederate States, and the admission of the State as another member of the Southern Confederacy. May 7.

Tennessee, the last to attach her fortunes to the chances of the new confederacy, it was fondly hoped by the North would have clung to the old Union. Though her Governor, who was known to be in league with the Confederates, had responded so defiantly to the President's requisition for troops, there was yet believed to be a loyalty to the Federal Government so strong, particularly in the eastern part of the State, that it could counteract the machinations of those political leaders of Tennessee who were striving to wrest her from the Union. This belief was encouraged by the vote of the State on the question of holding a convention for the consideration of the policy of seceding. By a large majority, the people of Tennessee decided against the convention. The Governor, though thus rebuked by this expression of popular will, gave it no heed, but persisted in his determination to force the State out of the Union. He accordingly convened the Legislature —the majority of which accorded with him in sentiment—for the purpose of accomplishing indirectly what seemed impracticable through the direct action of the suffrage of the people. The Legislature having met, both Houses passed at once, in secret session, a joint resolution authorizing the Governor to enter into a military league with the Confederate States. Three commissioners were accordingly appointed; and having held a conference with an agent of the new government, expressly delegated for the purpose, the following was agreed to:

"The State of Tennessee, looking to a speedy admission into the confederacy established by the Confederate States of America, in accordance with the Constitution for the Provisional Government of said States, enters into the following temporary convention, agreement, and military league with the Confederate States, for the purpose of meeting pressing exigencies affecting the common rights, interests, and safety of said States and said Confederacy:

"*First.* Until said State shall become a member of said Confederacy, according to the Constitutions of both powers, the whole military force and military operations, offensive and defensive, of said State in the impending conflict with the United States shall be under the chief control and direction of the President of the Confederate States upon the same basis, principles, and footing as if said State were now and during the interval a member of said Confederacy; said force, together with that of the Confederate States, to be employed for the common defence.

"*Second.* The State of Tennessee will, upon becoming a member of said Confederacy, under the permanent Constitution of said Confederate States, if the same shall occur, turn over to the said Confederate States all the public property, naval stores, and munitions of war of which she may then be in possession, acquired from the United States, on the same terms and in the same manner as the other States of said Confederacy have done in like cases.

"*Third.* Whatever expenditure of money, if any, the said State of Tennessee shall make before she becomes a member of said Confederacy, shall be met and provided for by the Confederate States.

"This convention entered into and agreed on, in the city of Nashville, Tennessee, on the seventh day of May, A.D. 1861, by Henry W. Hilliard, the duly authorized commissioner to act in the matter for the Confederate States, and Gustavus A. Henry, Archibald O. W. Totten, and Washington Barrow, commissioners, duly authorized to act in like manner for the State of Tennessee. The whole subject to the approval and ratification of the proper authorities of both governments, respectively.

"In testimony whereof, the parties aforesaid have hereunto set their hands and seals, the day and year aforesaid, in duplicate originals.

"HENRY W. HILLIARD,
"Commissioner for the Confederate States of America.
"GUSTAVUS A. HENRY,
"A. O. W. TOTTEN,
"WASHINGTON BARROW,
"Commissioners on the part of Tennessee."

The Legislature hastened to ratify this league, and thus secure the future secession of the State, by an act which, placing the military resources under the control of the Confederate States, would enable them to repress by coercion any appearance of dissatisfaction in Tennessee. There was, however, a manifestation of opposition, even in the Legislature, to this disregard of the voice of the people. The resolution ratifying the league was opposed in the Senate by a vote of six to fourteen, four not having voted at all;, and in the House by a vote of fifteen to forty-two, eighteen having withheld their votes.

After having thus deprived the people of all independence of action, the Legislature, with an affected regard for the popular will, formally submitted to the vote of the State a question which they had already decided by an act of their own, in defiance of the declared sentiment of a majority of their fellow-citizens. The following is a curious contrast to the league already formed with the Confederate States. The semblance of deference to popular will and the reality of arbitrary power, not seldom combined, was never more strikingly manifest than in these two documents emanating from the same source:

May 6.

"SEC. 1. *Be it enacted by the General Assembly of the State of Tennessee,* That immediately after the passage of this act, the Governor of this State shall, by proclamation, direct the sheriffs of the several counties in this State to open and hold an election at the various voting precincts in their respective counties on the 8th day of June, 1861 ; that the said sheriffs, or, in the absence of the sheriffs, the coroner of the county, shall immediately advertise the election contemplated by this act ; that said sheriffs appoint a deputy to hold said election for each voting precinct, and that said deputy appoint three judges and two clerks for each precinct ; and if no officer shall, from any cause, attend any voting precinct to open and hold said election, then any justice of the peace, or, in the absence of a justice of the peace, any respectable freeholder may appoint an officer, judges, and clerks to open and hold said election. Said officers, judges, and clerks shall be sworn as now required by law, and who, after being so sworn, shall open and hold an election, open and close at the time of day and in the manner now required by law in elections for members to the General Assembly.

"SEC. 2. *Be it further enacted*, That at said election the following declaration shall be submitted to a vote of the qualified voters of the State of Tennessee, for their ratification or rejection:

"DECLARATION OF INDEPENDENCE AND ORDINANCE DISSOLVING THE FEDERAL RELATION between the State of Tennessee and the United States of America.

"*First.* We, the people of the State of Tennessee, waiving an expression of opinion as to the abstract doctrine of secession, but asserting the right as a free and independent people to alter, reform, or abolish our form of government in such manner as we think proper, do ordain and declare that all the laws and ordinances by which the State of Tennessee became a member of the Federal Union of the United States of America are hereby abrogated and annulled, and that all obligations on our part be withdrawn therefrom; and we do hereby resume all the rights, functions, and powers which by any of said laws and ordinances were conveyed to the Government of the United States, and absolve ourselves from all the obligations, restraints, and duties incurred thereto; and do hereby henceforth become a free, sovereign, and independent State.

"*Second.* We furthermore declare and ordain, that Article 10, Sections 1 and 2 of the Constitution of the State of Tennessee, which requires members of the General Assembly, and all officers, civil and military, to take an oath to support the Constitution of the United States, be, and the same are hereby abrogated and annulled; and all parts of the Constitution of the State of Tennessee making citizenship of the United States a qualification for office, and recognizing the Constitution of the United States as the supreme law of this State, are in like manner abrogated and annulled.

"*Third.* We furthermore ordain and declare, that all rights acquired and vested under the Constitution of the United States, or under any act of Congress passed in pursuance thereof, or under any laws of this State, and not incompatible with this ordinance, shall remain in force, and have the same effect as if this ordinance had not been passed.

"SEC. 3. *Be it further enacted*, That said election shall be by ballot, that those voting for the Declaration and Ordinance shall have written or printed on their ballots 'Separation,' and those voting against it shall have written or printed on their ballots 'No Separation.' That the clerks holding said election shall keep regular scrolls of the voters, as now required by law in the election of members to the General Assembly: that the clerks and judges shall certify the same, with the number of votes for 'Separation,' and the number of votes for 'No Separation.' The officer holding the election shall return the same to the sheriff of the county, at the county seat, on the Monday next after the election. The sheriff shall immediately make out, certify, and send to the Governor the number of votes polled, and the number of votes for 'Separation,' and the number for 'No Separation,' and file one of the original scrolls with the clerk of the county court; that upon comparing the vote by the Governor in the office of the secretary of state, which shall be at least by the 24th day of June, 1861, and may be sooner if the returns are all received by the Governor, if a majority of the votes polled shall be for 'Separation,' the Governor shall, by his proclamation, make it known, and declare all connection by the State of Tennessee with the Federal Union dissolved, and that Tennessee is a free, independent government, free from all obligations to, or connection with, the Federal Government; and that the Governor shall cause 'the vote by counties' to be published, the number for 'Separation,' and the number for 'No Separation,' whether a majority vote for 'Separation' or 'No Separation.'

"SEC. 4. *Be it further enacted*, That in the election to be held under the provisions of this act, upon the Declaration submitted to the people, all volunteers and other persons connected with the service of this State, qualified to vote for members of the Legislature in the counties where they reside, shall be entitled to vote in any county in the State where they may be in active service, or under orders, or on parole, at the time of said election; and all other voters shall vote in the county where they reside, as now required by law in voting for members of the General Assembly.

"SEC. 5. *Be it further enacted*, That at the same time, and under the rules and regulations prescribed for the election hereinbefore ordered, the following ordinance shall be submitted to the popular vote. To wit:

"AN ORDINANCE for the adoption of the Constitution of the Provisional Government of the Confederate States of America.

"We, the people of Tennessee, solemnly impressed by the perils that surround us, do hereby adopt and ratify the Constitution of the Provisional Government of the Confederate States of America, ordained and established at Montgomery, Alabama, on the 8th day of February, 1861, to be in force during the existence thereof, or until such time as we may supersede it by the adoption of a permanent constitution.

"SEC. 6. *Be it further enacted*, That those in favor of the adoption of said Provisional Constitution, and thereby securing to Tennessee equal representation in the deliberations and councils of the Confederate States, shall have written or printed on their ballots the word 'Representation;' opposed, the words 'No Representation.'

"SEC. 7. *Be it further enacted*, That in the event the people shall adopt the Constitution of the Provisional Government of the Confederate States at the election herein ordered, it shall be the duty of the Governor forthwith to issue writs of election for delegates to represent the State of Tennessee in the said Provisional Government. That the State shall be represented by as many delegates as it was entitled to members of Congress to the recent Congress of the United States of America, who shall be elected from the several congressional districts as now established by law, in the mode and manner now prescribed for the election of members of Congress of the United States.

"SEC. 8. *Be it further enacted,* That this act shall take effect from and after its passage. W. C. WHITTHORNE,
  'Speaker of House of Rep.
    "B. L. STOVALL,
  "Speaker of the Senate."

The Tennessee Legislature, conscious that their arbitrary action in this matter was inconsistent with their professed deference to the popular will, issued a labored apology of their conduct. In regard to the secrecy of their session, they confessed that it was the first time in the history of the State that the "rule" had been adopted, but justified and strove to dignify it by some honored historic parallels. The people of Tennessee were reminded that the convention which framed the Declaration of Independence of the United States, and that which framed the Constitution of the United States, held their sessions in secret, and that the Senate of the United States not infrequently sits with closed doors. To those who had "taken occasion to condemn" them, they answered with the sneer that they "may be purer than those who framed the Declaration of Independence, but we very much doubt whether they will have greater hold upon public confidence."

In justification of their course, they declared that "the country was excited, and the public demands imperious;" that they desired to legislate uninfluenced and unretarded by the crowds that would have otherwise attended their deliberations, and that the western part of Tennessee was in an exposed condition, with no military defence whatever; that the towns and counties bordering on the Mississippi were liable to be assailed by the armed forces collected at Cairo, and they desired that no act on their part should form the pretext for such an invasion, so long as it could be avoided. "Our fellow-citizens of West Tennessee and of Arkansas are laboring night and day," they said, "to erect batteries on the river to prevent the descent of the enemy. A duty that we owed to them and to the cause of humanity demanded that we should not make our action known till the latest possible moment. If some desired light while we were at work, we equally desired to save the blood and property of Tennesseans."

This no doubt was a satisfactory excuse to the secessionists of Tennessee, but hardly a sufficient motive in the opinion of the loyal for depriving them of their constitutional rights, to uphold which that "enemy" so denounced by the Legislature was in arms.

Throughout Tennessee there was undoubtedly a strong attachment to the Union, but particularly in the eastern part of the State, a region bordering on the Alleghany range, where the people, possessed of but few slaves, had few interests in common with the lordly planters of the rest of the State. Inhabiting a country the land of which can only be cultivated profitably by the personal labor of the proprietors, the people of East Tennessee have learned to depend upon their own resources. They have thus become industrious and self-reliant, and acquired a respect for labor which, as it assimilates them to the people of the North, tends to withdraw their sympathies from the Southern slaveholders, who, with negroes to do their work, exult in the aristocracy of idleness.

The action of the Tennessee Legislature was particularly odious to the independent yeomen of East Tennessee, and they immediately called a convention to be held in Knoxville, "disapproving," as they declared, "of the hasty and inconsiderate action of our General Assembly, and sincerely desirous to do, in the midst of the troubles which surround us, what will be best for our country and for all classes of our citizens." The resistance, however, of this portion of the State proved at that time of little avail to the cause of the Union, and did not prevent the people of Tennessee, under the terrorism, doubtless, of the military power, from sanctioning, by a large majority of votes, the arbitrary action of the Legislature.

Though the Federal Government was disappointed in its anticipations of support in Tennessee, it found great encouragement in Virginia, where the people of the northwestern district, in spite of the secession of the State, had taken a bold stand for the Union. This portion of Virginia, bounded on the east by the Alleghany range of mountains, on the north and west by the free States of Pennsylvania and Ohio, and on the south by the Kanawha valley, watered by the river of that name which empties into the Ohio, has much of the geographical and social characteristics of the North. It is thus described, "The negro element is very small, there being but fifteen thousand slaves to three hundred and fifty-five thousand four hundred and ninety-two whites; while in the middle district, between the Blue Ridge and the Alleghanies, the proportion of slaves is forty-eight thousand and forty to two hundred and forty-three thousand one hundred and fifty-five whites; and in Eastern Virginia, lying between the Blue Ridge and the Atlantic, the number of slaves reaches the large proportion of four hundred and thirty-eight thousand four hundred and sixteen to four hundred and forty-eight thousand nine hundred and thirty-two whites.

"The proportion of the negro to the white population, moreover, has been rapidly decreasing in Western Virginia. The number of slaves, it is true, throughout the whole State, has lessened during the last ten years, but it is only in the middle and western districts, and especially in the latter, where the whites have much augmented in number. Of the whole increase of the white population of the State, from 1850 to 1860, estimated at one hundred and fifty-two thousand seven hundred and seventy-nine, no less than seventy-nine thousand eight hundred and twelve—more than one-half of the total increase—was in Western Virginia.

"A comparative freedom from slavery has produced not only a social diversity, but a difference of interest, which had long tended greatly to weaken the alliance of the western district with the rest of the State. There are, besides, natural influences which, at the same time, have continued to strengthen the sympathy of Western Virginia with the North. The abundant resources of coal and iron have attracted the enterprise of Northern capitalists and caused an immigration of working-men to a country where the slaves are so few as neither to degrade nor to compete with free labor. The close proximity, moreover, of the States of Pennsylvania and Ohio, between which Western Virginia is wedged, has naturally brought it into such an intimate social and trading relationship with them, that it has become emulous of the spirit of enterprise which, under the impulse of freedom, animates its neighbors. Its chief city, Wheeling, is already so alive with the zealous activity of commerce and manufactures, that it rivals in prosperity some of the most flourishing communities of the North. The whole region has immense resources for the support of a large and thriving population. With a wholesome climate, cooled by the bracing atmosphere of the mountains; with a soil of valley and hillside enriched by the flow of numerous rivers, and sources of wealth in its forests, its water power, its minerals, its navigable streams, and its railroad communications, Western Virginia presents a seductive invitation to enterprise and a certain promise of liberal reward. While the affinities of this district are thus naturally with its energetic neighbors of the free North, local political differences, apart from an original antagonism, have for a long time existed to interrupt its relations with the predominant slave power of the State."

"Presuming upon its political strength, Eastern Virginia had executed vast projects of improvement, especially for its own benefit, and imposed an unequal weight of the prodigal expenditure incurred, upon the western district. A tax was laid, but all slaves under twelve years of age were exempted. As Eastern Virginia was chiefly engaged in raising negroes for the Southwestern slave-markets, this exemption of a large portion of what was one of their most valuable products, was considered an unjust exception in favor of its own interests. Western Virginia complained grievously, and finally strove in consequence to separate from the eastern part of the State. Efforts to this effect had been made, and seemed at one time to have nearly succeeded.

An opposition to the action of the political leaders of Eastern Virginia in their movement toward wresting the

State from the Union, naturally came from the inhabitants of the west. At the convention which met on the 17th of April at Richmond, the delegates from Western Virginia protested almost unanimously against the act of secession which was passed. Such was the popular indignation to which they exposed themselves by their firm resistance to the prevalent disunion sentiment of that locality, that they barely escaped with their lives from the excited mob of the rebellious city.

Not satisfied with protests, Western Virginia determined to resist by action the violent disruption of its relations with the Union. Large meetings were held, and it was recommended at a **April 22.** gathering in Harrison County, that the people of all the counties of Northwestern Virginia should appoint delegates, not less than five in number, of "their wisest, best, and discreetest men," to meet in convention at Wheeling, on the 13th of May, to "consult and determine upon such action as the people of Northwestern Virginia should take in the present fearful emergency."

This recommendation met with general approval, and accordingly delegates, representing thirty of the fifty western **May 13.** counties, assembled at Wheeling. The long-desired object of many Western Virginians became the prominent subject of discussion, on the proposition of Mr. Carlile for the separation of the western district of Virginia from the rest, and its organization into a State to be called "New Virginia."

This, however, was not adopted, on the ground that it acknowledged the principle of secession, and thus seemed to justify the act of the secessionists of Virginia, against whom and their doctrines the loyal men of the West had arrayed themselves. Mr. Carlile's resolution of separation being, however, changed into one of inquiry as to its policy, became more acceptable, and in this form was adopted.

The convention, waiving for the present the question of separation, contented itself with passing resolutions denouncing the action of the secessionists of the State, expressing its own loyal attachment to the Union, recommending the citizens to vote against the act of secession to be submitted to their suffrage, and in case it should be passed, to appoint delegates to a general convention to meet for the purpose of devising such measures and taking such action as the welfare and safety of the people they represent might demand. Closing with this ardent appeal to the loyalty of the people of Northwestern Virginia, the convention adjourned:

"In obedience to the fourteenth* resolution of the convention which met in this city on the 13th instant, we earnestly conjure you to enter actively and immediately upon the great work of preparing your neighbors and friends,

---

* "*Resolved*, That each county represented in this convention, and any others that may be disposed to co-operate with us, be requested to appoint a committee of five, whose duty it shall be to see that all things that may be necessary to be done be attended to, to carry out the objects of this convention, and to correspond with the central committee."

as well as yourselves, for the firm, stern, and decided stand necessary to be taken and adhered to at all hazards, and maintained at any and every cost, if we would preserve to ourselves and transmit to our posterity that unity of government which constitutes us one people, which we justly regard as the palladium of our liberties and the main pillar in the edifice of our independence. In this way, and in this way alone, we can save ourselves from the innumerable evils consequent upon secession and all the horrors of civil war.

"Why should the people of Northwestern Virginia allow themselves to be dragged into the rebellion inaugurated by ambitious and heartless men, who have banded themselves together to destroy a government formed for you by your patriot fathers, and which has secured to you all the liberties consistent with the nature of man, and has, for near three-fourths of a century, sheltered you in sunshine and in storm, made you the admiration of the civilized world, and conferred upon you a title more honored, respected, and revered than that of king or potentate—the title of American citizen. Will you passively surrender it and submit to be used by the conspirators engaged in this effort to enslave you, as their instruments by which your enslavement is to be effected?

"Freemen who would remain free must prove themselves worthy to be free, and must themselves first strike the blow.

"What is secession? A deed not to be accomplished in the broad glare of a noonday sun, but a deed of darkness, which had to be performed in secret conclave by the reckless spirits who accomplished it, in contempt of the people, their masters under our form of government, but whom the leaders in this work of destruction have determined to enslave.

"What is secession? Bankruptcy, ruin, civil war, ending in military despotism. Prior to the adoption of the ordinance of secession in Virginia, and to the passage by the Legislature of the bill calling a convention, all was peace, and the great business interests of our State were uninterrupted. From the hour that it was proclaimed the ordinance of secession had been passed, business of every description has been paralyzed; State, corporation, and individual credit is prostrate, and bankruptcy and ruin stare us in the face, and war, civil war, with all its attendant horrors, is upon us. Secession, all now see, is war. It is preceded by war, accompanied and sustained by war, ushered into being by war.

"Who are to stand the brunt of this contest? Will it be those who have clamored loudest for secession, and who have done the most to bring on the present crisis? These are the first to flee from the very approach of danger. They hurry, in every train and by every coach, from the anticipated scenes of disturbance. Will the disunion majority of the Richmond Convention come into the ranks and shoulder the musket in the strife which they have inaugu-

NEW NATIONAL WORK ON THE LATE REBELLION.

Now Publishing, in Parts at 50 cents, and Divisions at $1.

THE GREAT CIVIL WAR:

A HISTORY OF

THE LATE REBELLION;

Being a complete Narrative of the Events connected with the Origin, Progress, and Conclusion of the War, with Biographical Sketches of Leading Statesmen and Distinguished Military and Naval Commanders, etc., etc.

By ROBERT TOMES, M.D.

Continued from the beginning of the year 1864 to the end of the War.

By BENJ. G. SMITH Esq.

Illustrated by numerous highly finished Steel Engravings, Colored Maps, Plans, etc., from Drawings by F. O. C. Darley and other eminent Artists.

THE four years' war, now happily ended—so remarkable for its sudden outbreak, its unexpected duration, and its entire termination—not only absorbed universal attention at home, but had, during its continuance, a paramount interest for the nations of Europe, and was the subject of constant comment and prophecy on the part of both the friends and enemies of national self-government. It not only displayed the astonishing resources of the country, and exhibited, even while the struggle continued, in the vast armies raised and the persistent spirit of the people, a capacity for war that entitles the United States to the first rank among military nations, but also demonstrated the enduring character of the government and institutions, which have proved themselves able to withstand even the fearful shocks of a gigantic civil war.

A history of this great war will be a necessity to every loyal American. To be without a knowledge of the causes and events of the great struggle for the preservation of the Union would be as inexcusable as to be ignorant of the events which led to its formation.

The present work will be a complete history of the war and of its immediate causes, from the election of Mr. Lincoln and the commencement of actual hostilities by the attack on Fort Sumter, to the evacuation of Richmond and the surrender of the armies of Lee, Johnston, and Kirby Smith. It will contain detailed accounts of the great battles, sieges, marches, and naval operations, a record of political events, remarks on foreign relations, statistical facts with regard to the resources of both the Northern and Southern States, descriptions of fortresses and battle-fields, and a large number of biographical sketches of distinguished commanders and statesmen, to which will be appended a copious and elaborate Index.

Not the least attractive feature of the work will be the large number of beautiful and costly steel engravings, comprising portraits of statesmen and military and naval commanders, Northern and Southern, who have become famous in the course of the war.

Among the illustrations are also splendid bird's-eye views of Fortress Monroe and vicinity, Charleston, Richmond, and New Orleans; representations of battle-scenes, views of forts and battle-fields, sea views, and a number of carefully prepared colored maps and plans, highly useful in making clear the movements and positions of armies.

CONDITIONS OF PUBLICATION.

The work will be printed in a clear, bold type, on superfine, calendered paper, and issued in Parts at Fifty Cents, and Divisions at $1 each.

The illustrations will comprise fifty-four portraits and thirty-six battle-scenes, plans, maps, bird's-eye views, etc.

A Part will be published every two weeks and a Division every month until completed, the whole not to exceed forty-five Parts, at Fifty Cents each.

No subscriber's name received for less than the whole work; and each Part or Division will be payable on delivery, the carrier not being allowed to give credit or receive payment in advance.

VIRTUE & YORSTON, 12 DEY STREET, & 544 BROADWAY, NEW YORK.

And Sold by their Agents in all the Principal Cities of the United States and Canadas.

To be Completed in Forty-five Parts, at Fifty Cents each.

rated? They will keep at a respectful distance from danger. They will fill the lucrative offices and secure the rich appointments which appertain to the new order of things. They will luxuriate on two or three or four hundred dollars per month, with horses, and servants, and rations to match, while the Union-loving people will be called upon, for the honor of Virginia and two shillings per day, to do the fighting and undergo the hardships of war. 'We are all Virginians,' say they; 'the State must be sustained, and, right or wrong, we must all fight for Virginia,' etc.

"What is it to fight for Virginia? What is it to sustain the State? Is it to urge her upon a course which leads to visible and gaping destruction? Is this the way and the only way in which we can testify our devotion to the commonwealth? If the feelings which actuated our Revolutionary fathers be not all dead in us, we shall exhibit our love for Virginia by repudiating this tyrannical rule which the Richmond Convention has endeavored to impose, and not suffer ourselves to be sold like sheep from the shambles. The people yet hold their destinies in their own hands; it is for them to accept or reject a tyranny worse many times than that from which the war of '76 delivered us—not the tyranny of one man, but of many.

"But, people of Northwestern Virginia, why should we thus permit ourselves to be tyrannized over and made slaves of by the haughty arrogance and wicked machinations of would-be Eastern despots? Are we submissionists, craven cowards, who will yield to daring ambition the rich legacy of freedom which we have inherited from our fathers, or are we men who know our rights, and knowing, dare maintain them? If we are, we will resist the usurpers, and drive from our midst the rebellion sought to be forced upon us. We will, in the strength of our cause, resolutely and determinedly stand by our rights and our liberties, secured to us by the struggles of our Revolutionary fathers and the authors of the Constitution under which we have grown and prospered beyond all precedent in the world's history; we will maintain, protect, and defend that Constitution and the Union with all our strength and with all our powers, ever remembering that 'Resistance to tyrants is obedience to God.'

"We utterly repudiate the war sought to be forced upon us without and against the consent and earnest protestations of the people who have not produced it, but who have, we regret to say, thus far offered no resistance, but have submitted to the filling up of armies and the quartering of troops in their midst; taking for the purpose our young men who had, in a time of profound peace, and with no expectation of ever being called upon to aid in a rebellion, attached themselves to the volunteer corps of our State. The people, stunned by the magnitude of the crime, have for a time offered no resistance; but as returning reason enables them to perceive distinctly the objects and purposes of the vile perpetrators of this deed, their hearts swell within them, and already

31

the cry has gone up from our mountains and our valleys, 'Resistance to tyrants is obedience to God.'

"Let us urge you, then, that our resistance may be effectual, to act in the spirit of the resolutions here appended, adopted by the Convention whose committee we are. Let all our ends be directed to the creation of an organized resistance to the despotism of the tyrants who have been in session in Richmond, and who are about to reassemble, that we may maintain our position in the Union under the flag of our common country, which has for so many years waved gracefully and protectingly over us, and which, when we behold upon its ample folds the stripes and the stars of freedom, causes our bosoms to glow with patriotic heat, and our hearts to swell with honest love of country. That this flag, the symbol of our might, challenges our admiration, and justly claims our every effort against those who have dared to desecrate and dishonor it, we all admit. Let us, then, see that we take the proper measures to make effectual those efforts.

"This Convention to assemble on the 11th proximo is looked to to organize our action. Its importance, its necessity will at once strike your minds; take immediate steps, therefore, to secure for your representatives in the Convention your most determined, resolute, temperate, and wisest men. We have already detained you too long; the time for action, prompt, firm, and decided, has come. In the hope that our action will be that of a united people, we take leave of you, confidently calculating that you will give your body, soul, strength, mind, and all the energies of your nature to the work of saving your country from becoming the theatre of a bloody war, brought upon you without your consent and against your will. Let us show Mr. Ex-Secretary Cobb, now President of the Montgomery Congress, that we are not willing to recognize the transfer of us made by the Richmond Convention, nor do we intend to allow our borders, as he says they will be, to be made the theatre of this war.

"Fellow-citizens, we ask you to read and ponder well the passage from Mr. Cobb's speech we recite:

"'The people of the Gulf States need have no apprehensions; they might go on with their planting and their other business as usual; the war would not come to their section; its theatre would be along the borders of the Ohio River and in Virginia.'

"The Convention between Virginia and the Confederate States, by which the control of all military operations is placed in the hands of President Davis, insures this result.

"Fellow-citizens, 'these are times when we must not stop to count sacrifices and costs, where honor, and character, and self-preservation are put in issue.' The patriot and sage, Daniel Webster, in a speech delivered at Washington in 1851, at the laying of the corner-stone of the addition to the Capitol, spoke as follows:

"'Ye men of the Blue Ridge, many

thousands of whom are nearer to this capital than the seat of Government of your own State, what do you think of breaking up this great association into fragments of States and of people? I know that some of you, and I believe that you all would be almost as much shocked at the announcement of such a catastrophe, as if you were informed that the Blue Ridge itself would soon totter from its base; and ye, men of Western Virginia, who occupy the slope from the Alleghanies to Ohio and Kentucky, what benefit do you propose to yourselves by disunion? If you secede, what do you "secede" from, and what do you "secede" to? Do you look for the current of the Ohio to change and to bring you and your commerce to the tide-waters of Eastern rivers? What man in his senses can suppose that one would remain part and parcel of Virginia in a month after Virginia had ceased to be a part and parcel of the United States?'

"Fellow-citizens of Northwestern Virginia, the issue is with you. Your destiny is in your own hands. If you are worthy descendants of worthy sires, you will rally to the defence of your liberties, and the Constitution, which has protected and blessed you, will still extend over you its protecting ægis. If you hesitate or falter, all is lost, and you and your children to the latest posterity are destined to perpetual slavery.

"JOHN S. CARLILE, JAS. S. WHEAT, A. WILSON, C. D. HUBBARD, F. H. PIERPONT, S. H. WOODWARD, C. TARR, G. R. LATHAM, JAMES W. PAXTON."

In sympathy with this spirited action of their political leaders, the people of Western Virginia showed a sentiment of patriotism, and an alacrity not surpassed even at the North, to rally to arms in defence of the Union. A general fast was kept at Wheeling, and the clergymen who preached on the occasion vied with each other in fervor of patriotic appeal. The churches were decorated with the stars and stripes. One loyal pulpit orator declared that he would have no fellowship with traitors, and if there was a secessionist in his congregation, he wished him to leave. Another prayed that the rebels "might be subdued or wiped from the face of the earth."* *May 10.*

Union military companies were formed throughout the loyal district, prepared to resist the advance of the troops in arms to uphold the Southern Confederacy, with which the Governor of Virginia and his fellow-conspirators had leagued the State. The first encounter took place at the town of Clarksburg, in Harrison County. *May 20.* Two companies of "Confederate military" having marched into the place, the court-house bell was rung, and immediately forth came two other companies of "Union military." The latter immediately summoned the former to surrender their arms, which after a brief parley was complied with. This was the bloodless beginning of that series of tragic conflicts in which the struggle in Western Virginia has abounded.

* New York *Herald*, May 10.

CHAPTER XXI.

Missouri.—Secession Governor and Political Leaders.—The Loyalty of the State undoubted at the North.—Majority of Inhabitants opposed to Slavery.—Proportion of Slaves to Free Population.—Small number of Slave Owners.—Free Labor.—The Foreign Population.—Germans.—Their Character and Enterprise.—Their Sentiments on Slavery.—The Action of the Secessionists.—Insulting Answer of the Governor to the President's Requisition.—Governor's Message.—Denunciation of the Federal Authority.—Sympathy with the Confederate States.—Secret Session of the Legislature.—The Governor's Call for Militia.—Pretext and Purpose.—Alertness of the Union Men of St. Louis.—Mustering of Union Volunteers.—Rapid Response to the President's Requisition.—Home Guards.—Guarding the Arsenal.—Graphic Account of the Rescue of Arms.—Captain Lyon.—His Spirited Conduct.—Mustering of his Forces.—March against the Governor's Secession Camp at Fort Jackson.—The Camp surrounded.—Disposition of Forces.—A Summons to Surrender.—Surrender of the Secessionists.—Dissatisfaction of the Secessionists.—An Excited Crowd.—Attack upon the Troops.—The Soldiers respond—Fatal Results. Official Justification.—Great Agitation in St. Louis.—Attack of the City Mob upon the German Home Guard.—Another Fatal Collision.—Death of the Innocent.—Major-General Harney.—His return to St. Louis.—Biography of Harney—His Headstrong Character.—Difficulties at Vancouver.—Recalled.—Appointed to the Command of the Western Department.—Visit to Washington. Capture on the way.—Release.—Return to St. Louis.—A Declaration of Loyalty.—Good Advice to Missouri.—Conciliatory Proclamation.—The "Military Bill."—Its Results.—Second Proclamation of Harney.—A Denunciation of the "Military Bill"—Energetic Movements—Secessionists dispersed at Liberty.—The affair at Potosi.—A Lady delivered of a Secession Flag.—League of Harney with the Leader of Secession Troops.—The first Effect—Harney Cajoled.—Impolitic Conduct.—Withdrawal of Harney.—Appointment of Lyon to a Brigadier-Generalship. Succeeds to the Command of Union Troops in Missouri.—Energy.

MISSOURI, though its Governor and many of its most influential political leaders were known to be in league with the conspirators of the South, contained so great a majority of inhabitants who, in interests and sentiment, were opposed to slavery, that none at the North doubted, whatever might be the attempts on its loyalty, of its adherence to the Union. Of its whole population of about one million three hundred thousand, the slaves constitute not more than a tenth part. Of the whites, there are nearly one hundred thousand of foreign birth. The slaveholders amount to little more than twenty thousand, and of these there are hardly a score who possess more than fifty negroes, while the larger proportion can number but one, two, or three on their slave-rolls.

With this small proportion of slaves and slave-owners, and large number of inhabitants dependent alone upon free labor, the prevailing political sentiment of the State has been in sympathy with that of the North. The larger proportion of the white population of foreign birth are Germans, who, with their patient industry and rigid economy, have become among the most thriving portion of the people. Good agriculturists, and ambitious of becoming landed proprietors, many have settled upon the fertile prairie districts of the State, and with the aversion to the aid of slave labor natural to those long accustomed to honest toil, cultivate

1861.

their farms themselves. Among them, too, are large numbers of plodding tradesmen, skilled artificers, and miners, who having availed themselves of the great natural resources of the State are among the most energetic and prosperous of those engaged in commerce, mining, and manufactures. This large and influential German population is, almost without an exception, opposed to slavery, and devotedly attached to that Union under whose liberal sway they have had free scope for the exercise of their industry, and hitherto secured the enjoyment of its fruits.

Notwithstanding the predominating sentiment of loyalty, the political leaders of Missouri were determined to make an effort to wrest the State from the Union, or to create by internal disorder a division in favor of the seceders, by which they hoped to embarrass the Federal authority in its efforts to suppress the Southern rebellion. The Governor, C. F. Jackson, had sent an insulting refusal to the demand of President Lincoln for troops: "Your requisition," he said, "in my judgment, is illegal, unconstitutional, and revolutionary in its objects—inhuman and diabolical, and cannot be complied with. Not one man will the State of Missouri furnish to carry on such an unholy crusade."

May 3. Again, in his message to the Legislature of Missouri convened to consider the policy of the State in relation to the civil quarrel, the Governor denounced the conduct of the Federal Government as unconstitutional, and tending toward "consolidated despotism," while in these words he manifested his own sympathy with the rebellious States, and indicated his disposition to commit Missouri to their destiny:

"Our interests and sympathies are identified with those of the slaveholding States, and necessarily unite our destinies with theirs. The similarity of our social and political institutions, our industrial interests, our sympathies, habits, and tastes, our common origin, territorial contiguity, all concur in pointing out our duty in regard to the separation now taking place between the States of the old Federal Union. Missouri has at this time no war to prosecute. It is not her policy to make an aggression, but in the present state of the country she would be faithless to her honor, recreant to her duty, were she to hesitate a moment in making the most ample preparation for the protection of her people against the aggressions of all assailants. I therefore recommend an appropriation of a sufficient sum of money to place the State at the earliest practicable moment in a complete state of defence."

The Legislature, the majority of which was ready to act in compliance with the seditious inclinations of the Governor, held its session in secret. Sustained by its acts, the Governor's next step was to call out the militia of the State and order them to be encamped, under the pretext to perfect their organization and drill, but in reality, as it was believed, to have an armed force under his control ready to further the objects of secession, by keeping in awe the loyal citizens of Missouri, and seizing the Federal property. The arsenal at St. Louis, with its abundant supplies of arms belonging to the United States, was only saved from the grasp of the disloyal Governor and his mob of secession followers by the prompt action of the Governor of the neighboring State of Illinois. The successful exploit by which this valuable property was secured, is well told in the following narrative:

"Captain James H. Stokes, of Chicago, late of the regular army, volunteered to undertake the perilous mission, and Governor Yates placed in his hands the requisition of the secretary of war for 10,000 muskets. Captain Stokes went to St. Louis, and made his way as rapidly as possible to the arsenal. He found it surrounded by an immense mob, and the postern gates all closed. His utmost efforts to penetrate the crowd were for a long time unavailing. The requisition was shown. Captain Lyon doubted the possibility of executing it. He said the arsenal was surrounded by a thousand spies, and every movement was watched and reported to the headquarters of the secessionists, who could throw an overpowering force upon them at any moment. Captain Stokes represented that every hour's delay was rendering the capture of the arsenal more certain, and the arms must be moved to Illinois now or never. Major Callender agreed with him, and told him to take them at his own time and in his own way. This was Wednesday night, 24th April.

"Captain Stokes had a spy in the camp, whom he met at intervals in a certain place in the city. On Thursday he received information that Governor Jackson had ordered two thousand armed men down from Jefferson City, whose movements could only contemplate a seizure of the arsenal, by occupying the heights around it, and planting batteries thereon. The job would have been an easy one. They had already planted one battery on the St. Louis levee, and another at Powder Point, a short distance below the arsenal. Captain Stokes immediately telegraphed to Alton to have the steamer City of Alton drop down to the arsenal, landing about midnight. He then returned to the arsenal and commenced moving the boxes of guns, weighing some three hundred pounds each, down to the lower floor.

"About seven hundred men were employed in the work. He then took five hundred Kentucky flint-lock muskets, which had been sent there to be altered, and sent them to be placed on a steamer as a blind to cover his real movements. The secessionists nabbed them at once, and raised a perfect bedlam over the capture. A large portion of the outside crowd left the arsenal when this movement was executed, and Captain Lyon took the remainder, who were lying around as spies, and locked them up in the guard-house. About eleven o'clock the steamer City of Alton came alongside, planks were shoved out from the windows to the main deck, and the boxes slid down. When the 10,000 were safely on board, Captain Stokes went to Captain Lyon and Major Callender and urged them, by the most pressing appeals, to let him empty the arsenal. They told him to go ahead and take whatever he wanted. Accordingly, he took 10,000 more muskets, 500 new rifle carbines, 500 revolvers, 110,000 musket cartridges, to say nothing of the cannon and a large quantity of miscellaneous accoutrements, leaving only 7,000 muskets in the arsenal to arm the St. Louis volunteers.

"When the whole were on board, about two o'clock on Friday morning the order was given by the captain of the steamer to cast off. Judge of the consternation of all hands when it was found that she would not move. The arms had been piled in great quantities around the engines to protect them against the battery on the levee, and the great weight had fastened the bows of the boat firmly on a rock, which was tearing a hole through the bottom at every turn of the wheels. A man of less nerve than Captain Stokes would have gone crazy on the spot. He called the arsenal men on board, and commenced moving the boxes to the stern.

"Fortunately, when about two hundred boxes had been shifted, the boat fell away from the shore, and floated in deep water. 'Which way?' said Captain Mitchell, of the steamer. 'Straight to Alton, in the regular channel,' replied Captain Stokes. 'What if we are attacked?' said Captain Mitchell. 'Then we will fight,' said Captain Stokes. 'What if we are overpowered?' said Captain Mitchell. 'Run her to the deepest part of the river, and sink her,' replied Captain Stokes. 'I'll do it,' was the heroic answer of Captain Mitchell; and away they went past the secession battery, past the entire St. Louis levee, and on to Alton, in the regular channel, where they arrived at five o'clock in the morning.

"When the boat touched the landing, Captain Stokes, fearing pursuit by some two or three of the secession military companies by which the city of St. Louis is disgraced, ran to the market-house and rang the fire-bell. The citizens came flocking pell-mell to the river in all sorts of habiliments. Captain Stokes informed them of the situation of things, and pointed out the freight-cars. Instantly men, women, and children boarded the steamer, seized the freight, and clambered up the levees to the cars. Rich and poor tugged together with might and main for two hours, when the cargo was all deposited in the cars, and the train moved off, amid their enthusiastic cheers, for Springfield."

The loyal men of St. Louis, the majority of whose citizens were of unquestioned fidelity to the Union, were also on the alert. Four regiments of volunteers were immediately mustered, ready to do service for the United States, so that the energetic Colonel Frank P. Blair, to whose efforts this success was greatly due, had the satisfaction of writing to Washington that Missouri, in spite of the Governor's insulting refusal, had responded faithfully, within a week, to the President's call for troops.

At the same time, several thousands of the citizens of St. Louis had enrolled themselves as a home guard, and were stationed at the arsenal to guard its important stores, and be in readiness for other loyal service. The Government at Washington had, with more than usual foresight and promptitude, sent orders to Captain Lyon, in command of the small Federal force of regulars at St. Louis, to enrol, if necessary, ten thousand men for the maintenance of the authority of the United States Government. This spirited young officer at once zealously applied himself to the work, and immediately, with the aid of Blair's regiments, was able to muster a force of nearly six thousand.

Lyon's first movement was to check the military operations of the Governor, who had encamped some eight hundred militia at Camp Jackson,* on the outskirts of the city of St. Louis. Lyon May accordingly marched with his whole 10. force through the streets of the city, which was greatly agitated by the then unusual event, to the undulating country beyond. On reaching the camp, he drew up the First and Third regiments, under the respective commands of Colonel Sigel and Colonel F. P. Blair, and his small detachment of United States regulars, on the northern side, where he also posted four pieces of artillery. The Second Regiment, under Colonel Borenstein, was so placed as to command the western, and Colonel Shuttner, with his force of volunteers, took position on the south. Guards were posted at the entrance to the camp to prevent any one either going out or in, and several pieces of flying artillery were placed upon the surrounding heights commanding the encampment. Having thus effectually surrounded in less than a half hour the Governor's force, which had no alternative but submission, Lyon summoned the general in command to surrender.

"HEADQUARTERS U. S. TROOPS,
ST. LOUIS, May 10.

"To GENERAL D. M. FROST:

"SIR: Your command is regarded as evidently hostile toward the Government of the United States. It is, for the most part, made up of those secessionists who have openly avowed their hostility to the General Government, and have been plotting for the seizure of its property and the overthrow of its authority. You are openly in communication with the so-called Southern Confederacy, which is now at war with the United States; and you are receiving at your camp, from the said Confederacy, under its flag, large supplies of material of war, most of which is known to be the property of the United States. These extraordinary preparations plainly indicate none other than the well-known

---

* The main avenue of Camp Jackson, recently under command of General Frost, had the name of Davis, and a principal street of the same camp that of Beauregard; and a body of men had also been received into that camp by its commander which had been notoriously organized in the interests of the secessionists; the men openly wearing the dress and badge distinguishing the army of the so-called Southern Confederacy. It is also a notorious fact that a quantity of arms had been received into the camp which were unlawfully taken from the United States arsenal at Baton Rouge, and surreptitiously passed up the river in boxes marked "marble." — General Harney's Proclamation, May 14.

purpose of the Governor of this State, under whose orders you are acting, and whose purpose, recently communicated to the Legislature, has just been responded to by that body in the most unparalleled legislation, having in direct view hostilities toward the General Government, and co-operation with its enemies.

"In view of these considerations, and your failure to disperse in obedience to the proclamation of the President, and of the eminent necessity of State policy and welfare, and obligations imposed upon me by instructions from Washington, it is my duty to demand, and I do hereby demand of you, an immediate surrender of your command, with no other conditions than that all persons surrendering under this demand shall be humanely and kindly treated. Believing myself prepared to enforce this demand, one half hour's time before doing so will be allowed for your compliance therewith.

"N. LYON,
"Captain Second Infantry."

The general in command of the so-called State troops, believed, however, to be in arms to sustain the cause of secession, finding that resistance would be of no avail, promptly surrendered himself and his whole force, while emphatically declaring that his men had been enrolled under the authority of the State with no hostile object.

The troops, when they discovered that they had been so unceremoniously disposed of, gave vent to their dissatisfaction, as they were marched out and placed under guard, in the "wildest yells, curses, and groans," in which they were joined by a portion of the large mob which had in the mean time gathered and followed the troops from the city. When Captain Lyon proceeded to take possession of the surrendered camp, the crowd became still more excited, and beginning with casting insults and imprecations upon the United States soldiers, finally threw at them stones and any other missile at hand. The troops, however, did not lose their self-control, and went calmly on. Finally, one of the mob fired a revolver and shot a soldier dead. As he fell, his comrades turned round and presented their muskets, when some of the crowd again fired. On the second discharge, one of the captains ordered his company to fire, which dispersed the throng, killing a large number, of whom several were women and children drawn to the spot by a fatal curiosity.

The following statement, given on the authority of Captain Lyon, explicitly justifies the conduct of the United States soldiers:

"The first firing was some half dozen shots near the head of the column, composed of the First Regiment, which was guarding the prisoners. It occurred in this wise: The artillery were stationed on the bluff northeast of Camp Jackson, with their pieces bearing on the camp. The men of this command were most insultingly treated by the mob; with the foulest epithets, were pushed, struck, and pelted with stones and dirt. All this was patiently borne, until one of the mob discharged a revolver at the men. At this they fired, but not more than six shots, which were sufficient to disperse that portion of the mob. How many were killed by this fire is not known. None of the First Regiment (Colonel Blair's) fired, although continually and shamefully abused both by the prisoners and the mob.

"The second and most destructive firing was from the rear of the column guarding the prisoners. The mob at the point intervening between Camp Jackson and the rear of the column, and, in fact, on all sides, were very abusive, and one of them, on being expostulated with, became very belligerent, drew his revolver, and fired at Lieutenant Saxton, of the regular army, three times, during which a crowd around him cheered him on, many of them drawing their revolvers and firing on the United States troops. The man who commenced the firing, preparatory to a fourth shot, laid his pistol across his arm, and was taking deliberate aim at Lieutenant Saxton, when he was thrust through with a bayonet, and fired upon at the same time, being killed instantly. Here the column of troops having received the order to march, Lieutenant Saxton's command passed on, and a company in the rear became the objects of a furious attack, when, several of their number having been shot, the company came to a halt, and fired with fatal effect. The mob, in retreating from both sides of the line, returned the fire, and the troops replied again. The command was then given by Captain Lyon to cease firing, and the order was promptly obeyed, as rapidly as it could be passed along the line.

"The sad results are much to be lamented. The killing of innocent men, women, and children is deplorable. There was no intention to fire upon peaceable citizens. The regular troops were over in the camp, beyond the mob, and in range of the firing. The troops manifested every forbearance, and at last discharged their guns, simply obeying the impulse, natural to us all, of self-defence. If innocent men, women, and children, whose curiosity placed them in a dangerous position, suffered with the guilty, it is no fault of the troops."

The fatal collision of the mob of St. Louis with the United States volunteers was the cause of great excitement, and increased the exasperation, of that portion of the populace favorable to the secessionists, against the Federal troops and officers. The Germans, prominent in the ranks of loyalty, were more especially the objects of the indignation of the infuriated disunionists, who sought the earliest opportunity of venting their rage and revenging upon them the fall of their confederates. On the very next May day after the capture of Fort Jackson, an occasion occurred which resulted in another tragedy. A body of German Home Guards having been enrolled at the arsenal and supplied with arms, proceeded to march through the city. Great crowds had collected, which received the troops with hootings and hisses, and a man out of the throng fired a revolver, shooting dead one of the soldiers. This discharge being immediately followed by two others from the neighboring houses, the troops suddenly turned round, presented their muskets, and fired a volley down the street. A promiscuous slaughter followed, in which innocent women and children again suffered the fate of the guilty. These two fatal collisions had resulted in the death and wounding of some fifty in all, and served to embitter still more the unhappy feeling already existing among the inhabitants of the same city.

The return, however, of Major-General Harney, the commander of the department of the West, to St. Louis, where he had established his headquarters, served for a time to compose the angry dissensions in Missouri, and to give hopes of saving that State from the evils of a civil conflict.

William Selby Harney was born in Tennessee in the year 1800, and entered the army as a second lieutenant of the First Infantry at the age of eighteen. He had acquired, during his long service, the reputation of an energetic, though arbitrary officer. His characteristic impulsiveness and headstrong disregard of consequences led him to assume possession of the island of San Juan, in Vancouver's Bay, during the dispute with Great Britain in regard to the boundary line between the northwestern possessions of that power and Oregon. This unauthorized act excited greatly the anger of England, which was only appeased by the recall of Harney and the conciliatory action of the veteran Scott, who was sent to supersede him in command.

At the beginning of the late civil war, Harney was the commander-in-chief of the Western Department, but was temporarily absent from St. Louis during the disturbances in that city, having been summoned to Washington. On his way he was taken prisoner by the Confederates at Harper's Ferry, but being soon released, he hastened, after a brief visit to the capital, to resume his duties in the West. Though the ties of birth and property attached him strongly to the slave States, he promptly declared his firm loyalty to the Union:

"The Government, whose honors have been bestowed upon me, I shall serve," he wrote, in a published letter, "for the remainder of my days. The flag whose glories I have witnessed shall never be forsaken by me while I can strike a blow for its defense. While I have breath I shall be ready to serve the Government of the United States, and be its faithful, loyal soldier."

To these expressions of loyalty the General added some pertinent advice to Missouri:

"Secession would, in my opinion," he emphatically declared, "be her ruin. The only special interest of Missouri, in common with the Confederate States, is slavery. Her interest in that institution is now protected by the Federal Constitution. But if Missouri secedes, that protection is gone. Surrounded on three sides by free States, which might soon become hostile, it would not be long until a slave could not be found within her borders. What interest could Missouri, then, have with the cotton States, or a confederacy founded on slavery and its extension? The protection of her slave property, if nothing else, admonishes her to never give up the Union. Other interests of vast magnitude can only be preserved by a steadfast adherence and support of the United States Government. All hope of a Pacific Railroad, so deeply interesting to St. Louis and the whole State, must vanish with the Federal Government. Great manufacturing and commercial interests with which the cotton States can have no sympathy, must perish in case of secession, and from her present proud condition of a powerful, thriving State, rapidly developing every element of wealth and social prosperity, Missouri would dwindle to a mere appendage and convenience for the military aristocracy established in the cotton States."

Immediately on his return to his post at St. Louis, General Harney strove with unquestioned sincerity, but uncertain vigor, to allay the civil strife in Missouri. In his first proclamation he assumed a highly conciliatory tone:

May 12.

"I most anxiously desire," he proclaimed, "to discharge the delicate and onerous duties devolved upon me so as to preserve the public peace. I shall carefully abstain from the exercise of any unnecessary powers, and from all interference with the proper functions of the public officers of the State and city. I therefore call upon the public authorities and the people to aid me in preserving the public peace.

"The military force stationed in this department by the authority of the Government, and now under my command, will only be used in the last resort to preserve peace. I trust I may be spared the necessity of resorting to martial law, but the public peace must be preserved, and the lives and property of the people protected. Upon a careful review of my instructions, I find I have no authority to change the location of the Home Guards.

"To avoid all cases of irritation and excitement, if called upon to aid the local authorities in preserving the public peace, I shall, in preference, make use of the regular army."

In the mean time, the Legislature, still in session at Jefferson City, passed a "military bill," the object of which was apparently to resist the Federal authority. The Governor was authorized to call out the militia, and a large sum was appropriated to arm and equip them. At the same time extraordinary powers were given to the Governor, by which he might control the State troops to his own purposes; which no one could doubt were in accordance with the interests of secession. No sooner had the "military bill" passed, than the Governor began to avail himself of the privileges it conferred, by mustering a military force, and ordering the telegraph and railroad bridges which communicated with St. Louis to be destroyed, in order to prevent the loyal troops of that city from marching to the rescue of the

State from the grasp of its secession conspirators.

General Harney now issued a second proclamation, to the gentle pleadings of which in behalf of loyalty he added a not very undecided declaration of the rebellious character of the "military bill."

May 17.

"It is with regret," he said, "that I feel it my duty to call your attention to the recent act of the General Assembly of Missouri, known as the 'military bill,' which is the result, no doubt, of the temporary excitement that now pervades the public mind. This bill cannot be regarded in any other light than an indirect secession ordinance, ignoring even the forms resorted to by other States. Manifestly its most material provisions are in conflict with the Constitution and laws of the United States. To this extent it is a nullity, and cannot and ought not to be upheld or regarded by the good citizens of Missouri. There are obligations and duties resting upon the people of Missouri under the Constitution and laws of the United States which are paramount, and which I trust you will carefully consider and weigh well before you will allow yourselves to be carried out of the Union, under the form of yielding obedience to this 'military bill,' which is clearly in violation of your duties as citizens of the United States."

To this proclamation succeeded an energetic movement toward repressing the secession demonstrations in various parts of the State of Missouri. Two hundred armed secessionists were dispersed from the arsenal at Liberty, and soon after the Federal arms met with other success. Some Union men having been driven from Potosi, in Washington County, Captain Lyon sent a small force, consisting of a hundred and fifty volunteers under the command of Captain Coles, to their relief. Arriving at Potosi before daylight, Captain Coles posted a chain of sentinels around the town, and stationed guards at the houses of the prominent secessionists. As the day broke, some hundred and fifty men found themselves thus imprisoned without hope of escape. Most of them were released on giving their parole and taking the oath not to take up arms against the United States, while the prominent leaders were held captive. Various munitions of war and other supplies intended for the secessionists were at the same time seized. On their way back from Potosi, the Union troops put to flight at De Soto a company of secession cavalry, captured a score or more of their horses, and their flag, secreted within the hoops of a lady of the place. The service of the surgeon of the United States volunteers was very appropriately put into requisition on the occasion. On entering, "the doctor thought he observed the lady of the house sitting in rather an uneasy position, and he very politely asked her to rise. At first the lady hesitated, but finding the doctor's persuasive suavity more than she could withstand, she slowly rose, when the bright folds of the rebel ensign appeared around the lady's feet. The doctor, bowing a graceful 'beg par-

May 13.

don, madam,' stooped, and quietly catching hold of the gaudy color, found in his possession a secession flag thirty* feet long and nine feet wide."

Having apparently checked the rising spirit of rebellion by judicious military movements, General Harney sought, by a *quasi* league with the leader of the so-called State troops, to establish a permanent truce with the seditiously disposed citizens of Missouri. He accordingly held a personal interview with Sterling Price, appointed by the Governor a major-general of the Missouri militia, and who, like him, was doubtless in league with the Southern leaders of rebellion. General Harney, persuaded by the artful plausibilities of the shrewd Price, was cajoled into an agreement, by which he pledged the Federal authority to withhold its power, and to leave the seditious Governor and his confederates to pursue their own designs, under the pretext of preserving order in the State. In a joint declaration, signed by General Harney and the major-general of the so-styled State Guard, it was announced that "General Price, having by commission full authority over the militia of the State of Missouri, undertakes, with the sanction of the Governor of the State already

May 21.

declared, to direct the whole power of the State officers to maintain order within the State among the people thereof; and General Harney publicly declares that this object being thus assured, he can have no occasion, as he has no wish, to make military movements which might otherwise create excitements and jealousies which he most earnestly desires to avoid."

Although the immediate effect of this compact was to tranquilize the public sentiment of Missouri, it soon became evident that the Governor and his confederates had been using General Harney to further their own seditious purposes. They continued to muster their military forces, and were evidently bent upon hostility to the Union men of the State. The Government at Washington becoming conscious of the impolitic action of General Harney, withdrew him from the Western Department. Lyon, who had been lately promoted to the rank of brigadier-general of volunteers, succeeded to the command of the Federal forces in Missouri. This energetic officer at once proceeded to assert the authority of the Union by the most decisive action. We shall soon have occasion to say more of him and his spirited achievements.

May 17.

---

* St. Louis *Democrat*, May 17.

CHAPTER XXII.

Spirit of Loyalty of the Free States of the West.—Attachment to the Union.—Interests in the Struggle.—The danger of being cut off from the Mississippi.—The Position of Illinois.—Her interest in the preservation of Communication.—Spirited Action.—Military Possession of Cairo.—Situation of Cairo.—The Key to the Northwest.—The motive for founding the City.—Marshy Site.—Artificial Dykes. Great Size and enormous Expense.—Illinois Central Railroad.—Population of Cairo.—Its Docks.—A Reservoir of Water.—Artificial Remedies.—Future Prospects.—Neighborhood of Cairo described.—Cairo as a Military Post.—Bird's Point. Its Position. Description of the place. Its Importance.—Danger of its Seizure.—Secured to the United States by General Lyon.—Communications with Cairo.—Columbus.—Paducah.—Military Possession of Cairo a blow to the Enemy.—Their Opinion.—Increased Military Energy of the United States.—Move across the Potomac.—The vote on Secession in Virginia.—Scruples of Government.—The crossing of the Potomac.—Arlington Heights occupied.—Entrenchments.—Opposition anticipated at Alexandria.—The animosity of the City.—Secession Flags.—Expedition against Alexandria.—The plan.—Movement of the Michigan Regiment.—Embarkation of the New York Fire Zouaves. The Steamer Pawnee.—Indiscreet haste of the Zouaves.—Landing at Alexandria.—Death of Colonel Ellsworth. The Michigan Regiment disappointed.—Escape of Virginia Troops.—Capture of thirty-seven Horsemen.—Occupation of Alexandria.—Sacrifice of a promising life.—Biography of Ellsworth.—Early Career.—Military Tastes.—His Company of Chicago Zouaves.—How shown and admired.—Application for a clerkship in the War Department.—Disappointment.—Made a Lieutenant in the Army.—Resignation.—Recruits the Fire Zouaves at New York, and becomes their Colonel.—Grief at his death.—A touching Letter.

1861. The free States of the West, actuated by a sentiment of loyalty which inspirited them to vindicate the honor and preserve the integrity of a Union to which they were fondly attached, exhibited the greatest alertness in coming to the rescue of the Federal Government. Finding, moreover, their interests deeply involved in a struggle, which, with the secession of Louisiana, Mississippi, Arkansas, Tennessee, and the unsettled condition of Missouri and Kentucky, threatened, by obstructing the navigation of the Mississippi River, to cut off that great channel of communication between the Northern lakes and the Gulf of Mexico, they felt, with all the impressiveness of a motive of self-preservation, the necessity of resisting the rebellion.

Illinois, from her geographical position, had been the chief State to profit from that bountiful provision of nature which united Lake Michigan and the Gulf of Mexico, and brought the northern city of Chicago into close relationship with tropical New Orleans. This State, accordingly, alive to the importance of securing a communication which had proved so great a source of inspiration to her enterprise and of the wealth that had crowned its efforts, eagerly strove to further the endeavors of the Federal Government to prevent the disruption of the Union. Her troops responded readily to the call of the Governor, and were soon enabled to hold in force the most important strategic point of the West. This was the city of Cairo, within her own borders.

Cairo is situated at the extreme south of Illinois, in Alexandria County, on the delta at the confluence of the Ohio with the Mississippi. On the east the former separates it from Kentucky, and on the west the latter separates it from Missouri. Cairo thus, by its position, commands the navigation of both rivers and the shores of the two neighboring States at this point. It is, as it were, the key to that extensive and important territory familiarly known as the Great Northwest, watered by the upper Mississippi, the Ohio, the Missouri, and their tributary streams. The city was founded with the expectation, from the natural advantages of geographical position, of its becoming a great trading emporium. Immense sums were expended in rendering it habitable. Naturally a swamp, the land was covered with water for the greater part of the year. Large dykes or levees were raised for two miles and a half along the borders of the Mississippi and Ohio, and joined by a transverse embankment, so as to close in the site and shut out the constant overflow of those rivers. Several attempts had been made in vain to protect the town from inundation, until finally the present works were constructed at an enormous expense. These now consist of vast dykes, from ten to thirty feet in height, with a breadth, at the top, from twenty to fifty feet, and at the bottom, from eighty to a hundred feet. Much of the structure was built at the expense of the Illinois Central Railroad Company, to which a great portion of the land belonged, and here its extreme southern dépot and works have been established. The inhabitants, largely increased during the war, have settled chiefly in the quarter bordered by the Ohio, where they have filled in the marshy site of the town almost to the height of the embankment, which protects it from the danger of inundation. The loading and unloading of freight is performed by means of large floating docks or wharf-floats, so contrived and moored that they can be adapted to the rise and fall of the river, and thus always present an even communication with the embanked shore.

After a heavy fall of rain, the enclosure within the levees or dykes, which forms a large artificial basin, collects the water. This, however, has been partially remedied by digging a deep canal through the centre of the town to receive the rain-fall. With this are connected drains which open through the dykes into the rivers. When their waters, however, are high, the heavy rains cannot be thus disposed of, and recourse is had to a steam-pump. The only effectual mode which has as yet been proposed of rendering this admirably situated city entirely free from the danger of inundation, is to fill up the whole basin with earth brought from the hills in the interior. In 1858 the river rose above a new embankment commenced the year previous, and destroyed almost the entire town.

The neighborhood of Cairo is thus described by a local observer:

"The nearest high land in any direction from Cairo is about nine miles distant, on the Central Railway, and all between are cypress swamps, with here and there a marshy opening, called a farm, and covered with a mass of heavy timber, vines and creepers, through which the sun cannot penetrate. The high land, commencing at the edge of this swamp, rises several hundred feet, often presenting mountainous aspects; the timber is maple, beech, hickory, and oak. Springs are frequent, and where farms are opened they well reward the laborer; but more than three-fourths of all this high land is an unbroken wilderness.

"On the Illinois side of the Ohio, above Mound City (six miles from Cairo), the shore is high and free from inundation, while on the Kentucky side the land is low and swampy, the distance to the hills being from six to twelve miles. The Illinois bank of the Mississippi is low, yet occasionally there are hills, as at Thebes, but above this point it is subject to overflow for 150 miles. The Mississippi shore of Missouri is swampy in every direction, and the nearest high land is as much as fifty miles distant, near Cape Girardeau, which is the only place where southern Missouri can reach the river with teams. From Cape Girardeau to the Gulf of Mexico extends a succession of cypress swamps, canebrakes, and bayous—the scene of desolation being varied only at long intervals by farms, always protected by a levee. On the east side of the river there are occasionally high lands and bluffs, on which the towns are situated. Opposite Cairo, in Missouri, is the little village of Bird's Point, from which a railroad extends twenty or thirty miles toward Little Rock, in Arkansas. In such a wilderness of swamps and waters, Cairo is really a place of refuge and a harbor of safety."

The importance of Cairo as a basis of military operations was recognized early in the struggle, and in the course of the month of May a force of over six thousand Illinois volunteers encamped there under the command of Brigadier-General Prentiss. They immediately commenced the construction of four entrenched camps, and mounted heavy guns upon the dykes.

The site of Cairo is commanded only in one direction. This is from the Missouri side of the Mississippi River, at Bird's Point, where the land rises two or three feet above the top of the Cairo dykes.

"Bird's Point consists of scarcely half a dozen unpretending houses and a wharf-boat, which is the principal feature of the town, inasmuch as it supports on its floating bottom the chief store, grocery, and commission-house of the town. * * * Standing upon even as low a situation as the deck of the wharf-boat, the housetops and spires within the Cairo levee are plainly visible, and within easy range of a battery at Bird's Point; and although the latter place is situated on low bottom land and subject to frequent overflows, yet the still lower situation of Cairo is so palpable, that, to a spectator at Bird's Point, it seems as if the great rivers which here mix their waters had been displaced from their beds to make room for the houses which are hugged within the huge embraces of the levee. The river here is very wide, and but for the murky turbulence of its water, and the steady onward motion of the current, would give one an idea of an arm of the sea."

There was great danger lest the secessionists of Missouri and Tennessee should seize this important position. Brigadier-General Lyon, however, was on the alert, and anticipated the movements of the enemy by promptly dispatching a regiment of Missouri volunteers, under Colonel Shuttner, to Bird's Point. Here they immediately fortified a camp, and thus bid defiance to attack.

The communications of Cairo through the Illinois Central Railroad with the North, give it every advantage of rapid reinforcement. In twenty-four hours troops can reach the place not only from Illinois, Missouri, and Kentucky, but from Indiana, Wisconsin, and Michigan.

About a score of miles below Cairo, on the Kentucky bank of the Mississippi River, is situated the town of Columbus, the Northern terminus of various Southern railways. This place had become of great interest, in connection with the rebellion, as an important strategic post, having been seized and held by the enemy. Paducah, again, forty miles to the east of Cairo, on the Kentucky side of the Ohio, at its confluence with the Tennessee, is another point of great importance, commanding as it does the mouth of the latter river, and connected as it is with the Southern series of railways. This important place fortunately was held in the possession of the United States troops.

The prompt military occupation of Cairo, and the preparations made for its defence, were heavy blows to the secessionists. They strove, however, to find consolation in the presumption that "this audacious movement has had good effect in developing the purpose of our enemies to prosecute the war in earnest, and in its inspiring influence upon the Tennessee and Kentucky mind. It conveys a threat which the people of those States will join their brethren of the Confederate States in resenting with promptitude."

They, nevertheless, were forced to acknowledge the importance of the possession of Cairo to the Federal troops.

"Geography," they admitted, "has made Cairo a strategical position of the utmost consequence. It is the key to the upper, as New Orleans and the Lake and the Balize are the key to the lower Mississippi. It can blockade St. Louis on the one hand, and Louisville on the other; while, if in possession of a considerable force, possessing heavy ordnance, and commanding the railroad leading south of that point, it would menace the city of Memphis, and open the way for an invading army to make that an advanced post of occupation. It is not pleasant to contemplate such a possibility. But it is good policy to face it fairly, if we would defeat it effectually."

The United States Government, with its rapidly accumulating forces, was

FIRST MOVEMENT INTO VIRGINIA.

beginning to present in every direction a more vigorous opposition to the enemy. Washington being considered temporarily out of danger, and the disaffected of Maryland no longer feared, General Scott ventured to make a move across the Potomac. Virginia, though previously in arms and leagued with the Confederate States in open resistance to the Federal authorities, had yet, with an affected regard for law, submitted the ordinance of secession to the vote of her people. In the middle and eastern districts of the State the vote was almost unanimous in favor of secession, while in the western it was nearly unanimous in opposition. The United States Government is supposed to have thus far withheld the assertion by arms of its authority in Virginia, that the people might enjoy in freedom the exercise of their suffrage. It was accordingly not until the day after the vote on secession had been taken that Scott threw across the Potomac, into the insurgent State, a portion of the troops encamped in and about the capital, which constituted already, such had been the military promptitude of the North, a force of nearly fifty thousand militia and volunteers.

May 23.

May 24.

The number of men detached for this purpose was nearly thirteen thousand, formed into two columns, one of which was sent to occupy Arlington Heights and the rest of the Virginia shore opposite to Washington, and the other Alexandria, on the Potomac River, about six miles south of the capital. The former, being the larger portion of the troops, crossed by the Long bridge at Washington and the iron bridge at Georgetown, and took possession of the high banks of the Virginia side of the river. Driving the scattered outpost guards of the enemy before them, they were permitted to occupy the ground with little opposition, and at once began to throw up fortifications.

At Alexandria, which had just voted almost unanimously for secession, and where an intense feeling of animosity to the Federal troops was known to prevail, greater opposition was anticipated. The town had been long flaunting its secession flags in the sight of the capital, the troops of the enemy were parading its streets, and its citizens were in arms apparently prepared for resistance. It was accordingly determined to surround the place, not only to secure its possession, but the capture of the armed force within. For this purpose the Third Regiment of Michigan militia, in command of Colonel Wilcox, accompanied by a detachment of United States cavalry, and supported by two pieces of Sherman's flying artillery, crossed the Long bridge into Virginia, with the view of marching to Alexandria by land and advancing upon the city in the rear. The Fire Zouave Regiment of New York, commanded by Colonel Ellsworth, was dispatched by water to take Alexandria in front. The steamer Pawnee had been previously moored in the Potomac off the town, so as to command it with her guns.

The Zouaves, however, reached their destination in advance of the Michigan troops, and impelled by an imprudent impetuosity hastened to land. The town was at once alarmed, and the enemy's troops succeeded in effecting their escape before the Michigan regiment, coming up in the rear, could cut them off. The landing of the Zouaves, and the subsequent tragedy in which their young Colonel lost his life, have been thus minutely detailed by one* who was at his death:

"It was not until our boats were about to draw up to the wharf," he says, "that our approach was noticed in any way; but at the latest minute a few sentinels, whom we had long before discerned, fired their muskets in the air as a warning, and, running rapidly into the town, disappeared. Two or three of the Zouaves, fancying that the shots were directed toward them (which they certainly were not), discharged their rifles after the retreating forms, but no injury to anybody followed. The town was thus put on its guard, but yet so early was the hour, and so apparently unlooked for our arrival, that when we landed, about half-past five o'clock A. M., the streets were as deserted as if it had been midnight.

"Before our troops disembarked, a boat, filled with armed marines, and carrying a flag of truce, put off from the Pawnee, and landed ahead of us. From the officer in charge we learned that the Pawnee had already proposed terms of submission to the town, and that the rebels had consented to vacate within a specified time. This seemed

* New York Tribune, May 26.

to settle the question of a contest in the negative; but in the confusion of mustering and forming the men, the intelligence was not well understood, and received but little attention. Indeed, I am quite sure that the Pawnee's officer did not seek Colonel Ellsworth, to communicate with him, and that the Colonel only obtained a meagre share of information by seeking it directly from the bearer of the flag of truce himself. No doubt this omission arose from the confused condition in which affairs then stood. But it would have caused no difference in the Colonel's military plans. No attack was meditated, except in case of a forcible resistance to his progress. On the other hand, the idea of the place being under a truce seemed to banish every suspicion of a resistance either from multitudes or individuals. It was just possibly this consideration that led Colonel Ellsworth to forego the requisite personal precautions, which, if taken, would have prevented his unhappy death. But I am sure none of us at that time estimated the probability of the danger which afterward menaced us. Perhaps the thought of actual bloodshed and death in war was too foreign to our experiences to be rightly weighed. But it certainly did not enter our minds then, as poor Ellsworth's fate has since taught us it should have done, that a town half waked, half terrified, and under truce, could harbor any peril for us. So the Colonel gave some rapid directions for the interruption of the railway course, by displacing a few rails near the depot, and then turned toward the centre of the town, to destroy the means of communication southward by the telegraph; a measure which he appeared to regard as very seriously important. He was accompanied by Mr. H. J. Winser, military secretary to the regiment, the chaplain, the Rev. E. W. Dodge, and myself. At first he summoned no guard to follow him, but he afterward turned and called forward a single squad, with a sergeant from the first company. We passed quickly through the streets, meeting a few bewildered travellers issuing from the principal hotel, which seemed to be slowly coming to its daily senses, and were about to turn toward the telegraph office, when the Colonel, first of all, caught sight of the secession flag, which has so long swung insolently in full view of the President's House. He immediately sent back the sergeant, with an order for the advance of the entire first company, and, leaving the matter of the telegraph office for a while, pushed on to the hotel, which proved to be the Marshall House, a second-class inn. On entering the open door the Colonel met a man in his shirt and trowsers, of whom he demanded what sort of flag it was that hung above the roof. The stranger, who seemed greatly alarmed, declared he knew nothing of it, and that he was only a boarder there. Without questioning him further the Colonel sprang up stairs, and we all followed to the topmost story, whence, by means of a ladder, he clambered to the roof, cut down the flag with Winser's knife, and brought it from its staff. There were two men in bed in the garret whom we had not observed at all when we entered, their position being somewhat concealed, but who now rose in great apparent amazement, although I observed that they were more than half dressed. We at once turned to descend, private Brownell leading the way, and Colonel Ellsworth immediately following him with the flag. As Brownell reached the first landing-place, or entry, after a descent of some dozen steps, a man jumped from a dark passage, and hardly noticing the private, levelled a double-barrelled gun square at the Colonel's breast. Brownell made a quick pass to turn the weapon aside, but the fellow's hand was firm, and he discharged one barrel straight to its aim, the slugs or buckshot with which it was loaded entering the Colonel's heart, and killing him at the instant. I think my arm was resting on poor Ellsworth's shoulder at the moment. At any rate, he seemed to fall almost from my own grasp. He was on the second or third step from the landing, and he dropped forward with that heavy, horrible, headlong weight which always comes of sudden death inflicted in this manner. His assailant had turned like a flash to give the contents of the other barrel to Brownell, but either he could not command his aim, or the Zouave was too quick with him, for the slugs went over his head, and passed through the panels and wainscot of a door which sheltered some sleeping lodgers. Simultaneously with this second shot, and sounding like the echo of the first, Brownell's rifle was heard, and the assassin staggered backward. He was hit exactly in the middle of the face, and the wound, as I afterward saw it, was the most frightful I ever witnessed. Of course Brownell did not know how fatal his shot had been, and so before the man dropped, he thrust his sabre bayonet through and through the body, the force of the blow sending the dead man violently down the upper section of the second flight of stairs, at the foot of which he lay with his face to the floor. Winser ran from above crying, 'Who is hit?' but as he glanced downward by our feet, he needed no answer.

"Bewildered for an instant by the suddenness of this attack, and not knowing what more might be in store, we forbore to proceed, and gathered together defensively. There were but seven of us altogether, and one was without a weapon of any kind. Brownell instantly reloaded, and while doing so perceived the door through which the assailant's shot had passed, beginning to open. He brought his rifle to the shoulder, and menaced the occupants, two travellers, with immediate death if they stirred. The three other privates guarded the passages, of which there were quite a number converging to the point where we stood, while the chaplain and Winser looked to the staircase by which we had descended, and the adjoining chambers. I ran down stairs to see if anything was threatened from the story below, but it soon appeared there was no danger from that quarter. However, we were not at all disposed to move from our position. From the opening doors, and through the passages, we discerned a sufficient number of forms to assure us that we were dreadfully in the minority. I think now that there was no danger, and that the single assailant acted without concert with anybody; but it is impossible to know accurately, and it was certainly a doubtful question then. The first thing to be done was to look to our dead friend and leader. He had fallen on his face, and the streams of blood that flowed from his wound had literally flooded the way. The chaplain turned him gently over, and I stooped and called his name aloud, at which I thought then he murmured inarticulately. I presume I was mistaken, and I am not sure that he spoke a word after being struck, although in my dispatch I repeated a single exclamation which I had believed he uttered. It might have been Brownell, or the chaplain, who was close behind me. Winser and I lifted the body with all the care we could apply, and laid it upon a bed in a room near by. The rebel flag, stained with his blood, and purified by this contact from the baseness of its former meaning. we laid about his feet. It was at first difficult to discover the precise locality of his wound, for all parts of his coat were equally saturated with blood. By cautiously loosening his belt and unbuttoning his coat we found where the shot had penetrated. None of us had any medical knowledge, but we saw that all hope must be resigned. Nevertheless, it seemed proper to summon the surgeon as speedily as possible. This could not easily be done; for, secluded as we were in that part of the town, and uncertain whether an ambush might not be awaiting us also, no man could volunteer to venture forth alone; and to go together, and leave the Colonel's body behind, was out of the question. We wondered at the long delay of the first company, for the advance of which the Colonel had sent back before approaching the hotel; but we subsequently learned that they had mistaken a street, and gone a little out of their way. Before they arrived we had removed some of the unsightly stains from the Colonel's features, and composed his limbs. His expression in death was beautifully natural. The Colonel was a singularly handsome man, and, excepting the pallor, there was nothing different in his countenance now from what all his friends had so lately been accustomed to gladly recognize. The detachment was heard approaching at last, a reinforcement was easily called up, and the surgeon was sent for. His arrival, not long after, of course sealed our own unhappy belief. A sufficient guard was presently distributed over the house, but meanwhile I had remembered the Colonel's earnestness about the telegraph seizure, and obtained permission to guide a squad of Zouaves to the office, which was found to be entirely open, with all the doors ajar yet apparently deserted. It looked like another chance of a surprise. The men remained in charge. I presume it was not wholly in order for me, a civilian, to start upon this mission, but I was the only person who knew the whereabouts of the office, and the Colonel had been very positive about the matter. When I returned to the hotel, there was a terrible scene enacting. A woman had run from a lower room to the stairway where the body of the defender of the secession flag lay, and recognizing it, cried aloud with an agony so heart-rending that no person could witness it without emotion. She flung her arms in the air, struck her brow madly, and seemed in every way utterly abandoned to desolation and frenzy. She offered no reproaches—appeared, indeed, almost regardless of our presence, and yielded only to her own frantic despair. It was her husband that had been shot. He was the proprietor of the hotel. His name was James T. Jackson. Winser was confident it was the same man who met us at the door when we entered, and told us he was a boarder. His wife, as I said, was wild almost to insanity. Yet she listened when spoken to, and although no consolation could be offered her by us for what she had lost, she seemed sensible to the assurance that the safety of her children, for whom she expressed fears, could not possibly be endangered.

"It is not from any wish to fasten obloquy upon the slayer of Colonel Ellsworth, but simply because it struck me as a frightful fact, that I say the face of the dead man wore the most revolting expression of rage and hatred that I ever saw. Perhaps the nature of his wound added to this effect, and the wound was something so appalling that I shall not attempt to describe it as it impressed me. It is probable that such a result from a bullet wound could not ensue once in a thousand times. Either of Brownell's onslaughts would have been instantaneously fatal. The sabre wound was not less effective than that of the ball. The gun which Jackson had fired lay beneath him, clasped in his arms, and as we did not at first all know that both barrels had been discharged, it was thought necessary to remove it, lest it should be suddenly seized and made use of from below. In doing this, his countenance was revealed.

"As the morning advanced, the townspeople began to gather in the vicinity, and a guard was fixed, preventing ingress and egress. This was done to keep all parties from knowing what had occurred, for the Zouaves were so devoted to their Colonel that it was feared if they all were made acquainted with the real fact, they would sack the house. On the other hand, it was not thought wise to let the Alexandrians know thus early the fate of their townsman. The Zouaves were the only regiment that had arrived, and their head and soul was gone. Besides, the duties which the Colonel had hurriedly assigned before leaving them had scattered some companies in various quarters of the town. Several persons sought admission to the Marshall House, among them a sister of the dead man, who had heard the rumor, but who was not allowed to know the true state of the case. It was painful to hear her remark, as she went away, that 'of course they wouldn't shoot a man dead in his own house about a bit of old bunting.' Many of the lodgers were anxious to go forth, but they were detained until after I had left. All sorts of arguments and persuasions were employed, but the Zouave guards were inexorable."

The Michigan regiment, though prevented by the impetuous movement of the Zouaves from fully effecting its object, succeeded, however, in capturing some thirty-seven of the enemy's cavalry. The rest had made off by the railroad extending into the interior of Virginia. The occupation of Alexandria was indeed secured, but at the sacrifice of a life suddenly arrested in its youthful promise of patriotic service. The friends of the Union mourned the fate of young Ellsworth, and honored his memory as that of a hero.

Elmer E. Ellsworth was born at Malta, Saratoga County, in the State of New York, on the 23d of April, 1837. His parents not being rich were unable to give him more than the advantages of an ordinary common school education. He, however, seemed to have some early inclinations for a military career, and an effort was made to obtain for him an admission into the academy at West Point. Not succeeding in this purpose, the lad was placed as a clerk in a trading establishment at Troy, and thence removed to the city of New York, where he remained engaged in similar occupations for several years. He subsequently emigrated to the West, and obtained the position of a clerk with an attorney in Chicago. He now commenced the study of the law, but devoted his leisure time to the study of military science.

About this time he was chosen captain of a volunteer company, whom he induced to adopt the uniform and drill of the French Zouaves, whose efficiency had been recently displayed in the Crimea. His soldiers soon became the pride of Chicago and the wonder of other cities, where, during a round of visits, they exhibited their striking costume and peculiar manners. On his return to the West he was chosen quartermaster of the northern division of Illinois, and paymaster-general of the State militia. He, however, still persevered in his legal studies, and was soon after admitted to the bar. On the election of his friend, Mr. Lincoln, to the Presidency, Ellsworth made application for the chief clerkship in the war department, but the secretary of war was prevented from bestowing it upon him in consequence of his pledge to a previous applicant. He, however, received, through the influence of the President, the commission of second lieutenant in the army. In the mean time, war with the South becoming imminent, young Ellsworth resigned his lieutenancy, and, offering his services to recruit a regiment, repaired at once to New York for the purpose.

The proverbial courage and energy of the city firemen led him to seek among them for the men suitable for the formation of a corps of Zouaves, of whom dash, daring, and activity are expected. He soon succeeded in enrolling a thousand firemen, and sailed, with the applause and good wishes of all New York, for Washington, at the head of his regiment, on the 29th of April. His tragic death has been already recorded.

There was an element of tender affection in the character of the youthful hero which endeared him to his family and friends, and served to increase the public regard for his memory. On the night previous to his departure on the fatal expedition to Alexandria, he wrote to his betrothed, and this reverential and pathetic letter to his parents, of whom he was the only surviving child:

"HEADQUARTERS 1ST ZOUAVES, CAMP LINCOLN,
WASHINGTON, D. C., *May* 23, 1861.

"MY DEAR FATHER AND MOTHER: The regiment is ordered to move across the river to-night. We have no means of knowing what reception we are to meet with. I am inclined to the opinion that our entrance to the city of Alexandria will be hotly contested, as I am just informed a large force has arrived there to-day. Should this happen, my dear parents, it may be my lot to be injured in some manner. Whatever may happen, cherish the consolation that I was engaged in the performance of a sacred duty; and to-night, thinking over the probabilities of to-morrow, and the occurrences of the past, I am perfectly content to accept whatever my fortune may be, confident that He who noteth even the fall of a sparrow, will have some purpose even in the fate of one like me.

"My darling and ever-loved parents, good-bye. God bless, protect, and care for you.   ELMER."

CHAPTER XXIII.

How the Virginians failed to take Fortress Monroe.—Efforts to counteract its Loss.—The importance of Fortress Monroe to the Union.—The danger to Norfolk.—Fortification of Virginia Rivers and Coasts.—Abundant Cannon from the Navy Yard.—Sewall's Point.—Its Position.—Raising of Fortifications by the Secessionists.—Attempt to prevent the Work by the Federal Cruisers.—Attack of the Star on Sewall's Point.—Official Report of Captain Eagle.—A lively Account by the Enemy.—Effect of the Attack.—The Reinforcement of Fortress Monroe.—Number of Troops.—Major-General Butler ordered to the Command of the Department of Virginia.—Arrival at Fortress Monroe.—His enthusiastic Reception.—Immediate Action.—A Foothold upon the Land of Virginia secured.—Increased Reinforcements at Fortress Monroe.—Expedition to Newport News.—Situation of the place.—No resistance.—Military possession.—Intrenchments.—Continued labor of the Enemy in fortifying their Coast.—The Works at Acquia Creek.—Position of Acquia Creek and its strategic importance.—Nature of the Batteries.—Attack by Captain Ward.—Silencing Batteries.—Hauling off the Freeborn.—Renewal of Attack.—Official Statement.—Unsuccessful attempt of the Harriet Lane upon an Enemy's Battery.—Spectators at Fortress Monroe.—Butler eager for Action.—The Expedition against Little and Big Bethel planned.—The Federal Troops.—Number and Commanders.—Brigadier-General Pierce.—Previous Military Experience.—The details of the plan of the Expedition.—A confused Statement explained.—The Reserves.—How they were to Co-operate.—Big Bethel.—Its Position.—Ignorance of Federal Officers.—March of Colonel Duryea.—Delays in Progress.—A Fire in the Rear.—A Counter-march.—No Enemy.—A fatal Blunder.—Return of Vermonters and Massachusetts Men.—The Blunder explained.—Who was to blame?—The General's self-justification.—Defence of Colonel Bendix.

1861.

THE Virginians having failed, through the rare and happy accident of its being held by a loyal officer at the time of their insurrection, in obtaining possession of Fortress Monroe, made great efforts to counteract the loss of so important a defence. This strong work, which held as it were in its grip the neck of Chesapeake Bay, and throttled Virginia by commanding its channels of communication with the sea, was also, as a basis of offensive operations, the most important possession retained by the Federal Government. The people of Norfolk especially felt themselves endangered by the proximity of the great fortress, where the Union could muster within its impregnable walls and under its commanding guns, armies and fleets ready to be directed at any moment upon the neighboring shores, and thus threaten the safety of their city.

The Virginians accordingly made haste to fortify that part of their coast more immediately exposed to an attack from Fortress Monroe. With the cannon left at the Norfolk navy-yard, after the blundering attempt at its destruction by the Federal officer in command, they were abundantly supplied with means of arming their defences. They accordingly raised fortifications on every point of land, and at every river's mouth where there seemed danger of an attack. Among these is Sewall's Point, at the confluence of the Elizabeth and James rivers, directly opposite to Fortress Monroe, and about four miles distant. This low spit of land not only commands the mouths of these two rivers, but presents a favorable place for the landing of troops to operate in the rear of Norfolk. The Virginians accordingly sent down gangs of negroes, and some soldiers, to raise batteries of sand, and to mount them with cannon. While thus occupied, commander Harry May Eagle, of the United States steamer 18. Star, who was on the watch, discovered the work in progress. "Several noises were heard during the night, but not distinct enough for me," reported Captain Eagle officially, " to trace them. At half-past five P.M. I heard distinct blows, as if from an axe securing timber platforms for gun-carriages inside of the embrasures, and immediately I ordered a shot to be fired over them. The rebels immediately hoisted a white flag with some design on it, and fired a shot that cut the fore spencer guys near the gaff. I immediately beat to quarters and returned their fire, which was continued by them. I expended fifteen round of grape, twelve ten-inch shot, thirty-two ten-inch shell, ten shell for thirty-two pounders, and forty-five thirty-two-pound shot, making a total of one hundred and fourteen shots, which," adds the captain, "I think did some execution among the rebels. I only desisted for want of ammunition, having only five eight-pound charges remaining for the pivot gun."

The action continued for an hour and a quarter, and although the official statement makes no allusion to the fact, it would seem that another Federal vessel bore a not ineffective part in the engagement. Captain Ward came up opportunely with the steamer Freeborn, and taking a position within five hundred yards of the shore, opened with thirty-two-pound round shot. " He soon drove the party out of the work, and was not long in hammering two or three of the embrasures into one. The defenders, with a mounted officer at their head, took refuge in a clump of trees near by, into which Captain Ward presently threw a shot, which had the effect of routing the party."

One of the enemy gave the following account of the affair, from which it would seem there was less " execution among the rebels" than Captain Eagle had expected.

"The enemy had three eight-inch columbiads, from which they kept up an incessant and rapid firing. Their guns were aimed with remarkable precision. Any one of their shots would have struck a boat of the size of theirs; but, thank God, not one did its diabolical work among us. Almost half their shot struck our battery, and several shells exploded on top of it. One tremendous bomb hit the muzzle of the cannon at which Lieutenant Moffet and myself were working, and exploded in the embrasure, not three feet from us, covering us with the turf and splinters of the battery, and so tearing up the embrasure as to make it large enough for three guns. Another shell passed within a foot of Robert Lockhart, as he ran out to plant the flag a little farther to the left than where it had been waving. He did not have time to get behind the battery after the cry of 'look out' was given and before the ball came. He fell flat on the ground, and that saved him. Privates Mayo and Porter had one ball pass between their legs while they were shoveling away sand from in front of their gun.

"The trees near the fort were completely peeled and trimmed by the grape and shell. A chain came whizzing just a foot above the battery, struck a tree about ten feet off, and cut it in two as smoothly as you could cut a sprig of asparagus. The shell, and grape, and thirty-two-pounders rained down among us all the time as thickly as hail, and all of us are the possessors of some of these trophies, gathered on the ground of our first successful battle-field."

The attack, however, upon Sewall's Point had the effect of putting the Virginians on the alert, to increase the strength of that place. They immediately concentrated two thousand troops there, and added "four of the heaviest guns" to the battery, which they continued to hold till the general advance of the Army of the Potomac, under McClellan, in March, 1862.

The United States Government, alive to the importance of Fortress Monroe, not only as a defensive work, but as a basis of operations, had hastened to strengthen its garrison and to place there a large body of troops. Before the close of May there were over five thousand men collected within its walls. To Butler, created a major-general, who had proved so energetic an officer at Annapolis and Baltimore, being succeeded at Baltimore by General Cadwallader—was given the command of the new military department of Virginia, embracing the eastern district to the summit of the Blue Ridge, and also the States of North and South Carolina. May 18.

Fortress Monroe was included within Butler's command, and thither he repaired and established his headquarters. His arrival was welcomed with enthusiasm, and honored by the usual military ceremonies. Salutes were fired, and there was a grand review, on the parade ground, of the troops, amounting to over four thousand men, who received their new chief with loud hurrahs. The General's first movement was to take possession of Hampton, separated from Fort Monroe, or rather the peninsula of Old Point Comfort, upon which the fortress stands, only by an artificial causeway and a narrow neck of land. A regiment of volunteers was detailed for the purpose of resisting any possible opposition, and they marched across the causeway. The Virginians, as soon as they observed the approach of the Federal troops, hurried to set fire to the bridge, where they had accumulated combustibles for the purpose. The advance guard, however, of the volunteers pushed on rapidly, and before the fire had done much damage, extinguished it and put the enemy to flight, with the loss of one field-piece. This was seized and thrown into the bay, and General Butler continuing his progress, and making his reconnoissance, selected the site for a permanent encampment upon the farm of a Mr. Segar, a unionist. Next day May 22.

two regiments were here encamped, and a foothold secured upon the mainland of Virginia.

Reinforcements continuing to pour into Fortress Monroe, General Butler was enabled again to make a successful advance into the territory of the enemy. Embarking twenty-five hundred men in transports at the wharf of the fort, consisting principally of Vermont and Massachusetts regiments, he dispatched them to take possession of Newport News. This place is situated on the left bank of the James River, on the same peninsula formed between that stream and the York River, to which Fortress Monroe itself is joined by a causeway and narrow neck of land. The expedition met with no resistance, and no attempt at it, beyond several ineffectual shots from the enemy's batteries on the opposite side of James River. Intrenchments were immediately begun after the landing of the troops, and Newport News, a post which commands the peninsula on which it is situated, and a small island in the stream which it was feared might be fortified by the Confederates, was thus secured.

May 27.

The enemy were vigorously providing for the defence of the Virginia coast, thus threatened by the increased force at Fortress Monroe, and by the accumulation, under the cover of its guns, of armed United States vessels in the Chesapeake Bay and its tributaries. The Confederates had not only erected batteries upon the Elizabeth, James, York, Rappahannock, and Potomac rivers, but upon the smaller streams which empty into them. One of the most formidable of these works had been constructed at the mouth of the Acquia Creek. This place had been judiciously chosen by the enemy as a point of the utmost importance in the defence of Virginia. Here is situated the eastern terminus of the Fredericksburgh and Potomac Railway, which, extending from the river to Fredericksburgh, continues from that city to Richmond, the capital of Virginia. The mouth of the Acquia, where it empties into the Potomac on the Virginia side of the river, is about fifty miles from Washington, and seventy-five from Richmond. The current of travel from the North to the South, after passing down the Potomac from Washington, usually took this direction, by rail, to the capital of Virginia and more Southern destinations.

Strong batteries had been raised on the shore and on high and commanding ground behind. These, Captain Ward, of the United States steamer Freeborn, determined to make an effort to reduce. He, accordingly, supported by the two steamers, Anacosta and Resolute, opened fire. After an incessant discharge, kept up for two hours, the three lower batteries at the railroad terminus were silenced. His ammunition, however, having been expended, and the enemy continuing to fire with great effect from their guns on the heights, Captain Ward was obliged to haul off the Freeborn. The other two small steamers, being unprovided with rifled guns, were unable to fire at a

May 31.

sufficiently long range to be of much aid, and they were accordingly prevented from taking any very effective share in the engagement.

On the next day the steamers Pawnee and Yankee joined Ward's flotilla, and the action was renewed. Captain Ward, in his report to the secretary of the navy, thus details the events of the cannonade:

"I have the honor," he wrote, "to report a renewal of the bombardment at Acquia Creek, commencing at eleven o'clock and thirty minutes in the forenoon this day, and terminating, from fatigue of the men (the day being very warm, and the firing on our side incessant), at 4.30 in the afternoon, being a duration of five hours. The firing on shore was scarcely as spirited at any time as yesterday. The heights were abandoned, the guns apparently having been transferred to the earth-works at the railway terminus, in replacement of the batteries there silenced by ours yesterday. During the last hour of the engagement only two or three shots were thrown from the shore, by a few individuals seen stealthily now and then to emerge from concealment, and who hastily loaded and fired a single gun. The bulk of the party had left half an hour before, and squads were observed from time to time taking to their heels along the beach, with a speed and bottom truly commendable for its prudence, and highly amusing to the seamen. I did not deem it advisable to permit so feeble a fire to wear out my men. Therefore, I discontinued the engagement. Several shots came on board of us, causing the vessel to leak badly, and, besides other injuries, clipping the port-wheel, the wrought-iron shaft being gouged by a shot which would have shattered it if of cast iron. Fortunately I have again neither killed nor wounded to report, though the shot at times fell thick about us, testing the gallantry and steadiness of my men, which I consider of standard proof for any emergency. I proceed to Washington to repair damages and refill my exhausted magazine. The Pawnee remains, meantime, below, to supply my place in the blockade. Captain Rowan, of that ship, joined me last night, replenishing my exhausted stores, and most gallantly opened the fire this morning, having followed my lead in shore toward the batteries. His ship received numerous wounds, both below and aloft, inflicted by the enemy's shot. On account of her size, she being more easily hit, she appeared to be their favorite mark, and was herself often a sheet of flame, owing to the great rapidity of her discharges. The enemy set fire to the large passenger and freight depot on the end of the long pier, as we were approaching, probably to remove it as an obstruction to their aim, but were not permitted to extinguish the flames during the whole five hours' cannonade. Consequently nearly the whole pier is destroyed, leaving only the charred piles remaining above the water to mark its former position.

* * * * * * * *

"More than one hundred shots have

fallen aboard and around us, any one of which would have struck a frigate. We had more than a thousand shots discharged at us within range, and have ourselves fired upward of three hundred shots and shells, with seventeen hundred pounds of powder. What damage we have inflicted remains to be seen. That we have received none not easily repaired, is truly remarkable. The Anacosta and Reliance were not permitted to come under damaging fire, their support having been necessary to embolden those engaged, by giving them confidence that if disabled in the machinery, assistance was at hand to drag them out."

The enemy, however, notwithstanding this spirited attack, persisted in holding their position, and by increased fortifications rendered the batteries of Acquia Creek among the most formidable of their defensive works.

The naval force, under Commodore Stringham, which had now gathered in Hampton Roads, and was blockading the Chesapeake, continued to be active, but, however spiritedly managed, seemed to effect but little in its attempts upon the enemy's batteries. The Harriet Lane, commanded by Captain Faunce, **June** started out on a cruise up the **5.** James River, to look out for batteries. Having discovered one at the mouth of the Nansemond, which joins the James at Hampton Roads, the Harriet Lane opened fire. Being within sight of Fortress Monroe, the soldiers thronged the ramparts to watch the scene. The cannonade of the steamer was briskly responded to by the enemy, who, with their guns of longer range and heavier metal, succeeded in effecting greater damage than they received. The Harriet Lane, after continuing the action for half an hour, in the course of which she was struck by several shot from a thirty-four-pound rifled cannon, hauled off and returned to her anchorage under the guns of the fort.

Reinforcements still continuing to pour into Fortress Monroe, the active Butler became eager for action. The outposts at Newport News and Hampton having been annoyed by a body of the enemy posted at Little Bethel, about eight miles distant from both encampments, General Butler resolved upon an attempt to surprise and capture it. He accordingly sent out an expedition for the purpose. This **June** was composed of two divisions— **9.** the one made up of the New York regiment of Zouaves, commanded by Colonel Duryea, and the Albany (N. Y.) regiment under Colonel Townsend, supported by a detachment of United States artillery, with three cannon, led by Lieutenant Greble. The other division was composed of the New York Steuben Regiment, commanded by Colonel Bendix, and detachments of the First Vermont and Third Massachusetts, under Lieutenant-Colonel Washburn. The whole expedition was placed under the command of General Pierce, a militia brigadier-general of Massachusetts, whose military service had hitherto been restricted to the holiday parades of Boston Common or the village green. The plan of the enterprise is thus set forth by General Butler himself:

"I ordered," he wrote, in his official report, "General Pierce, who is in command of Camp Hamilton, at Hampton, to send Duryea's regiment of Zouaves to be ferried over Hampton Creek at one o'clock this morning, and to march by the road up to Newmarket Bridge, then crossing the bridge, to go by a by-road, and thus put the regiment in the rear of the enemy and between Big Bethel and Little Bethel, in part for the purpose of cutting him off, and then to make an attack upon Little Bethel. I directed General Pierce to support him (Colonel Duryea) from Hampton with Colonel Townsend's regiment, with two mounted howitzers, and to march about an hour later. At the same time I directed Colonel Phelps, commanding at Newport News, to send out a battalion, composed of such companies of the regiments under his command as he thought best, under command of Lieutenant-Colonel Washburn, in time to make a demonstration upon Little Bethel in front, and to have him supported by Colonel Bendix's regiment, with two field-pieces."

From this not very perspicuous statement of General Butler, it may be inferred that Colonel Duryea's regiment from Hampton, and Lieutenant-Colonel Washburn's force from Newport News, were to move in advance, the former to the rear and the latter to the front of Little Bethel, while Colonel Townsend's regiment from Hampton, and Colonel Bendix's regiment from Newport News, were to move later and act as a reserve.

The two latter were to form a junction at a fork of the road leading from Hampton to Newport News, the two points from which they were separately to march, about a mile and a half from Little Bethel. "I directed," continues Butler, in his official report, "the march to be so timed that the attack should be made just at daybreak, and that after the attack was made upon Little Bethel, Duryea's regiment and a regiment from Newport News should follow immediately upon the heels of the fugitives, if they were enabled to cut them off, and attack the battery on the road to Big Bethel, while covered by the fugitives; or if it was thought expedient by General Pierce, failing to surprise the camp at Little Bethel, they should attempt to take the work near Big Bethel."

This Big Bethel is some four miles farther from Fortress Monroe than Little Bethel, on the road from the town of Hampton to Yorktown, of revolutionary renown. Its exact locality, the character of the surrounding country, the force of the enemy, the strength of their fortifications, or even the fact of their existence, was a mystery probably not only to the General-in-chief, but to all his subordinate officers. It was, however, soon to be solved with a fatal result.

Colonel Duryea having formed his regiment of Zouaves, seven hundred and forty strong, and sent skirmishers forward in advance, began his march from

Hampton at half-past eleven o'clock at night, toward Little Bethel. His men moved spiritedly forward, cheered with the prospect of a successful issue to their enterprise. The march for two miles was slow, in consequence of the tardy arrival of the howitzer which was to be placed at the head of the advancing column. There was again a delay at Hampton Creek, for want of surfboats, to convey the troops across. These, however, finally arrived, and the troops being transported to the other side, resumed their march, and soon came up with the two companies sent forward as skirmishers an hour and a half in advance of the main body. The whole force now pushed on with quickened step, without pausing a moment for rest, and at four o'clock in the morning fell in with the picket guard of the enemy at Little Bethel. This, consisting of four soldiers and an officer in command, being captured, the regiment began to move forward on the road toward Big Bethel. At this moment a heavy fire of musketry and cannon was heard in the rear. Believing it to be an attempt by the enemy to cut off his reserve, Colonel Duryea immediately gave the order to countermarch his men, and they at once proceeded in double quick time in direction of the cannonade. After having thus rapidly retraced their march for five miles, they discovered that there was no enemy in their rear, but that the firing had come from their friends brought into collision by a fatal blunder.

Lieutenant-Colonel Washburn, with his detachment of Massachusetts men and Vermonters, had also, in accordance with the plan of the expedition, moved on. Setting out from Newport News, he had marched within reach of the front of Little Bethel, when the cannonade heard in his rear startled him too, and induced him to march back again to meet an enemy, but only to discover that he and Colonel Duryea had been deceived by the same fatal blunder of our troops.

This was soon explained. Colonel Bendix having with his German regiment set out in due time from Newport News, reached the cross roads, and halted, to await the coming up of, and to form a junction with, the Albany regiment under Colonel Townsend, on their route from Hampton. "Up to this point the plan," says Butler, in his official report, "had been vigorously, accurately, and successfully carried out; but here, by some strange fatuity and yet unexplained blunder, without any word of notice, while Colonel Townsend was in column *en route*, and when the head of the column was within one hundred yards, Colonel Bendix's regiment opened fire, with both artillery and musketry, upon Colonel Townsend's column, which, in the hurry and confusion, was irregularly returned by some of Colonel Townsend's men, who feared they had fallen into an ambuscade. Colonel Townsend's column immediately retreated to the eminence near by, and were not pursued by Colonel Bendix's men. By this almost criminal blunder, two men of Colonel Townsend's regiment were killed and eight, more or less, wounded."

Every one was naturally anxious to free himself from the blame of what the General has termed an "almost criminal blunder." He in his own justification declared, that "to prevent the possibility of mistake in the darkness, I directed that no attack should be made until the watchword—Boston—should be shouted by the attacking regiment, and, in case that by any mistake in the march the regiments that were to make the junction should unexpectedly meet and be unknown to each other, also directed that the members of Colonel Townsend's regiment should be known, if in daylight, by something white worn on their arm."

The General seemed to impute the fault to Colonel Bendix's Germans, who, he declared, were the first to open fire. They, however, strenuously defended themselves, asserting that the mistake was mutual, and the attack on both sides simultaneous. The adjutant of the German regiment came to the rescue of its fame with the following declaration:

"Colonel Bendix had not received any order or intimation that our troops should wear white badges around the arm for the purpose of mutual recognition, and if he had, he would not have been able to distinguish such badge at the distance and in the dusk of the morning. Colonel Bendix's command did not wear such badges. The uniform of the Albany regiment was very similar to the uniform of the secession troops. It is doubtful which side opened fire. Many of the Albany boys admit that they fired first, mistaking the Steuben regiment for enemies, probably for the reason that the latter wore no white badges.

"When Colonel Townsend's troops approached the junction over a slight ridge, they appeared to be a troop of cavalry, because General Pierce and staff, and Colonel Townsend and staff, in a body, rode in advance of their troops, and without any advance guard thrown out, as customary, to reconnoitre and protect the head of the column. If the latter precaution had been taken, the unfortunate mistake would not have happened. It was known that our side had no cavalry."

CHAPTER XXIV.

Serious Effects of the Blunder at Little Bethel.—Inexperienced Leader.—Unwise Counsellors.—Second Advance of General Pierce.—Reinforcements.—Arrival of the Advance at Little Bethel.—A deserted Camp.—March to Big Bethel.—The Enemy reported in Force.—Battle given.—Spirit of the Men.—Plan of Battle.—Colonel Duryea's Zouaves.—The Struggle.—Retreat.—The Skirmishers.—Their Retreat.—Death of Greble.—Withdrawal of the Artillery.—Action of the New York Troops.—Relative Number of Troops Engaged.—Losses.—Enemy's Account of the Affair of Big Bethel.—Attempts at Justification by the Federal Officers.—Consoling Reflection of General Butler.—Censure of General Pierce.—Promises to Justify Himself.—Patriotism.—Gallant Behavior of the Soldiers.—Proofs.—Rescue of Guns.—Rescue of Body of Lieutenant Greble.—The Last to Retreat.—Death of Major Winthrop.—His Bravery.—His Lost Moments.—Admiration of the Enemy.—Life of Winthrop.—Adventurous Career.—Restlessness.—His Military Career.—Author of the Plan of Battle at Big Bethel.—Literary Tastes.—Success of his Posthumous Works.

GRIEVOUS as had been the blunder at Little Bethel, and fatal as it was to our own men destroyed by their comrades, it was still more serious in its effects upon the subsequent fate of the expedition. The inexperienced leader, counselled by those who were no more skilled in the art of war than himself, and piqued into an indiscreet activity by disappointment, determined to make an effort to redeem the unsuccessful beginning of the enterprise. He accordingly ordered his troops again to the advance. The enemy, in the mean time, were on the alert, and had fallen back from Little to Big Bethel, where the main body was posted under the cover of a strong battery of several heavy guns. General Pierce, without having made any reconnoissance, and entirely ignorant of the force of his antagonists or the nature of their position or defences, did not hesitate to push on his troops, against this concealed and unnumbered foe, at Great Bethel. He, however, had the prudence, as he advanced, to send back to General Butler for reinforcements, who sent forward Colonel Allen, with his New York city regiment, and Colonel Carr, with that of Troy (N. Y.)

1861.

Colonel Duryea, with his Zouaves, again assumed the advance, supported by Colonel Bendix and his Germans, and Colonel Townsend, with the Albany regiment. On reaching Little Bethel, from which a stray shot was fired by a retreating troop of cavalry, the camp was found deserted, and this being destroyed, our troops pushed on toward Big Bethel. Here the main body arrived at about ten o'clock in the morning, and halted in consequence of the intelligence brought back by those who had been sent forward to skirmish in advance. Captain Kilpatrick, who commanded these skirmishers, had evidently not underrated the strength of the enemy, for he reported that he had found them "with about from three

June 10.

thousand to five thousand men, posted in a strong position on the opposite side of the bridge—three earth-works and a masked battery on the right and left; in advance of the stream, thirty pieces of artillery and a large force of cavalry."

In face of this portentous report of the numbers and strength of position of the enemy, the troops were drawn up in line of battle, and prepared to give fight. The soldiers, though previously fatigued by their long and rapid march, and dispirited by the fatal mistake of the previous night, were at once reanimated by the prospect of a struggle. "It put a new spirit into the men, as the word passed down the line. They were no longer tired and sleepy. Each freshened up to his place in the ranks and closed up in column."

The skirmishers, now led by Lieutenant-Colonel Warren, were again thrown forward on the right and left, supported by the advance guard of Duryea's Zouaves and three pieces of United States artillery, under the command of Lieutenant Greble. The enemy at once opened fire from their batteries directly facing the road, but our men answered with a shout, and continued to press forward.

The enemy's fire was so heavy that it was found useless to attempt to meet it directly by discharges of musketry, and accordingly the Federal forces were deployed. Lieutenant Greble, with his three howitzers, being posted in the road toward the front, was left alone to face the batteries, while the rest assumed positions toward the enemy's right and left, with the view of flanking.

Colonel Duryea's Zouaves and Colonel Townsend's Albany regiment crossed from the road on the left through some cultivated farm-ground and orchards, to an open field on the enemy's right, with their skirmishers in advance, and the Germans, the Massachusetts men, and Vermonters passed into a forest on the right of the road, and toward the left of the enemy.

As the Zouaves advanced, the enemy opened their batteries upon them. Colonel Duryea, however, urged them forward at the double-quick step, until, finding the fire very "destructive," he thought it prudent to seek refuge in a neighboring wood, where he halted to rest his men, and to complete his preparations for charging the batteries in flank. After remaining two hours and a half in this imperfect cover, where they were still within range of the enemy's guns, the Zouaves returned to the open field and spiritedly advanced toward the rebel batteries, with the intention of making an attempt to carry them by storm. They had not proceeded far, however, before they discovered lying across their path an almost impassable swamp, with a small stream running through it. These proved to be insurmountable obstacles. They persevered, however, with great spirit till the order came from General Pierce to retreat. Colonel Duryea, now collecting such of his killed and wounded as he could find, withdrew his men and took to the road in the rear.

The Germans, at the same time, were

acting on the right in conjunction with the Zouaves on the left, and, like them, had made several spirited attempts at charging the batteries, but foiled by the same obstacles of morass and creek and heavy fire, were also forced to withdraw.

Lieutenant Greble, with his three pieces of artillery, had, in the mean time, been returning the fire of the enemy with considerable effect, and had steadily advanced until he reached within two hundred yards of the Confederate works.

The skirmishers, headed by Lieutenant-Colonel Warren, had made good progress. "We continued to advance," reported Captain Kilpatrick, in command, "clearing all before us, till we reached a point just on the edge of the woods where the fire was so hot and heavy that we were compelled to halt, and there we remained as directed by Lieutenant-Colonel Warren, till that gallant officer had made dispositions to turn their flanks. The enemy's fire at this time began to tell upon us with great effect. My men were falling one after another, as was the case of the rest of the command.

"Our object being now accomplished, to remain longer in this exposed position was useless; numbers of our men being killed and wounded, having received a grape-shot through my thigh, which tore off a portion of the rectangle on Colonel Duryea's left shoulder, passed through my leg, and killed a soldier in the rear, I withdrew my men to the skirts of the wood. We managed to reach Lieutenant Greble's battery and bring to his aid several of my men. The charge was then sounded, and Lieutenant Greble opened fire with grape and canister within two hundred yards of the enemy's lines. Captains Winslow, Bartlett, and myself charged with our commands in front; Captain Denike and Lieutenant Duryea (son of Colonel Duryea), and about two hundred of the Troy Rifles, upon the right; Colonel Townsend, with his men, to the left. The enemy were forced out of the first battery, all the forces were rapidly advancing, and everything promised a speedy victory, when we were ordered to fall back. Where this order came from, I do not know. We maintained our position till Colonel Townsend began to retire with his whole command. Being left thus alone, and no prospects of receiving aid, we ordered the men to fall back, which they did, and in good order, forming their line of battle about one hundred and fifty yards in the rear. A few minutes afterward, orders came from General Pierce to cease firing and retire."

Greble, after two hours of spirited work with his artillery, was struck by a cannon-ball in the head and killed instantly. With his death, the fall of the larger number of the artillerists, and the exhaustion of ammunition, it was found necessary to withdraw the guns, which was done by the Massachusetts men and Vermonters, under Lieutenant-Colonel Washburne. The body of the young lieutenant was borne off, lying upon one of those cannon which he had so gallantly served.

The New York regiment sent to reinforce the Federal troops, reached the battle-field in time to share in the engagement. The commander, Colonel Allen, in his official report, says: "Upon reporting to General Pierce, he directed me to proceed to the front and deploy my regiment in front of the battery, which I did, and so remained for one hour and forty minutes under a heavy fire of at least twenty guns, some of them rifled, and about four shell guns—the enemy deploying in my front with about 1,200 men and two guns, but made no advance. They, however, threw out two heavy flanking parties on my right and left, the former with two guns, and completely outflanked the entire brigade, at which time General Pierce deemed it proper to retire."

The number of Federal troops on the field of battle, including the reinforcements, amounted to about four thousand. Of these, sixteen were killed, thirty-four wounded, and five missing, making a total of fifty-three. The Federal loss, moreover, was increased by the fatal blunder, which resulted in killing two and wounding nineteen.

The enemy reported that their whole force engaged did not exceed eleven hundred men, under the command of General Magruder, and one killed and two wounded, as the total of their loss. One who served with them gave this account of the affair:

"On Monday morning, six hundred infantry and two guns, under General Magruder, left the camp and proceeded toward Hampton, but after advancing a mile or two, received information that the Yankees were coming in large force. We then retired, and after reaching camp the guns were placed in battery and the infantry took their places behind their breast-work. Everybody was cool, and all were anxious to give the invaders a good reception. About nine o'clock the glittering bayonets of the enemy appeared on the hill opposite, and above them waved the star-spangled banner. The moment the head of the column advanced far enough to show one or two companies, the Parrott gun of the howitzer battery opened on them, throwing a shell right into their midst. Their ranks broke in confusion, and the column, or as much of it as we could see, retreated behind two small farm-houses. From their position a fire was opened on us, which was replied to by our battery, which commanded the route of their approach. Our firing was excellent, and the shells scattered in all directions, when they burst. They could hardly approach the guns which they were firing, for the shells which came from our battery. Within our encampment fell a perfect hail-storm of canister shot, bullets, and balls. Remarkable to say, not one of our men was killed inside of our encampment. Several horses were slain by the shells and bullets. Finding that bombardment would not answer, the enemy, about eleven o'clock, tried to carry the position by assault, but met a terrible repulse at the hands of the infantry as he tried to scale the breast-works. The men disregarded sometimes the defences erected for them, and, leaping on the embankment, stood and fired at the Yankees, cutting them down as they came up. One company of the New York Seventh Regiment, under Captain Winthrop, attempted to take the redoubt on the left. The marsh they crossed was strewn with their bodies. Their captain, a fine-looking man, reached the fence, and, leaping on a log, waved his sword, crying, 'Come on, boys! one charge, and the day is ours!' The words were his last, for a Carolina rifle ended his life the next moment, and his men fled in terror back. At the redoubt on the right, a company of about three hundred New York Zouaves charged one of our guns, but could not stand the fire of the infantry, and retreated precipitately. During these charges the main body of the enemy on the hill were attempting to concentrate for a general assault, but the shells from the howitzer battery prevented them. As one regiment would give up the effort, another would be marched to the position, but with no better success, for a shell would scatter them like chaff. The men did not seem able to stand fire at all. About one o'clock their guns were silenced, and a few moments after, their infantry retreated precipitately down the road to Hampton. Our cavalry, numbering three companies, went in pursuit, and harassed them down to the edge of Hampton. As they retreated, many of the wounded fell along the road and died, and the whole road to Hampton was strewn with haversacks, overcoats, canteens, muskets, etc., which the men had thrown off in their retreat."

The Federal officers engaged in the unfortunate affairs of Little and Big Bethel strove to justify their conduct of the expedition, or to shift upon one another the responsibility of its failure. The commander-in-chief, General Butler, consoled himself with the thought, "in the unfortunate combination of circumstances, and the result which we have experienced, we have gained more than we have lost. Our troops have learned to have confidence in themselves under fire, the enemy have shown that they will not meet us in the open field, and our officers have learned wherein their organization and drill are deficient."

The militia Brigadier-General Pierce, who commanded the expedition, was so overwhelmed with censure, that he was forced to seek refuge within the columns of the newspaper, and persisting in the assertion of the excellence of his military conduct, promised a future justification of his skill as a commander:*

"CAMP HAMILTON, *June* 12, 1861.
"TO THE EDITORS OF THE BOSTON JOURNAL:

"Please correct the erroneous reports set afloat by my enemies. There were but seven killed of the forces that went from this camp, in the expedition to Little and Big Bethel, on the 10th of this month, and Colonel Townsend, of the Third Regiment New York Volunteers, who was formerly adjutant-gen-

* His justification was subsequently published. It cast the blame upon his superior in command.

eral of the State of New York, offers to certify that I gave my orders properly, and that, under the circumstances, the battle could not have been managed better.

"This I write that the public may not judge me before I have time to be heard.

"Captain Haggerty and Major Winthrop, of General Butler's staff, were with me, and advising me to do as I did. General Butler has not intimated to me, as yet, that he blames me at all. In haste, yours, E. W. PIERCE."

He subsequently confessed his incompetency as an officer by modestly retiring from the brigadier-generalship, and proved his patriotism by serving as a private in the ranks.

The soldiers unquestionably behaved with even more gallantry and firmness than might have been expected from raw troops, indiscreetly exposed to the batteries of a concealed and numerous enemy, and unskilfully managed by incompetent leaders. There were many instances of individual courage, which proved the spirit of the men and their capability, under proper command, of effectively serving the cause which they had so eagerly adopted.

During the retreat, Captain Wilson, of Colonel Carr's regiment of Troy (N. Y.), finding that a six-pounder had been left on the field, about fifty rods from the battery, shouted to his men: "Boys! there's a cannon: we must not leave it behind; we must take it with us." The whole company to a man cried out, "We'll take it;" and they were immediately marched back to obtain the piece. They had hardly reached it, when the enemy opened fire upon them, killing one of the brave fellows and wounding two others. The drag-ropes were detached, but the men tied them to the gun, in the midst of a shower of shot, and with a cheer ran it into the woods bordering the road. Captain Wilson, then, followed by five men, returned once more to the exposed spot to which the enemy's fire was hotly aimed, and securing the caisson, and also the body of poor Greble, who had fallen dead at his post, retired again to the cover of the woods, whence he retreated in safety with his hard-earned trophies. A score of men only, under the command of Lieutenant White, after firing their last charges from their howitzer, were left far in the rear, and being the last to leave the field, kept at bay a squadron of the enemy's cavalry and some infantry during their retreat to the main body.

The young Major Winthrop fell while gallantly urging on the troops, by his example and stirring words, to the attack. A fellow-officer who was with him during the engagement has testified to his spirit. "I made a reconnoissance," he said, "with Major Winthrop about twelve o'clock in the day, and can testify to his bravery and daring. He was very much exhausted, having wanted for sleep, food, and water, and the day had turned out very hot. We stuck our heads out of some underbrush, and instantly there was a perfect shower of balls rained upon us, which compelled us to withdraw a few paces. Major

Winthrop laid himself behind a tree, saying if he could only sleep for five minutes he would be all right. He remarked as he did this, that he was going to see the inside of that intrenchment before he went back to the fortress—his manner being that of cool, ordinary conversation. He continued self-possessed and cool throughout the whole engagement, up to the time when he received his death-wound, which happened by the side of Lieutenant Herringen, Company E, who remained with him and cared for him until life had fled. He was shot in the side."

The enemy found him to be the most conspicuous aim for their fatal shots. Their riflemen from their covers in the pits before the batteries had several times deliberately fired at him, as they declared he was constantly "conspicuous at the head of the advancing Federal troops, loudly cheering them on to the assault."

Theodore Winthrop was born in New Haven, Connecticut, in 1834, and was a descendant of the famous colonial governor of his name. He was possessed of a warm temperament, which gave the impulse to effort, but at the same time of a vagrant fancy, which hindered concentration and led to uncertainty of purpose. Educated at Yale College, and endowed with a natural taste for literature, he at one time aspired to be an author. Again his impulsive character, untutored by the discipline of routine, sought vent for its irregular forces in the adventure of exploration and travel. He crossed the Rocky Mountains to California, and again on his return he started with Lieutenant Strain on his bold expedition across the mountains, the jungles, and unnavigable rivers of the Isthmus of Darien. His physical strength, however, proved unequal to the trials of that adventurous exploration, and he returned to New York, his nominal home, to venture upon a new field of labor. He studied and began the practice of law. His errant fancies, however, were not favorable to the steady pursuit of the law, and he met with but little success. One of the fondest of his friends who knew him well, has said that "partly from ill-health, partly from temperament, a dreary sadness overhung his life and dispirited his efforts. Glad of his friends' success, and conscious of the kindred impulse, he still wistfully delayed. Of great industry and restless endeavor, he saw success slide by, and seemed to be waiting in melancholy patience the rising of a happier star. It has risen at last, and shines upon his grave."

On the fall of Sumter, he saw in the war which must ensue a new scope for his adventurous spirit and unemployed energies.

"On the Sunday afternoon after the fall of Sumter he was walking with a friend in the woods upon Staten Island, near his home. No man could have a clearer conception of the significance of that event. An American in the noblest sense, he felt that the time had come in which our liberties could be maintained only in the same way that they were won. 'To-morrow,' said his friend, 'we shall have a proclamation from the President.' 'Then to-morrow,' he answered, 'I shall enlist.' He did so. If he had hesitated before, there could be no hesitation now. Mother, sisters, brother, farewell! It is God who calls in the voice of my country."*

He joined, together with his brother, the Seventh Regiment, which was the first to leave New York to go to the defence of the capital. After his regiment was mustered out of the Federal service, young Winthrop was appointed aid-de-camp and military secretary to General Butler, whom he accompanied to Fortress Monroe. He was now fairly embarked for the war. With his natural hopefulness of temper, he was exceedingly sanguine of the success of the Federal arms.

"A few burned villages, a dozen guerrillas hung, one scouring skirmish or battle will pacify," he wrote, "a whole State. Under the discipline and *esprit du corps* of a regiment or an army the South may fight; but they will not have moral conviction enough to risk

* *Harper's Weekly.*

their separate lives except in assassinations, and those a few sharp examples will terminate. We heard their threats at Annapolis. We heard also the pitiful plaints of the timid who believed the threats. *No; if we are patient and well led*, we shall do our work without much massacre."

The equivocal honor of the plan of the expedition to Little Bethel has been claimed for him, and a memorandum with its main details was found among his papers after his death, and published. The fact that to so inexperienced a soldier recourse was had for the plan of the expedition, is a confession of incompetency on the part of his elders and superiors which betokened ill for its success.

Young Winthrop during his campaign wrote frequently for a Boston magazine, and his spirited account of the march of the Seventh Regiment, and its first experiences in actual warfare, was received with great popular favor. Since his death, several of his stories and two novels written by him have been published, awakening an interest naturally heightened by the heroic death of their patriotic author.

CHAPTER XXV.

The Call of the Country for the services of its Citizens.—The Sword laid aside for the pursuits of Peace.—States competing for a military leader.—George B. McClellan.—Proud position.—Hopes for the future.—A Bonaparte or a Washington?—Life of George B. McClellan.—Inheritance of paternal qualities.—Family Descent.—Military Education.—At West Point.—First of his class.—Enters the Army.—Organizes the Sappers and Miners.—His success.—Services and rewards in the Mexican Campaign.—Laborious work at Vera Cruz.—A dangerous Reconnoissance at Contreras.—In the fight.—Services at Churubusco.—Well-earned praise.—Brevetted Captain.—At Molino del Rey.—At Chapultepec.—One of the "five Lieutenants of Engineers who won the admiration of all."—In the same list with Beauregard.—McClellan accepts the command of the Sappers and Miners.—Two years at West Point.—Scientific Pursuits and Writings.—Superintendent of construction of Fort Delaware.—Married.—Chief Engineer in Texas.—Surveyor of North Pacific Railroad.—Services acknowledged by Jefferson Davis.—Secret Service in the West Indies.—Sent to the Crimea.—Report on European Armies.—The character of the work.—Description of the Storming of the Malakoff.—Practical views in regard to Coast Defences.—McClellan resigns his Army command.—Vice-President and Chief Engineer of the Illinois Central Railroad.—President and General Superintendent of the Ohio and Mississippi Railroad.—Summoned by the country to resume his Sword.—Services competed for by Pennsylvania and Ohio.—Accepts a Major-Generalship from Ohio.—Commissioned by the United States a Major-General.—Command of the Department of Ohio.—Personal appearance and character of McClellan.—Campaign in Western Virginia.—Movements of the Enemy.—Movements of General Patterson from Pennsylvania and McClellan from Ohio.—Proclamation of McClellan.—Crossing the Ohio into Western Virginia.

WHEN our domestic quarrel had become so exasperated that civil war 1861. was inevitable, and the country called for the services of all who were able to take up arms in its defence, there was one who, though he had laid aside the sword for the pursuits of peace, had given such proofs of military capacity, that States competed for him as the leader of their armies. This was George B. McClellan, afterward commander-in-chief of the United States forces, who held for some time the proudest position in the country, and seemed destined, should the capricious fortunes of war favor him, to acquire a military fame rivaling that of a Cæsar or a Bonaparte. Such was his popularity after taking command of the Army of the Potomac that high hopes of his ability to end the rebellion were anticipated, and that with a moderation of power and a disinterestedness of patriotism he might rise far beyond the imperial grandeur of the Roman and French emperors, and appear in moral greatness as the saviour of the republic next to Washington its revered founder.

George B. McClellan was born in Philadelphia, on the third of January, eighteen hundred and twenty-six. His father was a surgeon of that city, famous in his profession for skill, intrepidity, promptitude, and dexterity—qualities which his son was believed to have inherited, though exercised in a different sphere of duty. The family, as its name indicates, was of Scotch descent, and originally settled in New England, where some of its members are still to be found.

In 1842, young McClellan, at the age of sixteen, entered the Military Academy of West Point. After the usual course of four years of study he graduated in 1846, being twenty years old, at the head of his class. He entered the army as brevet second lieutenant of engineers, an honored corps into which the most distinguished students of West Point are only admitted. On the declaration of war against Mexico, Congress passed an act establishing a company of sappers, miners, and pontoon constructors to be added to the corps of engineers, and young McClellan was appointed its second lieutenant. Upon him and two other officers devolved the duty of organizing and drilling this new branch of service. The recruits were accordingly mustered at West Point, where they were practised in sapping, mining, constructing bridges, and preparing the materials for sieges. At the same time they were thoroughly drilled and disciplined as infantry soldiers. Colonel Totten, the chief of this department, declared in his report, that when this new company, composed of seventy-one men, left West Point for the war, they were in "admirable discipline," and warmly applauded the skill and energy displayed by McClellan and his associates in their work of organization and drill. Proceeding first to Camargo, in Mexico, and reporting for duty to General Taylor, the company was ordered to return to Matamoras, and act with the column about marching under the command of General Patterson.

At Matamoras the captain and nineteen men of the corps were invalided and left in the hospital. Lieutenant McClellan and his comrade, Lieutenant Gustavus W. Smith—afterward a general in the Confederate army—proceeded in command of the remainder of the company to Vera Cruz. "During the march from Matamoras to Vittoria," reported Colonel Totten, "the company, then reduced to forty-five effectives, executed a great amount of work on the roads, fords, etc., as it did in proceeding thence to Tampico, where it formed, with one company of the Third and one of the Seventh Infantry, a pioneer party, under Captain Henry of the Third Infantry. The detailed reports of these labors exhibit the greatest efficiency and excellent discipline under severe and trying circumstances, Lieutenant Smith having then but one officer, Lieutenant McClellan, under his command."

On arriving at Vera Cruz, the captain, invalided at Matamoras, resumed the command of the company, to which was attached also another subordinate officer. To the conduct of the sappers and miners at the siege of Vera Cruz, Colonel Totten paid this tribute: "During the siege of Vera Cruz," he said, "I was witness to the great exertions and services of this company, animated by and emulating the zeal and devotion of its excellent officers, Lieutenants Smith, McClellan, and Foster." During the whole work of the siege, the labors of the company were incessant. "The total of the company was so small," said Totten, "and demands for its aid so incessant, that every man may be said to have been constantly on duty, with scarcely a moment for rest and refreshment." The captain was unable, from continued illness, to take any very effective part in the onerous duties of the command, and soon after died, leaving the weight of labor and responsibility to rest upon his youthful subordinates, who proved themselves equal to the task, and earned another tribute from their superior, Colonel Totten, who declared that they "directed the operations with unsurpassed intelligence and zeal."

The same officer, in his reports of the services of the company, whether on the march, in the field, or in the trenches, had occasion but to repeat his praises both of men and officers. He said:

"Severe labors followed the surrender of Vera Cruz and its castle, and accompanied the march to the battle of Cerro Gordo, in which the company displayed, in various parts of the field, its gallantry and efficiency. It entered the city of Jalapa with the advance of Twiggs' division, and Puebla with the advance of Worth's. During the pause at the latter place, the instruction of the company in its appropriate studies and exercises was resumed by its persevering and zealous officers, and assistance was given by all in the repairs of the defences. Marching from Puebla with General Twiggs' division, the company was joined to General Worth at Chalon, and arrived in front of San Antonio on the 18th of August, having greatly assisted in clearing the road of obstructions placed by the enemy.

On the next day, the 19th of August, the company was placed at the head of the column commanded by General Pillow. Before the battle at Contreras opened, Lieutenant McClellan was ordered, together with another officer of engineers, to reconnoitre the position of the enemy. They, however, fell in with the advance guards of the Mexicans, and being fired upon, and losing their horses, which were killed, barely escaped in safety back to the lines. During the engagement which ensued, Lieutenant McClellan joined Magruder's battery. General Twiggs bore testimony to his good service on that day:

"Lieutenant George B. McClellan, after Lieutenant Calender was wounded, took charge of and managed the howitzer battery (Lieutenant Reno being detached with the rockets) with judgment and success, until it became so disabled as to require shelter. For Lieutenant McClellan's efficiency and gallantry in this affair, I present his name for the favorable consideration of the General in-chief."

On the next day, when the battle of Churubusco was fought and the victory won, McClellan again obtained the "honorable mention" of his commander, and a brevet rank. General Persifer F. Smith, with whose division the young Lieutenant served, declared in his report:

"Lieutenant G. W. Smith, in command of the engineer company, and Lieutenant McClellan, his subaltern, distinguished themselves throughout the whole of the three actions. Nothing seemed to them too bold to be undertaken, or too difficult to be executed, and their services as engineers were as valuable as those they rendered in battle at the head of their gallant men."

In the battle of Molino del Rey, too, which succeeded, McClellan was again conspicuous among the most active and brave. He was brevetted captain in acknowledgment of his services. He, however, declined the promotion, and was still only a lieutenant during the attack on Chapultepec. His services on this occasion, in erecting batteries before the engagement, and his gallantry in fighting during the battle, brought him once more within the notice of his superiors. General Scott named him in his dispatch as one of "those five lieutenants of engineers" who "won the admiration of all." The name of his famous competitor, Beauregard, was on the same honored list.

McClellan was thus with the army of General Scott during the whole of its victorious progress from Vera Cruz to the capital, and at every step the young Lieutenant won an increase of honor for his good conduct. He was brevetted captain for his service in Mexico, and returned in 1848 to West Point with his company of sappers and miners, of which he soon after became commander.

Here McClellan remained for more than two years, in comparative inactivity, but improved the time by study and devotion to the welfare of the service. He translated from the French, with which he is said to be thoroughly acquainted, a military work, which has been adopted as a text-book, and modifying in accordance with the latest system of tactics, the bayonet exercise, introduced it into the army.

During the summer and autumn of 1851, McClellan was charged with the superintendence of the construction of Fort Delaware, and in the spring of the same year was ordered to duty in the exploration of the Red River, under Major R. B. Marcy, whose daughter he married. While engaged in this work he was ordered to Texas, as chief engineer, under the command of General Persifer Smith of that department, and had been occupied for several months in surveying the rivers and harbors of the State, when he was transferred to the Pacific coast, to command the western division of the survey of the route for the North Pacific Railroad, to pass from the Mississippi to the Pacific Ocean.

Jefferson Davis, afterward President of the Southern Confederacy, then secretary of war of the United States, in his report to Congress thus acknowledged the services of McClellan as an explorer:

"The examination of the approaches and passes of the Cascade Mountains, made by Captain McClellan, of the corps of engineers, presents a reconnoissance of great value, and, though performed under adverse circumstances, exhibits all the information necessary to determine the practicability of this portion of the route, and reflects the highest credit on the capacity and resources of that officer."

Again he added: "Captain McClellan, of the corps of engineers, after the completion of his field operations, was directed to visit various railroads, and to collect information and facts established in the construction and working of existing roads, to serve as data in determining the practicability of constructing and working roads over the several routes explored. The results of his inquiries will be found in a very valuable memoir herewith submitted."

This public duty was followed by the performance of some secret service for the Government in the West Indies.

In 1855, McClellan received a commission of captain in the United States cavalry, and was appointed by the Government, together with Colonel Richard Delafield and Major Alfred Mordecai, to proceed to the Crimea and report upon the war then waging between Russia and the allied powers of France and England. The result of his observations was embodied in a work entitled, "Report on the Organization of European Armies and the Operations of the War." It is acknowledged to be a production showing a thorough mastery of the military art. Its demonstrations evince an exact knowledge of science and a broad view in the application of its principles. The author, in the freedom of his criticism, does not hesitate to disregard the pretensions of rank and authority, and submit the strategy and tactics of the most distinguished European officers to the test of his own judgment. This self-reliance, though it might be thought by some presumptuous in so young a man, came from a consciousness of power, derived not only from original genius but careful culture, which gave promise that McClellan would be the great leader the country required.

Of the clear and precise style of McClellan as a writer, the following description of the storming of the Malakoff presents a good illustration:

"In their admirable arrangements for the attack of the Malakoff, the French counted on two things for success: first, they had ascertained that the Russians were in the habit of relieving the guard of the Malakoff at noon, and that a great part of the old guard marched out before the new one arrived, in order to avoid the loss which would arise from crowding the work with men; in the second place, it was determined to keep up a most violent vertical fire until the very moment of the assault, thus driving the Russians into the bomb-proofs, and enabling the storming party to enter the work with but little opposition.

"The hour of noon was therefore selected for the assault, and the strong columns intended for the work were at an early hour assembled in the advanced trenches, all in admirable order, and furnished with precise instructions.

'The mortars maintained an unremitting fire until the moment appointed. The very instant the last volley was discharged, the storming party of Zouaves rushed over the thirty paces before them, and were in the work before the astonished Russians knew what had happened. It was stated that this party lost but eleven in entering the work. Other troops advanced rapidly to support the storming party, a bridge was formed by rolling up five ladders with planks lashed to them, a communication was at once commenced between the advanced trench and the bridge; brigade after brigade passed over, the redoubt was at once occupied by the storming party, and thus the Malakoff, and with it Sebastopol, was won. The few Russians remaining in the work made a desperate resistance. Many gallant attempts were made by Russian columns to ascend the steep slope in rear and regain the lost work; but as the road was narrow, difficult, and obstructed, the position strong, and the French in force, all their furious efforts were in vain, and the Malakoff remained in possession of those who had so gallantly and skilfully won it. With regard to the final retreat to the north side, it can only be said that a personal examination of the locality merely confirms its necessity, and the impression so generally entertained that it was the finest operation of the war; so admirably was it carried out that not a straggler remained behind; a few men, so severely wounded as to be unfit for rough and hurried transportation, were the only ghastly human trophies that remained to the allies. The retreat, being a more difficult operation than the assault, is worthy of more admiration, but the Russian retreat to the north side, and the French assault upon the Malakoff must each be regarded as a masterpiece of its kind, deserving the closest study. It is difficult to imagine what point in either can be criticised, for both evinced consummate skill, discipline, coolness, and courage."

The practical tendency of his mind and the character of his studies may be seen in the conclusions with which he has closed his report. From these it might be inferred that his efforts would early be directed to obtaining a disciplined army.

"It is believed that a calm consideration of the events so hastily and imperfectly narrated in the preceding pages must lead all unprejudiced persons among our countrymen to a firm conviction on two vital points:

"1st. That our system of permanent coast defences is a wise and proper one, which ought to be completed and armed with the least possible delay.

"2d. That mere individual courage cannot suffice to overcome the forces that would be brought against us were we involved in a European war, but that it must be rendered manageable by discipline, and directed by that consummate and mechanical military skill which can only be acquired by a course of education instituted for that special purpose, and by long habit.

"In the day of sailing vessels the successful siege of Sebastopol would have been impossible. It is evident that the Russians did not appreciate the advantages afforded by steamers, and were unprepared to sustain a siege.

"This same power of steam would enable European nations to disembark even a larger force than that which finally encamped around Sebastopol. To resist such an attack, should it ever be made, our cities and harbors must be fortified, and these fortifications must be provided with guns, ammunition, and

STANDARD ILLUSTRATED BOOKS.

BENSON J. LOSSING'S "LIFE OF WASHINGTON."
"BATTLES OF AMERICA BY SEA AND LAND."
"THE WAR WITH THE SOUTH," by Robt. Tomes, M.D.
Illustrated by F. O. C. DARLEY, and other Eminent Artists.

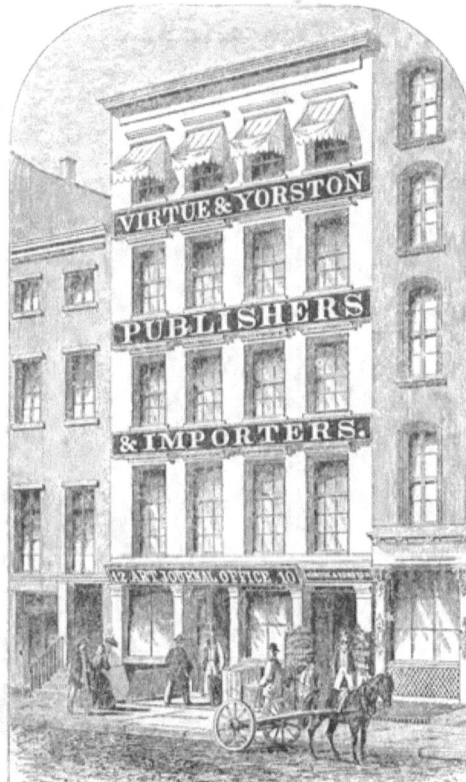

OFFICE OF

WEALE'S SERIES

OF

RUDIMENTARY,

SCIENTIFIC,

Educational

AND

CLASSICAL

WORKS

REISSUE

OF

𝕻𝖚𝖓𝖈𝖍,

&c., &c.

ILLUSTRATED

WORKS

ON THE SCENERY OF

The United States,

CANADA,

ITALY,

SWITZERLAND,

THE

BOSPHORUS,

The DANUBE,

&c., &c.

THE

TURNER GALLERY

Vernon Gallery,

WILKIE GALLERY,

Sculpture Gallery,

&c., &c.

12 DEY ST., and 544 BROADWAY,
NEW YORK.

New National Work on the Late Rebellion.

Part 7 — Illustrated by F. O. C. Darley and other Eminent Artists — Price 50c

VIRTUE & YORSTON,
12 DEY STREET, and 644 BROADWAY, NEW YORK.

To be Completed in Forty-five **Parts**, at Fifty **Cents** each.

instructed artillerists. To repel the advance of such an army into the interior, it is not enough to trust to the number of brave but undisciplined men that we can bring to bear against it.

"An invading army of fifteen thousand or twenty thousand men could easily be crushed by the unremitting attacks of superior numbers; but when it comes to the case of more than one hundred thousand disciplined veterans, the very multitude brought to bear against them works its own destruction; because, if without discipline and instruction, they cannot be handled, and are in their own way. We cannot afford a Moscow campaign.

"Our regular army never can be, and perhaps never ought to be, large enough to provide for all the contingencies that may arise; but it should be as large as its ordinary avocations in the defence of the frontier will justify; the number of officers and non-commissioned officers should be unusually large, to provide for a sudden increase; and the greatest possible care should be bestowed upon the instruction of the special arms of the artillery and engineer troops.

"The militia and volunteer system should be placed upon some tangible and effective basis, instructions furnished them from the regular army, and all possible means taken to spread sound military information among them.

"In the vicinity of our sea-coast fortifications it would be well to provide a sufficient number of volunteer companies, with the means of instruction in heavy artillery, detailing officers of the regular artillery as instructors, who should, at the same time, be in charge of, and responsible for, the guns and material.

"In time of war, or when war is imminent, local companies of regular artillery might easily be enlisted for short terms of service, or for the war, in the sea-coast towns. The same thing might advantageously be carried into effect on a small scale in times of peace."

After returning from Europe, McClellan, finding that the army, in those piping times of peace, did not offer a sufficient scope for his activity, resigned his commission and accepted the appointment of vice-president and chief engineer of the Illinois Central Railroad. After serving three years in this office, he accepted that of president and general superintendent of the Ohio and Mississippi Railroad. He was actively engaged in the performance of the civil duties pertaining to this position when, war becoming imminent, he was summoned to resume his sword. Governor Curtin, of Pennsylvania, strove to secure his services in organizing the militia of that State. The Governor of Ohio, however, was beforehand, and had already offered to him the command of the Ohio troops with the rank of major-general, which McClellan unhesitatingly accepted. A few weeks subsequently he was **May 14.** commissioned by the United States Government a major-general in the regular army and given the command of the department of Ohio, embracing the States of Illinois, Indiana, Ohio, and that part of Virginia lying north of the

Great Kanawha River and west of the Green Brier River and the Maryland line, with so much of Pennsylvania as lies west of a line drawn from the Maryland line to the north-east corner of McKean County. The following contemporary sketch of the personal appearance and character of this celebrated General is given, to show the estimation in which he was then held:

"McClellan, now thirty-five years old, is in the prime of life. A man of short stature and broad frame, with a tendency to corpulency, though of compact structure, he is possessed of great physical activity and powers of endurance. Not prone to loquacity, he is reticent of his own counsel, and when he speaks expresses himself in few words, and with the decisive tone which characterizes the energetic man of action, rather than the speculative discourser. His temperament is that of the prevailing Anglo-American type, a combination of the sanguine and nervous. He has the thoughtful forecast of the one and the rapid movement of the other. This commingling of the two temperaments is shown in the dark though not black hair, in the light-colored but piercing eyes, in the full but concentrated frame, in the small hands and feet, and in the rounded but well-knit limbs.

"A combined military knowledge and civil experience fit him eminently for the command of a mixed force of volunteers and regulars, enabling him to harmonize their discordant elements. He can appreciate fully the value of the disciplined soldier, and yet is not unconscious that important aid may be rendered by the citizen when aroused to take up arms in defence of his country. He has discovered, from actual contact, the character of his countrymen, and knows how gradually to subject their impatience of control to the stern requirements of military law."

The secessionists of Eastern Virginia, emboldened by the advance of the troops of the Confederate States, soon strove to overawe or subject the Union men of the Western District. Having accumulated a considerable force at Harper's Ferry, they moved towards Grafton and other points west of the Alleghanies. It became, therefore, a matter of moment with the Federal Government, in order to sustain its loyal supporters in Virginia, to counteract this movement of the secessionists. The neighboring States of Pennsylvania and Ohio, between which that part of the western district of Virginia most devoted to the Union is enclosed, naturally presented the proper basis for operations in that quarter. Accordingly, General Patterson, at the head of the Pennsylvania troops, was ordered to march upon Harper's Ferry, while General McClellan, in command of his Ohio force, was directed to cross the Ohio River and co-operate with him. Previous to doing this, however, it was necessary to give a check to the secession force advancing through Western Virginia. McClellan accordingly prepared to co-operate with the loyal Western Virginians, led by Colonel May Kelley, who were to march to meet the enemy at Grafton. Previous to moving his force across the Ohio, McClellan issued this proclamation:

"HEADQUARTERS, DEPT. OF THE OHIO,
CINCINNATI, May 26, 1861.
"TO THE PEOPLE OF WESTERN VIRGINIA:

"VIRGINIANS: The General Government has long enough endured the machinations of a few factious rebels in your midst! Armed traitors have in vain endeavored to deter you from expressing your loyalty at the polls. Having failed in this infamous attempt to deprive you of the exercise of your dearest rights, they now seek to inaugurate a reign of terror, and thus force you to yield to their schemes, and submit to the yoke of the traitorous conspiracy dignified by the name of the Southern Confederacy.

"They are destroying the property of citizens of your State, and ruining your magnificent railways. The General Government has heretofore carefully abstained from sending troops across the Ohio, or even from posting them along its banks, although frequently urged by many of your prominent citizens to do so. It determined to await the result of the State election, desirous that no one might be able to say that the slightest effort had been made from this side to influence the expression of your opinion, although the many agencies brought to bear upon you by the rebels were well known. You have now shown, under the most adverse circumstances, that the great mass of the people of Western Virginia are true and loyal to the beneficent Government under which we and our fathers have lived so long. As soon as the result of the election was known, the traitors commenced their work of destruction.

"The General Government cannot close its ears to the demand you have made for assistance. I have ordered troops to cross the river. They come as your friends and brothers—as enemies only to the armed rebels who are preying upon you. Your homes, your families, and your property are safe under our protection. All your rights shall be religiously protected.

"Notwithstanding all that has been said by the traitors to induce you to believe that our advent among you will be signalized by interference with your slaves, understand one thing clearly: not only will we abstain from all interference, but we will, on the contrary, with an iron hand, crush any attempt at insurrection on their part.

"Now that we are in your midst, I call upon you to fly to arms, and support the General Government; sever the connection that binds you to traitors; proclaim to the world that the faith and loyalty so long boasted of by the Old Dominion are still preserved in Western Virginia, and that you remain true to the stars and stripes.

"G. B. McCLELLAN,
"Major-General Commanding."

This was followed by a proclamation to the army.

"CINCINNATI, May 26, 1861.
"TO THE SOLDIERS OF THE ADVANCING COLUMN:

"You are ordered to cross the frontier and enter upon the soil of Virginia. Your mission is to restore peace and confidence, to protect the majesty of the law and to rescue our brethren from the grasp of armed traitors. You are to act in concert with the Virginia troops and to support their advance.

"I place under the safeguard of your honor the persons and property of the Virginians. I know that you will respect their feelings, and all their rights. Preserve the strictest discipline—remember that each one of you holds in his keeping the honor of Ohio and the Union.

"If you are called upon to overcome armed opposition, I know that your courage is equal to the task, but remember that your only foes are the armed traitors, and show mercy even to them when they are in your power, for many of them are misguided. When under your protection the loyal men of Western Virginia have been enabled to organize and arm, they can protect themselves, and you can then return to your homes with the proud satisfaction of having preserved a gallant people from destruction.

"GEO. B. MCCLELLAN,
"Major-General Commanding."

The 16th Ohio Regiment, commanded by Colonel Irvine, and the 14th, under Colonel Lander, a noted frontiersman, were on the next day after these proclamations thrown across the Ohio into Western Virginia. The former crossing the Ohio to Wheeling, and the latter at Marietta to Parkersburg, continued their progress through Western Virginia by the Baltimore and Ohio Railroad. Their advance was hailed by the people with great enthusiasm and demonstrations of loyalty, and many volunteers joined their standard. The campaign in Western Virginia had now fairly opened.

May 27.

CHAPTER XXVI.

Junction of the Ohio Troops with the Western Virginians.—Colonel Kelley takes possession of Grafton.—March to Philippi.—A severe march.—Delay.—Colonel Lander in advance.—Colonel Kelley mistakes the route.—The Enemy on the alert.—The Attack.—Retreat of the Enemy.—Pursuit.—Arrival of Kelley, who joins in the pursuit.—Kelley wounded.—Prospects of death.—Biography of Kelley.—Tributes of admiration.—Recovery of Kelley.—Comparative losses at Philippi.—Trophies.—Movement of General Patterson.—Attack on Romney.—March of Colonel Wallace. —A long and hard March.—Flight of the Enemy.—Good moral effect of the advance of the Federal Forces.— Spirited Skirmish of Corporal Hayes and his thirteen men.—Tribute from General Patterson.—The political action of the Union men of Western Virginia.—Convention at Wheeling.—Declaration of Grievances and Ordinance of Reorganization passed.—The motion to form a new State defeated.—New State Officers appointed.—Proclamation of Governor Pierpont.—Call upon the President for aid to put down the Insurrection in Virginia.—Answer of the Secretary of War.—Counter-manifesto of Governor Letcher.—Appeal of the Secessionist Governor to Western Virginia.—Effects of proclamations and counter-proclamations.—Increased civil rage in Virginia.

THE Ohio troops despatched by General McClellan, though delayed on the railway in consequence of the derangement of the tracks and the destruction of the bridges by the enemy, finally succeeded in forming a junction with the Western Virginians. Colonel Kelley, who commanded the latter, had with great promptitude marched upon Grafton. Upon reaching this place, the enemy, about fifteen hundred strong, retired, and the Western Virginians took possession of it, without striking a blow. Being now reinforced, not only by the Ohio troops, but by the Seventh and Ninth regiments of Indiana, Kelley determined to dislodge the enemy at Philippi, on the Monongahela River, twenty miles south of Grafton, where they were encamped with a force of two thousand men.

The Union force at Grafton set out at ten o'clock, in two divisions, one composed of the First Virginia Regiment, part of the Ohio Sixteenth and the Indiana Seventh, under the command of Colonel Kelley; the other, of the Indiana Regiment and the Ohio Fourteenth, which joined at Webster on the route, commanded by Colonel Lander. The former division proceeded by railroad as far as a small way station, five miles only from Grafton, and marched the rest of the distance, twenty-two miles, to Philippi. The latter was conveyed by railroad as far as Webster, and marched the remaining twelve miles to Philippi.

The march was performed during the night, with the view of coming upon the enemy before the break of day, and taking them by surprise. A severe storm was raging, and the night was so dark that it was exceedingly difficult to form the troops—the violence of the wind was such, that the word of command could hardly be passed from front to rear. Order was, however, finally

1861.

May 29.

June 2.

established, and the troops began their march. All night they toiled on through the darkness and storm, the soft earth yielding beneath their feet at every step. Thus impeded, the whole force was prevented from arriving at the time proposed.

The division under Colonel Lander, having the shortest distance to march, was the first to reach its destination, June but did not arrive until five o'clock 3. in the morning, instead of four, the hour when the joint attack was to have taken place, in accordance with the plan. It had been intended that Colonel Lander's march upon the enemy in front should have been simultaneous with a movement in their rear by Colonel Kelley, with a view to completely surround Philippi and close in upon the enemy. But Colonel Kelley, with his long march of twenty-two miles, impeded by the darkness and the storm, was greatly delayed, and, moreover, mistook the road, coming in below instead of above the town, where it was intended he should have cut off the retreat of the enemy.

Colonel Lander's force, as it approached Philippi in front, was discovered by a woman, who, after firing two discharges from a gun, sent her son across the hills to apprise the enemy of their danger.

Lander continued to push on, but when he reached a point commanding the town, and began to dispose his artillery and troops in order to be ready, when Kelley should arrive, to make the simultaneous attack proposed, he found the enemy on the alert. Their advance guards, posted on the neighboring heights and among the woods and brushwood on both sides of the road, opened a brisk fire. Lander hurriedly ordered his guns to be moved into position, and responded with a volley, while, at the same time, the infantry prepared to advance into the town.

"A moment's delay to the infantry," says their commander, Dermot, in his report, "was occasioned by want of knowledge on my part as to which of the two roads led to the bridge leading into the town across the river. At the forks of the road I halted my command, and, riding rapidly to the guns, got the desired information from Colonel Lander. So informed, I proceeded on the double-quick down the declivity of the hill, and here had a full view of the enemy, and I must confess that I never saw a flight determined on with greater promptness or executed with more despatch. The enemy was under the command of Col. G. A. Porterfield. What his strength was, is variously estimated. On my own judgment I would say from one thousand five hundred to two thousand, of which I should think five hundred were cavalry.

"They had no artillery but a swivel. I have conversed with many of the citizens of the town as to the strength of Colonel Porterfield's command. Some say the Colonel himself professed to have two thousand five hundred troops. It is my opinion that he had but magnified his own strength, with a view to intimidate the people and crush out the Union sentiment."

"When I first saw the enemy, it seemed to me he was pushing for the bridge, which I was rapidly approaching; but it turned out that it was necessary to converge towards the bridge to gain the street leading out of the town on the opposite side from that entered by my command. The bridge is a narrow structure, some three or four hundred feet in length, spanning the Valley River, a branch of the Monongahela. A small body of determined troops could have impeded our progress and crippled us at the bridge, and I apprehended resistance at this point.

"Toward it my men poured down the hill, in good order, and with an energy and determination that assured me in advance that victory was certain. In a moment I was at the mouth of the bridge; one of the passages was barricaded, the other clear; through it (Company B, commanded by Captain Morgan, in advance) my men pushed; the Seventh Indiana first, then Colonel Steedman's command, not including the artillery, then Colonel Crittenden's, and opened upon the enemy, then retreating in wild disorder. Both parties being upon the full run, and the distance between them being quite considerable, but little execution could be done. I pursued the enemy from the bridge through the town and for several miles beyond. At one time I thought I should be able to capture his entire baggage train; but the horses, to prevent this, were cut from many of the wagons and mounted, and the wagons and contents left as our booty. The wagons were filled with munitions of war, blankets, knapsacks, clothing, baggage of officers and men, and with a considerable amount of flour and forage."

It was not until Colonel Lander's division had thus begun the attack, that Colonel Kelley arrived with his force, and then, in consequence of having mistaken the road, at a point where, instead of cutting off the retreat of the enemy, he could only join in the pursuit.

This, however, he did with great spirit, though with less effect than if he had arrived but a moment sooner. With a " friendly cheer," Kelley's troops made their presence known to their comrades, and descending the declivity of the heights upon which they had first appeared, they were soon in quick pursuit of the enemy. Some followed and cut down those who had taken refuge among the wooded hills, and others gave chase to the fugitives upon the road, whom they pursued for several miles, "overtaking, killing, and wounding a number." Col. Kelley himself, "with a bravery amounting to rashness," was among the foremost of his men in the pursuit. He had thus reached the upper part of the town, when one of the enemy, concealed behind a fence, turned upon him and shot him in the breast. The wound was severe, and was thought to have been mortal. He himself despaired of recovery, and said to a friend at his side: " I expect I shall have to die; I would be glad to live if it might be that I might do something for my country; but if it cannot be, I shall have at least the consolation of knowing that I fell in a just cause."

When it was supposed that Kelley would not survive his wound, great regret was felt at the prospective loss to the service of so devoted a Unionist and spirited soldier. Although an Eastern man, having been born in Deerfield, New Hampshire, he had taken up his residence in Wheeling, and was among the first to sustain the cause of the Federal Government in Western Virginia. Educated at West Point, though latterly engaged in civil occupations, he continued to cherish his military tastes, and had served as the colonel of a city regiment in Wheeling. At the commencement of the war, he was urged to resume his position and lead his former comrades to battle for the Union. He did not hesitate a moment, but accepting the command on one day, he was on the next *en route* for the scene of war.

General McClellan, and Morris, the brigadier-general of the United States volunteers of Virginia, as soon as they heard that Kelley was wounded, hastened to make known to him their admiration of his gallantry and worth.

"Say to Colonel Kelley," wrote McClellan to Morris, "that I cannot yet believe it possible that one who has opened his career so brilliantly can be mortally wounded. In the name of the country I thank him for his conduct, which has been the most brilliant episode of the war thus far. If it can cheer him in his last moments, tell him I cannot repair his loss, and that I only regret that I cannot be by his side to thank him in person. God bless him!"

To this hearty testimonial of affectionate admiration, General Morris added his emphatic approbation of Kelley's conduct:

"I am extremely pleased and greatly gratified with your gallant and soldierly conduct in the expedition, which owes its success to your skill and bravery. I feel that your country owes you a deep debt of gratitude for your services on the occasion; and a grateful people cannot but render to you that honor you so richly deserve."

These despatches were borne by Morris' aide-de-camp to the litter of the prostrate officer, and as he was supposed to be dying, they did not hesitate to read them to him. His eyes filled with tears as he listened, but he was too weak to speak a word. The despatches were, after being read, put into his hands, and he held them with a fond grasp until he was removed from the litter to the bed in the next room, prepared for his comfort. Kelley finally recovered, and was made a brigadier-general for his services.

In this rout of the secessionists at Philippi, no one but Kelley, of our forces, was wounded, but it was supposed that the enemy had met with some loss of life. Their commander, Colonel Willy, was taken prisoner, and their camp was captured, with the secession flag, seven hundred and eighty stand of arms, a number of horses, and a quantity of blankets and provisions. Though, as a military operation, the rout of the enemy at Philippi was comparatively a failure, the moral effect proved so great in Western Virginia that that loyal district was temporarily relieved of all fears of the domination of the secessionists.

Major-General Patterson was, in the mean time, advancing through Pennsylvania from the north towards Maryland and Virginia, with the view of co-operating with General McClellan, about to approach from the west, in a combined effort against the secession troops gathered in force at Harper's Ferry. While Patterson was at Chambersburg, an attack was made upon Romney, in Virginia, by a portion of his advance troops stationed at Cumberland, in Maryland.

This was planned by Colonel Wallace, of the Eleventh Indiana Volunteers, who, having learned that several hundred troops were quartered at Romney, drilling, imprisoning Union men, and otherwise annoying loyal citizens, determined to rout them out. The Colonel, accordingly, started at ten o'clock in the morning from Cumberland with eight hundred men, and proceeded by railway twenty-one miles to New Creek station. Arriving in the afternoon, he began his march at four o'clock, with the hope of reaching Romney at an early hour next day. The road, however, leading across the mountains, through narrow passes and along high bluffs, proved difficult, so that after a long and fatiguing march of twenty-three miles, Colonel Wallace did not arrive before the town until past eight o'clock in the morning.

June 17.

The enemy were on the alert, and on the approach of their assailants their mounted picket guards fired and galloped into the town to arouse their comrades.

"In approaching the place, it was necessary," wrote Colonel Wallace, in his animated report of the affair, "for me to cross a bridge over the South Branch of the Potomac. A reconnoissance satisfied me that the passage of the bridge would be the chief obstacle in my way, although I could distinctly see the enemy drawn up on the bluff which is the town site, supporting a battery of two guns, planted so as to sweep the road completely.

"I directed my advance guard to cross the bridge on a run, leap down the embankment at the farther entrance, and observe the windows of a large brick house not farther off than seventy-five yards. Their appearance was the signal for an assault. A warm fire opened from the house, which the guard returned, with no other loss than the wounding of a sergeant. The firing continued several minutes. I led a second company across the bridge, and by following up a ravine got them into a position that soon drove the enemy from the house to a mountain in its rear.

"My attention was then turned to the battery on the hill. Instead of following the road, as the rebels expected, I pushed five companies in skirmishing order and at double-quick time, up a hill to the right, intending to get around the left flank of the enemy, and cut off their retreat. Hardly had my companies deployed and started forward, and got within rifle range, before the rebels limbered up and got off over the bluff in the hottest haste. Between their position and that of my men was a deep, precipitous gorge, the crossing of which occupied about ten minutes. When the opposite ridge was gained, we discovered the rebels, indiscriminately blent with a mass of women and children, flying as for life from the town. Having no horse, pursuit of the cannoniers was out of the question, as they went off under whip and spur. After that I quietly marched into the place, and took possession of the empty houses and a legion of negroes, who alone seemed unscared at our presence. After searching the town for arms, camp equipage, etc., I returned to Cumberland, by the same road, reaching camp at eleven o'clock at night. My return was forced, owing to the fact that there was not a mile on the road that did not offer half a dozen positions for the ruin or rout of my regiment by a much smaller force."

The Colonel was proud of the achievement of his men, and took occasion to direct the notice of General Patterson to the wonders they had accomplished. "I beg," he said, "to call your attention to the length of our march, eighty-seven miles in all, forty-six of which were on foot, over a continuous succession of mountains, made in twenty-four hours, without rest, and varied by a brisk engagement, without leaving a man behind; and what is more, my men are ready to repeat it to-morrow."

The loss of the enemy could not be ascertained with precision; two of them, however, were undoubtedly killed, and one wounded. A number of tents and a quantity of stores were captured, and some guns destroyed.

The Colonel, moreover, congratulated himself upon the impressive moral effect of his spirited demonstration.

"One good result," he said, "has come of it. The loyal men in that region have taken heart. Very shortly, I think, you will hear of another Union company from that district. Moreover, it has brought home to the insolent 'chivalry' a wholesome respect for Northern prowess."

The Indiana Volunteers, or Zouaves, as they termed themselves, soon had an opportunity of again displaying their spirit. A scouting party, consisting of thirteen mounted men, led by Corporal Hayes, a ranger of renown during the Mexican war, crossed from Maryland and proceeded on a reconnoitering expedition into Virginia. They proceeded within a quarter of a mile of Frankfort, half way between Cumberland, whence they had set out, and Romney, the scene of the former exploit of the Indiana men. Finding the place full of the enemy's cavalry, they turned back, and meeting forty-one mounted secessionists, charged full upon them, driving them back more than a mile, capturing seventeen of the horses and killing eight of their riders. In the collision, Corporal Hayes, the leader of the Indiana men, was wounded with sabre cuts and bullets. A man of great daring and strength, he had already

June 26.

killed two men with his own hand, when he himself was wounded, but he had still strength enough to wield his sabre with such effect, that he brought a third dead to the ground.

His comrades, however, were now forced to bear back their exhausted leader and halt. They had thus remained about an hour, when the fugitives of the enemy returned with a reinforcement of seventy-five men. Coming suddenly up, they forced the Indiana men to abandon their horses and seek safety by crossing Paterson Creek and landing upon a small island at its mouth. Here they were being closed in by the larger numbers of the enemy, and again compelled to fly, but not until they had fired upon their assailants with such effect, that twenty-three of them were made to bite the dust. The Zouaves finally reached their camp with the loss of only one man, who had been left behind wounded, and whom the enemy despatched, after his capture, with their bayonets. Major-General Patterson honored the spirited exploit of the Indiana men with a special mention in the orders of the day.

For a proper appreciation of the military events in Western Virginia, it is necessary to resume the history of the political action of the Union men of that loyal district. The Convention which had adjourned to meet at Wheeling now reassembled. At the opening of June the session a discussion arose as to 11. the policy to be pursued by Western Virginia. Some favored a separation and the formation of a new commonwealth, while others, who finally carried the day, advocated the reorganization of the existing State. Accordingly a Declaration of Grievances and an ordinance of reorganization having been reported by Mr. Carlile, the chairman of the "Committee on Business," they were submitted to the approval of the Convention. These were adopted by a vote of seventy in favor and three against, not, however, until the opinion of the members was tested on the question of forming a new State. A member offered the resolution, "that one of the leading objects of the Convention, after establishing a provisional government, is the separation of Western from Eastern Virginia." This, however, on a motion to lay it on the table, which was carried by a vote of fifty-seven to seventeen, was temporarily defeated.

The Declaration of Grievances, and the ordinance for the Reorganization of the State Government, having thus been carried by a large majority, was formally signed by all the members present. June On the same day, the Convention, in 20. conformity with this act, proceeded to the election of provisional State officers. Frank H. Pierpont, of Marion County, was unanimously chosen Governor, Daniel Paisly, of Marion County, Lieutenant-Governor, and Messieurs Lamb, Paxton, Van Winkle, Harrison, and Lazar members of the council.

These gentlemen, immediately upon being elected, were sworn into office, each taking this newly prescribed form of oath :

"I solemnly swear (or affirm) that I

will support the Constitution of the United States and the laws made in pursuance thereof, as the supreme law of the land, anything in the Constitution and laws of the State of Virginia, or in the ordinances of the Convention which assembled in Richmond on the 13th day of February last, to the contrary notwithstanding, and that I will uphold and defend the Government of Virginia as vindicated and restored by the Convention which assembled in Wheeling on the 11th day of June, 1861."

The Convention, after this momentous action, closed their session with passing ordinances adopting the former military laws of Virginia and recognizing the duty of the State to respond to the requisition of the President of the United States for militia and volunteers.

The new Governor soon after issued a proclamation causing the General Assembly to be composed of delegates to be elected as provided by the Convention of June 11th in its ordinance for the State Government. These delegates were accordingly chosen, and assembled at Wheeling, when Governor Pierpont delivered his first message.*

[margin: June 22. July 1.]

Following this independent action of Western Virginia, the new Governor became anxious about the safety of the commonwealth from "the banding together of large numbers of evil-minded persons, aided by men of like mind from other States, whose purpose was to invade the State," and confessing his want of a sufficient military force, to overcome them, earnestly called upon the President of the United States for assistance.

The secretary of war responded in behalf of the Federal chief magistrate, that a large additional force would be soon sent to the relief of the new Governor of Virginia, and at the same time took occasion to apologize for the apparent remissness hitherto of the Federal authority: "The full extent," wrote Secretary Cameron, " of the conspiracy against popular rights, which has culminated in the atrocities to which you refer, was not known when its outbreak took place at Charleston. It now appears that it was matured for many years by secret organizations throughout the country, especially in the slave States. By this means, when the President called upon Virginia, in April, for

---

* "TO THE SENATE AND HOUSE OF DELEGATES OF THE COMMONWEALTH OF VIRGINIA.—Gentlemen: You have been convened in extraordinary session in midsummer, when, under other circumstances, you should be at home attending to pursuits incident to this season of the year. The exigencies with which we find ourselves surrounded demand your counsels.

"I regret that I cannot congratulate you on the peace and prosperity of the country, in the manner which has been customary with Executives, both State and Federal. For the present, those happy days which, as a nation, we have so long enjoyed, and that prosperity which has smiled upon us, as upon no other nation, are departed.

"It is my painful duty to announce that the late Executive of the State, with a large part of the State officers, civil and military, under him, are at war with the loyal people of Virginia and the Constitutional Government of the United States. They have leagued themselves with persons from other States to tear down the benign Governments, State and Federal, erected by the wisdom and patriotism of our fathers, and under which our liberties have so long been protected and our prosperity secured. They have instituted civil war in our midst, and created a system of terror around us to intimidate our people.

"But while we are passing through this period of gloom and darkness in our country's history, we must not deits quota of troops, then deemed necessary to put it down in the States in which it had shown itself in arms, the call was responded to by an order from the chief spair, or fold our hands until the chains of despotism shall be fastened upon us by those conspiring against our liberties. As freemen, who know their rights and dare defend them, our spirits must rise above the intimidation and violence employed against us ; and we must meet and conquer every obstacle these men are attempting to interpose between us and our liberties. If we manfully exert ourselves we shall succeed. There is a just God who "rides upon the whirlwind and directs the storm." Let us look to him with abiding confidence.

"The fact is no longer disguised, that there has been in the South, for many years, a secret organization, laboring with steady perseverance to overturn the Federal Government, and destroy constitutional liberty in this country. The various conventions held in that portion of the country, for some years past, ostensibly for other objects, have only been the means of feeling the public pulse to ascertain if there was sufficient disease in the body politic for dissolution. The cry of danger to the institution of slavery has been a mere pretext to arouse and excite the people. In abandoning the Constitution of the Union, the leaders of the movement must have known that they were greatly weakening the safeguards and protection which were necessary to the existence of that institution.

"It has been urged that secession was necessary to protect the slave interest of the South. As is usual thing, those who are interested in a species of property, are the best informed in regard to their own rights, and the most tenacious in maintaining them. Secession has not originated among the large slaveholders of the South, nor has it found among that class its busiest and most ardent advocates. The sections of the country in which the largest slave interests have existed in this State, have heretofore been the most decided in support of the Union. The votes given at the last November and February elections in Eastern and Western Virginia, will show that the slaveholders themselves considered the safety of their property as dependent upon the maintenance of the Union. Another pertinent fact may be mentioned in this connection. It is, that in sections where slaves are numerous, it is always much easier to introduce a mob-law and intimidation to control the votes of the people. The constant apprehension of servile insurrection makes the matter an easy subject of control in a crisis like the present. Eastern and Western Virginia are illustrations of the truth of this statement.

"What affiliations this great conspiracy has had in the Northern States, remains yet unknown. The spirit which has been roused throughout the North has carried all opposition before it. But the extent of the treasonable plot has not been fully developed. Before the designs of the conspirators were made manifest, thousands of good men sympathized with the effort, as they regarded it, of the South to maintain their constitutional rights; but these have all abandoned them when the true purpose was ascertained. If there are any in the North, or in the border States, who still adhere to the conspiracy, they will attempt to aid its object by indirect means ; by opposing and caviling at the efforts to which the Government, in a struggle for existence, may use in its own defence, and by attempting to raise a popular outcry against coercion, and advocating a peaceable separation. A bold stand for secession would scarcely be attempted ; but those who sympathize with the leaders of rebellion will seek by covert and indirect means to aid the object of the conspirators.

"There is only one question now for each American citizen to decide in this controversy : Do you desire to stand by and live under the Constitution which has contributed so long and so greatly to the happiness and prosperity of the people, and to transmit its blessings to our posterity ? Or, do you desire the Union broken up, and an oligarchy or military despotism established in its stead? The leaders of the South are striving for the latter. The Government of the United States is exerting its whole force to maintain the integrity of the former. There can be no neutral ground. The secession leaders have declared that they desire no compromise, except the unconditional surrender to them of the objects they have been aiming to accomplish, and the consent of the Government to its own destruction. The very proposition of compromise places a false issue before the country. It implies that the Federal Government has committed some great wrong which ought to be remedied before peace can be restored ; when in fact the leaders in the South have controlled the legislation of the country for years, and the laws now in existence were made or suggested by themselves when in power.

"The position of this State is a peculiar one at this moment. Last November, at the Presidential election, it gave upward of sixteen thousand majority for Bell and Douglas, both Union candidates for the Presidency. Their principal competitor was loudly proclaimed as also true to the Union ; and throughout the canvass any imputation of favoring disunion was indignantly denied by the advocates of all the candidates. At the election for members of the Convention in February last, there was a majority of over sixty thousand votes given to the Union candidates ; and the people by an equal majority determined that no act of that Convention should change the relations of the State to the Federal Government, unless ratified by the popular vote. Yet the delegates to that Convention passed the ordinance of secession, and attached the State to the Southern league, called the Confederate States ; and to render the step irretrievable, and defeat the whole object of requiring a ratification of the people to render such acts valid, they put them into effect immediately ; and before the vote could be taken on the question of ratification, transferred the whole military force of our State to confederate in Virginia to his armed followers, to seize the navy-yard at Gosport; and the authorities of the State, who had till then shown repugnance to the plot, found themselves stripped of all actual power, and after-

the President of the Confederacy, and surrendered to him military possession of our territory.

"When the chains had been thus fastened upon us, we were called to vote upon the ordinance of secession. The same reign of terror which compelled Union men to vote as they did in the Convention, was brought to bear on the people themselves. Vast numbers were obliged, by intimidation and fear of threatened violence, to vote for secession. Many did not vote at all. Many, no doubt, were influenced by the consideration, that the measures already adopted had placed the Commonwealth helplessly within the grasp of the President of the Southern Confederacy, and that she could not escape from his power by the rejection of the ordinance.

"It is claimed that the ordinance of secession has been ratified by a majority of ninety-four thousand votes. Had the people of Virginia, then, so greatly changed? The best evidence that they had not is found in the fact that, wherever the vote was fully free, there was a much larger majority against secession than was given at the election in February to the Union candidates for the Convention. The means of intimidation and violence, which were resorted to over a large portion of the State, to compel an appearance of unanimity in favor of secession, show that the leaders of this movement felt that the hearts of the people were not with them.

"The proclamation of the President, calling for seventy-five thousand volunteer troops, is commonly relied upon to justify the ordinance of secession. That proclamation was issued on the 15th of April, 1861. It must not, however, be overlooked, that on the 6th of March, 1861, the pretended Congress at Montgomery provided by law for calling into the field a force of one hundred thousand volunteers; and that on the 12th of April the Secretary of War of the Confederate States publicly announced that war was commenced, and that the Capitol at Washington would be captured before the first of May. The intention to capture the capital of the Union was repeatedly proclaimed in influential papers at Richmond and other Southern cities before the 15th of April. It was, in fact, long a cherished object of the parties in this great conspiracy. Did they expect the President of the nation to yield the Capitol, and retire in disgrace, without adopting any measures of defence? Yet Virginia, we are told, seceded because the President, under such circumstances, called volunteers to the defence of the country.

"I need not remark to you, gentlemen, how fatal the attempted disseverance of the Union must prove to all our material interests. Secession, and annexation to the South, would cut off every outlet for our productions. We cannot get them to the Confederate States across the Alleghanies. The Ohio River and the country beyond it would be closed to our trade. With Maryland in the Union, our outlet to the East would be interrupted; while we could not carry our products across the Pennsylvania line, by the Monongahela or other route. In time of war we would encounter a hostile force, and in time of peace a custom-house at every turn.

"The interests of the people of Virginia were entrusted to the Richmond Convention. How have they fulfilled that trust? Why, if war was to come, was our land made the battle-field? Why was this Commonwealth interposed as a barrier to protect the States of the South, who undertook to overthrow the Union in utter disregard to our remonstrances? In the position in which the Richmond Convention have placed us, our homes are exposed to all the horrors of civil war, while the President of the Montgomery Congress can announce to the people of the Gulf States that 'they need now have no apprehension; they might go on with their planting and business as usual; the war would not come to their section; its theatre would be along the borders of the Ohio River, and in Virginia.'

"Have we done wrong in rejecting the authority of the men who have thus betrayed the interests confided to their charge?

"Under these circumstances the people of the State who desired to preserve a Virginia in the Union, by their delegates appointed at primary meetings, assembled at Wheeling on the 13th of May last, to consider the measures necessary to protect their constitutional rights and liberties, their lives and their property. Before a frank comparison could be had, differences of opinion were to be expected, and such differences accordingly then existed. That Convention, however, after three days' mature consideration, determined to call upon the loyal people of the State, after the vote was taken on the Secession ordinance, to elect delegates to a Convention to be held on the 11th day of June, 1861. All who witnessed the assembling of the last Convention, will bear witness to the solemnity of the occasion. Its action was attended with singular unanimity, and has resulted in the reorganization of the State government, as a member of the Union.

"Their journal and ordinances will be submitted to you. Plain principles vindicate their acts. The Constitution of the United States was adopted by the people of the United States; and the powers thus derived could be resumed only by the consent of the people who conferred them. That Constitution is the supreme law of the land. The Constitution of the State recognizes it as such, and all the laws of the State virtually recognize the same principle. The Governor, the Legislature, and all State officers, civil and military, when they entered upon the discharge of their duties, took an oath to support the Constitution of wards were manifestly permitted to retain the empty forms of office only because they consented to use them at the bidding of the invaders.

"The President, however, never supposed that a brave and free people, though surprised and unarmed, could long be subjugated by a class of political adventurers always adverse to them; and the fact that they have already rallied, reorganized their government, the United States. When the Convention assembled at Wheeling on the 11th of June, they found the late Governor, and many of the other officers of the State, engaged in an attempt to overthrow the Constitution they had sworn to support. Whatever they might actually effect, with the aid of their confederates, by unlawful intimidation and violence, they could not lawfully deprive the good people of this Commonwealth of the protection afforded by the Constitution and laws of the Union, and of the rights to which they are entitled under the same. The Convention attempted no change of the fundamental law of the State for light and transient causes. The alterations adopted were such only as were imperatively required by the necessity of the case; to give vitality and force to the Constitution of the State, and enable it to operate in the circumstances under which we are placed. They attempted no revolution. Whatever others may have done, we remain as we were, citizens of Virginia, citizens of the United States, recognizing and obeying the Constitutions and laws of both.

"I trust, gentlemen, you will excuse me for dwelling so long upon these important topics.

"Immediately on entering upon the duties of my office, I addressed an official communication to the President of the United States, stating briefly the circumstances in which we were placed, and demanding protection against invasion and domestic violence to which our people were subjected, and I am happy to inform you that the President, through the Secretary of War, promptly gave me very satisfactory assurances that the guarantee embodied in the Constitution of the United States would be efficiently complied with, by affording to our people a full protection. I transmit herewith copies of these communications.

"I also send you herewith a copy of a communication received from the Secretary of the Interior at Washington, certifying officially the apportionment of representatives in the XXXVIIIth Congress under the census of 1860. Virginia has thirteen representatives. Under the new apportionment she will have eleven only. Before the term of the XXXVIIIth Congress commences, it will be necessary, therefore, to redistrict the State, in conformity and checked the march of these invaders, demonstrates how justly he appreciated them.

"The failure, hitherto, of the State authorities, in consequence of the circumstances to which I have adverted, to organize its quota of troops called for by the President, imposed upon him the necessity of providing himself for their organization, and this has been done to some extent. But instructions have now with the principles established in the 13th and 14th sections of the 4th Article of the Constitution.

"The President of the United States has issued his proclamation convening an extra session of Congress, to meet at the National Capitol on the 4th of this month. The two senators from this State have vacated their offices. It is known to me that they are engaged in the conspiracy to overturn the Government of the United States, and in rebellion to its lawful authority. They have renounced the title of citizens of the United States, claiming to be citizens of a foreign and hostile State. They have abandoned the posts assigned to them by the State of Virginia in the Senate of the United States, to take office under the rebellious Government of the Confederate States. I recommend, therefore, the election of senators to fill the vacancies which have thus occurred. ° ° °

"The subject of the revenue will demand your attention. A recklessness has characterized the Legislature of the State for the last ten years, that has involved us in a most onerous debt. For many years past the western part of the State has been contributing in an unequal, an unjust proportion to the revenue, which has been largely expended on internal improvements, for the benefit of our eastern brethren, from which the west has received no advantage in any form. The proceeds of the heavy debt contracted on State account have also been applied to eastern railroads and internal improvements from which the west derives no benefit. The leaders of secession in the Gulf States have adroitly involved Virginia in an immense expenditure in support of their treasonable schemes; and to save their own people and property, have managed to transfer the theatre of war to our territory. Before they are driven out, the whole of the material interests of the State east of the Blue Ridge will probably be destroyed, including the internal improvements, upon which such lavish expenditure has been made. ° ° °

"You have met, gentlemen, in the midst of civil war, but I trust you may yet be assembled under happier auspices, when the strife shall be over, and peace and prosperity be restored to this once happy country. All which is respectfully submitted. F. H. PIERPONT."

been given to the agents of the Federal Government to proceed hereafter under your direction, and the company and field officers will be commissioned by you."

The secessionist Governor, John Letcher, met these declarations of independence, and the efforts to defend it, on the part of the new Governor, with a counter manifesto, asserting that Virginia had seceded by a vote of the majority of her people, and appealing to the Western Virginians "to yield to the will of the State."

"Men of the North-west," he said, "I appeal to you, by all the considerations which have drawn us together as one people heretofore, to rally to the standard of the Old Dominion. By all the sacred ties of consanguinity, by the intermixtures of the blood of East and West, by common paternity, by friendships hallowed by a thousand cherished recollections and memories of the past, by the relics of the great men of other days, come to Virginia's banner, and drive the invaders from your soil. There may be traitors in the midst of you, who, for selfish ends, have turned against their mother, and would permit her to be ignominiously oppressed and degraded. But I cannot, will not believe that a majority of you are not true sons, who will not give your blood and your treasure for Virginia's defence."

The Governor, at the same time, reminded the people of Western Virginia of the "magnanimity" of the Eastern districts, in consenting at last to an equalization of taxation, by which the cause of complaint of the former against the latter had been removed. "Let one heart," exclaimed the Governor, "one mind, one energy, one power nerve every patriot to arms in a common cause. The heart that will not beat in unison with Virginia is now a traitor's heart, the arm that will not strike home in her cause now, is palsied by coward fear.

"The troops are posted at Huttonsville. Come with your own good weapons and meet them as brothers!"

Such proclamations and counter-proclamations and appeals to diverse loyalties only served to quicken the rage of fellow-citizen arrayed against fellow-citizen, and more deeply to involve them in the perplexing horrors of civil war.

CHAPTER XXVII.

Failure in Missouri of General Harney's League.—Harney's Successor of "sterner stuff."—Life of General Lyon.—Birth and early Life.—Parentage.—His rustic home.—Early fondness for Mathematics.—A cadet at West Point.—Graduation.—Service in the Army.—Mexican Campaign.—Good deeds and just recompenses.—Service in California.—Indian Warfare.—In Kansas.—Sympathies with the Free-soilers.—Takes up the pen in their defence.—His writings and opinions.—Captain Lyon in command of the Arsenal at St. Louis.—His prompt action at the beginning of the Civil War.—Capture of Fort Jackson.—Seizure of the J. C. Swan.—Capture of lead at Ironton.—Lyon succeeds Harney.—Unsuccessful attempt of the secessionist Price to wheedle him.—Lyon refuses to be governed by the Harney League.—Alarm of the Secessionists.—The muster of the Secessionists in Jefferson City.—Personal interview of Governor Jackson with General Lyon.—Firmness of Lyon.—The Secessionists giving up all hope of promoting their cause by diplomacy.—Making a stand at Jefferson City.—Destruction of Telegraph and Railway bridges.—Proclamation of Governor Jackson.—Counter-proclamation of General Lyon.—General Lyon determines to root out the disunion plotters from Jefferson City.

1861. The league which General Harney had, with a too yielding confidence in their professions of peace, made with the secession leaders of Missouri, failed, as has been recorded, to check rebellion in that State. After his recall, and the succession to the command of General Lyon, a man of sterner stuff, Missouri promised to vindicate more decidedly its loyalty to the Union.

Nathaniel Lyon was born in Ashford, Wyndham County, Connecticut. His father was Amasa Lyon, a hard-working and thriving farmer of the place, where his intelligence and integrity won the appreciation of its inhabitants, who elected him a justice of the peace. His wife, whose family name was Kezia, was a descendant of the Knowltons, one of whom, Colonel Thomas Knowlton, had served in the French colonial war, and in the Revolutionary struggle, having commanded a Connecticut company at Bunker's Hill, and fallen on the plains of Harlem. Washington honored his memory with the tribute: "He would have been an honor to any country."

There is little record left of the boyhood of General Lyon. It was passed among the simple associations of his rustic home. In the winter he was sent to the village school, and in seed-time and harvest he aided his father or his neighbors in farm-work. An aged fellow-townsman in recalling, at the grave of the heroic soldier, his recollections of the country boy, said: "Nathaniel worked for me on my farm when he was a boy. He was smart, daring, and resolute, and wonderfully attached to his mother."

General Lyon, on the night before his last battle, while lying with a fellow-officer between two steep rocks, where the space was so narrow that there was hardly room to move, made light of the inconvenience, and playfully remarked, with a fond allusion to his home, that he was "born between two rocks." He referred to the position of the house where he was born, and the homestead of his family, which "stands about four miles from Eastford (Ashford was divided in 1847, and the name of the northern portion of the township changed to Eastford), on the road to Hampton. Leaving the little hamlet of Phœnixville," says his biographer,* "we climb a long hill, thence over a rough road to a valley, nestled in which, between two steep and rocky hills, about twenty rods from the highway, is the house—a small, old building, somewhat out of repair, with rusty clapboards, which were once painted red."

Though he found in the village school little opportunity for the development of his talent, he is reported to have shown a natural aptitude and fondness for the study of mathematics. This early taste probably induced his parents to obtain for him an appointment to a cadetship in West Point, where he entered at the age of eighteen. He graduated in 1841, ranking the eleventh of his class, a position which proved a fair degree of successful study. He commenced his military service, on leaving the academy, as a second lieutenant of infantry, and first entered upon active duty in Florida, during the campaign against the Seminole Indians. He was subsequently stationed at various points on our Western frontier, and on the breaking out of the war with Mexico, accompanied the army of Scott as first lieutenant. He took part in the siege

---

* The Last Political Writings of General Nathaniel Lyon, United States Army, with a Sketch of his Life and Military Services. New York, Rudd & Carleton, 1861.

---

of Vera Cruz, and at the battle of Cerro Gordo, where his good service was acknowledged by the commander of his regiment. "No sooner," said he, "had the height become ours, than the enemy appeared in large force on the Jalapa road, and we were ordered to that point. Captain Canby, with a small detachment, accompanied by Lieutenant Lyon, pressed hotly in their rear, and were soon in possession of a battery of three pieces which had been firing upon us in reverse."

At Contreras, too, he bore a gallant part, and in the pursuit aided in capturing several pieces of artillery, which were turned upon the fugitives. For his good conduct and spirit at Churubusco, he was recommended by his superior to "the special notice of the colonel commanding the brigade," and was rewarded for his services with the rank of brevet captain. At the capture of the Mexican capital, he was with the advance, and while fighting spiritedly at the Belen gate, was wounded with a musket-ball.

On the declaration of peace with Mexico, Lyon, now captain, was ordered to Jefferson barracks, in Missouri, preliminary to a proposed march across the Rocky Mountains to California. He was, however, finally despatched by sea around Cape Horn, and reached California soon after its acquisition by the United States. Here he was chiefly occupied with frontier duty, and proved his activity and his capability as a skirmishing officer in Indian warfare.

Subsequently ordered to the territories of Kansas and Nebraska, he found himself in the midst of the violent agitation to which that part of the country had become exposed. His sympathies were at once aroused in favor of the principles of the free-soilers, and with such fervor, that he was induced to take up the pen, though more used to the sword, in their defence. While stationed at Camp Riley, in Kansas, in the summer and autumn of 1860, he wrote a series of anonymous articles for the Manhattan *Express*, a weekly journal published at one of the neighboring settlements.

His private as well as his published writings show him to have been an earnest advocate of the Republican cause. Of the rebellious designs of the cotton States he seemed to have been fully conscious, and at the same time persuaded that they could be thwarted by a prompt exercise of executive authority. "There seems to be," he wrote, "little doubt that several of the Southern States will precipitate themselves into disaster and disgrace, if allowed to do so; but this can be prevented by the President, if he chooses to exercise his authority as becomes the chief magistrate of our great and powerful country. But unfortunately, Mr. Buchanan seems to regard himself as elected to submit tremblingly to any and every demand of the South, and I fear he can never rouse himself to take such action as our emergencies now require, as due to the country from him. Time must show: the only thing safe to predict is, that the conduct of the South must involve her people in suffering and shame."

Again he wrote, "Our cause is to honor labor and elevate the laborer; our candidate, Abe Lincoln." In the following exposition of the degradation of labor by slavery, he shows a thoughtful consideration of the subject.

"In countries," he wrote, "where slavery exists, labor devolves for the most part upon the slaves, and is therefore identified with slavery; and the white free laborer being valued by slave-owners, who control public opinion, only as so much physical organism (bone, muscle, etc.) for producing means, is degraded to the level of the slave, so far as his influence and moral status go, and is even lower in physical comforts, for the want of the intelligent care the slave-owner bestows upon the slave, and of which he, the free laborer, has become incompetent by a mental depravity corresponding to his moral degradation. This is a truth of philosophy and political economy, that man rises to a position corresponding to the rights and responsibilities devolved upon him; and therefore the only true way to make a man is to invest him with the rights, duties, and responsibilities of a man, and he generally rises in intellectual and moral greatness to a position corresponding to these circumstances; and it is the very want of them that makes the free non-slaveholding persons of the slave States so degraded and imbecile, that the slaves themselves feel a conscious superiority, in which they are encouraged by their owners, to the extent of thinking it better to be a nigger than a poor white man; and this is done to pacify the slave and thus secure this artificial system of securing the products of labor to the non-laboring classes, and also, by degrading white laborers, prevent their industry from competing with slave labor, to reduce thereby the value of slaves."

From Kansas, Captain Lyon was transferred to the command of the arsenal at St. Louis, where he was when the present civil war broke out. His prompt action in surrounding and capturing Camp Jackson, and his active measures toward checking the secession movement at Liberty and Potosi, have been already recorded. His subsequent action while commanding the Federal forces in Missouri, as a brigadier-general, was characterized by a spirit and promptitude which gave promise of security to the State and a certainty of renown to himself, which have won for him the gratitude of the country, and fixed him forever in its annals as among the bravest and most devoted of its heroes and patriots.

General Lyon, even while General Harney was in command, seeing how that officer had been deceived by the secession leaders, who, while pretending peace, were preparing for war, did not intermit his vigilance for a moment. He seized, on the very next day after the signing of the Harney league, the steamer J. C. Swan, at a point thirty miles below St. Louis, and caused her to be brought up and secured at the arsenal in the city.

This was the vessel which had been employed by the secessionists to convey the arms from Baton Rouge, which Lyon had seized after capturing Camp Jackson. He also succeeded, in spite of considerable resistance, in seizing five thousand pounds of lead at Ironton, on the Iron Mountain Railroad, while in transit to the Confederates in the South.

Price, the military leader of the secessionists, was evidently disturbed by the recall of his unsuspecting ally, and the transfer of power to the hands of the less confiding and more decided Lyon. Price, however, strove to wheedle him as he had done his predecessor, by fair words. In a proclamation issued to the brigadier-generals commanding the various military districts of Missouri, he expressed the desire that the State, in accordance with the Harney league, should exercise the right of determining its position in the contest, without the aid of any military force on either side. At the same time, alluding to the change in the command of the Federal forces, he said, with evident anxiety, though affected confidence, "The Government has thought proper to remove General Harney from the command of the Department of the West; but as the successor of General Harney will certainly consider himself and his Government in honor bound to carry out this agreement in good faith, I feel assured that his removal should give no cause of uneasiness to our citizens for the security of their liberties and property. I intend on my part to adhere both in its spirit and to the letter. The rumor in circulation, that it is the intention of the officers now in command of this Department to disarm those of our citizens who do not agree in opinion with the administration at Washington, and put arms in the hands of those who, in some localities of this State, are supposed to sympathize with the views of the Federal Government, are, I trust, unfounded. The purpose of such a movement could not be misunderstood, and it would not only be a violation of the agreement referred to, and an equally plain violation of our constitutional right, but a gross indignity to the citizens of the State, which would be resisted to the last extremity."

Notwithstanding this affected confidence, that General Lyon would thus carry out a league so dangerous to the loyalty of the State, and for the forming of which General Harney had been recalled, the secessionists became alarmed for their safety. Hurrying from the faithful St. Louis, they gathered together in Jefferson City, the capital of the State, where, under the sanction of the disloyal Governor, they were pursuing their machinations for wresting Missouri from the Union. Governor Jackson himself now strove, by a personal interview with General Lyon, to make with him an agreement such as had paralyzed the Federal authority under Harney's league. He proposed to disband the militia, or State guard as it was termed, provided Lyon would consent to disarm the Union volunteers. This the latter resolutely refused, insisting that the Federal Government should enjoy the unrestricted right to move and station its troops throughout the State whenever and wherever, in the opinion of its officers, it might be necessary, either for the protection of loyal subjects of the Federal Government or for repelling invasion.

General Lyon in this memorandum specified in detail his answer to the Governor's wily proposition. "General Lyon," he wrote, "sets forth as his conviction that if the Government withdrew its forces entirely, secret and subtle measures would be resorted to to provide arms and effect organizations which, upon any pretext, could put forth a formidable opposition to the General Government, and, even without arming, combinations would doubtless form in certain localities to oppress and drive out loyal citizens, to whom the Government is bound to give protection, but which it would be helpless to do, as also to repress such combinations, if its forces could not be sent into the State. A large aggressive force might be formed and advanced from the exterior into the State, to assist it in carrying out the secession programme, and the Government could not, under the limitation proposed, take posts on these borders to meet and repel such force. The Government could not shrink from its duties nor abdicate its corresponding rights; and, in addition to the above, it is the duty of its civil officers to execute civil process, and in case of resistance to receive the support of military force. The proposition of the Gov-

June 11.

ernor would at once overturn the Government privileges and prerogatives, which he (General Lyon) has neither the wish nor authority to do. In his opinion, if the Governor and the State authorities would earnestly set about to maintain the peace of the State, and declare their purposes to resist outrages upon loyal citizens of the Government, and repress insurrections against it, and, in case of violent combinations needing co-operation of the United States troops, they should call upon or accept such assistance, and in case of threatened invasion the Government troops took suitable posts to meet it, the purposes of the Government would be subserved, and no infringement of the State's rights or dignity committed. He would take good care, in such faithful co-operation of the State authorities to this end, that no individual should be injured in person or property, and that the utmost delicacy should be observed toward all peaceable persons concerned in these relations. Upon this basis, in General Lyon's opinion, could the rights of both the General and State governments be secured and peace maintained."

The Governor finding that the resolute Lyon was not to be shaken from his firm determination to uphold the Federal authority and sustain the loyal citizens of Missouri, lost all further hope of promoting secession by diplomacy, and appealed to arms. He hurried with his confederates to Jefferson City, the capital, destroying on the route the telegraph wires and railroad bridges, with the evident purpose of commencing war and resisting the Federal authority. At the same time the Governor issued an insurrectionary proclamation.*

* "To the People of Missouri : A series of unprovoked and unparalleled outrages have been inflicted upon the peace and dignity of this Commonwealth, and upon the rights and liberties of its people, by wicked and unprincipled men, professing to act under the authority of the United States Government; the solemn enactments of your Legislature have been nullified; your volunteer soldiers have been taken prisoners; your commerce with your sister States has been suspended ; your trade with your own fellow-citizens has been and is subjected to the harassing control of an armed soldiery ; peaceful citizens have been imprisoned without warrant of law ; unoffending and defenceless men, women, and children have been ruthlessly shot down and murdered ; and other unbearable indignities have been heaped upon your State and yourselves.

"To all these outrages and indignities you have submitted with a patriotic forbearance which has only encouraged the perpetrators of these grievous wrongs to attempt still bolder and more daring usurpations.

"It has been my earnest endeavor, under all these embarrassing circumstances, to maintain the peace of the State, and to avert, if possible, from our borders, the desolating effects of a civil war. With that object in view, I authorized Major-General Price, several weeks ago, to arrange with General Harney, commanding the Federal forces in this State, the terms of an agreement by which the peace of the State might be preserved. They came, on the 21st of May, to an understanding, which was made public. The State authorities have faithfully labored to carry out the terms of that agreement.

"The Federal Government, on the other hand, not only manifested its strong disapprobation of it, by the instant dismissal of the distinguished officer who, on his part, entered into it, but it at once began, and has unintermittingly carried out a system of hostile operations, in utter contempt of that agreement, and the reckless disregard of its own plighted faith. These acts have latterly portended revolution and civil war so unmistakably, that I resolved to make one further effort to avert these dangers from you. I therefore solicited an interview with Brigadier-General Lyon, commanding the Federal army in Missouri. It was granted, and, on the 10th instant, waiving all questions of personal and official dignity, I went to St. Louis, accompanied by Major-General Price.

"We had an interview on the 11th instant with General Lyon and Colonel F. P. Blair, Jr., at which I submitted to them this proposition : That I would disband the State Guard and break up its organization ; that I would disarm all the companies which had been armed by the State ; that I would pledge myself not to attempt to organize the militia under the military bill ; that no arms

PROCLAMATION OF LYON. 311

General Lyon responded to this manifesto of hostility of the Governor of Missouri, by issuing a counter-proclamation.*

or munitions of war should be brought into the State; that I would protect all citizens equally in all their rights, regardless of their political opinions; that I would repress all insurrectionary movements within the State; that I would repel all attempts to invade it, from whatever quarter and by whomsoever made; and that I would thus maintain a strict neutrality in the present unhappy contest, and preserve the peace of the State. And I further proposed that I would, if necessary, invoke the assistance of the United States troops to carry out these pledges. All this I proposed to do upon condition that the Federal Government would undertake to disarm the Home Guards; which it has illegally organized and armed throughout the State, and pledge itself not to occupy with its troops any localities in the State not occupied by them at this time.

"Nothing but the most earnest desire to avert the horrors of civil war from our beloved State could have tempted me to propose these humiliating terms. They were rejected by the Federal officers.

"They demanded not only the disorganization and disarming of the State militia, and the nullification of the military bill, but they refused to disarm their own Home Guards, and insisted that the Federal Government should enjoy an unrestricted right to move and station its troops throughout the State whenever and wherever it might, in the opinion of its officers, be necessary, either for the protection of the 'loyal subjects' of the Federal Government or for the repelling of invasion, and they plainly announced that it was the intention of the Administration to take military occupation, under these pretexts, of the whole State, and to reduce it, as avowed by General Lyon himself, to the 'exact condition of Maryland.' The acceptance by me of these degrading terms would not only have sullied the honor of Missouri, but would have aroused the indignation of every brave citizen, and precipitated the very conflict which it has been my aim to prevent. We refused to accede to them, and the conference was broken up.

"Fellow-citizens, all our efforts toward conciliation have failed. We can hope nothing from the justice or moderation of the agents of the Federal Government in this State. They are energetically hastening the execution of their bloody and revolutionary schemes for the inauguration of civil war in your midst; for the military occupation of your State by armed bands of lawless invaders for the overthrow of your State government; and for the subversion of those liberties which that government has always sought to protect; and they intend to exert their whole power to subjugate you, if possible, to the military despotism which has usurped the powers of the Federal Government.

"Now, therefore, I, C. F. Jackson, Governor of the State of Missouri, do, in view of the foregoing facts, and by virtue of the powers vested in me by the Constitution and laws of this Commonwealth, issue this my proclamation, calling the militia of the State, to the number of *fifty thousand*, into the active service of the State, for the purpose of repelling said invasion, and for the protection of the lives, liberty, and property of the citizens of this State. And I earnestly exhort all good citizens of Missouri to rally under the flag of their State for the protection of their endangered homes and firesides, and for the defence of their most sacred rights and dearest liberties.

"In issuing this proclamation, I hold it to be my solemn duty to remind you that Missouri is still one of the United States; that the Executive department of the State Government does not arrogate to itself the power to disturb that relation; that that power has been wisely vested in a convention, which will, at the proper time, express your sovereign will; and that, meanwhile, it is your duty to obey all the constitutional requirements of the Federal Government. But it is equally my duty to advise you that your first allegiance is due to your own State, and that you are under no obligation whatever to obey the unconstitutional edicts of the military despotism which has enthroned itself at Washington, nor to submit to the infamous and degrading sway of its wicked minions in this State. No brave and true-hearted Missourian will obey the one or submit to the other. Rise, then, and drive out ignominiously the invaders who have dared to desecrate the soil which your labors have made fruitful, and which is consecrated by your homes.

"Given under my hand, as Governor, and under the great seal of the State of Missouri, at Jefferson City, this 12th day of June, 1861.

"By the Governor. CLAIBORNE F. JACKSON.
"B. F. MASSEY, Secretary of State."

* "To THE CITIZENS OF MISSOURI: Prior to the proclamation issued by Governor Jackson, of date of June 12, it is well known to you that the Governor and Legislature sympathized with the rebellion movements now in progress in the country, and had adopted every means in their power to effect a separation of this State from the General Government. For this purpose, parties of avowed secessionists have been organized into military companies throughout the State, with the full knowledge and approval of the Governor. The establishment of encampments in the State at an unusual period of the year, and authorized for an indefinite period, could have had no other object than the concentration of a large military force, to be subjected to the provisions of the military law then in contemplation, and subsequently passed—a bill so offensive to all peaceable inhabitants, and so palpably unconstitutional, that it could be accepted by those only who were to conform to its extraordinary provisions for the

He at the same time marshalled his forces at St. Louis, and hurried to rout out the Governor and his secession bands from Jefferson City, the capital

purpose of effecting their cherished object—the disruption of the Federal Government. That bill provides for an obligation to the State on the part of all persons enrolled under its provisions irrespective of any obligation to the United States, when the Constitution requires all State officers to take an oath of allegiance to the United States. This of itself is a repudiation of all authority of the Federal Government, whose Constitution is the supreme law, on the part of the State Government, its officers, and such citizens as might choose to adopt the provisions of the bill, and, coupled as it was, on the part of the Legislature and the Governor, with declarations hostile to its authority and in sympathy with those who were arrayed in a condition of actual hostility against it, could leave no doubt of its object to carry out the provisions of this extraordinary bill, having in direct view hostilities to the Federal Government. It was so denounced by General Harney, who characterized it as a secession ordinance in his proclamation of 14th May last. That proclamation, doubtless, gave rise to an interview between General Harney and General Price, that resulted in an agreement which it was hoped would lead to a restoration of tranquillity and good order in your State. That a repudiation of the military bill, and all efforts of the militia of the State under its provisions was the basis of the agreement, was shown as well by this proclamation of General Harney immediately preceding it, as by a paper submitted to General Price, containing the preliminary conditions to an interview with him.

"This agreement failed to define specifically the terms of the peace, or how far a suspension of the provisions of the military bill should form a part of it, though from the express declaration of General Harney at the time of the conference, as well as from the foregoing paper, a suspension of any action under the bill until there could be a judicial termination of its character by some competent tribunal, must in good faith be regarded as a fundamental basis of the negotiation.

"Nevertheless, immediately after this arrangement, and up to the time of Governor Jackson's proclamation, inaugurating complaints of attempts to execute the provisions of this bill, by which most exasperating hardships have been imposed upon peaceful loyal citizens, coupled with persecutions and proscriptions of those opposed to its provisions, have been made to me as commander of the United States forces here, and have been carried to the authorities at Washington, with appeals for relief, from the Union men of all parties of the State who have been abused, insulted, and, in some instances, driven from their homes.

"That relief I conceive it to be the duty of a just government to use every exertion in its power to give. Upon this point the policy of the Government is set forth in the following communication from the Department at Washington:

"'ADJUTANT-GENERAL'S OFFICE,
WASHINGTON, May 27, 1861.

"'BRIGADIER-GENERAL W. S. HARNEY, COMMANDING DEPARTMENT WEST ST. LOUIS—Sir: The President observes with concern that, notwithstanding the pledge of the State authorities to co-operate in preserving the peace of Missouri, loyal citizens in great numbers continue to be driven from their homes. It is immaterial whether these outrages continue from inactivity or indisposition on the part of the State authorities to prevent them. It is enough that they continue, and it will devolve on you the duty of putting a stop to them summarily by the force under your command, to be aided by such troops as you may require from Kansas, Iowa, and Illinois. The professions of loyalty to the Union by the State authorities of Missouri are not to be relied upon. They have already falsified their professions too often, and are too far committed to secession to be admitted to your confidence, and you can only be sure of their desisting from their wicked purposes when it is not in their power to prosecute them. You will, therefore, be unceasingly watchful of their movements, and not permit the clamors of their partisans and the opponents of the wise measures already taken to prevent you from checking every movement against the Government, however disguised, under the pretended State authority. The authority of the United States is paramount, and whenever it is apparent that a movement —whether by order of State authorities or not—is hostile, you will not hesitate to put it down.

"'L. THOMAS, Adjutant-General.'

"It is my design to carry out these instructions in their letter and spirit. Their justness and propriety will be appreciated by whoever takes an enlightened view of the relations of the citizens of Missouri to the General Government, nor can such policy be construed as at all disparaging to the rights or dignity of the State of Missouri, or as infringing in any sense upon the individual liberty of its citizens. The recent proclamation of Governor Jackson, by which he has set at defiance the authorities of the United States, and urged you to make war upon them, is but a consummation of his treasonable purposes, long indicated by his acts and expressed opinions, and now made manifest. If, in suppressing these treasonable projects, carrying out the policy of the Government, and maintaining its dignity as above indicated, hostilities should unfortunately occur, and unhappy consequences should follow, I would hope that all aggravation of those events may be avoided, and that they may be diverted from the innocent, and may fall only on the heads of those by whom they have been provoked.

"In the discharge of these plain but onerous duties, I

of Missouri, where they were plotting against and making ready to attack the Union troops and overthrow the Federal authority.

CHAPTER XXVIII.

General Lyon's movement from St. Louis.—Occupation of the Railroad.—Force under Lyon.—Embarkation of Troops.—Arrival at Jefferson City.—Flight of the Enemy.—Their destructive proceedings.—General Lyon in pursuit.—Boernstein at the capital.—Route of General Lyon.—Reception by the way.—Rochefort.—First indication of the Enemy.—Dispersion of Scouts.—Disembarkation of General Lyon.—March of the Federal Troops.—Coming up with the Enemy.—Position of the Antagonist.—Opening Fire.—Battle of Booneville.—Flight of the Enemy.—Courage and coolness of General Lyon.—Pursuit of the Enemy.—Another Stand and another Rout.—A deserted Camp.—A half-cooked Breakfast.—The Federal Boats doing good service.—Capture of a Battery.—The stand at the Fair Grounds.—A third Rout.—The scattering of the Enemy.—The Killed and Wounded.—The Prisoners.—A warlike Parson.—Successful Appeal to an "old Rebel."—Comparative strength of Forces.—Approach to Booneville.—A civic and military Delegation.—Welcome to the Town.—Union Enthusiasm.—The Secessionists' Demand.—Danger to the Unionists.—The "Greatest Crime," etc.—General Lyon's Proclamation.—Forgiveness of Rebels.—Mildness and Severity.—Proclamation of Boernstein at Jefferson City.—The Missouri Convention taking Courage.—Convoked to reassemble.—The Congratulations of the Unionists.—Another Riot in St. Louis.—Attack upon the Federal Soldiers.—Tragic Results.—The Verdict of a St. Louis Jury.—General Lyon inspirited.—A bold move to the Southwest.—Sterling Price and Ben McCulloch.—Departure of Lyon.—An Augmenting Force.

GENERAL LYON'S first movement was to send the Second Regiment of Missouri Volunteers, under the command of Colonel Siegel, by land, along the Pacific Railroad, to occupy the line, and thus prevent any further destruction, by the secessionists, of the bridges. This detachment proceeded, without any show of opposition, as far as the Gasconade River, where the enemy had destroyed the bridge. On the next day, Lyon embarked his troops in two divisions; one consisting of the Second Battalion of the First Regiment of Missouri Volunteers, commanded by Lieutenant-Colonel Andrews, one section of Totten's light artillery, and two companies of regulars under Captain Lathrop; and the other of the First Battalion of the First Regiment of Missouri Volunteers under Colonel Blair, another section of Totten's artillery, and a detachment of pioneers, numbering in all about two thousand men. Each division was embarked on board of a river steamer at the wharves of St. Louis, and together with the men a large supply of horses, baggage wagons, camp equipage, ammunition, and provisions was put on board, evidently with the view of a long march. General Lyon and his staff embarked with the second division, and the two steamers proceeded up the Missouri

1861.
June 12.
June 13.

shall look for the countenance and active co-operation of all good citizens, and I shall expect them to discountenance all illegal combinations or organizations, and support and uphold, by every lawful means, the Federal Government, upon the maintenance of which depend their liberties and the perfect enjoyment of all their rights.

"N. LYON,
"Brigadier-General U. S. Volunteers Commanding."

to Jefferson City, the capital, situated on that river, near the centre of the State.

On the second day after embarking, General Lyon reached Jefferson City, but on marching into the place found that Governor Jackson, General Sterling Price, and their secession confederates and bands, had retreated the day before to Booneville, some forty miles farther up the Missouri, within the interior of the State. They had striven to conceal their destination, but the people of Jefferson City had no doubt of the direction of their flight, and being loyally disposed, freely gave all the information they possessed to the Federal officers. In their retreat the secessionists had sought to hinder pursuit, by seizing the cars and locomotives, which they carried along with them, and by destroying the bridges and telegraphs, as they hurriedly pushed forward.

Lyon promptly hurried on in pursuit. Embarking again in the steamers, to which was added a third, he moved with his troops up the Missouri, having left three companies of Boernstein's regiment under the command of the Colonel himself, at Jefferson City, to protect the capital. On passing the little town of Marion, on the Missouri River, the inhabitants manifested their loyalty by heartily cheering the expedition. Having reached Providence during the night, the steamers hauled up until daybreak, when they continued their course. At Rochefort the sullenness of some of the people indicated that the Federal forces had arrived in a part of the State where they were less welcome. Though the citizens were little disposed to be communicative, the information was obtained from them that the enemy were in considerable force some miles below Booneville.

The expedition, after pressing into the service a steam ferry-boat at Rochefort, continued its course up the river, until it reached a point within eight miles of Booneville. Here was seen the first indication of the enemy in a battery on the bluff or high embankment of the river, and some scouts appeared, who hastened, on seeing the steamers, to convey information of their approach to the main body of the secessionists. The boats now moved at once to the shore, where there was a stretch of alluvial land or "bottom" a mile and a half in width between the water and the bluff, on the south side of the river, and making fast, the troops disembarked without opposition.

Scouts were now sent in advance, and the main body followed them, marching along the river road. The troops had thus proceeded about a mile and a half to the point where the road ascends the bluffs, when a firing was heard, indicating that our scouts were engaged with the picket guards of the enemy, whom they succeeded in driving back. The Federal troops continued to push on, marching up the gentle slope of the ascent for nearly half a mile, when their advanced guard came galloping back with the information that the enemy

June 15.

June 16.

BATTLE OF BOONEVILLE.   315

were in full force, posted advantageously upon the summit of the rising ground, about three hundred yards in front.

Their position was on the crest of the hill along which the road ascends. Colonel Marmaduke, in command, held the road itself with a troop of horsemen and a battalion of infantry. On his left was a brick house occupied by a portion of his force, and to the rear, in a lane leading to the river, was formed the main body of his left wing. Behind this again stretched a wheat-field, in which had gathered small bodies of men apparently without form or order. The enemy's right wing was posted behind a "worm" fence, which divided the wheat-field where the men were formed from a neighboring field of Indian corn.

The Federal troops, as soon as they discovered the position of the enemy, formed on the ridge of rising ground facing them and separated only by a shallow valley with a scattered growth of oak. On our right there were also some trees, while on the left there was a field of Indian corn. The regular troops were posted, with Colonel Blair's regiment of Missouri Volunteers, on the left, and the Germans, also volunteers, under Lieutenant-Colonel Shaeffer, on the right.

Captain Totten, of the light artillery, opened the engagement by firing a shell from a twelve-pounder, among the enemy's force in the road. This was immediately followed by another well-aimed shell, which fell among the throngs in the wheat-field, and forced them to a hasty retreat. The battle thus begun, our men on the right and left advanced in good order and soon opened with a volley of musketry, which was spiritedly returned by the enemy. The regulars on our right marched boldly along the field of Indian corn, until they reached the ascent which led to the crest upon which the enemy were posted. They now began to move more cautiously, creeping along and firing when a good opportunity for a shot presented. The volunteers sent to support them gallantly followed the example of the regulars and spiritedly joined in the attack. The Germans on the right were advancing no less firmly and persistently and engaging the enemy's left. The secessionists were forced back by the steady advance of our men, and the effective firing of Totten's artillery. They, however, as they retired, still made a show of resistance.

Two bombshells, sent by Totten against the brick house, within which the enemy had sought cover, penetrated the wall and effectually routed them out. After this the secessionists gave way more rapidly before the steady advance of our troops, and were soon forced to abandon their position, which the Federalists occupied in twenty minutes after the first shot fired by Totten, which opened the engagement.

"The commander, General Lyon," says an eye-witness of the battle, "exhibited the most remarkable coolness, and preserved throughout that undisturbed presence of mind shown by him alike in the camp, in private life, and on the field of battle. 'Forward, on the extreme right;' 'give them another shot, Captain Totten,' echoed above the roar of musketry, clear and distinct, from the lips of the general who led the advancing column."

The enemy continued to retreat and the Federalists to pursue without further collision, until the latter had advanced about a mile and a half, when the former made a stand in some woods near their encampment. Two shells, however, and a volley of musketry soon put them again to the rout, and they fled in confusion towards Booneville. Their deserted camp, which our men now occupied, was found to contain a considerable quantity of provisions, arms, and ammunition. The evident haste with which, after the landing of the Federalists, they had advanced to meet them, proved how unexpected had been their arrival. The breakfasts of the men were found in the course of preparation in the camp; the half-baked bread, the partially fried pork, the ham with the knife sticking in the meat, and the pots of coffee still on the fire, showed how sudden had been their movement. Our troops gave them no opportunity of resuming the cooking of their morning's meal, or of breaking their long morning's fast. A company being left to guard the camp, General Lyon led the rest of his force on to Booneville.

In the mean time, while the main body of the Federalists had been acquitting themselves so satisfactorily on land, the artillerists under Captain Voorhies, and the company of infantry in command of Captain Richardson, who had been reluctantly left behind to take charge of the boats, contrived also to do some effectual service. After the troops began their march, Richardson went ashore with his men, and captured a battery of two iron six-pounders, posted on the river about five miles below Booneville. He then moved on with one of the boats, the McDowell, towards the town, with the view of co-operating with the land force.

This he was able to effect, when Lyon had marched within a mile of Booneville, where the secessionists, again at the fair grounds, seemed disposed to make a stand. Captain Richardson being from his position on the river in their rear, first discovered their intention, and was enabled to fire upon them with great effect. A shot from his howitzer, followed by a fire from Totten's artillery, and a volley of musketry from Lyon's main body, which had in the mean time become aware of the enemy's purpose, soon scattered them for a third time. The secessionists now continued their flight, dispersing in various directions. Some crossed the river, some went south, but the chief portion, after having passed through the town, escaped up the Missouri in boats to the west.

In the course of the attack and pursuit by the Federal forces, there were but three of them killed, ten wounded, and one missing. It was difficult to estimate the loss of the secessionists, but it is supposed to have been large. Eighty were taken prisoners, of whom twenty-six were captured by the chaplain of the First Regiment. "He had charge," says the authority before quoted, "of a party of four men, two mounted and two on foot, with which to take charge of the wounded. Ascending the brow of a hill, he suddenly came upon a company of twenty-four rebels, armed with revolvers, and fully bent upon securing a place of safety for their carcasses. Their intentions, however, were considerably modified, when the parson ordered them to halt, which they did, surrendering their arms. Surrounded by the squad of five men, they were then marched on board the Louisiana, prisoners of war. The parson also captured two other secessionists during the day, and at one time, needing a wagon and horses for the wounded, and finding friendly suggestions wasted on a stubborn old rebel, placed a revolver at his head, and the desired articles were forthcoming. In time of peace the preacher had prepared for war."

The enemy were reported to have been four thousand strong, and the Federalists only two thousand, of whom less than half were actively engaged. Governor Jackson is supposed to have discreetly kept at a distance from the battle, and to have been among the first to seek safety in flight while General Sterling Price was prevented by an inopportune attack of illness from taking command of the secession forces.

As General Lyon was approaching the town of Booneville, he was met by some of the officials and leading citizens bearing a flag of truce. They were anxious to impress upon the victors, that the greater proportion of their fellow-citizens were favorable to the Federal cause. General Lyon received them in a conciliatory spirit, and assured them that, if no resistance should be offered to the entrance of his troops, no harm need be feared. Soon after Major O'Brien, a military officer of Booneville, presented himself, and the town was formally surrendered. The Federal troops now advanced, headed by General Lyon and the civic and military representatives of the place. On passing through the principal street, they were met by a party of citizens waving the United States flag and cheering lustily for the Union, to which the Federal troops gave a hearty response. The "stars and stripes" now suddenly fluttered out from house window and church steeple, and Booneville proclaimed itself once more a loyal town.

"One can hardly imagine," declares a writer who was present on the occasion, "the joy expressed and felt by the loyal citizens when the Federal troops entered the city. Stores which had been closed all day, began to open, the national flag was quickly run up on a secession pole, cheers for the Union, Lyon, Blair, and Lincoln were frequently heard, and everything betokened the restoration of peace, law, and order. 'True men' are reported to have said, 'that had the troops delayed ten days longer, it would have been impossible for them to have remained in safety. Irresponsible vagabonds had been taking guns wherever they could find them, and notifying the most substantial and prosperous citizens to leave.' One worthy citizen, the proprietor of the City Hotel, was said to have denounced 'the whole secession movement as the greatest crime committed since the crucifixion of our Saviour.'

On the next day after entering Booneville, General Lyon released his prisoners, most of whom were youths and had been misled, as he believed, by the artful devices of older conspirators.

<small>June 18.</small>

In the mean time Colonel Boernstein, who had been left with a battalion of the Second Regiment of Missouri Volunteers, in command of Jefferson City, the capital, was effectually keeping in check the secessionists, and striving to soothe the disaffected with proclaiming summary punishment for treason and security for property. "Your personal safety," he said, "will be protected, and your property respected. Slave property will not be interfered with by any part of my command, nor will slaves be allowed to enter my lines without written authority from their masters; and, notwithstanding we are in times of war, I shall endeavor to execute my instructions with moderation and forbearance, and at the same time shall not suffer the least attempt to destroy the Union and its Government, by the performance of any unlawful act."

Under the protection of the military rule of Boernstein, at the capital, and inspirited by the success of the Federal troops under Lyon, the members of the Convention of the State of Missouri took courage. Having already, as early as February, refused by a large majority to consider the question of secession, they now prepared to execute the will of the people whom they represented, in thwarting the action of the secessionist Governor and his confederates of the Legislature. The Convention was accordingly called to reassemble in Jefferson City, on the twenty-second day of July.

Lyon having by his prompt movement swept the eastern part of Missouri, from St. Louis to Booneville, clear of the secession leaders and their bands, the unionists began to congratulate themselves that the State was now secure in the enjoyment of a loyal tranquillity. There was, however, even in St. Louis, some unwillingness to submit quietly to the Federal power. The military authorities having considered it prudent to station guards on the various railways leading from the city, had detailed a regiment commanded by Colonel Kallman for that duty. After detailing the necessary number of men, the rest of the regiment returned, passing through St. Louis, when a collision took place with the citizens.

<small>June 17.</small>

The event was thus related by one of the journals* of that city.

"Forming at the dépôt in good order, they marched quietly down Broadway and Seventh Street without interruption or disturbance of any kind, so far as is known, till Company B reached St. Charles Street. At that point a half-drunken or crazed individual insulted

---

* St. Louis Democrat.

the troops with language so abusive and threatening, that several of them took him into custody. The captain came up, inquiring into the circumstances of the case, and, on the prisoner's protesting that he meant no harm, ordered his release. This took place in Olive Street. In a moment afterward a pistol was fired from a second-story window on the east side of the street, just south of Olive, a second almost simultaneously from near the pavement, and instantly a third from the window above.

"Some of the troops noticed that an attack was in contemplation, and began arranging caps on their muskets, a movement perceived by spectators, who were as yet unaware of the cause. During this quick movement one of the muskets accidentally exploded, and this occurred near the time of the first firing of the pistol as described.

"Colonel Kallman gave the order to halt, pistol shots still firing from the windows. The order was promptly obeyed, and the troops, till then marching four abreast, wheeled westward and formed into double file, fronting east. No order to fire was given. Captain Risech, of Company I, marching in the rear, was shot so as to be disabled from command, and a soldier at the same time fell senseless in the ranks. The troops began firing briskly up to the windows of the Missouri engine-house and Recorder's court-room, and the second story of the building adjoining on the north. The fire of the pistols was returned, but soon ceased, the officers below passing along the ranks and ordering the troops to stop firing. The terrible scene, which lasted scarcely a minute and a half or two minutes at the furthest, was thus terminated."

There were no less than six victims of this tragic occurrence, all of whom were private citizens, while the soldiers escaped with but some slight wounds. The coroner's jury, after a long investigation of ten days, rendered a verdict which, while it exonerated citizens and the military officers, imputed the blame to the soldiers. They declared that the "wounds were inflicted without any provocation or discharge of firearms from the citizens then present, and also without any order to fire having been given by the officers of the said companies."

General Lyon, inspirited by his success in the north and east, and trusting to the loyalty which his triumphs had encouraged to manifest itself, now boldly determined to push on to the southwest, where Sterling Price and Ben McCulloch, the Texan ranger, had formed a junction and mustered a strong force. Lyon accordingly, with his characteristic self-reliance, left Booneville, with only two thousand men. This meagre band, however, rapidly increased on the march by the accessions of the loyal men of the country, who welcomed and offered their services readily to the victorious leader of the Federal troops. The events of this campaign and its fatal results will be related in the due course of this narrative.

July 3.

CHAPTER XXIX.

Unabated spirit of the North.—Large mustering of Troops.—The Force at Washington.—The Potomac Line.—Commanders.—Force at Fortress Monroe.—Force in the neighborhood of Harper's Ferry.—Force in Western Virginia.—Force at Cairo.—Force in Missouri.—Force in Maryland.—The Line on the Potomac.—Topography of the Country.—The dangers of the ground.—Fortifications.—Arlington Heights.—Alexandria.—The ghost of a city.—Deserted Streets.—Abandoned Houses.—Closed Warehouses and Shops.—Military Occupation.—Present Inhabitants.—Soldiers and Negroes. Description of Vienna.—Description of Fairfax Court House.—The Position of the Enemy in Virginia.—Manassas Junction.—Position and Fortifications.—Distances and Communications.—Exploit of Lieut. Tompkins at Fairfax Court House. A spirited Charge.—The result.—The affair at Vienna.—A clear field reported.—Orders to General Schenck.—Departure of Schenck.—His Force.—How it was disposed of.—A sudden stoppage.—A Masked Battery.—A Conflict.—Killed and Wounded.—Conduct of the Engineer.—Criticism upon the management of the Expedition.—The Enterprise denounced.—The sacrifice.—Gallantry of Federal Troops.—An account of the Enemy. Tribute to a "Few."—The Enemy's Batteries on the Potomac.—Captain Ward's Reconnoissance of Matthias Point.—An Attack planned.—Landing of Men.—Federal Batteries raised on the Virginia Shore.—A sudden surprise from the Enemy.—Death of Captain Ward.—An official criticism on the expedition.

THERE was no abatement of the military spirit of the loyal North. With each development of secession there was an increased vigor shown on the part of the defenders of the Union. In two or three months after the fall of Fort Sumter it was estimated that two hundred and twenty-five thousand men, militia and volunteers, had already mustered into the service of the United States. Of these there were some sixty thousand who had marched to the protection of the capital, one half of whom were stationed in and about the city of Washington, under the command of Brigadier-General J. K. T. Mansfield, and the other half on the opposite and south side of the Potomac, under the command of Brigadier-General T. McDowell.

Twelve thousand men were at Fortress Monroe and its environs, in command of Major-General B. F. Butler. Twenty thousand had marched from Pennsylvania under Majors-General Robert Patterson and W. H. Keim to the neighborhood of Harper's Ferry, to which point Major-General George Cadwallader with six thousand was also proceeding. This combined force was intended to co-operate with Major-General George B. McClellan, who, crossing the Ohio from the west, was in Western Virginia at the head of twenty-five thousand men. Seven thousand had gathered at Cairo, under the command of Brigadier-General B. M. Prentiss; and Brigadier-General Lyon was supposed to be able to muster throughout the State of Missouri a force of nearly thirteen thousand. Major-General N. P. Banks, who had succeeded Cadwallader, was keeping Baltimore and Maryland in check with over ten thousand. The rest of this large army was still in camp in the various Northern and Western States, ready to

1861.

march to any point to which it might be directed.

The line of the Federal forces on the south side of the Potomac opposite to Washington extended from Alexandria on the east in the direction of Vienna on the west, a distance of about sixteen miles, and again to the north toward Fairfax Court House, over twelve miles from the capital. The whole country is rolling, composed of hills and shallow valleys, and intersected with numerous small streams. The ground is very favorable for defence. Its approaches, winding in narrow roads or lanes about the hills, are readily commanded by fortifications, while a march through it would be greatly exposed to surprises from ambuscades and concealed batteries. There is hardly a spot which a commanding officer would select for the manœuvering of a large force in regular battle.

The most commanding heights had been seized by the Federal forces, upon which they had raised entrenchments and redoubts. Among these was Arlington Heights, directly opposite and commanding the capital, formerly the property of George Washington Custis, the descendant of Washington's wife, and belonging at this time to Mrs. R. E. Lee, wife of the celebrated General in the Confederate service. Here General McDowell had his headquarters.

Alexandria, on the Potomac, about seven miles from Washington, was also held in force by the Federal troops, and its approaches commanded by the construction of an earthen redoubt. This city ordinarily contained about ten thousand inhabitants, mostly engaged in commerce. Grain, flour, and tobacco were its principal exports, and its domestic trade was in negroes, for the sale of whom there were two thriving slave-pens. On the possession of Alexandria by our troops, the greater portion of the leading people, who were devoted to the cause of secession, abandoned the place and allowed it to become little more than barracks for soldiers or a refuge for the negroes whom their masters could not compel to fly with them. Its communications with the interior, by means of canals and railways, and with other ports by the Potomac, were cut off by the war. An eye-witness at this time pictures the city as "a ghost of its former self." Warehouses and mills on the wharves are closed, save perhaps here and there one which has been opened as a guard-house for soldiers or a receptacle for munitions of war. The little river steamboats still ply between Washington and the town, but convey only armed soldiers, or a few privileged visitors, who can neither embark nor disembark without submitting their 'passes' to a vigilant sentinel. The main street, still bearing in its name, 'King,' a reverential reminiscence of colonial loyalty, is silent except to the rumbling of heavy baggage wagons or the clatter of the mounted dragoon. Most of the shops are closed and their shutters heavily barred with iron. The few which remain open, show the timid anxiety of their occupants, by the darkened windows and half-opened doors. The villas

41

in the suburbs are deserted, with the vines hanging from the verandahs in tangled neglect, and the gardens overgrown with weeds. The public halls and hotels are turned into barracks, and private mansions and school-houses into military hospitals; churches and churchyards are locked and abandoned by priest and sexton. Soldiers are on guard at the corner of every street. But few of the ordinary inhabitants of the town are to be seen, except some "poor whites," who may be still slinking out of hovels or into the groggeries, and the negroes, who are idly chatting as they lie in groups upon the door-steps, or striving to support their sudden independence by selling fruits and pastry and other delicacies to lounging soldiers."

Vienna, towards which the other extremity of the Federal line of occupation extended on the south side of the Potomac, is a small village on the Loudon and Hampshire Railroad, about fifteen miles from Alexandria and nearly twelve from Washington. It was near this point that the Federal troops were imprudently exposed to an attack from the enemy, which will soon be narrated.

Fairfax Court House, though of inconsiderable size, is a place of more importance than Vienna. It is situated on the turnpike road leading from Alexandria to Centreville, and is about fifteen miles both from Washington and Alexandria. This was also the scene of an early skirmish, between a troop of Federal cavalry and the enemy, in which our soldiers were enabled by the gallantry of their leader to acquit themselves with more credit than in the blundering expedition to Vienna.

The enemy had, in the mean time, while the Federal forces had been crossing the Potomac and occupying the country bordering on that river, been mustering a large number of troops in Virginia.

Their main force was posted at "Manassas Junction," a railway station where the Manassas Gap Railroad joins that between Orange and Alexandria. The place derives all its importance from its strategic position, as it commands the land communications from the north with Richmond. Here Beauregard was in command, and exercising all his skill as an engineer in fortifying the post. The distance of Manassas Junction, to the south-west, from Alexandria is about twenty-seven miles; from Washington, south, thirty-two; and from Richmond a hundred and thirty-five miles north.

From Manassas Junction the enemy's line extended toward Acquia Creek on their right; in the direction of Harper's Ferry on their left, whence a considerable body was manœuvering with the view of subjecting Western Virginia, and in front to Fairfax Court House.

It was at this last place that Lieutenant Tompkins performed his spirited exploit. Being ordered on a scouting expedition, he set out from the camp on the Potomac, at half-past ten o'clock at night, with a company of United States cavalry numbering seventy-five men. He reached Fairfax Court House next morning before daylight, at three o'clock. Having surprised and captured the enemy's picket guard, the Lieutenant boldly pushed into the town. As he entered, he was met by a fire from the windows of the houses. He then charged on the troops he found there, and drove them from the town. They, however, being reinforced by several companies, were encouraged to return, when Tompkins, finding himself greatly outnumbered, retreated in good order, bringing with him as trophies five prisoners fully armed and equipped and two horses.

"My loss," the Lieutenant officially reported, "is three men missing, three slightly wounded, and twelve horses lost. The loss of the rebels is from twenty to twenty-five in killed and wounded. From observations I should judge that the rebels at that point numbered fully one thousand five hundred men." The Lieutenant himself was reported to have lost two horses killed under him, but to have escaped with but a slight wound from the fall of one of them.

The affair which occurred at Vienna was less successful. A detachment of Connecticut troops having been sent out to reconnoitre, reported, although one of the men had been wounded by a concealed shot, that the railroad from the Federal lines to two miles beyond Vienna was clear of the enemy. On the same night, however, General McDowell learned that the secessionists were about to obstruct the road, by destroying the bridges and tearing up the rails. He accordingly ordered Brigadier-General Schenck, of the Ohio Volunteers, formerly member of Congress, to reconnoitre the ground and station guards at the various exposed points of the road. Schenck accordingly mustered six hundred and sixty-eight rank and file, with twenty-nine field and company officers of the First Ohio Volunteers, and started on the expedition from his camp three miles beyond Alexandria. Placing his men in the railroad cars he proceeded on his route along the Loudon and Hampshire Railroad, upon which the village of Vienna is situated, at a distance of about fifteen miles from the city of Alexandria.

In accordance with his orders, Schenck stationed one hundred and thirty men at the crossing of the road, and sent one hundred and seventeen men to Falls Church to reconnoitre in that direction. He then went on, leaving one hundred and thirty men to guard the railroad and the bridge between the crossing and Vienna. He had now only four companies left, consisting of two hundred and seventy-five men. With this remnant of his force he proceeded toward Vienna."

"On turning the curve slowly, within one quarter of a mile of Vienna," said the Brigadier in his official report, "*we were fired upon by raking masked batteries* of, I think, three guns, with shells, round shot, and grape, killing and wounding the men on the platform and in the cars before the train could be stopped. When the train stopped, the engine could not, on account of damage to some part of the running machinery, draw the train out of the fire. The engine being in the rear, we left the cars, and retired to the right and left of the train through the woods.

"Finding that the enemy's batteries were sustained by what appeared about a regiment of infantry, and by cavalry, which force we have since understood to have been some fifteen hundred South Carolinians, we fell back along the railroad, throwing out skirmishers on both flanks; and this was about seven P.M. Thus we retired slowly, bearing off our wounded five miles to this point, which we reached at ten o'clock."

The loss reported was five killed, six wounded, and ten missing. The General had good ground of complaint against the engineer, who, he says, "when the men left the cars, instead of retiring slowly, as I ordered, detached his engine with one passenger car from the rest of the disabled train and abandoned us, running to Alexandria, and we have heard nothing from him since. Thus we were deprived of a rallying-point, and of all means of conveying the wounded, who had to be carried on litters and in blankets."

The conduct of the expedition was severely censured. A writer* who accompanied it, and wrote a graphic description of it, while he did not withhold his admiration of the courage of the Ohio troops and their leaders, did not hesitate to rebuke the imprudent management of the enterprise. He wrote: "However wise or necessary this plan of dropping squads behind might be in an ordinary advance, it certainly was of doubtful expediency in this case. There were no villages or groups of houses along the route, among which the enemy's men could have established themselves in force, and the only point from which an attack could be seriously apprehended was Vienna itself. Had the entire regiment—and a larger body would have been better—been pushed rapidly down to Vienna, we should have been more fully prepared to encounter and act against an ambush; and, had all proved quiet, nothing would have been lost, since we had the advantage of railroad speed, by stationing the guards on the return, instead of the advance. It is true that the entire course of the road is through a valley, and that the hills on either side, and the heavy thickets which screen them, appear to offer excellent situations for ambuscade; but the roads in the neighborhood are few, and those which exist are quite impracticable for the ready transportation of troops, not to speak of artillery. Decidedly the suspicious spot was Vienna and its vicinity. A certain disposition to tardy caution was frustrated by the carelessness of the engine-driver. He had been directed to stop at the distance of a mile from the town, whence skirmishers were to be thrown out, and proper reconnoissances to be made. Instead of doing so, he shot ahead until within half a mile or less, so that this single chance of averting the impending danger was wasted. The train was rounding a gentle curve, and the men were laughing, quite unconscious of peril, when the first round of shot fell among them, tearing five of them to pieces, and wounding many

---

* Correspondent of the New York Tribune.

THE AMBUSH AT VIENNA.

others. The rebels' guns had been carefully planted in the curve, and were hidden until the worst part of their work was accomplished. The first discharge was the most fatal. The four companies were disposed upon open platform cars, and were first of all exposed to the enemy's fire. The engine was at the rear of the train. It was fortunate that most of the men were sitting, for the shot flew high, and only those who stood erect were struck. Major Hughey was among the foremost, but was unharmed. General Schenck and Colonel McCook were in a covered car behind the troops. The Colonel instantly sprang out, and gathered the best part of his men together. The enemy's field-pieces had been stationed to command the line of the railroad and nothing else. They were at the termination of the curve, to the left of the track, and elevated a few feet above the grade. With the exception of that company which was the most exposed, and which suffered the most, the men promptly assembled near Colonel McCook, who proceeded to form them in line of battle, and to lead them into the protection of a little wood, or thicket, at the right of the track, apart from the range of the battery. Meanwhile shot and shell continued to assail the train, and those who lingered near it. The engine-driver, in a panic, detached his locomotive and a single car, and dashed off at full speed. The rebel artillerists then directed their range, so as to menace Colonel McCook's three companies, upon which the Colonel quietly marched them over to the left of the track, into another clump of trees, where he collected all his little force, and arrayed them boldly in line. The shot from the rebels now flew very wild, cutting the trees overhead and around, and, in their hurry, they made the frequent blunder of discharging their shell without opening the fuse. But, notwithstanding this, Colonel McCook's position was far from comfortable. He saw that he was prodigiously outnumbered, and that if the enemy could only keep their wits for a few minutes, he must inevitably be captured, or venture a struggle at fearful odds. He had only about one hundred and eighty men, while the rebel force exceeded two thousand. Their field-pieces alone, decently managed, would have destroyed the little Ohio band in a twinkling. But the Ohio men never flinched, and this was the reward of their bravery: the rebels observing such a mere handful bearing themselves undaunted before their superior host, were at first amazed, and then startled into the conviction that powerful reinforcements must be close at hand. How else, it seemed to them, could this sprinkling of troops hold their ground. It could be nothing but the confidence of overwhelming strength that sustained them. And this is not conjecture. The information since received from Vienna proves it to have been their real belief. Disheartened by this belief, they became irresolute, their fire slackened, they wavered, and, in a few minutes, broke up their lines and slowly retired. At the same time

Colonel McCook, having secured his wounded, also withdrew, his two thousand assailants making no attempt or motion to oppose his retreat."

The enemy, too, gave their version of the affair at Vienna, claiming a victory, which they said they had won with a force of six hundred Carolinians, a company of artillery, and two companies of cavalry. They, moreover, insisted that the attack was an extemporaneous one, and that they "had scarcely time to place two cannon in position" when the Federal troops first showed themselves. One "well-directed shot," which raked the railroad cars, was sufficient, they asserted, to cause consternation and dismay, and force the Federalists to fly to the woods. "A few of the party," however, they confessed, "exhibited some bravery, and endeavored, by shouts, to rally their flying comrades, but it was impossible."

The enemy had possession, on their right, to the south of Alexandria, of the Virginian bank of the river Potomac, and here they had been zealously at work, protecting themselves with batteries. Captain Ward, of the steamer Freeborn, and in command of the flotilla of the Potomac, was on the alert, and was eager to prevent the completion of these batteries. Accordingly, having discovered that the enemy were about to erect works at Matthias Point, a commanding position fifty miles below Washington, where the river narrows and makes an abrupt turn, first to the north and then to the south, Captain Ward determined to try to dislodge them. His plan was, to effect a landing upon the point under cover of the guns of his steamer, and after driving away the enemy, to destroy the works in progress and cut down the trees which concealed them from the river. He accordingly obtained from Captain Rowan, in command of the Pawnee, stationed above on the Potomac, off the mouth of Acquia Creek, two boats' crews, and these, together with some of his own men, numbering in all about forty, armed and equipped with axes and building materials, he sent ashore at Matthias Point, while he closed in with his own steamer to cover their landing.

June 27.

The men succeeded in reaching the land without resistance, and selecting a position began at once to construct sand-bag breastworks. Under cover of the guns of the Freeborn they remained at work unmolested for four hours and a half. At five o'clock in the afternoon, however, when returning to their boats, with the view of going on board the steamer to obtain cannon to mount upon the work, a large number of the enemy suddenly made their appearance, and fired upon them a volley of musketry.

The men hurried in confusion to their boats, and as they pushed off, left some of their comrades behind. The Freeborn, in the mean time, brought her guns to bear upon the enemy, who were, however, greatly protected by the brushwood, behind which they had sought cover, and whence they kept up a direct fire upon the steamer. The gunner at the bow guns being wounded, Captain Ward took his place himself, and was sighting the piece, when a Minié ball struck him in the abdomen and killed him almost on the instant.

That the enterprise of Captain Ward, however gallantly conducted, was an imprudent one, seemed to be the opinion of some of his fellow-officers. Captain Rowan, of the Pawnee, says "the Resolute returned, with a request from Captain Ward that I should send her back, if I had no more important service for her. I immediately despatched the Reliance to Captain Ward, knowing the danger to which our people would be exposed if he contemplated a landing at Matthias Point, as I feared was his intention, judging from the nature of the order he gave me, to furnish him with such equipments as were necessary to cut down trees on the Point and burn them;" and Captain Rowan continues with the declaration, that "Lieutenant Chaplin and his command" (whom he sent to the aid of Ward, and complimented for their gallantry) "escaped utter destruction by a miracle."

CHAPTER XXX.

Occupation of Harper's Ferry by the Enemy.—Their Force.—General Johnston.—His Life and Character.—The advantages of position at Harper's Ferry.—The defences of the place.—The movement of the Federal Forces upon Harper's Ferry.—Combination of Federal Generals.—Alarm of General Johnston—Evacuation of Harper's Ferry.—Destructiveness.—A lively description by a Secessionist.—A conflagration.—A picture.—Route of Johnston.—Advance of the Federalists.—Movement of General Patterson.—Crossing the Potomac.—Coming up with the Enemy.—Battle of Falling Waters A droll description.—The Secessionists routed.—Flight to Bunker Hill.—Pursuit by General Patterson.—Arrival at Martinsburgh.—Losses at Falling Waters.—Harper's Ferry unoccupied.—Return to Harper's Ferry of a detachment of the Enemy.—Their proceedings on the occasion.—Terror and destruction.—Combined movement of the Secessionists.—Subjection of Western Virginia intended. The Secession force under General Garnett.—The encampment at Laurel Hill.—Distribution of Troops.—March of General Wise.—Position of Johnston.—Advance of General McClellan.—Proclamations.—Disposition of his forces.—Skilful strategy.—General Rosecrans sent against the enemy.—Battle of Rich Mountain.—Flight of the Enemy. Losses. A rich Capture.—Advance of McClellan to Beverly. Sudden disappearance of the Enemy.—McClellan in possession of Beverly.—The retreat of the Enemy.—Possession of their camp.—McClellan's movement to cut them off.—Importance of Beverly.—The enemy's works—Inner and outer works.—Rifle Pits.—Abattis.—Redoubts.—McClellan's reports.—Surrender of Pegram and his force. Correspondence on the occasion.—Coming up with Garnett.—Battle of Carrick's Ford.—Death of Garnett.—Account of the Battle.—Reports of McClellan.—A glowing tribute to his Soldiers.—Failure of a well-laid plan.—Escape of the Fugitives.—An enemy's account of the Battle of Rich Mountain.

1861.

EVER since the abandonment and unfortunately incomplete destruction of the public works at Harper's Ferry by Lieutenant Jones, already described in an earlier part of this narrative, the enemy had occupied the place. A large force, amounting to nearly twenty thousand men, was here mustered under one of their ablest officers, General Johnston.

Joseph Eccleston Johnston was born in Virginia, in 1804, and at an early age entered the military academy of West Point. After a career of successful study in this institution, he received the commission of second lieutenant of artillery. In 1836, he became first lieutenant, and was appointed to the lucrative position of assistant commissary of subsistence. In 1838, such was his high professional repute, he was promoted to a first lieutenancy in that *corps d'élite* the Topographical Engineers, in which rank he served during the Indian war in Florida, and was brevetted captain in reward for his services. In 1846, he was promoted captain in full, and during the Mexican war served with distinction, first in the engineer corps, and subsequently with the voltigeurs. He was brevetted twice for good service and gallant conduct. At the end of the war he resumed his position as an officer of engineers, and after a long service in the bureau of that department, was appointed, by General Scott, in June, 1860, quartermaster-general. Notwithstanding this late appointment to so important a post, which would seem to have been a proof of great reliance placed in his fidelity by the commander-in-chief of the United States, Johnston was among the earliest of the Federal officers of Southern origin to abandon the Union and give in his adherence to secession. At this time, although fifty-seven years of age, a man of great energy, he was esteemed one of the ablest officers in the service of the Southern Confederacy. With great ability as a strategist and a man of inflexible spirit, he proved to be as a leader and conspirator a most persistent and formidable antagonist. A square and compact head, a firm compression of the upper lip and a certain fulness of animal development about the lower lip, chin, and neck, are the external indications of those qualities of calculation, firmness, and brute courage which are known to characterize him.

Johnston seemed determined to hold Harper's Ferry as a basis of operations. Commanding the Ohio and Baltimore Railroad, the great avenue of communication between the valley of the Ohio and the sea, through Chesapeake Bay, and being separated from Maryland only by the river, and from Pennsylvania by a narrow stretch of the former State, Harper's Ferry was favorably placed for operating in Western Virginia, Maryland, or even in Pennsylvania. The enemy seemed determined to hold the position, and raised works of defence commanding the various approaches not only on the Virginia but the Maryland side of the river, where they occupied the high banks in force.

The Federal forces now moved from three different points with the view of driving the secessionists from Harper's Ferry. General McClellan was advancing from the Ohio through Western Virginia; General Stone, detached from the army before Washington, was moving up the Potomac; and General Patterson marching with his column from Pennsylvania in the north, with the view of closing in upon the enemy's position at Harper's Ferry.

General Johnston becoming alarmed,

determined to evacuate the place. Before leaving, however, he strove to render it untenable by and useless to his antagonists. All the machinery of the public works left, after the incomplete destruction by Lieutenant Jones, had been already removed to Richmond and there utilized, greatly to the advantage of the enemy. Johnston, however, destroyed all the remnant of the arsenals and workshops, the great railway bridge over the Potomac, and a portion of the railroad itself. A secessionist officer has given a lively description of the evacuation.

"On Thursday, June 13, just as the troops were in a fair way for the enjoyment of the holiday from military duty, consequent upon the fast-day, an order was circulated among the different regiments for immediate preparations for march. This was the first intimation we had of General Johnston's purpose to evacuate Harper's Ferry. Instantly the whole place was in a stir. Hundreds of baggage-wagons were laden, burly, big-bellied broad treads, and stuffed with provision stores, while ammunition was carefully deposited in safe trains, and from every side arose the swelling strains of music as the troops took up the line of march.

"The necessity of this step was rendered the more apparent by the fact that intelligence had been received of the rapid approach of General McClellan's division of the Federal army toward Winchester. Thus we were to be intercepted, and our small force completely hemmed in by the constantly augmenting numbers of the Northerners, and either cut to pieces or compelled to surrender. Our commander very prudently chose to take neither horn of the dilemma, but resolved to desert Harper's Ferry and boldly strike into the valley of Virginia, where he could attack the enemy. We are thus to be made the offensive party, and shall certainly, in good time, make a proper report of our interview with the blustering Hoosiers and Buckeyes.

"The companies of Captains Desha and Pope were quickly under arms, and moved to the armory yard, where, having stacked their rifles, they awaited orders. The Kentuckians, under Colonel Duncan, reported themselves at the same place, and were subsequently removed to Camp Hill, overlooking the battery. A large number of men left by railway for Winchester, and others, for lack of transportation, marched afoot. During the day there was an indescribable scene of excitement. Broadway, in its palmiest day, never witnessed such a jam as this little town. The business houses were closed, families were attempting to move their effects, and every street and avenue was crowded with loaded wagons. Officers were dashing hither and thither, and soldiers were on the *qui vive* for movement. Loads of provisions, that it was found impossible to transport, were dumped in the river. There was a general rush by the boys for sugar and bread. It was, indeed, in more senses than one, a *fast* day. In the first place, we had no regular meal, and every movement was made at the most accelerated rate of speed.

"During the afternoon, the pickets of the enemy were distinctly observable on the Maryland Heights, and Captain Desha and Lieutenant Rogers took a crack at them with their rifles, which caused the tories to disappear rather suddenly.

"Just after dark, Captain Desha's company was ordered to accompany Major Whiting, the chief engineer, across the Potomac, and make preparations for blowing up the bridge. This was an undertaking of no inconsiderable hazard. The enemy was known to be in the immediate vicinity, and it was thought not unlikely that they might attempt to force a passage of the bridge. I have slept in many places and under many disadvantages, but never before above a foaming, turbulent river, and just above a terrible mine that in an instant could flash the structure into a myriad of fragments. The night, however, passed quietly, and in the early grey of the morning we were visited by Major Whiting. The immense bridge, over three quarters of a mile in length, was thoroughly saturated, the torch lit, and just as we reached the Virginia shore the magnificent structure was hurried into mid air, falling a shapeless mass of ruins into the rapid stream. The burning *debris*, with the clouds of lurid flame, presented a picture worthy an artist's study. In an hour or two the massive and extensive armory buildings were ignited, and the conflagration that ensued was of the most terrific and impressive character. In order to prevent the flames extending to private property, the troops were detailed to act as firemen, under Captain Fauntleroy, of the Confederate navy, and right manfully did they discharge their arduous duty. Not a penny's worth of that which did not belong to the Government was destroyed."

After evacuating Harper's Ferry, General Johnston retreated along the valley of the Shenandoah to Winchester, in order to secure his communications with the main body of the secessionists at Manassas Junction and the city of Richmond.

It is here necessary to recur to the progress of the Federal forces, which had caused this sudden and important movement of the enemy from Harper's Ferry.

General Patterson left Chambersburg, in Pennsylvania, on June 8th, with nearly twenty thousand men, on his march southward through Maryland. From Cumberland and Hagerstown, in the latter State, he marched to Williamsport, on the Potomac, about twenty-five miles northwest of Harper's Ferry. Here he crossed the river into Virginia, a movement effected without opposition or difficulty. The enemy, however, although they made no show of resistance to the passage of the troops over the Potomac, were in considerable force at a short distance from the ford by which the Federal army was passing.

This was the enemy's rear guard, consisting of three or four thousand men, with cavalry and artillery under the command of General Jackson, encamped

June 18.
July 2.

at a place called Falling Waters, near Hainesville.

The advance of the Federal army, consisting of the Wisconsin First and the Pennsylvania Eleventh and Twelfth Regiments, with artillery and cavalry, was immediately thrown forward by Patterson, while his main body was still crossing the river to attack the enemy at Falling Waters. The commencement of the engagement is thus drolly described by a participator:

"The battle commenced about nine o'clock, as no other battle probably ever commenced in the history of war. Colonel Perkins' battery was in advance, and the Colonel himself a quarter of a mile in the lead of his men, when, upon making a turn in the road, he came suddenly upon two mounted officers. Military salutes were passed, hands were shaken all round, and the strangers asked Colonel Perkins what company he belonged to, and when he had got in. The Colonel replied that he belonged to Company C, and had just arrived. One of the strangers observed, reflectively, 'Company C! Company C!' and just then the first piece of the battery showed itself around the turn, when he exclaimed, 'Artillery, by God!' and fled for his life with his companion. Colonel Perkins immediately shouted to his men, 'Now, boys, come on, we've got 'em.' In less than a minute the battery was in operation, and blazing away right and left, while the rebels could be seen in all directions, trying to form their men."

The infantry in support of the battery came promptly into line after the first shot, and poured such rapid volleys of musketry upon the enemy that they did not find time to form. They accordingly retired in confusion, turning and shooting irregularly as they went. However, on reaching a farm belonging to a person of the name of Porterfield, they succeeded in forming, and made a brief stand. Although covered by the house and barn, behind and within which they sought refuge, they were soon again forced to fly, being shelled out by the artillery. They were pursued beyond Hainesville, when our wearied men awaited the coming up of their comrades, and the secessionists continued their retreat to Martinsburgh. Joined by the secession troops in occupation of that place, they again fell back until they reached the main body under General Johnston, encamped at Bunker Hill.

General Patterson followed closely with his whole force, and took possession of Martinsburgh without resistance, on the day after it had been abandoned by the enemy. The loss of the Federal troops engaged in the affair at Falling Waters, was three killed and ten wounded; that of the enemy was estimated to amount to nearly thirty killed and fifty wounded. Their force in the battle was said to have numbered five thousand men, while the unionists were less than three thousand.

Harper's Ferry, for some good strategic reason, doubtless, was not occupied by the Federal troops, and General Johnston, emboldened by the fact, sent back a detachment to the place, which destroyed the fine bridge over the Shenandoah, the railroad bridge, and many of the public buildings and private dwellings.

Co-operating with the army under General Johnston, whose retreat from Harper's Ferry and subsequent manœuvres until he reached Winchester have been already alluded to, were two other columns of Confederate troops, thrown into Western Virginia with the object of subjecting that loyal district. One of these columns, estimated to number about ten thousand men, under the command of General R. S. Garnett, a Virginian, and formerly an officer of repute in the Federal service, had marched into the valley of Cheat River, the principal and eastern branch of the fork of the Monongahela. Garnett had his headquarters at Beverly, on the eastern side of the ridge called Laurel Hill, which lies parallel to the Alleghany range of mountains. Detachments of his command were distributed in various parts of Western Virginia, at Bealington, Buckhannon, Romney, and at points approaching Philippi and Grafton, which had been seized by the unionists under General Kelley.

The third column of secession troops, under the command of Wise, the former Governor of Virginia, had advanced from the extreme southwest of the State beyond the Greenbrier Mountains, into the valley of the Kanawha.

Johnston was thus to the east of the Alleghanies, between that range and the Blue Ridge, and so placed that he might co-operate either with the Confederate line extending from Manassas to the Potomac, or give aid to Garnett, who was not far from him, though on the other side of the mountains, while Wise was to act in co-operation with the whole to the extreme west beyond the Alleghanies.

General McClellan* having now, in

---

* General McClellan, on entering Virginia, issued these proclamations :

"HEADQUARTERS DEPARTMENT OF THE OHIO,
GRAFTON (VA.), June 23, 1861.

"TO THE INHABITANTS OF WESTERN VIRGINIA : The army of this department, headed by Virginia troops, is rapidly occupying all Western Virginia. This is done in co operation with and in support of such civil authorities of the State as are faithful to the Constitution and laws of the United States. The proclamation issued by me under date of May 26, 1861, will be strictly maintained. Your houses, families, property, and all your rights will be religiously respected. We are enemies to none but armed rebels, and those voluntarily giving them aid. All officers of this army will be held responsible for the most prompt and vigorous action in repressing disorder and punishing aggression by those under their command.

"To my great regret I find that the enemies of the United States continue to carry on a system of hostilities prohibited by the laws of war among belligerent nations, and of course far more wicked and intolerable when directed against loyal citizens engaged in the defence of the common Government of all. Individuals and marauding parties are pursuing a guerrilla warfare, firing upon sentinels and pickets, burning bridges, hooting, and even killing citizens because of their Union sentiments, and committing many kindred acts.

"I do now, therefore, make proclamation and warn all persons that individuals or parties engaged in this species of warfare, irregular in every view which can be taken of it, thus attacking sentries, pickets, or other soldiers, destroying public or private property, or committing insult to any of the inhabitants because of their Union sentiments or conduct, will be dealt with in their persons and property according to the severest rules of military law.

"All persons giving information or aid to the public enemies will be arrested and kept in close custody; and all persons bearing arms, unless of known loyalty, will be arrested and held for examination.

"GEO. B. MCCLELLAN, Major-General U. S. A.,
"Commanding Department."

"TO THE SOLDIERS OF THE ARMY OF THE WEST: You are here to support the Government of your country, and protect the lives and liberties of your brethren, threatened person, entered Western Virginia, from Ohio, disposed his force so as to counteract this combination of the Confederates for the subjection of the loyal valley of the Kanawha. He first sent a detachment, under the command of General Cox, up the Kanawha River to meet Wise advancing in that direction, and keep him in check, while he himself, with his main body, having reached Clarksburgh, on the Baltimore and Ohio Railroad, marched directly from that place against the enemy under Garnett, encamped at Laurel Hill, near Beverly. At the same time a detachment was sent to Philippi to act with the Western Virginians there under Kelley, and move to Bealington in order to prevent the retreat of the enemy by the Cheat valley; another body of troops was despatched to West Union, in case they should strive to escape by that way over the Alleghanies and form a junction with Johnston at Winchester.

The only other means of retreat was through the Cheat Mountain Gap, above Beverly, which the self-reliant McClellan determined himself to close, by a victory which he confidently calculated upon.

Having reached Buckhannon on his march, and after some spirited skirmishes with the enemy's advance in that neighborhood, McClellan's scouts discovered a large body of the enemy, under Colonel Pegram, in an entrenched camp in Rich Mountain Gap of the Laurel Hill range. This position, twenty-six miles east from Buckhannon and four from Beverly, commanded the road to Staunton, a town situated to the west of the Alleghanies.

July 7.

After a thorough reconnoissance, McClellan sent a detachment under Colonel, now General, Rosencranz, to make a circuit through the woods and attack the position at Rich Mountain, while he himself led his main body against Garnett's principal camp at Laurel Hill.

After a long and rapid march, eight miles of which were through a dense

by a rebellious and traitorous foe. No higher or nobler duty could devolve on you, and I expect you to bring to its performance the highest and noblest qualities of soldiers—discipline, courage, and mercy.

"I call upon the officers of every grade to enforce the highest discipline, and I know that those of all grades, privates and officers, will display in battle cool, heroic courage, and will know how to show mercy to a disarmed enemy. Bear in mind that you are in the country of friends, not of enemies—that you are here to protect, not to destroy. Take nothing, destroy nothing unless you are ordered to do so by your general officers. Remember that I have pledged my word to the people of Western Virginia, that their rights in person and property shall be respected. I ask every one of you to make good this promise in its broadest sense.

"We have come here to save, not to upturn. I do not appeal to the fear of punishment, but to your appreciation of the sacredness of the cause in which we are engaged. Carry into battle the conviction that you are right, and that God is on our side. Your enemies have violated every

moral law; neither God nor man can sustain them. They have without cause rebelled against a mild and paternal Government; they have seized upon public and private property; they have outraged the persons of Northern men merely because they came from the North, and of Southern Union men merely because they loved the Union; they have placed themselves beneath contempt, unless they can retrieve some honor on the field of battle.

"You will pursue a different course; you will be honest, brave, and merciful; you will respect the right of private opinion; you will punish no man for opinion's sake. Show to the world that you differ from our enemies in these points of honor, honesty, and respect for private opinion, and that we inaugurate no reign of terror wherever we go.

"Soldiers, I have heard that there was danger here. I have come to place myself at your head, and share it with you. I fear now but one thing, that you will not find foemen worthy of your steel. I know that I can rely upon you. Geo. B. McClellan, Maj.-Gen. Com'g."

mountain forest and in a dark night with a severe storm of rain, Rosencranz halted his troops next morning in view of the enemy's pickets. The Federal force numbered sixteen hundred men; that of the secessionists, estimated at two thousand, was strongly entrenched on the west side of the mountain, at its foot. They had felled and "rolled whole trees from the mountain side and lapped them together, filling in with stones and earth from a trench outside," testifies General Rosencranz's guide, who thus gives an artless and interesting account of his personal experience in the battle.

"We started," he says, "about daylight, having first taken something to eat (but got nothing more until six o'clock next night, when some of them got a little beef), and turned into the woods on our right. I led, accompanied by Colonel Landor, through a pathless route in the woods, by which I had made my escape about four weeks before. We pushed along through the bushes, laurels, and rocks, followed by the whole division in perfect silence. The bushes wetted us thoroughly, and it was very cold. Our circuit was about five miles. About noon we reached the top of the mountain, near my father's farm. It was not intended that the enemy should know of our movements; but a dragoon with despatches from General McClellan, who was sent after us, fell into the hands of the enemy, and they thus found out our movements. They immediately despatched two thousand five hundred men to the top of the mountain with three cannon. They entrenched themselves with earth-works on my father's farm, just where we were to come into the road. We did not know they were there until we came on their pickets, and their cannon opened fire upon us. We were then about a quarter of a mile from the house, and skirmishing began. I left the advance and went into the main body of the army. I had no arms of any kind. The rain began pouring down in torrents, while the enemy fired his cannon, cutting off the tree-tops over our heads quite lively. They fired rapidly. I thought, from the firing, they had twenty-five or thirty pieces. We had no cannon with us. Our boys stood still in the rain about half an hour. The Eighth and Tenth then led off, bearing to the left of our position. The bushes were so thick we could not see out, nor could the enemy see us. The enemy's musket balls could not reach us. Our boys, keeping up a fire, got down within sight and then pretended to run, but they only fell down in the bushes and behind rocks. This drew the enemy from their entrenchments, when our boys let into them with their Enfield and Minié rifles, and I never heard such screaming in my life. The Nineteenth, in the mean time, advanced to a fence in a line with the breastworks, and fired one round. The whole earth seemed to shake. They then gave the Indiana boys a tremendous cheer, and the enemy broke from their entrenchments in every way they could. The Indiana boys had previously been ordered to fix bayonets. We could

BATTLE OF RICH MOUNTAIN.

bear the rattle of the iron very plainly as the order was obeyed. Charge bayonets was then ordered, and away went our boys after the enemy. One man alone stood his ground, and fired a cannon, until shot by a revolver. A general race for about three hundred yards followed through the bush, when our men were recalled and reformed in line of battle, to receive the enemy from the entrenchments at the foot of the mountains, as we supposed they would certainly attack us from that point; but it seemed that as soon as they no longer heard the firing of the cannon they gave up all for lost. They then deserted their works and took off whatever way they could. A reinforcement, which was also coming from Beverly to the aid of the two thousand five hundred, retreated for the same reason. We took all their wagons, tents, provisions, stores, and cannon, many guns which they left, many horses, mules, etc. In short, we got everything they had, as they took nothing but such horses as they were on. We found several of these in the woods. One hundred and thirty-five of the enemy were buried before I left. They were for the most part shot in the head, and hard to be recognized. Some six hundred, who had managed to get down to the river at Caplinger's, finding no chance of escape, sent in a flag of truce, and on Saturday morning they were escorted into Beverly by the Chicago cavalry, which had been sent after them, Gen. McClellan having in the mean time gone on there with his main column."

The enemy lost a hundred and fifty killed and about three hundred wounded and captured. The Federal loss was reported to have been but eighteen killed and some thirty-five wounded. The struggle lasted only forty minutes, when the enemy fled precipitately, abandoning everything, camp and camp equipage, provisions, artillery, and ammunition, to our victorious troops.

In the mean time, while Rosencranz was routing the enemy at Rich Mountain, General McClellan was advancing toward Beverly. He arrived at night before the enemy's fortified position at Laurel Hill, and waited but for the break of morning to plant his cannon on a commanding position and begin his attack. The morning came, and it was discovered that the enemy had fled, **July 12.** abandoning their strong position, which was occupied by a detachment of troops under General Morris, while McClellan himself delayed not a moment in pushing forward to Beverly to prevent their retreat in that direction.

The enemy thus headed off by the prompt movement of McClellan, were forced to countermarch and seek another outlet of escape. They now fled down the valley toward St. George. McClellan at once despatched Captain Benham, with a detachment from his own force, to join General Morris and the troops left in occupation of the enemy's abandoned camp, and followed the fugitives in rapid pursuit.

General McClellan, in his report of the action under Rosencranz, gave a **July 12.** characteristically terse yet comprehensive account of the victory:

"HEADQUARTERS DEPT. OF OHIO,
RICH MOUNTAIN, VA., *July* 12, 9 A. M.

"COLONEL E. D. TOWNSEND:

"We are in possession of all the enemy's works up to a point in sight of Beverly. We have taken all his guns, a very large amount of wagons, tents, etc.—everything that he had. A large number of prisoners were also taken, many of whom are wounded, and several of whom are officers. The enemy lost many killed. We have lost, in all, perhaps twenty killed and forty wounded, of whom all but two or three belong to the column under General Rosencranz, which turned the position of the enemy. The mass of the rebels escaped through the woods, entirely disorganized.

"Among the prisoners is Dr. Taylor, formerly of the army. Colonel Pegram was in command of the enemy's forces.

"General Rosencranz's column left camp yesterday morning, and marched eight miles through the mountains, reaching the turnpike two or three miles in the rear of the enemy, and defeated an advance force and captured a couple of guns. I had a position ready for twelve guns near the main camp, and as the guns were moving up, it was ascertained that the enemy had retreated.

"I am now pushing on to Beverly. A part of General Rosencranz's troops are now within three miles of it. Our success is complete, and almost bloodless. The behavior of our troops in action and toward the prisoners is admirable.

"G. B. MCCLELLAN, Maj.-Gen. Com."

McClellan's own movement on Beverly, though effected without a struggle with the enemy, was still more important than that of Rosencranz. The position which they had abandoned at Beverly, on the approach of the Federal troops, was considered of great importance naturally, and had been strengthened by elaborate works. These consisted of a line of entrenchments nearly a mile in extent, stretching on both sides of the main road which runs from Philippi to Beverly. Divided by this road they extended up the slopes of the hills on either side, and commanded one of the most important mountain passes. Rifle pits were dug to the depth of three feet, while the earth was thrown up so as to form breastworks to each, which were further protected by large bushes. Trees had been cut down and their trunks and branches so prepared and disposed as to form an abattis, which extended for several hundred yards in front of the approaches. On the summits of two commanding elevations of ground were built redoubts of logs and earth, with embrasures for six cannon and loopholes for musketry. Within the outer works were others, consisting of entrenchments with two salients for cannon. This was intended as a cover under which the enemy, in case he had been driven from his exterior fortifications, might make a stand. The work seemed so formidable, and the natural position of Beverly so strong, that if the secessionists had been disposed to hold their ground, it would probably have cost a severe struggle and great loss of life to have driven them from it.

NEW NATIONAL WORK ON THE LATE REBELLION.

Now Publishing, in Parts at 50 cents, and Divisions at $1.

THE GREAT CIVIL WAR:

A HISTORY OF

THE LATE REBELLION;

Being a complete Narrative of the Events connected with the Origin, Progress, and Conclusion of the War, with Biographical Sketches of Leading Statesmen and Distinguished Military and Naval Commanders, etc., etc.

By ROBERT TOMES, M.D.

Continued from the beginning of the year 1864 to the end of the War,

By BENJ. G. SMITH, Esq.

Illustrated by numerous highly finished Steel Engravings, Colored Maps, Plans, etc., from Drawings by F. O. C. Darley and other eminent Artists.

The four years' war, now happily ended—so remarkable for its sudden outbreak, its unexpected duration, and its entire termination—not only absorbed universal attention at home, but had, during its continuance, a paramount interest for the nations of Europe, and was the subject of constant comment and prophecy on the part of both the friends and enemies of national self-government. It not only displayed the astonishing resources of the country, and exhibited, even while the struggle continued, in the vast armies raised and the persistent spirit of the people, a capacity for war that entitles the United States to the first rank among military nations, but also demonstrated the enduring character of the government and institutions, which have proved themselves able to withstand even the fearful shocks of a gigantic civil war.

A history of this great war will be a necessity to every loyal American. To be without a knowledge of the causes and events of the great struggle for the preservation of the Union would be as inexcusable as to be ignorant of the events which led to its formation.

The present work will be a complete history of the war and of its immediate causes, from the election of Mr. Lincoln and the commencement of actual hostilities by the attack on Fort Sumter, to the evacuation of Richmond and the surrender of the armies of Lee, Johnston, and Kirby Smith. It will contain detailed accounts of the great battles, sieges, marches, and naval operations, a record of political events, remarks on foreign relations, statistical facts with regard to the resources of both the Northern and Southern States, descriptions of fortresses and battle-fields, and a large number of biographical sketches of distinguished commanders and statesmen, to which will be appended a copious and elaborate Index.

Not the least attractive feature of the work will be the large number of beautiful and costly steel engravings, comprising portraits of statesmen and military and naval commanders, Northern and Southern, who have become famous in the course of the war.

Among the illustrations are also splendid bird's-eye views of Fortress Monroe and vicinity, Charleston, Richmond, and New Orleans; representations of battle-scenes, views of forts and battle-fields, sea views, and a number of carefully prepared colored maps and plans, highly useful in making clear the movements and positions of armies.

CONDITIONS OF PUBLICATION.

The work will be printed in a clear, bold type, on superfine, calendered paper, and issued in Parts at Fifty Cents, and Divisions at $1 each.

The illustrations will comprise fifty-four portraits and thirty-six battle-scenes, plans, maps, bird's-eye views, etc.

A Part will be published every two weeks and a Division every month until completed, the whole not to exceed forty-five Parts, at Fifty Cents each.

No subscriber's name received for less than the whole work; and each Part or Division will be payable on delivery, the carrier not being allowed to give credit or receive payment in advance.

VIRTUE & YORSTON, 12 DEY STREET, & 544 BROADWAY, NEW YORK.

And Sold by their Agents in all the Principal Cities of the United States and Canadas.

www.ingramcontent.com/pod-product-compliance
Lightning Source LLC
Chambersburg PA
CBHW030358230426
43664CB00007BB/649